W9-ACL-421

POLITICS IN BRAZIL, 1930–1964

POLITICS IN BRAZIL, 1930–1964

An Experiment in Democracy

THOMAS E. SKIDMORE

OXFORD UNIVERSITY PRESS   New York   Oxford

Oxford University Press
Oxford New York Toronto
Delhi Bombay Calcutta Madras Karachi
Petaling Jaya Singapore Hong Kong Tokyo
Nairobi Dar es Salaam Cape Town
Melbourne Auckland

and associated companies in
Beirut Berlin Ibadan Nicosia

For Felicity
who made it a book

ACKNOWLEDGMENTS

I have been fortunate in receiving the advice and suggestions of a number of friends and colleagues who took the time to read this book at various stages during its preparation: Nathaniel Leff, Riordan Roett, Roberto Cavalcanti de Albuquerque, Richard Ullman, Robert Packenham, John Wirth, Albert Hirschman, Frank Bonilla, and Melvin Croan. Brady Tyson loaned me his very useful clipping collection. Any American writing on Brazilian political and economic history must depend upon the generous and helpful counsel of Brazilian scholars, whose patience in such matters seems limitless. I am greatly indebted to Hélio Jaguaribe and Octávio Dias Carneiro for many hours of stimulating conversation on the period covered in this book, as well as numerous helpful suggestions on the manuscript. Márcio Rego Monteiro not only gave me many insights into the history of economic policy-making in postwar Brazil; he also allowed me to use a number of books and official publications which I could have found elsewhere only with great difficulty. Former Ambassador Lincoln Gordon has been generous with his time and hospitality, both in Rio de Janeiro and in Washington, where he is now (fall 1966) Assistant Secretary of State for Inter-American Affairs. His thoughtful and detailed criticisms have been much appreciated, if not always incorporated. My friend Paul Samuelson read the sections on economic history, in a valiant attempt to expunge the more egregious errors in economics. He was also kind enough to permit me to call upon the editorial talents of his extraordinarily able research assistant. Martha Wailes, Inez Crandall, Emmy Norris, Norma Wasser, and Katherine

Herrlich lent expert typing assistance. The major typing burden fell on Diana Meister, who cheerfully nursed the manuscript through more than one incarnation. Anil Khosla made innumerable trips to the library and was a valuable research assistant, as was Ferne Gurvitz. Many of the printed sources were located in the Harvard College Library, the Harvard Business School Library, and the Library of Congress, whose staffs were most helpful. I am indebted to the Committee on Latin American Studies of Harvard University for a grant which helped to cover research expenses, and to the Ibero-American Studies Committee of the University of Wisconsin for a research grant which made possible the completion of this book. Finally, I must express my gratitude to Robert L. Wolff, who first turned my attention south. My debt to my wife is indicated in the dedication. Her name ought to be on the title page. The errors and infelicities that escaped her expert eye (and those of previous readers) remain my responsibility.

T. E. S.

Madison, Wisconsin
January 1967

CONTENTS

List of Abbreviations and Terms Used in Text

AMFORP American and Foreign Power Co.

ANL Aliança Nacional Libertadora
(National Liberation Alliance)

AP Ação Popular (Popular Action)

ARENA Aliança Nacional Renovadora
(National Renovation Alliance)

BNDE Banco Nacional do Desenvolvimento Econômico
(National Bank for Economic Development)

CGT Comando Geral dos Trabalhadores
(General Labor Command)

CNI Confederação Nacional da Indústria
(National Confederation of Industry)

CNTI Confederação Nacional dos Trabalhadores da Indústria (National Confederation of Industrial Workers)

coronelismo The system of political bossism (by "coronels") widespread in rural areas during the Old Republic (1889–1930)

CVSF Comissão do Vale do São Francisco
(São Francisco Valley Commission)

DASP Departamento Administrativo do Serviço Público
(Administrative Department of Public Service)

DIP Departamento de Imprensa e Propaganda
(Department of Press and Propaganda)

DNOCS Departamento Nacional de Obras Contra as Sêcas
(National Department of Anti-Drought Works)

DOPS	Departamento de Ordem Política e Social (Department of Political and Social Order)
dispositivo militar	Contingent of military officers who actively support a politician or a group of politicians
dispositivo sindical	Contingent of labor union officials who actively support a politician or a group of politicians
ECLA	Economic Commission for Latin America
Electrobrás	Government–owned and operated electric power company
entreguismo	Pejorative term used to describe those Brazilians ("entreguistas") who are accused of favoring excessive foreign influence in their country
FPN	Frente Parlamentar Nacionalista (Nationalist Parliamentary Front)
golpe	Coup d'état; "golpistas" are those who favor a coup
IBAD	Instituto Brasileiro de Ação Democrática (Brazilian Institute of Democratic Action)
IBRA	Instituto Brasileiro de Reforma Agrária (Brazilian Institute of Agrarian Reform)
IMF	International Monetary Fund
IPES	Instituto de Pesquisas e Estudos Sociais (Institute for Social Research and Study)
ISEB	Instituto Superior de Estudos Brasileiros (Higher Institute of Brazilian Studies)
MDB	Movimento Democrático Brasileiro (Brazilian Democratic Movement)
NOVACAP	Companhia Urbanizadora da Nova Capital (Urban Authority for a New Capital [Brasília])
PCB	Partido Communista Brasileiro (Brazilian Communist Party) pro-Russian
PC do B	Partido Communista do Brasil (Communist Party of Brazil) pro-Chinese
PDC	Partido Democrata Cristão (Christian Democratic Party)
Petrobrás	Federally-owned and operated oil industry
PL	Partido Libertador (Liberation Party)
PR	Partido Republicano (Republican Party)
PRP	Partido Republicano Paulista

(Republican Party of São Paulo)
also:
Partido de Representação Popular
(Popular Representation Party)

PSD   Partido Social Democrático
(Social Democratic Party)

PSP   Partido Social Progressista
(Social Progressive Party)

PTB   Partido Trabalhista Brasileiro
(Brazilian Labor Party)

PUA   Pacto de Unidade de Ação
(Pact for Unity of Action)

SALTE   Loosely co-ordinated plan for federal government expenditures proposed in 1948. Name comes from first letters of Portuguese words for health (saúde), food (alimentação), transportation (transporte), and energy (energia).

SPVEA   Superintendência do Plano de Valorização Econômica da Amazônia (Superintendency of the Plan for the Economic Valorization of the Amazon Valley)

SUDENE   Superintendência do Desenvolvimento do Nordeste (Superintendency for the Development of the Northeast)

SUMOC   Superintendência da Moeda e Crédito
(Superintendency of Money and Credit)

SUNAB   Superintendência Nacional do Abastecimento
(National Superintendency of Food Supplies)

UDN   União Democrática Nacional
(National Democratic Union)

UNE   União Nacional dos Estudantes
(National Union of Students)

INTRODUCTION

I began this book in an attempt to investigate the causes of the fall of former President João Goulart on April 1, 1964. It soon expanded well beyond the originally intended format because I found it impossible to explain the political system in which Goulart operated without examining the origins of that system in the decade following the Revolution of 1930 and the process of redemocratization which brought an end to the Vargas dictatorship of 1937–45.

All Brazilians, regardless of political position, seem agreed that April 1, 1964, was a watershed in postwar Brazilian history. Events since then have only served to strengthen that view. I am convinced that the overthrow of Goulart brought to an end the era of democratic politics that began in 1945. Whatever subsequent Brazilian politics may bring, the political process will be fundamentally different from what it was between 1945 and 1964. If this supposition is correct, then it is not too early to begin an assessment of the complex chapter that began with the rise of Getúlio Vargas and ended with the fall of João Goulart.

The overthrow of President João Goulart can be interpreted on several levels. First, one can analyze the immediate political deadlock which, given the attitudes of the protagonists, was bound to be broken by some radical departure from established constitutional processes. Or one can regard this political conflict as a part of the deeper institutional crisis resulting from the failure to create political institutions and processes that could channel and direct the rapid social and economic changes which have transformed Brazil since 1930. Finally, one can note that the deepening political crisis was the inevitable corollary of the dramatic slowdown in economic growth that became evident after 1962 and was compounded by the large burden of short-term foreign debts. These three levels of interpretation might be called the political, the social, and the economic, although the second involves the relationship between political institutions and social change, and the third involves the relationship between political institutions and economic development.

These interpretations are not, of course, separable. For purposes of analysis, however, it is useful to differentiate them. On the first level, one must begin by examining the manner in which Goulart's personal motivations and political style catalyzed the deepening conflicts among the arbiters of Brazilian political power. Here one must guard against an overemphasis either of Goulart's "personalistic" ambitions or of the lines of group conflict (economic interests, social classes, and geographic regions).

To understand how group conflict played a role in the political impasse, one must turn to the second level of interpretation and look at Goulart's fall within the context of the institutional crisis which has characterized the relationship between the Brazilian polity and Brazilian society since 1945. The polarization so evident by March 1964 had roots far deeper than the immediate controversy surrounding Goulart's actions as President. Both his supporters and his opponents (significantly, many politically active Brazilians abhorred the dichotomy which forced them to choose between the two camps) found themselves operating within a political system whose implicit rules and social basis they were now questioning. Nearly all sectors could see that the rationale of political relationships was threatened by the disequilibrium between the existing political institutions and the society on whose behalf they were supposed to operate. The immediate conflict arose over how severe the disequilibrium was, and how it could be corrected.

Underlying all political events, especially since the early 1950's, has been the need to make painful choices in economic policy. By 1964, the basic question was how to resume rapid economic growth and how to direct the benefits of such growth to a constantly larger share of the Brazilian population. The choices had become as delicate as they were unavoidable: the balance between industrialization and agriculture, the possible sources of capital (if foreign capital, how much public and how much private?), the need to correct regional imbalances, the distribution of income as affected by wage, tax, and welfare policies, and the further problem of how to accomplish all these objectives while holding inflation within manageable limits.

Decisions on economic policy raised large political questions, because every policy tended to rebound to the benefit of some groups and to the detriment of others. Furthermore, inability to maintain a high overall economic growth rate—a failure evident after 1962—created intense pressures on the national political leadership. Every government had to make immediate and far-reaching economic decisions, which in turn required political machinery adequate to sustain them in the process of conceiving and implementing their economic policies. In addition, all governments had to maintain a political consensus assuring them a reasonable measure of support from a majority of the most powerful political sectors. Such a consensus is what João Goulart had irretrievably lost by the end of March 1964.

Unfortunately, the period from 1930 to 1945 has been little studied by historians. Even the factual outline of the postwar era is often difficult to establish. I have not attempted to write an exhaustive history of Brazilian politics between 1930 and 1964. The reader should not, therefore, expect to find a complete account of the principal problems and accomplishments of every government during this period. Rather, I have written an interpretation of what I regard as the most important factors determining the trend of Brazilian politics since the Revolution of 1930. Certain themes are emphasized: the changing institutional context of politics (the expansion of the electorate, the strengthening of the central government), the electoral weakness of liberal constitutionalism, the remarkable survival of the political "ins," the inexperience and division of the left, and the growing political involvement of the military. Throughout the analysis I have given much attention to the pressure felt by politicians to find a satisfactory strategy of economic development and to deal with the recurrent financial crisis. No account of modern Brazilian politics can afford to ignore the manner in which economic pressures have restricted the options of the political elite. Those pressures have also constituted an invitation to statesmanship. In responding to this challenge, the history of Brazilian political leadership since 1930 is a record both of success and of failure. Although the style and the institutions of politics may change, the essential challenge remains: how can Brazil reconcile her democratic ideal with the social tensions resulting from the gap between the rapid economic change of her recent past and the enormous tasks of development yet to be accomplished?

POLITICS IN BRAZIL, 1930–1964

The territory of Rio Branco has been renamed Roraima.

I

THE VARGAS ERA: 1930–1945

1930: Revolution of the Elite

In November 1930 the leader of an armed opposition movement, Getúlio Vargas, became provisional President of Brazil. The higher military had ten days earlier deposed the incumbent government of President Washington Luiz (1926–30) and thereby prevented it from inaugurating the candidate (Júlio Prestes) who, by the official returns, had defeated Vargas in the presidential election the preceding March. For the first time since the creation of the Republic in 1889, the "government" candidate failed to gain the presidency.

A bitter struggle over the presidential succession was nothing new in the history of the "Old Republic" (1889–1930).[1] Under the Constitution of 1891 the presidency was the chief prize in national politics. Since the President was constitutionally prohibited from succeeding himself, there was often a political upheaval every four years (the length of the presidential term), as the incumbent leadership sought agreement among the leaders of the major state political machines on the nomination of a successor. Once the nomination was agreed upon, however, it was tantamount to election because the state governments had the power to administer elections and did not hesitate to manipulate the returns to fit their pre-election agreements. With the support of the political leaders of enough states to insure an electoral majority, the nominee endorsed by the incumbent regime need have little fear of defeat. As the twentieth century wore on and cities grew, manipulation of the electorate became more difficult. But the results in the cities could still be neutralized by the electoral "herds" of the backcountry bosses (known as "colonels") who ruled their patriarchal domains with an iron hand. Although this political system of *coronel-ismo* was on the wane as a result of the economic changes that were undermining the traditional social structure of Brazil's backward interior, it was still assumed to be an important factor during the pre-election negotiations in 1929.[2]

President Washington Luiz thought he had secured sufficient support to insure the election of his presidential nominee, Júlio Prestes. The official election returns seemed to confirm his calculations. Prestes, whose ties to the incumbent President were reinforced by the fact that both were from the state of São Paulo, received 1,091,709 out of the 1,890,524 votes cast. But the opposition, which had campaigned under the label of the "Liberal Alliance" (*Aliança Liberal*), angrily rejected the official result.[3] The political leaders of the states of Minas Gerais and Rio Grande do Sul, who dominated the opposition alliance, especially resented Washington Luiz's attempt to install another São Paulo politician in the presidency.

After past elections, especially those of 1910 and 1922, the losing candidates had claimed fraud in the counting of votes as well as claiming that force, threats or bribes had been used at the ballot box. And for a short time after the election of Júlio Prestes was officially announced in April, it appeared that the opposition might again restrict its protest to mere words. On May 30 Vargas issued a "manifesto," denouncing the "frauds and intimidations" practiced by the electoral officials "whose tricks and stratagems are stimulated and encouraged by the electoral legislation itself." But the defeated candidate tempered his attack with the assurance that he still believed the necessary modification "in our political habits and customs" could take place "within the existing order" (*dentro da ordem e do regime*).[4] Certain of the revolutionaries were, however, less willing to be satisfied with words, and finally organized a full-fledged conspiracy aimed at seizing power by armed rebellion. A few weeks after the election, young radicals such as Oswaldo Aranha and Lindolfo Collor made contact with disgruntled leaders of the Liberal Alliance in Minas Gerais and Paraíba. But the political patriarchs of Rio Grande do Sul (Borges de Medeiros) and Minas Gerais (António Carlos) were at first cautious; since neither wished to initiate a revolt, each waited for the other.

The event which catalyzed the opposition into armed rebellion was the assassination of its former vice presidential candidate, João Pessoa of the northeastern state of Paraíba. On July 26 Pessoa fell before the bullets of the son of a bitter local political enemy of the former governor. His death was not atypical of the bloody clan politics in the northern coastal backwaters. At this tense moment in national politics, however, it had traumatic effect because Washington Luiz had supported the political group to which the assassin was linked. The wavering conspirators among the opposition were swept along in the wave of indignation which the radicals promoted in order to create a revolutionary atmosphere. Borges de Medeiros now supported the revolution and aided greatly in recruiting military commanders into the conspiracy. A revolutionary general staff was organized, with Colonel Góes Monteiro as its chief. The date of the revolt was set for October 3.[5]

The revolt began as scheduled, with Vargas exhorting the rebels in Rio Grande do Sul to lead the march on Rio de Janeiro. "Rio Grande, on your feet for Brazil! You cannot fail to meet your heroic destiny!" The "people" were rising "to re-acquire liberty, to restore the purity of the republican regime, to achieve national reconstruction," Vargas proclaimed.[6]

The conspiracy was supported by politicians of the Liberal Alliance and a group of revolutionary young military officers (tenentes). If this had been the limit of the rebels' strength, they would have constituted a serious but not necessarily a mortal threat to the incumbent government. With the military behind him, President Luiz could have imposed his new President on the country, as previous regimes had done against severe protests of the opposition in 1910 and 1922. But as the rebels marched on Rio de Janeiro from south (Rio Grande do Sul), north (Paraíba), and west (Minas Gerais), Washington Luiz found that he lacked the support of the military.

The incumbent President had been assured by his Minister of War, General Sezefredo dos Passos, that he could count on the armed forces to back him against the rebels. But many senior generals stationed in Rio de Janeiro were disturbed at the prospect of a civil war against what was now a formidable armed opposition in the states of Rio Grande do Sul, Santa Catarina, and Paraná. The leader of the dissident officers, Army Chief of Staff General Tasso Fragoso, later explained their apprehensions: "It seemed that an electric shock had passed through the political atmosphere." He held the President responsible "for the state of unrest and distrust in which we find ourselves. Unfortunately he set out on a rocky path and has already brought grave misfortunes upon the country." As for supporting Washington Luiz against the rebels, "No one wanted his son to put on a uniform and die fighting for a man frankly divorced from the common interest." [7]

Some three weeks after the rebels began their march on Rio de Janeiro, Washington Luiz still did not yet appreciate how his authority had crumbled. By late October the revolt had reached such proportions that the generals in Rio decided to take matters into their own hands.

The dissident military, led by Generals Tasso Fragoso and Mena Barreto, moved on October 24 to seize power from the President and his military ministers. Tasso Fragoso explained that the commanders in Rio were forced to act because "agitation had erupted everywhere," presenting them with the threat of a "national revolution such as had never been seen." [8]

The dissident generals issued a manifesto calling upon Washington Luiz to resign; they even forced an interview to make a personal appeal. Ever confident, Washington Luiz defied their ultimatum. Only after the personal intervention of Cardinal Leme of Rio de Janeiro was the President convinced that his position was lost and that he must leave office and abandon his plan to inaugurate Júlio Prestes in December. [9]

The Junta ruled Rio de Janeiro in its own right for ten days before finally delivering power on November 4 to Getúlio Vargas, the acknowledged leader of the opposition movement. Any inclination on the part of the Junta to perpetuate themselves in power had been cut short by the growing pressure from the rebels, whose military forces were closing in on the capital city. In his speech accompanying the investiture of Vargas as "Provisional President," General Fragoso noted that the military had decided to intervene out of a desire that "Brazilians cease spilling blood on behalf of a cause which was not endorsed by the national conscience." [10] As in 1889, when the Republic replaced the Empire, control at the critical moment was assumed by the higher military and then transferred to a new cadre of civilian politicians. In 1930 the Army and Navy commanders found themselves cast in a position which was to become increasingly familiar in subsequent Brazilian history: the role of final arbiter in domestic politics.

The shift in political leadership resulting from Vargas' assumption of the presidency became known as the "Revolution of 1930." Subsequent events confirmed the accuracy of that description, at least in the political sphere. In the decade and a half after Vargas assumed power, nearly every feature of the political system and the administrative structure was subjected to the zeal for reform. Many of these changes remained juridical fictions. Enough were implemented by 1945, however, to have transformed irrevocably the world of government and politics which had produced the revolutionaries of 1930.

Seen from the perspective of November 1930, the revolution may have appeared as merely another chapter in the history of the quarrels among the slowly changing elite which had dominated Brazilian politics since independence in 1822. In one sense, that interpretation was correct. Brazil's social structure and political forces had not changed overnight. The country remained overwhelmingly rural (over 70 percent of the employed males were in agriculture as of 1920).

There were two factors, however, which distinguished the events of 1930 from all previous power struggles in the history of the Republic. First, the Revolution of 1930 brought the end of the republican structure created in the decade of the 1890's. The revolutionaries were pushing on an open door, it later became evident, as the "Old Republic" quickly collapsed under the weight of its internal divisions and the pressure of the world-wide economic crisis. Second, there was widespread agreement before 1930 on the urgent need for a basic overhaul of the political system. The depth of this discontent with the existing system and the exact character of the proposed remedies varied enormously because it was a loosely knit coalition which revolted against the incumbent leadership of the Old Republic. Some of the revolutionaries envisioned little more than constitutional changes in the narrow juridical sense. Others were prepared to fight for ambitious plans of economic and social change, involving full-scale national reorganization. But there was in common a willingness to experiment with new political forms in a desperate attempt to discard the old. The effort resulted in seven years of agitated improvisation, including a regionalist revolt in São Paulo, a new constitution, a popular front movement, a fascist movement, and an attempted Communist coup. In 1937 an exhausted Brazil ended her political experimentation and began eight years of authoritarian rule under the *Estado Nôvo*.

The man who presided over the entire era of 1930 to 1945 was Getúlio Vargas. There was little in Vargas' background before 1930 to suggest that he was about to become the dominant figure of Brazilian politics for the next twenty-five years. A short, plump man with a passion for cigars, he seemed possessed of an ambition hardly distinguishable from many other members of the political elite during the Old Republic. He was born in 1883 of a wealthy ranching family in Rio Grande do Sul, near the Argentine border, where the tradition of border warfare was still alive. Vargas first embarked on a military career but after a brief stint as a cadet switched to law, the preferred training for Brazilian politicians. After a brief career as a lawyer in Rio Grande do Sul he entered state politics and then became a federal deputy in 1924. He rose quickly in the political world of Rio de Janeiro, becoming Finance Minister in Washington Luiz' government in 1926. Rio Grande do Sul had been "allocated" the Finance Ministry, a post for which Vargas, as the chief of his state's congressional delegation, was the logical nominee. Although Vargas remained minister less than two years, he gained valuable experience in cabinet-level politics at a time when the new President was radically reorganizing the national government's financial policy.

In 1928 Vargas was called back to Rio Grande do Sul to become Governor, thereby ending his association with the federal financial policies that were soon to become disastrously unpopular. Vargas became Governor under the aegis of Borges de Medeiros, the long-time political leader of Rio Grande do Sul, who was now barred by a recent political agreement from succeeding himself as Governor. Upon assuming the highest office in his native state, Vargas soon exhibited an extraordinary ability to bring together the warring political factions in the state. It was this talent more than any other that was to sustain Getúlio in his first years of power in Rio de Janeiro. His other talents became obvious only later.[11]

The "Revolutionary" Coalition of 1930

An understanding of Brazilian politics after 1930 requires a closer analysis of the heterogeneous coalition that made the Revolution of 1930.

The basic division to be made is between the revolutionary and non-revolutionary supporters of the change of power. Although even the revolutionaries as a group had no clear-cut program, one can distinguish two major positions.[12] First, there were the liberal constitutionalists, who wished to implement the classic liberal ideals—free elections, constitutional government, and full civil liberties. The liberal-constitutionalist position was strongest in the state of São Paulo and found its most certain support in the small but growing middle class of a few major cities. Its most distinguished precursor during the Old Republic was Ruy Barbosa, whose unsuccessful campaign against the government candidate in 1910 was a high point of liberal opposition to the state party machines that manipulated the presidential succession. At the outset of the Vargas era the liberal constitutionalist position was best represented by the Democratic Party of São Paulo, organized in 1926 and opposed to the government candidate (Júlio Prestes, who had been governor of São Paulo) in 1930.[13]

Second, there were the semi-authoritarian nationalists, whose main concern was "national regeneration" and modernization. Its adherents were willing to experiment with non-democratic political forms in order to achieve the social and economic changes about which they talked vaguely but passionately. The chief proponents of this position in 1930 were the intransigent young military (called lieutenants or *tenentes*) who had staged a series of abortive revolts in 1922 and 1924 in Rio de Janeiro, São Paulo and Rio Grande do Sul.[14] Their dissatisfaction with the Old Republic went deeper than its failure to fulfill the liberal constitutionalist ideals outlined in the Constitution of 1891. They looked to fundamental change, however imprecisely articulated, in public administration, social services, and the level of national consciousness. They were fearful, moreover, of resorting to elections too soon after the revolution, because they knew that the traditional state political machines would undoubtedly manipulate any elections for their own purposes. In essence, the tenentista doctrine was elitist and anti-political. These ambitious junior officers wanted to force Brazil's emergence as a modern nation, and believed it could be achieved in the short run only by a totally uncompromised cadre of non-political technocrats with an unswerving sense of national mission. After the revolution the tenente viewpoint was best represented by the "October 3rd Club" (the name recalled the day on which the successful revolt of Vargas began), an organization founded in 1931 which included both military and like-minded civilians. Although the tenentes as a group began to lose influence after 1932, and virtually disappeared after 1934, it was the position identified with their more militant wing that Vargas embraced after 1937.[15]

Apart from the tenentes, the supporters of radical change were fragmented. Brazil's meager industrialization and patrimonial social culture had not produced any mass movement or even a unified political leadership on the left. The labor union movement (of extremely modest proportions in 1930) was rent by struggles among anarchists, Trotskyites, Communists, and radicals. The "Workers' and Peasants' Bloc" (*Bloco Operário e Camponês*) failed to exert any significant weight in the events of 1930. The Communist Party dismissed the revolution by calling it "struggle among two factions of the national bourgeoisie, a struggle between two branches of the Army." [16]

The "bolshevik threat" was, however, an important concern of the "bourgeois" leadership. The military junta, for example, issued a manifesto on October 27 appealing for calm, warning the populace to beware of "the elements pernicious to the social order, who are trying to infiltrate the working class with ideas injurious to public order." [17] This obsession with heading off any proletarian "agitation"—a force of negligible potential in the Brazil of the 1930's—became more marked in the calculations of almost all sectors of the traditional political elite after the installation of the Vargas government.

The "non-revolutionary" supporters of Vargas' accession to power were made up of three groups. Although none of these groups considered itself revolutionary, each, for reasons of its own, opposed the incumbent political leadership and was prepared to aid or at least acquiesce in its overthrow.

First, there were the higher military. Generals such as Tasso Fragoso, who headed the junta that transferred power to Vargas, were resentful over what they considered the shortsighted and unpopular policies of the incumbent political elite. They were also restless over the unwillingness of the civilian governments to look more kindly upon the technical requirements of the armed forces—the need for new equipment and more generous budgets.[18] Furthermore, the military had come to find themselves the targets of overtures by civilian politicians who sought their aid in the political battles. The election of President Arthur Bernardes in 1922 began a period of bitter political strife into which the Army had been plunged by an alleged insult to military honor by Bernardes. Proof of the "insult," an alleged letter from Bernardes printed in the opposition newspaper, Correio da Manhã, was later proved to be a forgery.[19] But the gap between the senior military and the political leadership had been opened.

During the 1920's the military were repeatedly asked to enforce a state of siege in order to save federal and state governments. They were irritated and disturbed that elected governments should need to be propped up constantly. This frustration spilled over in October 1930 and proved to be the final cause of Washington Luiz' premature departure from the presidency. Many of the senior officers, therefore, believed that the depth of discontent in the country proved that Brazil needed reforms in 1930. Their concern should not be confused with the zeal for change expressed by the tenentes, however. The latter were separated from their leaders not only by the gap of years but also by career ambitions and by a different vision of the world.[20]

Coffee growers also supported the revolution. Although the federal government was committed to a coffee support program, the Washington Luiz regime insisted on maintaining a fixed exchange rate for the Brazilian currency, thereby giving the export sector a declining income as foreign prices for coffee fell. Furthermore, the government refused to take any special steps to ease the forcelosures which resulted from the financial collapse. It also refused to supply further credit to the Coffee Institute of São Paulo for purchases of surplus stocks, deciding instead to lower the previously fixed price of Brazilian coffee on the world market, thereby hoping to increase total sales. This tactic, which completely contradicted Washington Luiz' previous policy, failed, since the demand for coffee was actually declining. Coffee growers were thus angered by the double shock of the suspension of the surplus purchase program and the disastrous decline in world prices (approximately 50 percent between September 1929 and January 1930). In the aftermath of the 1929 crash, Washington

Luiz therefore found himself in the worst of all possible worlds: foreign exchange earnings tumbled and holders of Brazilian currency rushed to convert their holdings into gold. Brazil's hard-won gold and foreign exchange reserves were quickly exhausted, and coffee growers blamed their losses on the government's policy. Although Júlio Prestes had promised to change his predecessor's financial policies, he was the inevitable victim of the coffee growers' resentment against his sponsor.[21]

Finally, there were many dissident members of the established political elite who were anxious to use a coup for their own purposes. Their dissension had in many cases originated in routine political rivalries within states and among states. Leaders of opposition clans within state politics, for example, were happy to gain local power by means of a military coup in Rio de Janeiro. On the national level, the proprietors of political machines in Minas Gerais and Rio Grande do Sul, leaders in the Liberal Alliance, were angered by the attempt of Washington Luiz to impose another Paulista, Júlio Prestes, in the presidential palace. They supported the "revolution" not because they wanted basic social and economic change, but as a rationale for their resort to armed revolt against the "ins," who had ignored their interests in the negotiations to choose a "government" candidate in 1929. These frustrated politicians in both major and minor states were to provide indispensable continuity between the Old Republic and the successive stages of the Vargas era. Indeed, it was the essence of Vargas' political skill to be able to use these non-ideological politicians for his own purposes—which amounted both to keeping himself in power and to transforming the political system which they had helped overturn in 1930.[22]

New Political Forces: 1930–1935

The group which felt most deeply the obsolescence of the elitist politics in Brazil before 1930 was the small but growing class whose economic base lay in the city. They were middle-class in economic position, although frequently not in attitude, if one interprets "middle class" by the standards of nineteenth-century western European class behavior. They were employed in commerce, light industry, the professions, and the bureaucracy. Although this group had by no means fully articulated a class mentality which might place them in conscious opposition to the agrarian-dominated export economy, they were the largest single group of supporters of liberal constitutionalism. Their principal national stronghold was in the city of São Paulo.[23]

The chief political goal of the middle class, as expressed in liberal constitutionalism, was more "authentic" representation: voting must be honestly supervised and the ballots honestly counted. If a literacy requirement were enforced, this would mean increasing political power for the middle class voters who looked upon the cities as their natural political preserve. In the months after the revolution the liberal constitutionalists bombarded Vargas with demands that he reform the electoral system. As delay followed delay, they grew suspicious of the President's motives and placed the blame on the tenentes and their agents around Vargas.[24]

Their concern was compounded by the fact that the Provisional Government had taken unto itself sweeping powers. On November 11 the "Chief of the Provisional Government" issued a decree over the signature of his new ministers which gave his government the right (the revolution was "legitimizing" itself) to exercise not only executive power but also full legislative authority "until a Constituent Assembly is elected and establishes the constitutional reorganization of the country." All legislative bodies from the National Congress down to municipal assemblies were abolished. The position of "Interventor" on the state level was created as a counterpart to the "Chief of the Provisional Government" at the national level. The Interventor was given full executive and legislative powers and was responsible directly to the Provisional Government in Rio.[25]

This extraordinary concentration of power (notably absent under the extreme federalism of the Republic created in 1889) made the Vargas regime the immediate focus of a power struggle among the divergent elements in the revolutionary coalition. For the first few months there was tenuous agreement on two measures: the need to purge the "corruption" of the old politicians and the need to make new governmental provisions to satisfy working-class needs. An investigating tribunal was set up in December 1930 to punish the "malefactors" of the Old Republic, but it drew little attention, proved nothing, and disappeared before the end of 1931. Having displaced the old political elite, the revolutionaries found little advantage in persecuting the losers who were so decisively driven from power. For the working class the Provisional Government created in December 1930 a new Ministry of Labor formed by—an interesting comment on the Brazil of 1930—splitting off part of the Ministry of Agriculture. The "social question" was no longer to be considered "a matter for the police"; now it was to be "solved" by concessions from the new political elite before pressure from below might force more basic changes.[26]

The issue on which the revolutionaries split was the question of when and how Brazil ought to be "reconstitutionalized." The liberal constitutionalists pressed for immediate elections. By late 1931 the advocates of early elections included also the leaders of the "revolutionary" states of Rio Grande do Sul and Minas, who saw how elections would increase their bargaining power with the new federal government and thereby preserve a measure of the great political independence they had enjoyed since the 1890's. The tenentes, on the other hand, through the "October 3rd Club," were demanding that Vargas continue indefinitely his rule by provisional authority. They argued that the structural changes Brazil needed would be frustrated by immediate elections which would only return to office the traditional elite or their well-meaning but indistinguishable successors among the liberal constitutionalists.

Vargas' Machiavellian political style encouraged each of these groups to press their claims. The tenentes, for example, exercised considerable influence within the provisional government for the first year. Their leaders were liberally used by Vargas as political lieutenants in several important areas, such as João Alberto, the Interventor in São Paulo, and Juarez Távora, the political viceroy of the Northeast.[27]

But Vargas also gave ground to the advocates of early reconstitutionalization. On February 24, 1932, Vargas published the new Electoral Code, satisfying a principal desire of the liberal constitutionalists. The tenentes retaliated the next day by sending a mob to storm the offices of the anti-tenente newspaper, *Diario Carioca*. The assault took place with the apparent blessing of Vargas' police chief in Rio. The tenentes' opponents of all persuasions charged that the tenentes were on the verge of seizing power within the Vargas government. The tenentes seemed to share this view, or, at the least, they hoped to emerge as the dominant force within the highest councils in Rio. In early March a delegation from the October 3rd Club called upon Vargas to ask that he repudiate the idea of a Constituent Assembly. Vargas promised that "the return to a constitution system cannot and will not be a return to the past under the banner of the professional mourners of the deposed regime who today, invoking the principle of autonomy, demand a birth certificate for every local interventor. . . ." The jibe was aimed at São Paulo's resentment over the "foreigners" sent from Rio to administer Brazil's richest state. But Vargas also warned against "the practice of violence, whatever its origins" and tried to reconcile the multiple pressures on him by urging all the civilian and military revolutionaries to "unite against the efforts at intrigue, defeatism and 'sabotage' by the enemies of yesterday." He concluded by pointedly suggesting to the tenentes that they should continue their work of *"peaceful* propaganda." [28]

The threat of violence was greatest, however, to the south. Vargas knew that his opponents in São Paulo had gone beyond verbal protests and were plotting an armed revolt. The conspiracy in São Paulo had several sources. A major one was the disillusionment of the liberal constitutionalists over Vargas' delaying tactics on new elections. On January 13, 1932, the Democratic Party (the party of the liberal constitutionalists) broke openly with the Provisional Government and by mid-February had organized a "United Paulista Front" (*Frente Única Paulista*) which included the "League of Paulista Defense" (*Liga de Defesa Paulista*) and one wing of the former Paulista Republican Party (*Partido Republicano Paulista* or PRP).

This heterogeneous coalition was proof that the Vargas government had succeeded in alienating almost every political element in São Paulo. The opposition was led by the Democratic Party, which had opposed the PRP nominee in 1930 (Júlio Prestes) and supported the revolution of October. They were now disillusioned over not having been handed the perquisites of power which their PRP rivals had enjoyed in the past, and they were embittered by the arbitrary attitude of Vargas' first Interventor in São Paulo, the disastrously unpopular tenente João Alberto. They had also been alarmed by the radical tendencies of revolutionary Police Chief Miguel Costa, who organized popular militias and approached the "social question" in a manner which threatened to undermine the new political elite's paternalistic strategy.[29]

The pre-1930 state political leadership, the Paulista Republican Party (PRP) joined the opposition movement out of a desire for revenge against the "revolutionaries" who had prevented the inauguration of Júlio Prestes, the PRP standard-bearer. They stressed the "invasion" of São Paulo by "outsiders," thus appealing to the strong regionalist pride shared by the middle class and the old-line politicians. Vargas' opposition in São Paulo also included many coffee growers who felt the new federal government had still done too little to protect coffee prices. Finally, there were the disgruntled military officers who resented their replacement by the tenentes in the brief and incomplete purge of the officer corps after the October Revolution. General Bertoldo Klinger was their leader. They happily offered their services as the coordinators of a Paulista military conspiracy against the government in Rio.

In March, Vargas' equivocal attitude toward the tenentes provoked the resignations of Maurício Cardoso, Minister of Justice, and Lindolfo Collor, Minister of Labor. Both were natives of Rio Grande do Sul, to which they returned to help form an opposition movement (*Frente Única Gaúcha*). On March 29, Rio Grande do Sul broke openly with Vargas, whose efforts at reconciling the opposition there were as unsuccessful as in São Paulo.

In Minas Gerais the leadership was split over the question of armed resistance to the Vargas regime. One wing of the *Frente Única,* led by Arthur Bernardes, maintained active contact with the conspiracies in São Paulo and Rio Grande do Sul, while the Governor, Olegário Maciel, preserved an equivocal attitude which nonetheless led the conspirators to believe that Minas would join the revolt.

It now appeared that Vargas had provoked the combined opposition of Brazil's three most powerful states: São Paulo, Minas Gerais, and Rio Grande do Sul. A last-minute mission by João Neves da Fontoura on June 9 failed to convince Getúlio to renounce the tenentes. Instead, he replaced his War Minister, General Leite de Castro, with General Espírito Santo Cardoso, the candidate of the tenentes and a figure who could assure Vargas of the loyalty of a majority of the officer corps.[30]

Although the opposition loomed formidable, Vargas had made several strategic concessions both to São Paulo and to the liberal constitutionalists as a whole. The new Electoral Code, issued on February 24, 1932, was followed by a decree on March 15 establishing May 3, 1933, as the date for elections to the Constituent Assembly. The tenentista opposition to these measures of reconstitutionalization was unavailing. Vargas also met a chief complaint of São Paulo on March 1, when he named Pedro de Toledo Interventor, thus satisfying the demand for an Interventor who was both "civilian and a Paulista." But, as Vargas well knew, the opposition in São Paulo was based upon a deep-seated regional antagonism that any strong federal government was bound to exacerbate. The state and city of São Paulo had such a superiority complex toward the rest of Brazil that a movement in opposition to the federal government could gain many supporters who failed to agree on any principles except their passionate identification as Paulistas.

On July 9, 1932, São Paulo rose in armed revolt. The rebellion was immediately christened the "Constitutionalist Revolution" and the city of São Paulo mobilized for a full-scale civil war. Factories were hastily converted to the production of crude munitions. Middle-class housewives contributed their jewelry in a "Campaign of Gold" to finance the war effort, while their sons volunteered for duty in the trenches. The working class, however, remained relatively indifferent to the appeal to arms.[31]

The liberal constitutionalists, led by the Democratic Party, made a fatal error in launching the revolt. As was perhaps inevitable, they allowed demands for constitutional reform to become mixed, and finally identified, with regionalist separatism. This meant that the liberal constitutionalists forfeited any support for their principles which might well have been forthcoming from urban centers in other parts of Brazil, especially in the states of Minas Gerais and Rio Grande do Sul. Such aid was essential if they were to have any hope of success, and its absence dealt a death blow to the "constitutionalist" movement.

The support from Minas Gerais and Rio Grande do Sul which had seemed certain now failed to materialize. In part, this was because Paulista rebels began the revolt prematurely, before their allies in Minas Gerais and Rio Grande do Sul had time to organize themselves. The Gaúcho Front in Rio Grande do Sul was caught by surprise.

When the indecisive Interventor, Flores da Cunha, opted for Vargas, the dissidents who favored aid for the Paulista rebels revolted against the state government but were contained and soon defeated. Minas Gerais, under the leadership of Olegário Maciel, the Governor, and Benedito Valladares, now unknown but later to become Governor, also jumped to Vargas' side. The pro-Paulista dissidents in Minas, like their Riograndense counterparts, revolted without success against their state government.[32]

In both states it was the political patriarch from the Old Republic who led the rebels—Borges de Medeiros in Rio Grande do Sul and Arthur Bernardes in Minas Gerais. Both failed and were arrested. Their adherence to the "Constitutionalist Revolution" of 1932 helped to brand that movement as simply the counter-revolution of the old-style "oligarchs." This impression was reinforced by the fact that the old-line Paulista Republican Party joined the revolt in São Paulo, although in fact the Democratic Party in São Paulo, with the enthusiastic support of the middle class, organized the conspiracy and the old-line elements followed.

Vargas had been careful to line up his support for the confrontation with São Paulo. He cultivated the leaders of Minas Gerais and Rio Grande do Sul, arguing that the Paulista conspiracy could not benefit them. Most important, he had made sure of his military support, which remained firm except for a few scattered commanders in remote outposts such as Mato Grosso. General Góes Monteiro directed the federal forces in the Paraíba Valley, blocking a Paulista march on Rio de Janeiro. State military forces from Minas Gerais and Rio Grande do Sul invaded the state of São Paulo, aiding the federal troops in their encirclement of the capital city. Aerial bombardment by the federal forces aroused the indignation and alarm of Paulista businessmen, who called for a truce on the grounds that even the principles of constitutionalism did not justify the destruction of Brazil's wealthiest and most productive center. After a two-month siege, the rebels surrendered to the superior federal forces.

It looked as if the heartland of liberal constitutionalism had committed suicide. Vargas' primary intention, however, was to suppress São Paulo's crudely provincial self-assertion. In a characteristic gesture, he immediately extended the olive branch to the liberal constitutionalists by declaring that he intended to carry out the earlier promises of elections and a new constitution. He also appeased the Paulistas by instructing the Bank of Brazil to take over the war bonds that the Paulista banks had floated to finance the state's war effort.

The elections for the Constituent Assembly were held as scheduled on May 3, 1933. Observers agreed that they were remarkably honest compared to pre-1930 elections.[33] The tenentes, who retained their anti-political attitude and had never tried to mobilize wide public support, were split over the question of elections. A radical wing opposed elections altogether, while another group organized halfheartedly for the campaign. Some of them were elected, however, and they managed also to force a modification in the traditional method of representation to be followed in the elections for the Constituent Assembly—the Electoral regulations provided for professional syndicates which were each to elect their own representatives. From these representatives in turn was chosen a total of forty to participate in the Assembly itself, the rest of the members being elected within each state.

In the voting of the Assembly, these syndicate members voted with the tenentes, and carried a proposal that the Constituent Assembly become the first Chamber of Deputies, with power to elect the President. This was extremely important to the tenente group, because they felt that if there had to be elections, they should be indirect, on the grounds that the general electorate could never be counted upon to favor radical change. The established state leadership capitalized on their control of local politics to extract their own victories from the elections. The Constituent Assembly began its deliberations on November 15, 1933, and by mid-July of the following year produced the legal basis for Brazil's new constitutional order.

The Constitution of 1934 was a hybrid product. As a juridical document, it realized to a remarkable degree the ideals both of political liberalism and of socio-economic reformism. The liberal constitutionalists could take satisfaction from the fact that, although the federal structure was much like that of the Old Republic, there were now guarantees of free elections, ensured by the Electoral Code of 1932 and the new Electoral Tribunal, a federal authority with powers to supervise elections and count the returns. There was also a new and more intricate set of guarantees of an impartial judiciary. The tenentes, on the other hand, could point to the Constitution's assertion of new government responsibility in the areas of economic development and social welfare, especially as spelled out in the constitutional provisions on the "Economic and Social Order." A new labor tribunal system was established, for example, and the power to fix minimum wages was given to the federal government. In July 1934, Getúlio was elected by the Chamber of Deputies for a term which extended until the direct election scheduled for January 1938. The elections for state legislatures (which subsequently elected the state governors) were held in October 1934, and confirmed the hold of the established leadership in the principal states—Armando de Salles Oliveira in São Paulo, Flores da Cunha in Rio Grande do Sul, and Benedito Valladares in Minas Gerais.[34]

The apparent ease with which both the liberal constitutionalists and the tenente group were able to incorporate their views into the new Constitution was not an accurate indication of the political strength of either position. The middle class of the large cities, which constituted the liberal constitutionalists par excellence, still lacked leadership, partly because of the discredit which the Paulistas, their natural leaders, had brought upon themselves by the debacle of 1932. The tenentes, on the other hand, the most influential advocates of state-directed social and economic change, had never commanded a wide popular following. They were manipulators who gained access to Vargas and his political advisers in the two years after 1930 and thus were able to set the tone of thinking on many social and economic questions. After mid-1932, however, they lost most of the cohesion they earlier enjoyed, and subsequently only those tenentes whom Vargas *chose* to use in his government were influential.[35]

The formalization of the new political system in 1934 occurred, therefore, at a moment when the political lines produced by the revolution of 1930 had grown irrelevant. If the uneasy compromise embodied in the new Constitution had been the product of a balance among opposing political forces, it might have enjoyed greater prospects for longevity. But the political groups most closely identified with the positions of liberal constitutionalism and of socioeconomic reformism were by 1934 being superseded by a new genre of political activism. Politics in Brazil, just as in Europe of the early 1930's, was becoming radicalized.[36]

On the left, one faction of the Communist Party of Brazil, the "legalist" wing, organized a popular front movement called the National Liberation Alliance (*Aliança Nacional Libertadora* or ANL). Although the movement depended heavily on Communist Party organization, it succeeded in rallying large numbers of perplexed middle-class voters who were prepared to supplement their earlier liberalism with a dose of the progressivism symbolized by the appeal of Luís Carlos Prestes, the honorary president of the ANL. Although himself a Communist, Prestes' role in the ANL was to attract those voters who still admired him as the courageous leader of the rebel column ("Prestes Column") which had dramatized the tenente cause in the 1920's by successfully eluding federal armies in the Brazilian interior for two and a half years.[37]

Suddenly it appeared that the left had come to life. More than 1,600 local branches of the ANL had sprung up by the end of May 1935. The "progressive" elements within the middle class were at last joining with the militant labor unions to support a radical program. The platform of the ANL, announced in February, called for the cancellation of "imperialist debts," the nationalization of foreign-owned businesses, and the liquidation of latifundia.[38]

Radicalizers were equally active on the right. Since 1932 a fascist movement called Integralism (*Integralismo*) had also been gaining strength. The Integralista leader, Plínio Salgado, used the trappings of continental fascism—green shirts, mass street rallies, street violence against radicals of the left—to exploit the growing middle-class suspicion that perhaps the economic and political problems of the Depression could be solved only by turning to extremist methods of the right.[39]

Most significant was the fact that Integralismo and the National Liberation Alliance constituted the first national political movements with sharply ideological orientation. The components of the loosely knit Liberal Alliance (*Aliança Liberal*), which had made the Revolution of 1930, had been local political groupings held together only by a common desire to overthrow the narrow governing elite of the Old Republic. Now they had been overshadowed by more ambitious, better disciplined, wider based, and more radical national movements.

The Collapse of Democracy: 1935–1937

If politics had come alive with such vigor in 1934, how was a coup possible just three years later? The answer lies in the great skill with which Vargas manipulated one extreme against the other, producing in the minds of the military and the middle class profound pessimism about the viability of open politics.[40] In Brazil, as in the entire Western political world, liberalism was steadily losing ground.

Even before the National Liberation Alliance was fully organized in 1935, the increasingly conservative Congress began to debate the menace of the "subversives." On March 30 the majority, led by Raul Fernandes, pushed through a National Security Law giving the federal government special powers to repress "subversive" political activities. Vargas had already been maneuvering since late 1934 to discredit the emerging popular front movement on the grounds that it was Communist-led.

An overconfident Luís Carlos Prestes soon gave Vargas an opportunity to use the new security law. On July 5, the anniversary of the first tenente revolt at Copacabana Fort (1922), Prestes gave a violent speech attacking Vargas' failure to carry out the ideals of 1922; what Brazil needed was a "popular government" which was truly "revolutionary and anti-imperialist." Grievously overestimating the prospects for a mass-based revolution from the left, he ended with the cry "Down with Fascism! Down with the hateful government of Vargas! For a revolutionary national popular government! All power to the National Liberation Alliance!" [41]

Vargas quickly answered. On July 13 police raided the headquarters of the Alliance, confiscating documents later used to prove that the movement was foreign-financed and Communist-controlled. The Alliance was closed by government order for six months. Many leaders of the left were arrested, while the congressional majority left judgment on the repressive measures to the Supreme Court, which refused to act on the Alliance's petition for judicial measures against the suppression. The "legal road" to power for the extreme left had been barred. The Congress, dominated by its middle class and agrarian members, along with the syndical delegates, was apprehensive over the "bolshevik" threat and ready to give Vargas the special powers he wanted for his own purposes. As for popular support, Vargas knew that the Integralistas were always at work, harassing the left in the politics of the street.[42]

At this point the revolutionary wing of the Brazilian Communist Party, which had rejected the popular front approach and had urged an armed uprising instead, played into Vargas' hands so perfectly that many participants later concluded that these events were engineered by government agents who had infiltrated both the Aliança Nacional Libertadora and the Communist Party itself. In late November of 1935, military revolutionaries in the northern garrisons of Natal and Recife began a barracks revolt, murdering senior officers in their beds. But the rebels in the north had failed to coordinate their coup with the plotters in the south. By the time the Communist military rebels made their move in Rio de Janeiro, the local commands had been fully alerted and the revolt was easily crushed by government forces. Vargas now had the ideal justification for repression of the left: incontrovertible proof of the danger of armed treason.[43]

The emergency powers of the federal government were rapidly augmented. On November 25 Vargas requested a state of siege from the Congress; it was approved. In December the Chamber of Deputies agreed to tighten the National Security Law and also passed three constitutional amendments. One authorized the President to dismiss summarily any civil servant, while another strengthened Vargas' control over the military by giving him the power over promotion of all officers and where they should be posted. The third gave the President even greater temporary emergency powers.

Ruthless police methods quickly eliminated the fledgling political movements on the left. The Communist Party leadership was imprisoned (Luís Carlos Prestes eluded his captors until March 1936) and their offices raided. In the months after the abortive Communist revolt thousands of political suspects, both military and civilian, were imprisoned. To dramatize the "subversive" threat, the prisoners were herded onto an ancient naval vessel, the "Pedro I," which was converted into a floating jail and anchored in the bay fronting one of Rio's more populous quarters. In the Federal District (greater Rio de Janeiro) the popular reform regime of Mayor Pedro Ernesto was suppressed. The political system had begun to close.

During 1936 the congressional acquiescence in rule by emergency powers continued unabated. Four times that year the Congress voted to extend the state of siege for ninety days. The repression extended even to members of Congress—in March one senator and four deputies were arrested and in July the Chamber agreed to their trial. In September a new National Security Tribunal (*Tribunal de Segurança*

Nacional) was approved by the Congress, giving Vargas a new instrument to harass and repress his opposition.

Despite the repression of the left, planning began in 1936 for the presidential election which would be held in January 1938. Vargas had been elected as Brazil's first President under the new Constitution by the Constituent Assembly of 1933–34, but he was also prohibited from succeeding himself. By mid-1937 two candidates had emerged. A newly formed political alliance, the Brazilian Democratic Union (*União Democrática Brasileira*), supported Armando de Salles Oliveira, the Governor of São Paulo, who had just finished a successful administration. He was an authentic spokesman for liberal constitutionalism (the party which first nominated him was called, characteristically, the *Partido Constitucionalista*), proclaiming his faith in Brazil's ability to govern by the democratic process while warning of the "bolshevik" agitation and infiltration which had reached into the ranks of the apprehensive middle class. Brazil, he explained, was fortunate to have escaped from the "anguish of European peoples"; his country did not need totalitarian methods to ward off the "bolshevik onslaughts"—instead, Brazil could fortify her democratic tradition by borrowing the "powerful methods of propaganda" developed in Italy, Portugal, and Germany. Salles Oliveira proudly pointed out that a system of social legislation "capable of satisfying the aspirations of the working classes" had been enacted without "pressure from powerful parties or the violence and tumult of unexpected strikes." What Brazil now needed, he argued, was an authentic "social democracy" fortified against subversion from both the right and the left.[44]

The other principal candidate was José Américo de Almeida, a former *tenente* and novelist-politician from the northeastern state of Paraíba. He had been a leader in the Liberal Alliance of 1930 and an important spokesman for authoritarian nationalist policies (as urged by the tenentes) in the first two years after the Revolution of 1930. In his presidential campaign of 1937, José Américo attempted to mobilize lower-class voters by arguing that only through the exercise of the franchise could they gain their social and economic rights. He was generally regarded as the government candidate, lacking only the formal endorsement of Vargas.[45]

But Vargas conspicuously declined to endorse anyone. Although it was difficult to estimate the relative strength of the two candidates—

this was to be the first direct presidential election since the Revolution of 1930 and the new Electoral Code issued in 1932—Armando de Salles Oliveira had a reasonable chance of winning the election. Vargas, wishing as always to preserve maximum room for maneuver, adopted a strategy of equivocation, allowing the impression to grow that José Américo was the official candidate, while at the same time encouraging speculation over the possibility of some surprise move from the presidential palace. The Integralistas waited in vain for Vargas to clarify his attitude, and finally nominated their "Führer," Plínio Salgado, in June 1937.

As the campaign continued, close advisers of Getúlio argued that only he could save Brazil from the extremes of right and left. Indeed, support for some kind of "continuist" solution was widespread among the military and political elites. Vargas needed little encouragement to believe in his own indispensability. Since the Communist revolt of 1935, Vargas had been considering the possibility of a coup. The ease with which the Congress voted him emergency powers encouraged thoughts of an authoritarian regime which would eliminate the divided political forces and give the President a free hand to carry forward Brazil's "reorganization" as he saw fit.

During the first six months of 1937, Vargas pursued a dual strategy: on the one hand he appeared to cooperate with preparations for the presidential campaign by negotiating with state leaders; at the same time, however, he was working to isolate the more refractory of them. A new series of "interventions" were carried out in Mato Grosso, Maranhão, and the Federal District, replacing the elected leadership with men in Vargas' confidence. Of the three major states whose opposition Vargas feared, Rio Grande do Sul was the first to feel the pressure from Rio de Janeiro. In April it was put under a state of siege, thus aiding the local opponents of Governor Flores da Cunha, who was attempting to throw Rio Grande's weight behind the candidacy of Armando de Salles Oliveira. Rio Grande do Sul was a important obstacle to Vargas' plan of disarming his opposition because Flores da Cunha had the largest state militia in Brazil under his command.

The politicians in the Congress now began to sense the possible implications of Vargas' moves. Having been continuously willing to give Vargas emergency weapons against the left, they realized that their own fortunes in the election depended on a more compliant executive. For the first time since November 1935, the Congress refused to renew the state of siege requested in June of 1937. Vargas thereupon adopted a new strategy aimed at maneuvering his opponents into an untenable position by unleashing the "subversives." He released a group of left-wing political prisoners, thereby dramatizing the "threat" from the left for the middle class, the conservative state politicians, and the military. The freeing of prisoners continued into September. Vargas also entered into contact with the Integralistas, who grew confident that they would emerge the winners in the coming showdown. Plínio Salgado's nomination for President was communicated to Vargas on June 14. Street fights between the Green Shirts and their disorganized hecklers on the left broke out repeatedly; in August, thirteen fatalities resulted from a clash in Campos, a city in the state of Rio de Janeiro. The presidential campaign was now under the growing cloud of anti-democratic violence.

Given the division and indecision of the conservative and center politicians, Vargas knew that the position of the Army would be crucial in any attempt at a coup. Since the change of War Minister in June 1934, the Army had succeeded in reestablishing the discipline which had been undermined during the revolts of the 1920's, the Revolution of 1930, and the São Paulo revolt of 1932. In December 1936, General Eurico Dutra became War Minister, thus assuring Vargas of strong support from a known advocate of a coup. In July 1937, General Góes Monteiro, a persistent advocate of a more centralized and authoritarian regime, was named Army Chief of Staff, further strengthening Vargas' hand. In the two years since the Communist revolt of 1935, Góes Monteiro, Vargas' military *éminence grise,* had pursued his own plan of neutralizing the states whose political leadership had gone into opposition to the federal government—Bahia (Juracy Magalhães), Pernambuco (Lima Cavalcanti), Rio Grande do Sul (Flores da Cunha), and São Paulo (the supporters of Salles Oliveira). For Góes Monteiro and Dutra, the goal was a "strong Army within a strong state." Their efforts to give the national Army a monopoly of military force coincided with Vargas' own plans for a personal dictatorship.[46]

By strategic transfers Góes Monteiro filled the Army posts in the doubtful states with commanders who could be counted upon to isolate and, if necessary, seize control of the state militia and local police forces. Góes Monteiro did a tour of duty himself in Rio Grande do Sul in January 1937 in order to make certain that the Army command there could deal with Flores da Cunha's state brigade. But Flores da Cunha was in a weak position within Rio Grande do Sul. The state of siege imposed on the state in April had aided his local enemies who were remnants of the *Frente Única Gaúcha*.

By September 1937, Vargas' military commanders had succeeded in isolating the opposition in the principal states. Minas Gerais, which had earlier in 1937 (April) agreed to a pact of mutual defense with Rio Grande do Sul and Bahia, turned cautious. São Paulo, having furnished the principal opposition candidate, also grew wary of a link with Rio Grande do Sul, whose "treachery" in 1932 had left the Paulistas powerless against the troops of Vargas.

Plans for a coup now waited on some new dramatic move in Rio de Janeiro. Growing impatient with the maneuvering of Vargas, Góes Monteiro resorted to a familiar stratagem: the Army General Staff suddenly "discovered" a document purporting to be the battle plan for a Communist revolution. They produced a crude forgery known as the "Cohen Plan," fabricated, as the title suggested, by the Integralistas and handed to Góes Monteiro by an Integralista officer, Captain Olímpio Mourão Filho. It was passed on to Dutra and Getúlio, who approved its use to prepare *their* coup. On September 30, Dutra denounced the Communist plot revealed in the "Cohen Plan" and the next day, October 1, the Congress approved the suspension of constitutional rights which it had denied Vargas the preceding June. Minas Gerais supported the measure, with Rio Grande do Sul and São Paulo opposing.[47]

Preparations for the coup were now accelerated. Congressional Deputy Negrão de Lima was sent on a mission to prepare the wavering states to support stronger federal measures. Rio Grande do Sul remained the most important obstacle. Flores da Cunha's local opposition (which included Vargas' brother Benjamin) had already begun impeachment proceedings against the Governor. On October 14, the Riograndense state militia was federalized by order of Góes Monteiro and the local Army commander he had appointed. On October 18, Flores da Cunha fled to Uruguay, depriving Salles Oliveira of his most powerful supporter against Vargas' coup.

Dutra and Góes Monteiro were now certain of their strength. Francisco Campos, a young revolutionary of 1930 from Minas Gerais, had been at work for some time drafting a new constitution. As November began, there was a growing fear among the supporters of Salles Oliveira and José Américo de Almeida that the election scheduled for January of 1938 might be postponed or canceled. On November 8, the Justice Minister, José Carlos de Macedo Soares, resigned; he had finally realized that the "constitutional reform" which he had been actively discussing with the military commanders was about to occur under auspices very different from what he had imagined. The date of the coup had in fact been set for November 15, the forty-eighth anniversary of the proclamation of the Republic.[48]

The drift of events became so obvious that Salles Oliveira decided to make a last-minute appeal to the military. In a statement read to the two houses of Congress on November 9, the former Governor of São Paulo attacked the "small group" around the President who had a "long-prepared plan" to subvert Brazilian institutions. "It is the duty of the Army and Navy to keep watch over the ballot boxes and make certain that they give the country a government of authority. . . ."[49]

Salles Oliveira was not in a strong position to offer the military such lessons in democracy. Earlier he had praised the Army's "unselfish heroism" as the answer to "bolshevik" aggression.[50] He had proudly noted in October 1936 that "the Brazilian Congress demonstrated that it was not afraid of the responsibility of giving the Executive the means of defending the nation in crises which the Constitution had not foreseen." Now the presidential candidate saw his own political career and the hopes of the liberal constitutionalists threatened by the same fate that had befallen the left. Salles Oliveira's statement closed with an ingenuous plea: "The nation turns to its military leaders: in suspense, it awaits the gesture which kills or the word which saves."[51]

The gesture was not long in coming. The next morning, troops surrounded the Congress and turned its members away with the news that it had been closed. Vargas had taken the precaution of first confirming that the Governor of São Paulo, Cardoso de Melo Neto, did not endorse the position of Salles Oliveira. Eighty members of the Chamber of Deputies immediately declared their support for Getúlio.

Vargas had prepared the ground so effectively in the states that only two governors had to be replaced—Juracy Magalhães in Bahia, who resigned in protest, and Lima Cavalcanti in Pernambuco. At the same time, Vargas promulgated a new constitution, giving himself authoritarian powers and providing for a plebiscite in six years to choose a new President. The new constitutional forms were an imitation of the European corporatist and fascist models, especially in Portugal and Italy.

In his radio broadcast of November 10, Vargas explained that Brazil must forgo the "democracy of parties" which "threatens national unity." He described the Congress as an "inadequate and costly apparatus" whose continuation was "inadvisable." Brazil had no alternative but to institute a "strong government of peace, justice, and work," concluded the new dictator, "in order to adjust the political organism to the economic necessities of the country." To underline his point. Vargas announced in the same speech Brazil's decision to suspend all interest and amortization payments on her foreign debt.[52] All political parties were abolished on December 2 and the new consolidation of federal power began.

The coup of November 10 was the triumph of Vargas' long-evident desire to remain in office beyond his legal term, which was to expire in 1938. Since 1935 he had been maneuvering his opponents into a position where he could either discredit or repress them, while at the same time carefully cultivating the support of well-established power groups such as the coffee growers and the higher military. To appease the coffee growers, for example, Vargas had in October 1937 reduced the ceiling on Brazilian coffee prices in an effort to increase sales (and, hopefully, total export earnings) abroad.[53] As for the military, the Army command had been planning an authoritarian solution of Brazil's political crisis since the Communist revolt of November 1935. The higher military were skeptical of Brazil's ability to withstand the confusion and indecision of open political competition, and they were frightened by the prospect of further gains by radicals of the left— who, if ever in power, might succeed in removing the Armed Forces as the ultimate arbiter of political conflict. Finally, the coup of 1937 was possible because the middle class, that small but important social group which would hold the balance in any system of free elections restricted to literate voters, was confused and divided. Some middle-class voters remained loyal to their traditional liberal constitutional-ism and pinned their hopes on Armando de Salles Oliveira in the campaign of 1937. Others despaired of their original liberalism and turned toward the radicalism of either left or right. In so doing, they in effect conceded that liberal formulae were no longer applicable to Brazil and they were therefore prepared, if unconsciously, to accept with little protest the special brand of authoritarianism which Vargas suddenly imposed in November of 1937. The coup of November 1937 closed the political system. With it, all questions of voting strength in the elections scheduled for January 1938 became academic.[54]

The higher Army officers justified the authoritarian turn on the grounds that free political competition had proved bankrupt and even dangerous to national unity and national security. The immediate evidence for this claim was Vargas' charge that the executive must be strengthened against "extremists." Vargas had been shrewdly maneuvering to increase his own power from the time he first reached the presidency in 1930. From 1935 to 1937, however, he was able to move into a vacuum resulting from the total collapse of the alliance of forces which overthrew the Old Republic in 1930.

With the coup of November 1937, Vargas began the second half of his fifteen-year tenure. It was to last until the military forced his retirement in October 1945. The introduction of the Estado Nôvo, Brazil's milder version of Europe's fascist mode, dramatized and confirmed the long-standing division between the two principal positions inherent in the revolutionary movement of 1930. Since the fall of incumbent President Washington Luiz in that year, national politics had consisted of a series of uneasy compromises between liberal constitutionalists and authoritarian nationalists, presided over by political opportunists (often representing the old-line state oligarchies) or by idealists who felt drawn in both directions. The open political system, with its uncertain balance of forces, had been eroded by violence from the left and right. The coup of 1937 finally settled the direction of Brazil's historic path at a critical juncture. The goals of social welfare and economic nationalism, much debated earlier in the decade, were now to be pursued under authoritarian tutelage. The result was a deepening of the dichotomy between a narrow constitutionalism which had neglected social and economic questions and a nationalistic social welfarism which had become unequivocally anti-democratic.[55]

In the wake of the coup, one political group still appeared to enjoy full freedom—the radicals of the right. Salgado and his Integralista followers mistakenly thought they were to be the principal beneficiaries of Vargas' move. Their arch-enemies on the left had been eliminated; now it appeared that the Integralistas were to furnish the cadres and perhaps the leadership for the new Brazil. But Vargas had no intention of delivering his political victory to the Green Shirts. The ostensible political arm of the Integralistas (called the *Ação Integralista Brasileira*) was suppressed on December 2, 1937, along with all other political parties. In their ensuing resentment, the Integralistas played into Vargas' hands in circumstances almost as strange as those surrounding the abortive Communist military rising of 1935.

In May 1938, a small band of armed Integralistas, aided by some non-Integralista anti-Vargas military, attacked the presidential palace. Although a part of the palace guard collaborated with the attackers and the local military garrison was slow to send reinforcements, the loyalist guards helped Vargas and his gun-wielding daughter, Alzira, to hold off the attackers until they were driven away by the police.[56] Now Vargas had the same justification for repressing the Integralistas that he had been given by the Communists in 1935. Since his handwritten constitution of the Estado Nôvo gave him ample powers, the remaining Integralista organization (the "non-political" sporting clubs had survived the decree of December 2, 1937) could be quickly broken up and the leaders imprisoned or exiled. The last of the two national political movements which had emerged in the early 1930's had now been smashed. From 1938 until late 1944, the Estado Nôvo rested upon the support of the Armed Forces, Vargas' own police, and the disorganization, demoralization, and debilitation of the opposition.

It is important to understand that, unlike his European mentors in fascism, Vargas did not organize any political movement on which to base his authoritarian regime. There was no Vargas party, no Estado Nôvo movement, no government cadres in Brazilian society. The Estado Nôvo in its undiluted form, between 1937 and 1943 (when Vargas began to prepare for the return of elections), represented a hiatus in the development of party politics organized on class or ideological lines—a form of politics which itself had only begun to take form in Brazil in the early 1930's. Every significant political group had been outmaneuvered and suppressed. The Communists and radical leftists suffered the most brutal repression. The Integralistas disappeared, in part because of repression, in part because the logic of their authoritarianism was undermined by Vargas' more Brazilian form of dictatorship.

The liberal constitutionalists had lost most. Whereas the Communists could claim that their suffering demonstrated the dialectic of history and could hope that the Vargas dictatorship would further prepare the masses for revolution, the liberals saw their ideals of free elections, civil liberties, and impartial justice repudiated without arousing significant protest. At first glance, it might appear that those identified with semi-authoritarian social and economic change had lost least. But if Vargas implemented some of the tenentes' ideas after 1937, and even used some of the former tenente leaders, they had long since lost any identity as a group, or any coherence as a political position.

In sum, the Estado Nôvo was a hybrid state, not dependent on articulate popular support in Brazilian society, and without any consistent ideological basis. Vargas hoped to preempt for his own political advantage the direction of social change and economic growth in Brazil. Despite the corporatist trappings, his Estado Nôvo was a highly personal creation.[57]

Brazil proved unable to find a democratic solution to the alternating paroxysm and paralysis which had followed the demise of the Old Republic. As the eight-year dictatorship wore on, Brazil continued to undergo a process of rapid economic and social change which was rendering any return to the pre-1930 political system steadily less possible. By the end of the Estado Nôvo in 1945, the social basis of politics had changed irrevocably. Although Brazil had not embarked upon a full-fledged industrialization program by 1945, there were important beginnings. Accompanying this limited economic development was a continued growth in the proportion of Brazilians living in urban areas and a sharp growth in the absolute size of the literate population. The political consequences of these economic and social changes were striking. The dynamic urban centers of the industrializing triangle—with its three corners located in Belo Horizonte, Rio de Janeiro, and São Paulo—had created a significant block of urban voters. There were still large areas of rural Brazil where the old-style "clientelistic" politics persisted, but national politics, if and when free elections were held, would inevitably become a more open and less predictable game.[58]

New Patterns of Government and Politics

The Estado Nôvo brought irreversible changes in the institutions of political life and public administration. Most important, Vargas transformed the relationship between federal authority and state authority, and thereby moved Brazil much closer to a truly national government.

In 1945, Brazil inherited a federal executive which was immeasurably stronger than the one the revolutionaries had seized in 1930. The process by which the federal government was steadily strengthened at the expense of state and local government began in November 1930 and was accelerated after 1937. There was a political and an administrative aspect to the process, although the two were closely related.

The federal government increased its powers in the administrative sphere in two different ways. First, many functions previously exercised by state and local government were shifted into the area of federal competence. Before 1930 many of the most important functions of government had been exercised by the states, which enjoyed wide autonomy. States such as São Paulo, for example, were in the habit of directly negotiating foreign loans to be used for facilities such as railroads and docks, or for the financing of the coffee support program. In the fundamental areas of education and labor, responsibility under the Old Republic had been left almost entirely to the states. Immediately after the revolution of 1930, the situation began to change. For many years critics of the old order had been arguing that Brazil's enormous social needs demanded a national effort by a strong federal government.[59] Even before the Constitution of 1934 had codified this new role, the Vargas government, in its provisional status, gained by decree of November 11, 1930, broader powers than any previous government had ever enjoyed. A new Ministry of Labor, Industry, and Commerce was created in November 1930, and supervision over the production and marketing of coffee was transferred from state to federal auspices, in return for a higher level of support. New federal institutes of pine (1941), tea (1938) and salt (1940) were set up after 1937; these government-sponsored cartels represented the assumption of federal responsibility in areas in which no government had previously claimed authority.[60]

This leads to the second method by which federal administrative predominance grew: federal activity in new areas. The Vargas years saw a repudiation in Brazil of the "gendarme" theory, which held that the state should be a policeman, not a participant. Increasing federal intervention in the economy required new federal agencies which, in turn, further weakened the relative power of the states and municipalities. Federal ownership in industries such as railways and shipping, and mixed public-private corporations—a favored technique for stimulating investment in basic industries after 1938—responded to the policy direction of Rio de Janeiro. In this system, regional influences could be brought to bear only through the channels of national government.

New federal responsibility in two other areas—social welfare and labor union organization—further increased federal power. Although federal activity in these areas accelerated under the Estado Nôvo, and was considered by Vargas to be the cornerstone of his new political style after 1943, it had been initiated even before the Constitution of 1934. Income-flows channeled through the social welfare institutes and labor syndicates, although not part of federal revenues, were nonetheless transfer payments supervised by federal and not state or municipal authorities. The effect was to increase direct federal contact at the local level, thereby undermining the foundation of the *política dos governadores* ("politics of the governors") which had prevailed before 1930.

The power of state and municipal government was also eroded by the restricting of traditional sources of tax revenue. Tax jurisdictions were revised by the constitutions of 1934 and 1937, in the latter case eliminating what had been a major source of state revenue—interstate (called "export") taxes. This was an important step in creating a national market.[61]

Along with the overall growth of federal responsibility went a growth in federal bureaucracy. The latter was institutionalized under Vargas with the creation of DASP (*Departamento Administrativo do Serviço Público*), the federal agency set up in 1938 with functions roughly equal to the combined roles of the Bureau of the Budget and the Civil Service Commission in the United States. DASP became an important instrument for raising administrative standards, but it was also a means by which Vargas could increase his personal control (and, for his successors, the powers of the President) over federal administration.[62]

All of these additions to federal administrative authority and competence had great political repercussions. The federal executive gained enormous patronage power, both in the sense of federally controlled jobs and in the sense of the favoritism or discrimination inherent in the exercising of the growing administrative powers. It included, for example, control over low-interest loans from the Bank of Brazil, public works projects, differential exchange rates, and import controls. This increase in the political leverage of the presidency was felt most strongly in those parts of the country which were most dynamic politically—the urbanizing areas. Thus Vargas was able to use the greatly strengthened federal executive to forge what Brazil had failed to achieve before 1930: a more truly national polity.

The growth of new political institutions on the federal level therefore served two purposes: it was part of the process of unifying the sprawling country administratively; and it helped enable the President to articulate a national network of political alliances.

The increased centralization under Vargas was a reaction to the decentralization imposed by the Republican constitution-writers of 1889–91, who had wished to undo what they regarded as the harmful overcentralization of the Empire (1822–89). Except for the Paulistas, who still treasured their uniquely efficient regionalism, the majority of those who welcomed the end of the Old Republic in 1930 hoped for a more centralized Brazil. This was especially true of the urban classes, who had failed to win what they considered their rightful political representation from the agrarian-dominated political elite. Both the liberal constitutionalists and the tenentes knew that their goals had greatest prospects for success under a strong federal regime. If it came to a choice between anarchy and authoritarianism, a surprisingly large number of the revolutionaries of 1930 were willing to opt for the latter, if only implicitly.

In effect, they were unwilling to fight the dictatorship without first seeing what it might accomplish. Indeed, many of the institutional innovations of the Estado Nôvo were merely logical extensions in the growth of the federal executive which had begun in Vargas' first phase. With the exception of a few institutions, such as the propaganda and press censorship agency (*Departamento de Imprensa e Propaganda* or DIP) and the secret police, the administrative structure of the Estado Nôvo was as much a response to the challenge of effectively governing and rapidly transforming the country as it was a set of devices to facilitate Vargas' personal rule. This fact helps explain why the Estado Nôvo began and ended with relatively little social tension.[63]

In addition to the administrative changes, what were the political techniques which Vargas used to increase his own power and that of the federal government? Once installed in the presidency in 1930, he had been faced with the immediate problem of consolidating the new regime's power. Since 1889 national politics had been the prerogative of the leaders of the most powerful states. Minas Gerais and São Paulo had been the leaders in this system, with Rio Grande do Sul and Rio de Janeiro growing in importance, and Bahia and Pernambuco declining in relative power. From 1930 until 1945 Vargas strove to replace this quasi-confederation with a strong federal executive (redounding to Vargas' greater personal power, of course) at the expense of the state political machines. By the midpoint of the period, 1937, Vargas had succeeded to a remarkable extent in neutralizing the local political oligarchs who previously had been the key to national politics.

It was this outmaneuvering of the opposition in the principal states which enabled Vargas to capitalize upon the division, demoralization, and ineptitude of the political forces generated by the Revolution of 1930. Even before the coup of 1937, Vargas had amply demonstrated his extraordinary talents of political persuasion. He seldom failed to cultivate a minority faction in a state where the leadership was hostile. By assiduously maintaining intimate political contacts with the "opposition," Vargas was able to hold out the promise of federal endorsement if the pro-Vargas faction should reach power. Since the patronage powers of the federal government were growing enormously, federal favor could be of great value to a local politician. It could mean influence over the growing operations of the federal authorities in his locality. Without Vargas' support, such influence was far more difficult. After the coup of 1937, it was impossible. But even before the

Estado Nôvo, Vargas demonstrated how effectively he could use persuasion, cajolery, and the promise of spoils to exploit for his own benefit the traditional power struggles within the political leadership of the major states.

There were other assets which Vargas enjoyed in his dealings with state politicians. For those who harbored national ambitions, Vargas' blessing was almost indispensable after 1935, and a *sine qua non* after 1937. With the rapidly growing federal responsibility in so many fields, as staked out by the actions of the provisional government of 1930–34 and by the Constitution of 1934, any Brazilian politician who wished to help direct his country's destiny had to contemplate national politics or federal administration. The leverage which Vargas thereby gained is obvious.

One of Vargas' constant targets was the extreme regionalism of some states, of which the São Paulo revolt of 1932 was the leading example. Vargas appealed to the higher sentiment of nationalism and was thus able to cut across conflicting regional sympathies. After the coup of 1937, Vargas adopted a more direct approach: in late November 1937, the dictator held a public ceremony at which he burned the traditional state flags.

Both before and after 1937, Vargas made frequent use of "Interventors." This was the title, as noted earlier, given to the federally appointed Governor who was also invested with legislative powers. Where states were rebellious, Vargas resorted to using military officers as Interventors. Although their power was limited by their own ability to gain the cooperation of local power centers, some Interventors proved highly successful deputies of federal authority. By using a bevy of such devices, Vargas was able, in the major states, to undermine the traditional political clans and to create in their place a network of nationally oriented local alliances. In the Vargas era, these alliances were designed to be loyal to the President himself. Perhaps the most successful case of Vargas' cultivation of a state leadership was Minas Gerais, where his Interventor, Benedito Valladares, was a valuable ally in the preparations for the coup of 1937. After Vargas' fall in 1945, these pro-Vargas state leaderships proved to be responsive to orders from other holders of national power, demonstrating that Vargas had fashioned a system of national government which would outlast him.[64]

In explaining Vargas' political success after 1930, one should also note that he managed to make himself the symbol, in the eyes of many of the younger generation, of a sense of national purpose. From 1930 to 1932 he had been able to exploit the ideas, enthusiasm, and administrative ability of the small group of younger military, known as the tenentes, and their civilian allies, such as Oswaldo Aranha. Even after most of their number had become disillusioned or had been discarded by Vargas, there were other idealists who identified their hopes with the revolutionary President. Francisco Campos, a young lawyer from Minas Gerais and author of the Constitution of 1937, is the most famous example. There were many others, like José Américo de Almeida. Some were to desert Vargas before the coup of 1937. The reasoned support of younger intellectuals, usually of middle-class background, helped to furnish at each stage an aura of legitimacy for a leader who was not given to ideological self-justification. Such intellectual legitimacy was important for many Brazilians who quietly approved Vargas' policies but wished to be given some rationale for the President's actions.[65]

Although Vargas himself was not given to nourishing a "cult of personality," he allowed his propaganda agency (DIP), through both its national and its state offices, to chant his praises in publications such as the monthly *O Brasil de Hoje, de Ontem e de Amanhã* (first published in 1939). Yet Getúlio undoubtedly looked on such adulation skeptically. He approved it as long as it continued to absorb the energy of some otherwise restless intellectuals and filled a vacuum left by the suppression of democratic politics. But Vargas' reliance on these instruments borrowed from European fascism was in no sense irreversible. He was well aware of the irreverent humor that his countrymen, especially the Cariocas (residents of the city of Rio de Janeiro), aimed at the would-be dictator. Vargas later explained that during the years from 1930 to 1945 "popular jokes were my guide, indicating a safe path in the midst of the pleasant smile and the delicate venom distilled from the good humor of the Carioca." He concluded that it was "this profound respect for the popular intelligence" that "created the identity of minds and the communion between the actions of the government and the will of the people." [66]

Despite his immodesty, Vargas was justified in pointing to his masterful knowledge of Brazilian psychology as one of his greatest political assets. Visitors to Brazil during the Estado Nôvo, such as journalist John Gunther and constitutional lawyer Karl Loewenstein, were fascinated by the way in which Vargas' political dominance was in part based on his chameleon-like ability to embody the national character. His exasperated enemies invariably labeled him "Machiavellian." This description was accurate; Getúlio would also have found it flattering.[67]

But what about the role of political parties? As noted in the analysis of new political forces, the Estado Nôvo was an authoritarian, nonparty way out of Brazil's political inexperience and the resulting political deadlock of the mid-1930's. A genuine innovation on the level of political parties would have been the creation of truly national organizations. Neither the liberal constitutionalists nor the tenentes had been able to accomplish this before the first national parties—the Integralistas and the Communists—unwittingly abetted Vargas' plan to impose his authoritarian rule. Since Vargas took great care not to create any government party, the Estado Nôvo produced no new parties. The brief operation of the Electoral Code of 1932 had, however, demonstrated how important party organization would be under free elections. The lesson was not lost on Vargas, who nevertheless postponed as long as possible any thought of organizing his own political movement. The "non-political" system of the Estado Nôvo offered the perfect medium for his great talents of conciliation and manipulation which in turn depended upon highly personal contact with opponents and allies.

During the last two years of the Estado Nôvo (1943 to 1945), Vargas was farsighted enough to realize that his dictatorship could not survive the war. His fascism, although second-hand, was bound to be shaken by the coming demise of fascism in Europe, toward whose defeat the Brazilian Army was contributing an expeditionary force. In 1943 Vargas therefore endorsed the efforts of one of his most trusted political lieutenants, Labor Minister Marcondes Filho, who began propounding the rationale for a new political movement. Vargas was anticipating the moment when the political system would be reopened, and power would rest on the electoral process.

This attempt to build a new political base was part of a three-pronged effort by Vargas to preempt the left of the political spectrum. First came the extensive social welfare legislation (such as medical and pension benefits), designed to gain worker loyalty for the paternalistic government which had implemented these programs. The doctrine to justify this system was *trabalhismo,* which Marcondes Filho spelled out in his famous radio broadcasts, "A Hora do Brasil," starting in 1942. Furthermore, the new union structure was administered under close control from the Ministry of Labor, thus giving the government an important source of influence within the urban economy, as well as a vast patronage instrument for converting potential opponents into political clients. Government control over the unions (*Sindicatos*) took several forms. First, only those unions recognized by the Ministry of Labor were legal. As the union organization increased after 1941 under government pressure, the Labor Ministry was able to place its agents (later termed *pelegos* or "political henchmen") in positions of leadership, thus excluding the independent labor militants (including especially anarcho-syndicalists and Communists) who had been active in the fledgling labor movement before 1937. The "bureaucratization" of the union structure was given a further institutional basis with the introduction of the compulsory labor union membership dues (*impôsto sindical*) in the amount of one day's wages per year deducted from the worker's pay-check. The funds were then distributed to the government-recognized unions by the Ministry of Labor. This paternalistic organization imposed upon the labor sector by Vargas was part of the overall corporatist economic structure that the Estado Nôvo government laid out for the entire urban society.[68]

Vargas' third tactic was to be a Labor Party based on a coalition of the government-dominated labor unions and the "progressive" forces that Vargas hoped to lead by embracing programs of industrialization, economic nationalism, and social welfarism. In a speech in 1943 discussing his postwar political plans, Vargas promised that workers would have a prominent role among the "new groups that are full of energy and enthusiasm, capable of faith and of carrying out the tasks of our development." In 1944 he called on the workers of São Paulo to join the government-supervised unions and thus participate in the necessary "change of mentality" required by the "rapidity of the transformations in economic life." [69]

The last two years of the Estado Nôvo therefore foreshadowed the beginning of a new ("third") phase in Vargas' political career. During his first phase (1930 to 1937), he played the role of the political arbiter and conspirator for dictatorial powers. The second covered the dictatorship of the Estado Nôvo. Now, after 1943, Vargas was in effect laying the groundwork for his later emergence as a "democratic" leader who would rely on support from a new popular movement as well as from more established groups such as rural landowners, São Paulo industrialists, and the bureaucracy. Before we can understand how the "third" Vargas was able to return to power in 1950 after having been forced from office in 1945, we must first examine those innovations in the area of economic policy, which, along with the changes in political institutions, were to make the era from 1930 to 1945 a watershed in modern Brazilian history.

New Directions in Economic Policy

Under the Old Republic, the Brazilian economy had been highly dependent upon a few agricultural crops—coffee, cocoa, cotton, and rubber. Brazil exported these products, using the resulting foreign exchange to import nearly all the manufactured goods consumed at home. This was a continuation of Brazil's historical role in the world economy: a supplier of tropical and semi-tropical primary products to the North Atlantic economies. In the seventeenth century, Brazil grew relatively prosperous from her sugar exports to Europe; in the eighteenth century, gold and diamonds replaced agricultural exports without altering Brazil's "peripheral" position in the world economy. In the later nineteenth century, coffee emerged as the new major export earner.

But the specter of overproduction and the accompanying problem of violent price fluctuations had become acute by this century. In order to maximize her foreign exchange earnings, Brazil resorted to the practice of withholding stocks of coffee and rubber (a major export product in the second decade) from the world market. This policy was based on the assumption that world demand for both products was relatively insensitive to price. A marketing policy which kept surplus stocks from depressing the market could keep prices high, and thereby maximize total foreign exchange receipts. The marketing controls were known as "valorization" plans and were bitterly attacked by many Brazilian followers of strict laissez-faire economics, who argued that such attempts at manipulation would prove self-defeating in the long run and only irritate Brazil's customers and creditors in the short run.[70] But the temptation to maximize export earnings was too strong, especially for the exporters and the state governments (in the case of coffee—São Paulo, Minas Gerais, and Rio de Janeiro) they controlled. Successive federal governments were torn between the possible advantages of valorization schemes on the one hand and the counter-arguments of Brazilian economic liberals (including some Finance Ministers) and foreign creditors and customers on the other hand. By the 1930's, Brazil was effectively committed to this form of state intervention in a vital sector of the economy. It was a somewhat paradoxical situation: Brazil exported primary products and imported finished goods, as the principles of economic liberalism suggested; but she also attempted to maximize her comparative advantage by marketing controls—a clear violation of Manchester-school liberal economic doctrine.[71]

In the area of industrialization, however, the apologists of pure economic liberalism had carried the day before 1930. There were periodic attempts by advocates of industrialization to gain higher tariff protection and more liberal credit to infant industry. But they were largely unsuccessful. Except for a few items such as textiles, virtually all manufactured goods were imported. State intervention on behalf of industry, in contrast to the export sector, collided with the predominant view of Brazil's "natural" role as a dependent economy, exchanging primary products for finished goods.[72]

The crash of 1929 highlighted Brazil's dependence on her few export crops. In a desperate effort to compensate the coffee growers for the disastrous fall in coffee prices, the federal government after 1930 expanded its purchases of surplus coffee stocks. Although the coffee growers' decreased earnings were greatly compensated by this "socialization of losses," such programs could not arrest the decline in Brazil's foreign exchange earnings, for world commodity prices simply could not be stabilized by state marketing monopolies within a single producing country. With the loss in export earnings, Brazil's capacity to import declined still further. Despite drastic reductions in imports, the balance of payments showed a growing deficit (with occasional brief improvements as in 1934 and 1935), finally forcing the Vargas government to default on its foreign debts in 1938 and 1939.[73]

The fragility of Brazil's position amidst the world economic anarchy had become dramatically evident. The principles of economic liberalism, even when modified by the valorization programs, had failed. The Vargas government even resorted to burning huge quantities of surplus coffee, to insure that it would never reach the market. Although such action could not keep coffee prices in New York and London up to their pre-Depression levels, it did encourage industrialization in a manner which was apparently unappreciated at the time by either the government or the relevant economic sectors.

The federal government's purchase of coffee surpluses, by creating a major source of deficit financing or "pump priming," prevented Brazil from experiencing the grave collapse in domestic demand which the loss in export earnings would otherwise have brought. The resulting maintenance of internal demand, coupled with a progressive currency devaluation rapid enough to keep imports roughly in line with the reduced capacity to import, turned out to be a powerful stimulant to the growth of domestic light industry. Consumers now sought Brazilian sources for the products they had previously bought from abroad. At the same time, investment which once had gone into the export sector was attracted by the higher profits to be earned in industrial production.[74]

This spurt of "spontaneous" industrialization was aided in the later 1930's by a conscious policy of state intervention, as the Estado Nôvo's repudiation of political liberalism carried with it a willingness to deviate from the doctrine of economic liberalism. Private businessmen were encouraged to continue their own efforts, while the federal government expanded its authority to direct the economy in two major ways: the "managing of stimulants," such as taxes, exchange controls, import quotas, credit controls, and wage requirements; and direct intervention by means of public investment, in such areas as railroads, shipping, public utilities, and basic industries such as oil and steel.

In the first area, the Estado Nôvo saw the establishment of the first minimum wages; at the same time, the Labor Ministry created the apparatus of government-controlled unions, which became an important instrument for state intervention in wage policy. Other devices for managing stimulants were introduced or strengthened: the pension institutes and savings banks whose capital funds could be directed into

government-favored investments, the import-licensing and foreign exchange authorities, and the Bank of Brazil, with power to direct loans
to borrowers designated by the government.[75]

In the second area—direct public investment, either by means of a
mixed enterprise or purely public-enterprise system—there were important precedents set during the Estado Nôvo: the National Steel
Commission was created in 1940 and the National Steel Company
was officially founded in 1941. Aided by loans from the Export-
Import Bank, it built the huge steel plant at Volta Redonda.[76] Other
mixed corporations were founded before 1945 in areas such as iron
ore, alkali processing, aircraft and truck engine production, and river
valley development in the São Francisco valley.

The intervention of the federal government in the Brazilian economy, although it had already been justified in terms of economic nationalism and military defense, was greatly accelerated by the Second
World War. Brazil's formal entry into the war in 1942 provided the
occasion for a full-scale economic mobilization effort under the direction of João Alberto, the former tenente and interventor in São Paulo.
The obvious need for raw materials and manufactured goods vital to
the war effort gave new urgency to the Vargas government's program
of state-financed enterprises.[77]

Because the Brazilians were providing vital bases for the Battle of
the Atlantic and for the communications life-line to North Africa, the
United States government was anxious to aid in Vargas' mobilization
effort. The American government had already committed itself to the
assistance of Brazil's basic economic development in 1940 by making
available long-term loans from the Export-Import Bank in return for
the assurance of Brazilian bases. The first major commitment was a
$20 million loan for the new National Steel Company. This support
for public investment in basic industry in an underdeveloped country
reflected a mixture of motives from the North American standpoint.
On the one hand, it demonstrated the desire of Roosevelt's New Deal
administration to give economic substance to the Good Neighbor Policy. At the same time, it represented an attempt to realize long-
standing North American ambitions for greater commercial penetra-
tion in Latin America through the new and unorthodox measure of
United States government aid for programs of state-directed industrialization. American willingness was undoubtedly increased by a

knowledge that Vargas had actively negotiated with Nazi Germany for assistance in setting up a steel industry.

In 1942 the American involvement in Brazilian economic development became even greater when the Roosevelt administration sent a technical mission to help plan Brazil's mobilization. The work of this mission, headed by Morris Llewellyn Cooke, was the beginning of a long and close relationship between economic planners within the two governments. The American Technical Mission contributed significantly to what was the first systematic survey of Brazilian resources, although the mission's recommendations for postwar American assistance were not followed.[78]

Vargas used the occasion of the war effort to elaborate a policy of industrialization, a goal toward which he had been moving since 1937, although as late as 1940 he had still not committed himself unequivocally to systematic industrial development. In 1943 Vargas announced proudly that by such enterprises as iron and steel plants, aluminum and copper factories, and mineral exports, Brazil was forging "the basic elements for the transformation of a vast and scattered agrarian community into a nation capable of providing its fundamental necessities." For the military the point was made unmistakably obvious in a speech in 1944: "Our first lesson from the present war," Vargas noted, was that "the only countries that can really be considered military powers are those that are sufficiently industrialized and able to produce within their own frontiers the war materials they need." [79]

During the Estado Nôvo, Vargas also increased the appeal to Brazilian sentiments of economic nationalism. Nationalist opinion ranged from elementary suspicion of foreign profiteers to sophisticated theories of international economic stratification. The practical effect of economic nationalism was to create support for policies of industrialization, as well as increased state intervention in the economy.[80]

The higher military favored national control over the sectors they considered essential to national security.[81] This coincided with the brand of economic nationalism expressed by the militant lieutenants who had played an important role in undermining the pre-1930 regime and had provided leadership cadres in the first two years of Vargas' rule. Intellectuals and students, who were to play an influential role in politics in the years after Vargas' fall, were drawn to the arguments of economic nationalism. And public intervention in key economic sectors also offered political appeal to the newly enfranchised urban working class, whose political power was obvious should elections be held. Finally, some features of state direction of the economy appealed to Brazilian businessmen and consumers. Most obviously, anti-foreign measures which placed foreign capital at a relative disadvantage might be attractive to domestic entrepreneurs hard-pressed to compete with the superior resources of outside investors. Also, some businessmen and consumers believed they had a stake in seeing the domestic market develop, and recognized that this required a large measure of state intervention in a country at an early stage of development.[82]

In sum, Brazil's industrialization between 1930 and 1945 was the product of two factors: "spontaneous" import substitution resulting from the collapse of the capacity to import, the maintenance of domestic demand by the coffee support program, and the shift in private investment from the export sector to industrial production for the domestic market; and direct and indirect state intervention.

The growth of state responsibility in the economic sector did not result from popular demand or from pressure brought to bear by the entrepreneurial sector; rather, it was the response of the political elite. The only important group that solidly backed industrialization was the higher military, who badly wanted a modern steel industry. The policy was justified by a logic compounded of arguments based on considerations of economics, national security, and emotional nationalism. The question of industrialization per se was not widely debated in this period, even within business circles.[83] By the end of the 1930's, however, the historic arguments of the export sector about Brazil's "natural" role as primary-product exporter began to fall of their own weight. The prolonged world depression had shown underdeveloped countries how vulnerable the international division of labor had rendered them. If Brazil was to emerge from the status of an agricultural export economy to that of an industrialized nation, a considerable "cake of custom" would have to be broken. It was this process which the authoritarian regime of the Estado Nôvo helped make possible. The new policy of industrialization, which Vargas explicitly endorsed only after the beginning of the war, was not the victory of a dynamic urban sector; it was a policy imposed from the top during a dictatorship. The rationale for such a policy was in the air—corporatist and fascist doctrines in Europe, the New Deal in North America, state socialism in the Soviet Union. By 1945 the direction of government policy was irreversible. Vargas, responding in part to pressure from the higher military, had committed all subsequent governments to the responsibility of directing the national economy on a large scale. Even the character of such tutelage would later seem difficult to change. The Depression demonstrated that Brazil had little choice but to industrialize if she wished to transform herself into a modern nation and a world power. The initial pressure for state-sponsored industrialization came from the military, whose support had been the *sine qua non* of Vargas' coup in 1937. The ideas and policy rationale came from businessmen-advisers such as Roberto Simonsen and Euvaldo Lodi. It was the resourceful politician Vargas, however, who became the best-known patron of industrialization. In the area of economic policy, as in the sphere of political institutions, it was to prove far easier to overthrow the dictator than to repudiate his legacy.

The End of the Estado Nôvo
and the Dutra Years

The Dictator Loses Control

As the tide of war shifted toward the Allies in 1943, Vargas began to plan for the new political atmosphere that would be created by an Allied victory. In 1944 he received reports of criticism of the Estado Nôvo among the Brazilian officers fighting alongside the American Fifth Army in Italy. The Brazilians had become aware of the anomaly of fighting for democracy abroad while representing dictatorship at home.[1]

On November 10, 1943, the sixth anniversary of the coup of 1937 and the date on which the plebiscite provided in the Constitution of 1937 was to have been held, Vargas spoke to the nation and promised that after the war "in the appropriate environment of peace and order and surrounded by guarantees of liberty and opinion we shall readjust our political structure and devise ample and suitable formulas for the consultation of the Brazilian people." [2] Six months later, on April 15, 1944, he repeated his promise, assuring Brazilians that they would be able to "declare themselves and choose their representatives within democracy, law and order." [3]

During the Estado Nôvo, Vargas' efficient censorship of public opinion had silenced the voices of dissent. Before 1945 there was only one significant statement by the opposition. In October 1943 a group of intellectuals and politicians from Minas Gerais issued a cautious manifesto calling for Brazil's redemocratization and citing the political history of Minas Gerais as proof that freedom of opinion and constitutional government were natural aspirations for Brazilians.[4]

As 1945 began, protest began to seep through the curtain of censorship. On January 26 the First Congress of Brazilian Writers called for "complete freedom of speech" and demanded a government elected by "universal, direct and secret vote." [5] On February 22 was heard a more sensational voice of protest, José Américo de Almeida, a candidate in the abortive presidential campaign of 1937, gave a lengthy interview in which he explained why presidential elections must be held and why it would be "inappropriate" for Vargas to run.[6] The failure of the censors to prevent publication of the interview (the government censorship bureau, DIP, still operated) was a clear sign that the dictator was giving ground in the face of the opposition. The relaxation of government controls emboldened the protesters. Few now doubted that Brazil was on the eve of the reopening of her political system.

Questions about the timing of the constitutional changes were partially allayed when the government issued an "Additional Act" on February 28, amending the Constitution of 1937. The Act provided that within 90 days a decree would be issued setting a date for elections. Just before Vargas issued the Act, the first presidential candidacy was launched. Major General Eduardo Gomes, a former tenente and now a leading Air Force Commander, was put forward as the candidate of the liberal constitutionalists, soon to campaign under the label of the Democratic National Union (*União Democrática Nacional* or UDN).

In early March Vargas held a news conference, his first in several years. He pointedly defended the Constitution of 1937 and was evasive about running for President. Public protest now spilled into the streets. The newly organized university student union in Rio de Janeiro held a rally; a similar student demonstration in Recife provoked violence from the police and led to the death of two students.

The public mood had turned ugly. Vargas calmed the scene by announcing on March 11 that he would not run for President. The following day a movement was launched to nominate the War Minister, General Dutra. This was immediately interpreted by the opposition as a diversionary tactic by Vargas. By supporting an "official" candidate who was eminently acceptable to the Army officer corps, the incumbent dictator might be able to influence the policies of his successor. Furthermore, Dutra's candidacy would undercut Gomes' potential support among pro-government circles for whom victory was more important than principle. In early April, Dutra, although still War Minister, tacitly accepted nomination.[7]

The pressure now increased to discard the authoritarian remnants which obstructed free political activity. In mid-April the government announced a political amnesty and released hundreds of political prisoners, including some, like the famous Communist leader Luís Carlos Prestes, who had languished in prison throughout the Estado Nôvo.

Getúlio spoke to a large rally on May 1, explaining that his own mission was completed. He reviewed his achievements, particularly in the area of economic development and social legislation, and concluded by endorsing the candidacy of Dutra.[8] On May 23 Prestes spoke to his own mass rally in Rio de Janeiro, signaling the beginning of political activity by the newly legalized Communist Party.[9]

Attention now centered on the impending decree which would set the election date. It was issued on May 28 and the date was set for December 2, 1945. The presidential campaign picked up steam. A new political party, the Social Democratic Party (*Partido Social Democrático* or PSD) which had been formally organized on May 9, endorsed Dutra's candidacy on July 1. In early August, Dutra resigned as War Minister and was replaced by General Góes Monteiro, an architect of the coup of 1937. In mid-August the UDN formalized its campaign for Gomes, publishing a program on August 17. Thus far, the Brazilians had been presented with two candidates. There seemed little doubt that the return of democratic institutions was imminent. The air of confidence was soon shattered, however, by agitation on the left and equivocation in the presidential palace.

In early August a group of Vargas supporters began a movement to postpone the presidential election while proceeding with elections for a Constituent Assembly. Their aim was to "redemocratize" Brazil under the dictator's auspices. The opposition to Vargas had been arguing for the opposite: the election of a new President *before* the writing of a new constitution. The difference was crucial, since the incumbent government could exercise great influence over the deliberations of any Constituent Assembly.

Those who wanted Getúlio to remain President or declare himself a candidate in the upcoming election were labeled *queremistas* (after the Portuguese verb *queremos* meaning "we want" as in "We Want Vargas"). Their motto was "A Constituent Assembly With Getúlio!"

Prominent along the leaders of this movement were members of the Communist Party as well as the Vargas lieutenants, such as Hugo Borghi, who had begun organizing a new Brazilian Labor Party (*Partido Trabalhista Brasileiro* or PTB).[10]

Vargas assumed an equivocal attitude toward the Queremista Movement. He gave it no overt encouragement, but neither did he attempt to prevent its growth. When the September 2 deadline for the filing of presidential candidates passed, it appeared that Vargas had finally ruled out any possibility of asking Dutra to stand aside in favor of himself. On September 29 the American ambassador, Adolph A. Berle, Jr., delivered a speech in which he expressed "confidence" that Brazil would hold elections on December 2, as scheduled. The speech, which had been personally cleared with Vargas by Ambassador Berle, caused an uproar on the left. The Queremistas and Communists denounced American "intervention" and described the upcoming elections as "the manipulation of reactionaries." [11]

After issuing the decrees designed to "redemocratize" Brazil, Vargas had taken a tack to the left in his domestic policy. In June he had issued an "anti-trust" decree creating a commission authorized to expropriate any organization conducting business in a fashion detrimental to the national interest. The decree, effective August 1, was aimed at holding down the cost of living by prohibiting monopolistic practices. It mentioned specifically "national or foreign enterprises known to be connected with associations, 'trusts' or 'cartels.' " The decree provoked enthusiasm on the left and indignation on the right. The UDN issued an immediate protest branding the decree as "nothing more than an instrument of the Nazi fascist type with which the dictatorship threatens the entire Brazilian economy." The opposition's anger was especially strong because the decree was rumored to be directed primarily against the newspaper chain owned by an outspoken anti-getulista, Assis Chateaubriand. United States business interests were also disturbed over the decree for obvious reasons. They discreetly sought changes in the enforcement regulations.[12]

On October 3, the fifteenth anniversary of the call to arms in 1930, the Queremistas staged a rally outside the Palácio Guanabara. It was the movement's strongest demonstration yet. Getúlio addressed the gathering, stating firmly that he was not a candidate in the election. But he added that the public had the "right" to demand a Constituent

Assembly, and he warned that "powerful reactionary forces, some occult and some public" were opposed to the calling of such an assembly. "I can assure you that insofar as it is within my power the people can count on me." He acknowledged the gathering as "a representation of the popular will," and thanked the crowd for "this civic demonstration of such great significance." [13]

Getúlio's enigmatic stance stimulated further speculation about his real attitude toward the impending elections. Might the former dictator be planning a repetition of 1937, when he unleashed the left in order to justify his own coup? Or might he be contemplating a new political era based on militant labor support, such as Perón had mobilized in Argentina since his coup in 1943? On October 10 Getúlio gave the opposition new reason to distrust his intentions. He issued a decree advancing the date for state and local elections to the same day as the national elections—December 2. Since the decree also required that incumbent office holders who wished to stand for governorships would have to resign thirty days before the elections, the opposition feared that the newly appointed local officials, who would be named by Vargas, could manipulate the elections for the benefit of the incumbent President's candidate.[14]

Tampering with the electoral regulations at such a late date provoked deep suspicion among many military officers. The UDN, equally fearful, immediately protested the October 10 decree. Perón's triumphal return to power in Argentina on October 17, after having been deposed only eight days earlier, gave the Brazilian dictator's opponents an example of liberals' failure elsewhere. On October 25 Vargas made a further move that proved too much for the generals. He informed João Alberto, chief of police of the Federal District, that he would be replaced by the President's brother—Benjamin Vargas, an unsavory figure known more than anything else for his connections with the shadier side of public affairs.[15]

João Alberto communicated Vargas' decision to the War Minister, Góes Monteiro, with whom João Alberto had concluded an informal agreement that if one left office the other would follow suit. Góes Monteiro, however, was in no mood to resign. In a whirlwind of activity he mobilized officer opinion in support of a coup to depose the equivocating President. Góes Monteiro became certain of his support after extensive soundings among the senior officers. Dutra went to the palace on the afternoon of October 29 to present Getúlio with an ultimatum: withdraw his brother's nomination or face deposition by the Army. Vargas refused, still unconvinced that Góes Monteiro would carry out the ultimatum.

It was too late, however. Góes had already mobilized the local Army garrison and the presidential palace was virtually cut off when Dutra returned to the War Ministry with Vargas' reply. Despite Justice Minister Agamemnon Magalhães' desperate efforts to arrange a compromise solution, Góes was determined to complete the showdown. That evening he sent General Oswaldo Cordeiro de Farias to the presidential palace to inform Vargas that his term was at an end. At first Getúlio refused to accede, but finally gave in when his old colleague explained how any resistance would be impossible. When Cordeiro de Farias asked if the President had thought about his future plans, Vargas immediately replied, "I want to go directly from here to São Borja." Vargas' departure was quickly arranged, and on October 30 he took up his "exile" in Rio Grande do Sul.[16]

General Góes Monteiro took full responsibility for deposing the President, issuing successive declarations on October 29 explaining why the action was necessary. Vargas was induced to publish a statement making clear that he had acquiesced in his own deposition. He contented himself with the assurance that "history and time will speak for me," and he reminded Brazilians that he had always sought to defend their "aspirations and legitimate interests." Most significantly, he announced that "I have no grounds for ill will against the glorious Armed Forces of my country whose prestige I have always sought to enhance." [17]

The manner in which Vargas had departed was all-important. As Góes Monteiro was later to remind the UDN, the dictator was sent from office not by the power of the civilian opposition, but by decision of the Army command.[18] It was not, therefore, a victory earned by the political influence of the liberal constitutionalists. Rather, it was an act of stewardship by the generals. As had been true in the critical moments in October 1930 and November 1937, it was the military, not the politicians, who were the immediate custodians of power.

The Rebirth of Democratic Politics

With Vargas safely gone, General Góes Monteiro then consulted the two presidential candidates, Gomes and Dutra, on the question of choosing an interim President. They agreed that it should be, as the UDN leaders had been arguing ("all power to the judiciary"), the Chief Justice of the Supreme Court, José Linhares. Góes Monteiro left no doubt that the national elections would be held on December 2, as scheduled. The new President, Linhares, repealed Vargas' decree which had advanced the date of state elections. He replaced the Interventors and suspended all mayors until after the election. The replacements for these officials were largely members of the judiciary, who were instructed to be impartial in the upcoming elections.

Linhares also appointed a caretaker Cabinet. Góes Monteiro, who insisted upon resigning as War Minister, was prevailed upon by his military supporters to assume the newly created post of Commander in Chief of the Army, where he continued as the power behind the scenes. Although Linhares' government was characterized as "non-political," it lost no time in repealing the anti-trust decree issued by Vargas in June. It also engaged in a brief crackdown on the Communist Party, raiding party offices. This suppression was short-lived, however, and the party resumed its campaign activities.

Vargas' departure from power in 1945 had immediate and profound consequences for the Brazilian political scene. First, although the central figure of recent Brazilian history was retiring from the scene, the shadow of his personality would continue to dominate Brazilian politics for years to come. Second, Vargas' retirement meant the creation of a new legal structure to accompany the new democratic era. Brazilians would need a new constitution to replace Francisco Campos' authoritarian document of 1937. Political parties—the most important vehicle of modern democracy—would have to be founded and nurtured. Third, the return to democratic politics would offer greater possibilities for the expression of disagreement and conflict. The urban middle class and labor groups centered in the more developed regions would be likely to benefit, since they would hold an important block of votes in any national election in which the franchise was limited to literates (as it turned out to be in the Constitution of 1946).

What of the more traditional power groups, especially the land-owners, who had manipulated politics so freely before 1930? They remained strongest in the areas untouched by significant economic change. With the return of free elections these areas could be expected once again to display the political vices common in the Old Republic. Their back-country bosses could still deliver votes on demand, but their importance would depend on how rapidly the urban share of the total national electorate grew. This growing contrast between the developing and the traditional regions within the country—a contrast often at its most dramatic within individual states—had become even more acute in the fifteen years since the Revolution of 1930.[19]

The most basic division in Brazilian politics as of mid-1945 was between the "ins" and the "outs." In traditional Brazilian political terminology, the contrast was expressed by the terms *situacionistas* (proprietors of the status quo) and *oposicionistas*. The "ins" of 1945 were those who had tacitly supported Vargas through the Estado Nôvo and who were now a ready source of votes for the candidate who seemed most likely to continue his basic policies. The "outs" were those who had been excluded from power since 1937, especially the liberal constitutionalists. Each group deserves closer analysis.[20]

The "Ins." In the process of transforming the Brazilian political system, Vargas had created a network of leaders and groups on whom he could count for support and cooperation. Even under the authoritarian system imposed by the coup of 1937 his political style required an astute combination of coercion and cajolery, directed at the old-style political and social cadres which have provided the continuity of modern Brazilian history. Vargas' political network, untested, of course, by an election during his own rule, was made up of three major groups. First, there were the politicians and bureaucrats who had benefited from the Vargas years and who preferred a minimum of change in the system they knew. They were the men who had run Vargas' most important political creations—the new state machines and the much-enlarged government apparatus. The second group among the "ins" were the landowners and industrialists who had prospered under Vargas and who harbored grave uncertainties about the stability of a more open political system. Prominent in this number were coffee growers and other large landowners who appreciated Vargas' complete silence on the agrarian question; there were also the bankers and businessmen who had learned to deal profitably with the growing central control over credit and business regulations. The third group was the newest element among the "ins." It was made up of the urban workers at whom Vargas aimed his social welfare legislation and paternalistic union organization strengthened in the 1940's.

The first two elements among the "ins" had their own party par excellence, founded in 1945. It was the Social Democratic Party (*Partido Social Democrático* or PSD). It bore no resemblance to a European social democratic party, being closest in Brazilian political tradition to the state political machines which bore the title of *Partido Republicano* during the Old Republic. The organizers of the PSD began organizing in March 1945 when elections had become inevitable. The manner in which the party was founded gave a clue to its later characteristics. The Interventors in many states simply called together pro-government public figures, asking them to gather the signatures necessary for founding a party under the new electoral regulations. Final direction came from on high, as Vargas personally supervised the organization of the PSD in order to support the official candidacy of Dutra.[21]

Although the newly formed PSD used much of the language of the liberal constitutionalists, it was more the creature of the traditional politicians in the rural areas than of the middle-class opposition in the cities. The party was especially strong in Minas Gerais, where the Interventor, Benedito Valladares, had been a close collaborator of Vargas since his emergence to power in late 1933. Paradoxically, the PSD also attracted support from progressive businessmen such as Roberto Simonsen, who regarded continued state intervention as essential for further industrialization. This combination of *nouveau* industrialists and old-style state politicians was to give the PSD its uniquely "non-ideological" position in the postwar era.[22]

The organized urban workers—a privileged minority within the total labor force—were represented among the "ins" by the new Brazilian Labor Party (*Partido Trabalhista Brasileiro* or PTB). Vargas later revealed, in a moment of candor, why the PTB was founded. "Since the mentality of the workers was not well-adapted to that of the old politicians, there was created a new political organization called the Brazilian Labor Party." [23] The PTB represented Vargas' effort to undercut the Communists on the left and to preempt for his own benefit the increasingly important working-class vote. The party was organized by Vargas' lieutenants and advisers, such as Alexandre Marcondes Filho, the minister of labor, and Alberto Pasqualini. As Minister of Labor since 1943, Marcondes Filho had consolidated the labor laws and helped to produce the mystique of *trabalhismo* on which a political movement could be based.

The election strategy of the PTB was complicated by the fact that the party had been deeply implicated in the Queremista movement. Vargas' abrupt departure demoralized and divided the PTB. Some favored supporting Dutra; others, deprived of their leader, were attracted by the militancy of the Communist Party; still others lost interest in the presidential race and concentrated on supporting Vargas for election in as many congressional races as possible, thereby hoping to pile up an impressive total vote for the deposed President.

The "Outs." The "outs" of 1945 proved to be a smaller group than might have been expected. Most important among the heterogeneous opposition were the liberal constitutionalists. In 1930 they had supported Vargas in the belief that they were beginning a new democratic era in Brazil, thereby giving the emerging urban areas a predominant influence. Instead, they saw their hopes for a liberal regime shattered as Vargas led Brazil into the authoritarian regime of the Estado Nôvo. In late 1944, as the rising tide of Allied victory made redemocratization a palpable hope, the liberal constitutionalists organized a new political movement, the *União Democrática Nacional* (UDN). The title, National Democratic Union, indicated their intention of forming a united opposition front, an attempt which proved largely unsuccessful. With Vargas forced by the Army to resign, the liberals hoped to resume the unfinished business of fifteen years ago. Their presidential candidate was Brigadier Eduardo Gomes, a well-known Air Force commander who had been one of the young military rebels of the 1920's and a revolutionary of 1930, but who had opposed the authoritarian turn of events in 1937.[24]

Eduardo Gomes inherited the mantle of Armando de Salles Oliveira, the leading opposition candidate in the abortive presidential campaign of 1937. In that campaign Salles Oliveira had spoken for the frustrated Paulistas whom he had served as Governor from 1935 to 1937. He had struggled, however, to make his appeal national. Forced into exile by the coup of November 1937, he lived in exile until returning to Brazil on April 7, 1945. He reached Brazilian soil mortally ill and died on May 17, thus having time only to witness the birth pangs of Brazil's democratic revival.

Salles Oliveira had always recognized that Brazilian politics were subject to a military veto. It was his appeal to the Army on the eve of the 1937 coup which forced Dutra and Góes Monteiro to advance the date of the coup by five days. Throughout his exile, Salles Oliverira continued his appeal to the Army as the only force which could end the dictatorship it had underwritten in 1937. His constant appeals were convincing proof of the liberal constitutionalists' weakness. Unable to dissuade the Army High Command from the coup of 1937, they could hope to reenter the political arena only by convincing the military to return Brazil to its democratic path. It never occurred to Salles Oliveira throughout his exile either to attack the Army for having snuffed out democracy in 1937, or to organize a revolutionary movement. Either move would have violated the implicit rule of Brazilian politics to which he, as a leading member of the political elite, was an instinctive subscriber.

To attack the Army would have been to attack the logic of the system itself and would have led to the conclusion that the Army's role in 1937 was ill-conceived. For the liberal constitutionalists, it was not the Army's *right* to intervene, but the results of their intervention which had harmed Brazil. By recognizing the Army's role as power arbiter, and by even glorifying that role, the liberal constitutionalists hoped for a new intervention for their benefit.

Writing from exile in New York City in December 1939, Salles Oliveira put it thus: "Outside of the Army there is no solution for the Brazilian crisis. Only the Army can bring about unity because it is the only national force not demoralized by the authoritarian lunacy." He went on to say that he regarded the Army "with unlimited confidence" and suggested that the Brazilian people wanted the Army to assume power "in this hour of supreme threats so as to assure internal order and external respect until the nation, united, can deliberate." [25]

One month after Vargas' promise of November 1943 to redemocratize Brazil after the war, Salles Oliveira published (from Buenos Aires this time) another "Letter to the Brazilians." In this message he identified the liberal constitutionalists' hopes more closely with the Army: "The Army is the image of the people, in these days of war more than ever. It has the virtues and defects of the people." Sensing that officer opinion was turning against the Estado Nôvo, Salles Oliveira sympathized with their anguish. "The truth is that the Army suffers and in a certain sense is more unhappy than the people because the military insignia are sensitive antennae which must have picked up long ago the fateful warnings of the humiliation of the country." [26]

The liberal constitutionalists' identification with the officer corps had a natural class basis. The Brazilian officer corps was recruited largely from the middle class, on which the liberal constitutionalists also depended. It was therefore logical that politicians such as Salles Oliveira should assume that they shared a common interest with the military. [27]

Even as the dictator steadily gave ground during the first nine months of 1945, the liberal constitutionalists, organized in the UDN, looked to the Army to protect their rights. In October 1945, for example, the UDN sent a stream of complaints to the War Minister about partisan actions of incumbent government officials who allowed violence, it alleged, to hobble the UDN's campaign efforts. [28] After the Queremista rally of October 3, the UDN protested that "continuism was in the wind, as evidenced by the 'subversive character' of the rally." [29] On October 29 the Army finally did what the liberal constitutionalists had hoped for long ago—it deposed Vargas. The fact that it was the Army which deposed the dictator deprived the opposition, especially the UDN, of the opportunity to claim credit for averting the threat to Brazilian democracy.

With Vargas out of office, one of the UDN's chief goals had been accomplished, although sheer anti-Vargas sentiment continued to hold the party together. The burden of its campaign now had to rest on the appeal of its candidate and its stand on substantive questions of political and economic organization. Gomes, the UDN candidate, counted on the support of merchant groups in the principal cities, including the Northeast, as well as some landowners to whom the PSD also appealed. He included among his backers many prominent members of the Brazilian political elite such as former President Arthur Bernades (Minas Gerais) and Oswaldo Aranha, former ambassador to Washington and foreign minister. Aranha supported the UDN candidate partly because he resented having had his own presidential ambitions cut short when Vargas forced him to resign as foreign minister in 1944. Gomes was backed also by the majority of the press led by newspaper magnates Assis Chateaubriand (owner of the newspaper chain *Diários Associados*), Herbert Moses (*O Globo*), and Paulo Bittencourt (*O Correio da Manhã*).[30]

Gomes' program stressed the juridical aspects of Brazil's redemocratization. In the area of economics Gomes and the UDN called for a cautious policy of industrialization. They warned against the use of the Bank of Brazil "for the creation of new and the financing of unviable industries." They called for the "collaboration of foreign capital," opposed "protective tariffs" and recommended a "financial cleanup." The UDN platform of August 17 favored protecting industry only if it "were fitted with modern equipment which reduces the cost of production." Herbert Levy, later to be a principal leader of the UDN, stressed the Communist danger and warned that the elite must adapt so as to "assume control of the transformations which have become imperative in our time." [31]

In essence, the UDN was recommending a return to the principles of liberalism in both politics and economics (economic "liberalism" in the Manchester sense). Their formula was to dismantle the apparatus of wartime controls, abolish the barriers obstructing the free flow of men and capital, and thereby allow the spontaneous economic forces to operate. They did not, however, propose to abolish the social welfare legislation nor, interestingly enough, dismantle the corporatist structure, especially the government-manipulated labor union system, left by Vargas.

Because of the issue's importance in postwar Brazilian politics, it is worth stressing that the UDN position on industrialization was equivocal. Although they claimed to favor the continuation of industrialization, it was not clear what position they would take if Brazil's industrial growth should be impeded by the operation of the rules of classical economics. Furthermore, the merchant groups and urban consumers who made up an important part of the UDN's constituency were certain to oppose economic policies which would make finished goods more costly in the short run.

A very different group of "outs" in the 1945 elections were the Communists. Underground since the abortive revolt of 1935, they reemerged with the resumption of open politics. The party's candidates and Marxist dogma found a wide receptivity, especially among the younger generation, which had known little but the barren intellectual and political tutelage of the Estado Nôvo. The Brazilian Communist Party (*Partido Communista Brasileiro* or PCB) was in a difficult position in 1945. It was the only Communist party in Latin America to have attempted a violent revolution. The disastrous failure of that revolt in 1935 had proved to be a formidable political liability. The revolt had begun with the murder of Army officers, thereby furnishing evidence for anti-Communist generals such as Góes Monteiro and Dutra, who asserted that the "bolshevik threat" justified measures of suppression. Militant anti-communists, including many liberal constitutionalists, constantly cited 1935 as proof that the Communist Party had no place in a democratic system.

But the general amnesty in April 1945 and the new Electoral Code of May had permitted the Communist Party to reemerge as a political force. The atmosphere of triumph over fascism abroad, based on a U.S.-U.S.S.R. alliance in which Brazil had participated, helped to resuscitate the reputation of the Brazilian Communist Party at home. The party therefore enjoyed the moral prestige of identification with the "heroic" Russian people who had withstood the Nazi onslaught in Europe. The new atmosphere was symbolized by Vargas' recognition of the Soviet Union in April 1945.

Luís Carlos Prestes himself was the party's greatest asset. As the romantic "cavalier of hope" from the 1920's, he still enjoyed a wide personal following, including some members of the middle class. After his release from prison in mid-April, he addressed a huge rally in Rio de Janeiro on May 23, calling for "national unification" aimed at "a Constituent Assembly." He referred to the "Communists and conscientious anti-Fascists," as "the chief pillar of order and law in these days of agitation when disorder is preached and there is open talk of military coups." [32]

Much to the surprise of many supporters, Prestes outlined a popular front strategy which included support for Vargas' continuation in power. The Communist policy was to support the call for a Constituent Assembly while at the same time favoring postponement of the presidential elections. The strategy of the Communists therefore coincided with that of the Queremistas and raised suspicion that there was a deal between Vargas and Prestes. Had Vargas "unleashed" Prestes in return for the latter's support of the Queremista movement? It was certainly true that the Communists had been prominent in helping to organize the Queremista rally outside the presidential palace on October 3. They were also busy infiltrating the official labor union movement and were encouraging "anti-fascist" Queremista labor rallies.

After Vargas was deposed on October 29, the Communist Party leadership was thrown into momentary confusion. The brief crackdown on the party provoked fears that its legal status might be at an end. But it was permitted to continue in operation and proceeded to nominate its own candidate for President. In mid-November the party chose Yeddo Fiúza, a civil engineer, a former mayor of Petropolis, and a non-Communist. As Prestes made clear in a campaign speech in Recife in late November, the PCB believed that Brazil was not yet ready for a Communist government. The error of November 1935 must not be repeated; Prestes exhorted his listeners to support the "civilian candidate," Fiúza, as the first step in the revolution of the "national bourgeoisie." At the same time, however, the PCB continued its vigorous campaign to elect its own deputies and senators to the new Congress.[33]

Elsewhere on the left there was little significant activity. Within the UDN was a small "democratic left" (*Esquerda Democrática*) wing which in fact broke away in 1946. Neither then nor later was it able to gain influence in what itself was a minority party. Equally significant was the fact that the resumption of free political competition failed to produce any independent socialist party of importance. Instead, the left was preempted by the Communist Party and by the fledgling Brazilian Labor Party, which was actually a pillar among the "ins," and largely supported Dutra (the PSD candidate) in the rest of the presidential campaign.[34]

The Election of 1945 and the Constitution of 1946: A New Brazil?

On the eve of the election of December 2, 1945, the situation was as follows: both the "ins" and the non-Communist "outs" had nominated high military officers, hoping to invest their campaigns with a non-partisan tone. General Dutra, the colorless but respectable candidate of the "ins," seemed to promise a continuation of the Vargas system without the authoritarian trappings. His campaign was low key, aimed at capitalizing on the support of the political network of old and new *situacionistas* inherited from Vargas. These "ins" were relying on the expected strength of their electoral machine in the rural and urban areas of the major states, especially Minas Gerais, São Paulo, and Rio Grande do Sul. The liberal opposition politicians had no particular geographical stronghold, and seemed to base their confidence on the belief that their role in mobilizing public opinion against Vargas had earned them a natural right to a turn in power. The Communists offered a radical critique of the entire political and economic system, while hoping to gain votes through a "non-revolutionary" appeal.

Although the opposition, especially the UDN, complained bitterly about the advantages which the "official" candidate enjoyed, the Dutra supporters were disturbed by the stolid general's inability to stimulate voter enthusiasm. In September the principal leaders of the PSD met and agreed unanimously that Dutra's candidacy was no longer "viable." João Alberto, chief of police of the Federal District and a leading Dutra supporter, confessed that the general's campaign had become "waterlogged" (*pesada*). They decided that an emissary should be sent to Dutra asking him to withdraw in favor of a new official candidate. But the mission aborted when Góes Monteiro, a leader of the PSD and a firm supporter of Dutra, threatened to resign if the ultimatum carried Vargas' approval. Vargas denied any knowledge of the group's decision, and the matter rested.[35] Even after Vargas was deposed, the Dutra supporters continued to worry. Dutra was irritated that Vargas had done little since October 29 to back him in the campaign. Virtually on the eve of the election, November 28, Vargas was finally induced to issue a new statement endorsing the PSD candidate. His support for Dutra was halfhearted, however, and Vargas warned that "I shall be at the people's side against the President if the candidate's promises are not fulfilled."[36]

The elections held on December 2 were, it was generally agreed, impartially supervised and passed without major incident. Dutra's supporters need not have worried. The former War Minister emerged the 55 percent of the national vote, including a comfortable margin of victory in the three key states of Minas Gerais, Rio Grande do Sul, and São Paulo. Gomes received 35 percent of the vote. Most surprising was the relatively large vote for the communist candidate, Fíuza, who received 10 percent of the national total. In the congressional elections the Partido Social Democrático (PSD) won 42 percent of the vote (151 seats), the União Democrática Nacional (UDN) 26 percent (77 seats), the Partido Trabalhista Brasileiro (PTB) 10 percent (22 seats), and the Partido Communista Brasileiro (PCB) 9 percent (14 congressmen plus one senator).[37] The remaining votes and seats went to minor party candidates. The conclusion was inescapable: even with Vargas replaced by a lackluster candidate, the ex-President's loose alliance of "ins" could survive a free election.

The elections of December 2, 1945, set the scene for Brazil's redemocratization. Having inaugurated its new President in January 1946, the country prepared to rewrite its constitution for the fourth time since the fall of the Empire in 1889. The Brazilian Institute of Lawyers appointed a panel of distinguished legal scholars to propose a replacement for the authoritarian structure imposed in 1937. The new Congress met as a Constituent Assembly and debated successive drafts.[38]

In September 1946 they approved a final version, and Brazil had a new Constitution. As in 1934, it incorporated the hopes of both the liberal constitutionalists and those who favored a strong federal government. As in 1934, elaborate guarantees were included to assure free elections and civil liberties. But there was no return to the decentralized system prevailing before 1930. Indeed, the delegates to the Constituent Assembly of 1946 made no secret of their opposition to a revival of the old *política dos governadores*. The much-enlarged executive, created by Vargas, remained virtually intact, even though the liberal opposition had charged during the 1945 election campaign that it had been used for electoral purposes by the Social Democratic Party. The electorate was defined as excluding illiterates and enlisted men in the armed forces. This exclusion of over half the population from the Brazilian polity was later to be the target for reform proposals and bitter debate.[39]

The Dutra Years

Dutra quickly proved to be a blandly non-political President. His term was characterized by frequent appeals for a return to "tranquillity," the Brazilian equivalent of "normalcy." [40] Dutra enjoyed a political honeymoon during his first year, when the UDN cooperated with his government in the immediate tasks of postwar reconstruction. It was not until after the approval of the new Constitution in September that politics became unabashedly partisan. In that month President Dutra chose a new Cabinet, moderately conservative in character. The new Foreign Affairs Minister for example, Raúl Fernandes, was a prominent member of the UDN. The War Minister, General Canrobert Pereira da Costa, was an outspoken anti-Communist. The Finance Minister, Corrêa e Castro, pledged to follow orthodox monetary procedures in order to arrest the inflation born of wartime shortages. The UDN, however, chafed over its minimal role in the new government. Its leaders felt that the Dutra regime, which rested on the jerry-built political machine of the PSD, had allowed too many Vargas appointees to remain in office. Despite the efforts of some UDN leaders, the party went into open opposition to the Dutra government.[41]

In December 1946, the Dutra government's problems were complicated when the popular former dictator broke openly with the government. Vargas had been active in organizing the fledgling Brazilian Labor Party in Rio Grande do Sul. Although elected as senator under the aegis of President Dutra's PSD, Vargas urged Brazilian workers to join the PTB. Getúlio was following the characteristic strategy of keeping a foot in both camps, thereby hoping to maintain a broad base of support for a political comeback. He tried to explain away the uproar caused by his apparent disloyalty to the party of President Dutra, but the die was cast. Along with a democratic constitution, Brazil had resumed partisan politics.[42]

Political Lines: Fluidity and Rigidity. Dutra's most implacable opposition came from the Communist Party of Brazil. The *Partido Communista Brasileiro* (PCB) emerged in 1945 as the strongest Communist party in Latin America. In the December election, the party had elected to the Constituent Assembly fifteen members who bitterly criticized the neo-liberal provisions written into the Constitution of

1946. There were periodic clashes between the police and Communist organizers. The Communists were quick to criticize the strong appeal which the Dutra government made to foreign investors. In March 1946 Prestes went so far as to declare that he would side with the Soviet Union in the case of a war between that country and Brazil. In May 1946 the Dutra government purged all government employees known to be members of the Communist Party. In August the PCB was given a perfect opportunity for propaganda. General Eisenhower, the hero of the European theater, in which Brazilian troops had fought, visited Rio de Janeiro. At an official reception, UDN leader Octávio Mangabeira somehow managed to kiss the American general's hand. Ultra-nationalists were outraged. They succeeded in creating such an uproar that the matter reached the Congress, which finally voted to approve Mangabeira's behavior.[43]

Clearly, the Brazilian Communist Party was finding fertile ground for its activities. Prices were rising rapidly, and the Communists were successfully infiltrating the leadership of many trade unions. Building on its impressive vote in the elections of 1945, the party appeared to be securing a mass base. The state and supplementary congressional elections of January 1947 confirmed its position. The PCB retained its rank as the fourth most powerful party, and added two new congressmen, bringing the total to 17 congressmen and one senator, while electing 46 members in 15 state legislatures and winning a plurality of 18 in the Municipal Assembly of the Federal District. In the state of São Paulo, the PCB actually replaced the UDN as the party third in total vote.[44]

Faced with this increasing strength, the Dutra government decided on repression. A legal procedure had been included in the Constitution of 1946 by which "anti-democratic" parties could be barred from open participation in politics. The clause was invoked by government prosecutors, and the PCB was declared illegal by court decision in 1947. This action was supported, not surprisingly, by the Army, which had been a bastion of official anti-Communist ideology since the attempted Communist coup of November 1935. It was also supported by most of the liberal constitutionalists, who followed the pattern of 1935–37 and swallowed their doubts about depriving "anti-democrats" of their democratic rights. They clearly agreed with the "ins" that the Communists' militancy, combined with the alarming growth in their vote-getting powers, might prove a truly disruptive force.[45]

The official suppression of the Brazilian Communist Party also coincided with the beginnings of the Cold War. Brazilian anti-Communists could therefore find abroad a ready rationale for their actions.

The Dutra government took advantage of this occasion to crack down also on left-wing labor leaders. A leftist Workers' Federation (*Confederação dos Trabalhadores do Brasil*), organized in 1946, was declared illegal, and the federal government "intervened" in 143 unions (out of a total of 944) "to eliminate extremist elements." [46]

The other important voice of opposition to the Dutra government came from the ex-dictator, now restive in his self-imposed "exile" in Rio Grande do Sul. Vargas campaigned actively in the elections of January 1947, supporting PTB candidates for Congress and PSD candidates for governorships. He was already mapping out the strategy which would, he hoped, return him to the presidential palace.

The suppression of the Communist Party created a vacuum on the left. The PTB, whose creation Vargas had encouraged in 1945 specifically to mobilize working-class support for his own benefit, quickly moved to take over the ground relinquished by the PCB. During the government campaign to outlaw the Communists, Vargas had sought to dissociate the PTB from communism, which he rejected as "devoid of constructive idealism." [47] Analysis of the elections for State Assembly in São Paulo in January 1947 showed that the working-class vote was divided between the PCB and the PTB. With the disappearance of the former, the PTB was certain to benefit. [48]

At this stage of his career, Vargas typified in a preliminary manner a new populist style of politician. The term "populist" is an imprecise term, which has come to be used to describe a style of politician produced in a situation where a mass urban electorate is receptive to a colorful leader who relies on a direct, emotional appeal, based on economic issues of varying ideological sophistication. The populist politician would have been unthinkable before 1930, since his success presupposes a relatively free vote. He is a personalistic leader whose political organization centers upon his own ambitions and career. He is feared, naturally, by the right—for the havoc he might wreak upon the status quo. He is scorned by the disciplined Marxist left for his irresponsibility, and for his "mystification" of the masses. In the last twenty years, the populist politicians have proved to be formidable vote-getters in Brazil. [49]

The most remarkable populist of the Dutra era was Adhemar de

Barros. The product of an old Paulista family, he had been Vargas' Interventor in São Paulo from 1938 to 1941. Thoroughly familiar with the techniques of the "ins," he undoubtedly could have continued as a successful manipulator of that system after Vargas' forced resignation. But Adhemar had a driving ambition which impelled him to come up with a new political formula. By mixing generous patronage, lavish public works, and colorful campaigning in a manner reminiscent of Tammany Hall or of Huey Long without the violence, he proved remarkably successful. To the surprise of almost all the old-line politicians, Adhemar swept into the governorship of São Paulo in 1947.

Adhemar's election was a *tour de force*. During the campaign he made an explicit bargain with the Communist Party for their support. This earned him a large number of working-class votes. It also aroused the anger of conservative politicians and Army officers who questioned aloud Adhemar's right to be inaugurated. Nevertheless, Adhemar succeeded in attracting a large segment of the middle class, thus proving to some observers (and this was not lost on Vargas) that neither the PSD nor the UDN was a satisfactory vehicle for middle-class opinion. Adhemar was permitted to take office, where he began a colorful four-year governorship. Among his more candid supporters, the slogan was *"Rouba mas faz"* (He steals but he gets things done).[50]

The personalistic and "corrupt" political style which Adhemar adopted was a logical response to the sudden growth in the number of voters. The elitist politicians of pre-1930 could hardly expect to find their former methods successful in the world of the mass electorate created by the accelerating process of urbanization. As a populist, however, Adhemar was somewhat deceptive. He did not constitute any *apparent* threat to the established social and economic order. His approach was, in essence, the social welfarism of the 1930's carried to its electoral extreme, combined with a shrewd willingness to cooperate with existing power centers in São Paulo. At the same time, Adhemar was building his own party, the Progressive Social Party (*Partido Social Progressista* or PSP), which in 1950 was to gain the largest number of votes in the state.[51]

By the end of the Dutra presidency, there had not yet appeared a significant populist politician of the left. Adhemar had not sought to exploit popular feelings of economic nationalism, an approach later to be the stock-in-trade of left-wing populists. But the new style and its effectiveness had been amply demonstrated.[52]

Economic Cross-Currents. The economic history of the Dutra presidency may be divided into two phases: 1946–47 and 1947–50. The first period saw an attempt to return to the principles of laissez-faire liberalism, a policy that was shaken by the rapid exhaustion of Brazil's foreign exchange reserves and the resulting deficit in the balance of payments in 1947. The reintroduction of exchange controls in June 1947 marked the beginning of the transition to the second period, which saw a speedup in "spontaneous industrialization" and a turn toward rudimentary forms of overall planning for federal expenditures.[53]

The men who wrote the Constitution of 1946 were strongly influenced by the ideas of economic liberalism, from which the Estado Nôvo had deviated. Since the end of the Estado Nôvo coincided with the end of the war, the anti-Vargas politicians and lawyers were attempting to reject the state intervention which had been identified with both. In part, they were motivated by a desire to avoid continuing in the future what they regarded as the illegitimate political use of economic controls in the past. At the same time as the new Constitution was emerging in 1946, the Dutra government quickly dismantled the ad hoc apparatus of direct wartime controls. The new government's answer to the war-induced inflation was to open up the country to importation of finished goods from abroad. This seemed all the more logical in view of the large foreign exchange reserves accumulated during the war. The Ministers of Finance in 1946 and 1947 therefore sought to satisfy pent-up demand *and* to combat rising prices by a generous import policy.

Coupled with this turn to a policy of free exchange rates and free capital movements was a constrictionist policy towards the domestic economy. Preoccupied with the rising price level, the Dutra government in 1946 undertook no effective measures to expand domestic industrial capacity. Minister of Finance Correia e Castro in his annual Report for 1946 (dated May 1947), noted that bank credit must be "organized in the classical mold," and warned against "opportunistic banking maneuvers." He stressed that "the return to the norms of free trade" would create "a climate of confidence conducive to an increase in production."

As for Brazil's economic destiny, the Finance Minister was frank.

He described Brazil as "essentially an agrarian country," and added, "the essence of the Latin American economy, and Brazil is an integral part of this area, is a certain concentration of effort in the export of primary products and foodstuffs, as well as in the import of a wide variety of manufactured goods and processed foodstuffs." [54]

The economic policy of the early Dutra regime, based on a minimum of controls in every sector, soon proved self-defeating. The foreign exchange reserves, which in 1945 had totaled $708 million, were virtually gone after a year and a half. The small foreign balances left were in blocked accounts, leaving total foreign liquid assets at only $92 million by the end of the first quarter of 1947. The policy of satisfying domestic demand by maintaining a high level of imports had collided with the fact of Brazil's limited capacity to import. In essence, Brazil had tried to revert to the level of import expenditure which had prevailed in 1929. But aggregate income had increased by 50 percent over 1929, while the importing capacity had remained the same. An equilibrium could be reached in the short run, therefore, only by adopting one of two measures: devaluation, or exchange controls. By choosing the latter, the Dutra regime, probably without realizing the implications of its own action, furnished a powerful stimulus to Brazil's industrialization.[55]

In June 1947, the government introduced a set of exchange controls which set up a drastic system of import licensing while maintaining Brazil's high valuation of its own currency. Although the government claimed not to have deviated from its declared policy of fighting inflation by maintaining imports, in practice the import regulations worked against consumer goods and in favor of essential items such as fuels, equipment, and machinery. Since domestic demand remained high, there was a powerful incentive for Brazilian industry to expand. Furthermore, the maintaining of a high official value on the cruzeiro acted as a disincentive to the export sector, thereby diverting investment into production for the domestic market. The resulting surge in Brazil's economic development, like the import substitution of the 1930's, has been described as a phase of "spontaneous industrialization."

This process was in no sense the product of a deliberate policy on the part of the Dutra government. On the contrary, it was the result of measures aimed at the solution of such short-term problems as domestic inflation and disequilibrium in the balance of payments. The exchange controls of 1947 acted in a manner similar to the coffee support policy in the 1930's, which has already been discussed. Although neither policy was intended primarily to promote industrialization, both had that effect. From the standpoint of those who favored Brazil's industrialization, they were both examples of "sleepwalking" in the making of economic policy.[56]

The industrialization of the last two years of the Dutra period was aided by an easier credit policy. This included loans from the Bank of Brazil to several key sectors of private industry—as, for example, to the Klabin firm, which built a cellulose factory in Paraná, and the Acésita firm, for a specialty steel operation in the Rio Doce Valley. By the end of the Dutra presidency, Brazil could point to an impressive record of economic growth. Between 1945 and 1951 there was a 6 percent annual real growth in total production and a 3.2 percent annual increase in per capita output.[57]

The years after 1947 also saw the beginning of a change in the Dutra government's attitude toward the need to coordinate its public expenditures. It therefore proposed, in May 1948, the SALTE Plan.[58] This constituted little more than a first attempt at the coordination of public expenditure on a five-year basis. The SALTE Plan was incorporated into the federal budget proposal for 1949, but was never fully enacted. In operation for only a year, the SALTE Plan ran into financial difficulties and was discontinued in 1951.[59]

The abortive SALTE program, which encompassed only public investment, was as close as the Dutra government came to planning on a national scale. Planning on a regional level, however, was written into the Constitution of 1946, which called for plans to develop the São Francisco and Amazon River Valleys and a plan to combat the drought in the Northeast. Each program was guaranteed a fixed percentage of the federal tax returns (1 percent for the São Francisco Valley, and 3 percent each for the Amazon and the Northeast). The commissions for the São Francisco Valley (*Comissão do Vale de São Francisco or CVSF*) and the Amazon Valley (*Superintendência do Plano de Valorização Econômica de Amazônia or SPVEA*) were created in 1948. Neither was to prove a particularly effective agent for economic development, but their creation and continued financial support by the federal government showed that there was no aversion to planning in practice, despite the influence that advocates of economic liberalism had enjoyed in 1945 and 1946. In short, planning during the Dutra years was pursued on a regional and sectoral basis, accompanied by a deliberate soft-pedaling of the principle of state intervention in the economy.[60]

By the late 1940's, however, there were signs of a wide-ranging debate over the question of Brazil's optimal strategy for economic development. In 1948 the United States and Brazil agreed to set up a joint technical commission, designed to resume the economic cooperation established by the Cooke mission that President Roosevelt had sent during the Second World War. The commission was empowered "to analyze the factors in Brazil which are tending to promote or to retard the economic development of Brazil." The United States delegation was headed by John Abbink, and the Brazilian delegation by Octávio Gouvêa de Bulhões. The commission's findings, published in June 1949, became known as the "Abbink Report." The Report reflected the strongly neo-liberal economic views of its co-chairmen, Bulhões and Abbink. It largely neglected the area of manufacturing industry, and came out in favor of orthodox financial and fiscal policies: "Can a balanced and rapid economic development, of a kind which will bring lasting benefit to all the people of the nation, be achieved in Brazil under conditions of rapidly and continuously mounting prices? The Commission is convinced that it cannot." The Report also stressed the need for "a balanced development of Brazil's resources by private enterprise." The commission saw a need for measures to restructure Brazil's domestic capital market, which, never well-organized, had been thrown into disarray by the rapid inflation of 1941–46 and the distorting effect of the speculative boom in urban real estate. Finally, the Report emphasized the serious deficiencies in the areas of transportation and energy, and acknowledged that these bottlenecks would require vigorous state action.[61]

The publication of the Abbink Report stimulated criticism from a group of young economists who had just begun editing an economic journal for the National Confederation of Industry in Rio de Janeiro. They questioned the theoretical basis of the Report, especially the assumption that inflation in an underdeveloped country such as Brazil was necessarily the result of an attempt at "overutilization" of available resources. They suggested an alternative interpretation that would take account of the different conditions in underdeveloped economies where disguised unemployment could coincide with rising prices. "What ought to predominate in economic policy," they argued, "is the increase in real income, above all in an underdeveloped country, even though it presupposes a certain increase in prices."

These critics were advancing an early version of the "structuralist" theory. They criticized the Report for stressing the need to eliminate the "symptoms" which, they held, would only disappear when the underlying structural deficiencies had been overcome. Although they acknowledged the value of some of the commission's technical work, they concluded that "the policy of credit restriction recommended by the Report is contrary, in the present situation, to the objective of economic development, which first requires, for a more productive utilization of the factors of production, an adequate expansion of credit." Octávio Gouvêa de Bulhões replied, defending the Report for which he had been largely responsible. This debate was an overture to the subsequent controversy over economic development between "monetarists" and "structuralists." [62]

Vargas Returns

Vargas had been caught unprepared by the sudden end of the Estado Nôvo. Although the return of free elections became virtually certain in early 1945, the incumbent dictator was unable to prevent his own removal as the prelude to his country's return to the liberal democratic path from which he had diverted it in 1937. Few believed, however, that he could remain outside politics for long.

Dutra had hardly settled into the presidential palace before Vargas' admirers began to organize for his candidacy in the presidential election of 1950. The 1945 election proved that Vargas enjoyed wide popular support. He was elected to the federal Senate from two states —Rio Grande do Sul and São Paulo. After some hesitation, he chose to accept election as a PSD senator from his home state of Rio Grande do Sul. Although he appeared to withdraw from politics, his ranch at São Borja became a mecca for aspiring politicians; and it was soon clear that the central personality of the period was not the newly elected President, but the recently deposed one.

Elected senator, Getúlio appeared infrequently in the body he described in his maiden speech as a "backwater where the ripples from elsewhere die down." During 1946 he assumed the pose of the former President who harbored no rancor from the bitter political wars of his fifteen years in power. He hoped that his conspicuously conciliatory attitude would disarm his enemies, led by the UDN politicians who continued, after 1945, to make political capital of their long opposition to the Estado Nôvo. In the face of their denunciation, Getúlio exploited the remarkable Brazilian propensity to forgive and forget in politics. In December 1946 he delivered a long speech in the Senate, justifying his coup of 1937 as having been Brazil's only alternative to an imminent civil war. The implication of Vargas' explanation was clear. Free political competition had been the norm from which the country diverged for an emergency period. But normal times had now returned. The dictator of yesterday had become the elder statesman of today—ready, if summoned by his countrymen, to run for high office.[63]

By 1949, Vargas' patient strategy began to pay off. Mixing discretion, magnanimity, and tact, he gradually succeeded in changing his image from Vargas the dictator to Vargas the democrat. UDN politicians discovered that mere attacks on the mistakes of Estado Nôvo brought diminishing returns. The rhetoric of 1945 had become increasingly irrevelant to the problems of 1950.

In his new role as a democratic politician, Vargas needed a party. His initial efforts went into building up the Brazilian Labor Party, which had been founded under his guidance and inspiration in 1945. In his statement endorsing Dutra on the eve of the presidential election in 1945, Vargas urged all Brazilian workers to join the PTB. In 1946 he called for support of the PTB as the party "most likely to bring about the happiness of all Brazilians." In the state and supplementary congressional elections of January 1947 he campaigned for PTB congressional candidates, attacking the "plutocracy" of "capitalist democracy" in which political liberty was a "fraud" because "social equality" was lacking.[64]

While working to build this new party, Vargas was careful not to neglect his old contacts. From the outset he was shrewd enough to see that the party lines were too fluid and party commitments too unreliable for a national politician to identify himself exclusively with one party. Indeed, his party affiliation *as a senator* was with the

PSD. When asked in late 1946 how he could reconcile his efforts to build up an opposition party (the PTB), with his status as a senator in President Dutra's party (the PSD), he candidly explained: "I have many friends whom I greatly value in the PSD all over Brazil. A political stand taken on matters of doctrine does not constitute an insult to anyone nor does it exclude the possibility of collaboration." [65] It was precisely on the "collaboration" of the PSD and the PTB that Getúlio based his political comeback in the 1940's. During a speaking tour in Minas Gerais during the 1947 elections, for example, Vargas endorsed Governor Bias Fortes, a venerable PSD politician of the old style, while urging at the same time the election of PTB congressional candidates. The Vargas strategy was clear: hold the loyalty of the traditional political chieftains in the countryside through the PSD, while building electoral strength in the cities by means of the PTB.

In his role as PTB leader, Vargas spelled out his political philosophy of trabalhismo—a mixture of social welfarism, working-class political activity, and economic nationalism. It was his up-to-date version (now in a democratic rather than an authoritarian context) of the social philosophy which had been expressed in corporatist terms during the Estado Nôvo.[66]

Trabalhismo was not the only political movement at work in the cities, however. The Communist Party had shown strength in 1945 and 1947, especially in the Federal District and São Paulo. Its legal suppression in 1947 soon removed it as a publicly identifiable separate force. A more dynamic vote-getting force in São Paulo was the movement of the populist politician, Adhemar de Barros. Adhemar had put together a formidable electoral machine, the PSP, which extended well into the interior of the state of São Paulo. After two years as Governor of São Paulo, Adhemar represented a force more powerful in that state than either the PTB or the PSD. If Getúlio wanted to reach the presidency, he could not do so without Adhemar's help. Adhemar had presidential ambitions himself. But he felt it was too early to test them, and he needed Getúlio's help for his long-range plans. By supporting Vargas' return he might ensure endorsement later as Vargas' successor and thereby gain a powerful springboard to highest office.

It was not only among the politicians that Vargas had to lay the groundwork for his candidacy. There was also the opinion of the military to be considered. Getúlio had been installed in the presidency in November, 1930 by a military junta, elevated to a dictatorship in 1937 by the military, and summarily deposed in 1945 by the military. In each case there were vigorous debates among the higher Army officers over the course the Armed Forces should take. In each instance there was sufficient agreement for the high command to assume a united front. In 1937 and again in 1945 the key figures in Getúlio's career had been Generals Dutra and Góes Monteiro. As Vargas now planned his political comeback, Dutra was the stiffly correct President, while Góes Monteiro, although no longer in a formal position of command in the Army, was still an influential senior commander, widely honored within the officer class as the author of the "movement of October 29" which had removed Getúlio from the presidential palace in 1945.

Vargas and Adhemar de Barros sent their emissaries in late 1949 to learn from Góes Monteiro how the military would react to the idea of Getúlio's candidacy. Góes assured the Vargas lieutenants that "the Armed Forces harbored no resentments or prejudices against him, nor would they oppose his taking office if elected, as long as he respected not only the Constitution, but also the inalienable rights of the military." Góes' support was sealed by an emotional reconciliation with Getúlio during which the details of the campaign strategy were discussed. Vargas tried to convince him to accept the vice presidential nomination on the PSP-PTB ticket, but Góes was already committed to support the candidate selected by Dutra and the PSD. That made it doubly important for Vargas to have Góes' assurance that the majority of the military would not veto his candidacy.[67]

In early 1950 the PSP, always the personal instrument of Adhemar de Barros, offered Getúlio its nomination for the presidential election of October 3, 1950. In June the PTB met and also nominated Vargas. On June 7, he accepted both nominations. The scene for the election campaign of 1950 was now set. Vargas had reemerged on the national stage as the champion of trabalhismo and the authorized candidate of his nearest rival in populism, Adhemar de Barros.

The PSD, haven of many getulistas from the days of the Estado Nôvo, decided to nominate its own candidate, Cristiano Machado, an unexceptionable lawyer-politician from the PSD stronghold of Minas. The PSD nomination came at the insistence of Dutra, who had taken umbrage at Vargas' attacks on the incumbent government, and wanted to insure "continuity" in the presidency by choosing his own successor. But Dutra was naive and relatively ineffective in the art of negotiation with PSD chieftains. Only in the state of Minas Gerais did the Machado candidacy have a following that offered Getúlio any real threat. Elsewhere Vargas had concluded "understandings" with the PSD (or their dissident factions, as in Rio Grande do Sul) which ensured that they would give less than enthusiastic backing to Machado, if not tacit support for Getúlio. This strategy was facilitated by Vargas' intimate contacts with the ex-Interventors who were now PSD stalwarts. Ernani do Amaral Peixoto, running for Governor of the state of Rio de Janeiro, was one of the more prominent. He was also Getúlio's son-in-law. PSD support in that state was minimal for Machado.[68]

Getúlio's natural opposition, the UDN, renominated Eduardo Gomes, their candidate of 1945. Despite the victory of the "ins" in 1945, the UDN had not abandoned their hope that the return of more normal political conditions would help them gain the presidency. Immediately after his defeat in December 1945, Gomes explained that the election of Dutra had been influenced by "some transitory factors" which were the "left-overs of an evil government," such as "the fascist submission of workers to the State, the neglect of education" and "pauperism." By 1949, the UDN leaders hoped, these "transitory factors" would cease to carry much weight. They subbornly refused, however, to adapt their campaign strategy to the new political atmosphere of postwar Brazil. During the campaign Gomes actually went so far as to advocate repeal of the minimum wage law. He also accepted the formal support of Plínio Salgado's latter-day Integralistas, now organized in the *Partido de Representação Popular* (PRP).[69]

The election campaign proceeded along the lines Vargas had planned. His opposition was divided. Unable to agree on a "union" candidate, both the UDN and the PSD had put their own candidates in the field. Against them Vargas constructed a formidable alliance. It was a marriage of convenience between old and new political forces in Brazil. The old were represented by the traditional-style politicians—especially of the PSD—for whom politics was less a matter of policy and principle than of power and patronage. They viewed the exercise of office as a process of satisfying their "clients," usually the proprietors of the rural social structure. The new political forces were represented by the populist politicians who had demonstrated an ability to win the votes of the growing masses—including both the working class and the lower middle class—in the major cities. Adhemar de Barros was the leading practitioner of this new-style politics; and Vargas himself assumed this role in his efforts to build the PTB. Getúlio's alliance, then, rested on Adhemar's PSP (of crucial importance in São Paulo), the PTB, and the PSD where its loyalty was negotiable. In one state, Pernambuco, Vargas found the PSD stubbornly wedded to Machado and was forced to ally with the UDN, the party whose *raison d'être* was opposition to getulismo. One could hardly have found greater proof of the non-doctrinal character of parties in the economically backward states!

Getúlio had strong personal reasons for wishing to regain the presidency. Although he claimed that he harbored no bitterness over being deposed in 1945, in private he talked passionately of his impending "revindication." [70] Throughout the campaign he defended his record from 1930 to 1945, especially in economic policy. His "unceasing effort," he explained, had been to "transform into an industrial nation" a country "paralyzed by the myopia of rulers wedded to the existing monoculture and to the simple extraction of primary materials." Brazilians now had the opportunity to "resume the impetus lost in 1945." He pledged that "as long as I have breath I shall continue to fight against the fossilized and myopic apostles of inaction, the apologists of stagnation and apathy." [71]

Vargas spared Dutra in his attacks, but not the Finance Minister, Manuel Guilherme da Silveira Filho, whom Getúlio described as "the great organizer of defeats." [72] Vargas derided the orthodox financial policies which had cost Brazil her foreign exchange reserves in 1946 without sufficiently strengthening her industrial base. In essence, he advocated a speed up in industrialization—a policy of the kind that was later to be labeled "developmentalism." At the same time he claimed credit for having launched Brazil's drive to industrialize.

Vargas also campaigned on the need to expand and strengthen social welfare legislation originated in the 1930's. In 1946 he had pronounced the death notice of the "old liberal and capitalist democracy" which "is founded in inequality." In its place was emerging, he argued, "socialist democracy, the democracy of the workers." Now, in the 1950 campaign, he protected himself from the "reactionaries" by quoting the *Rerum Novarum* of Pope Leo XIII, "which many people cite without really understanding." [73]

All this was Vargas' language of trabalhismo, but the old Machiavellian was too shrewd to offer the same message everywhere. In Rio de Janeiro, a center of Communist strength in 1945 and 1947, he sensed that something stronger was needed and came forward as the populist: "If I am elected on October 3, as I take office the people will climb the steps of Catete with me. And they will remain with me in power." [74] In Minas Gerais he was the sober statesman, in Bahia the eloquent disciple of Ruy Barbosa's liberalism, in the Northeast the champion of a crusade against the drought.

As for Getúlio's opponents, Machado never undertook a serious national effort, concentrating instead where his strength was already proven. Gomes, on the other hand, moved about frenetically in search of votes, and his party, the UDN, supported their candidate with a wealth of publicity based on their control of most of the established newspapers and radio. Vargas countered the mass media with sound trucks and fliers, and his campaign itinerary was a model of effectiveness. Indeed, he knew Brazil as neither Gomes nor Machado could.[75]

On October 3 the electoral issue was joined and Getúlio emerged victorious. Much to the shock of the UDN and the surprise of the PSD, he captured nearly an absolute majority of the vote for President, receiving 3,849,040, or 48.7 percent of the total vote. Gomes ran a weak second, with 29.7 percent, and Machado third, with 21.5 percent. Vargas' election strategy had paid off handsomely.

This winning strategy had also left Getúlio with a number of electoral debts. He owed his most important debt to Adhemar de Barros, the Governor of São Paulo. Nearly a quarter of Vargas' national vote came from Adhemar's state, where the President-elect's total of 925,493 was almost three times that of Gomes (357,413) and six times the vote of Machado (153,039). In the Federal District, Adhemar's electoral machine was also an important aid, helping Getúlio to win 378,015 votes—more than double Gomes' vote of 169,263. Adhemar's dramatic and highly effective support, therefore, gave him a strong claim to a voice in the new government, but it was the voice of a highly personal political movement couched in a populist tone, and deliberately ambiguous on key problems of public policy.

Vargas also owed a clear debt to the PSD, the organization of the "ins" which he had himself launched in 1945. Despite the party's nomination of Machado, local PSD leaders had been willing to negotiate with Vargas. Minas Gerais was a good example. Although it was a strong PSD state, Vargas succeeded in neutralizing Machado's strength. During the campaign he refrained from endorsing either the UDN or the PSD candidate for governor. He did, however, negotiate with local PSD leaders on his own behalf. As a result, he managed to divide the total vote in Minas almost equally among himself (418,-194), Gomes (441,690) and Machado (409,402). This was no small triumph in view of the strength of the PSD machine in Minas.

What did Vargas owe to the PTB? It was effective mainly in Rio Grande do Sul and the Federal District, but even in these areas its importance was secondary. Although the party was growing rapidly—it had doubled its congressional vote between 1945 and 1950—it could not claim to have contributed the decisive margin for Getúlio's victory. Furthermore, the PTB had been powerfully molded to Vargas' personal cast. Instead of emerging as an independent party capable of producing its own cadre of leaders, it was exploited as simply another instrument at the service of Vargas' short-term coalition politics.

III

A New Vargas Era: 1951–1954

On January 31, 1951, the sash of office was handed to Getúlio Vargas by outgoing President Dutra. A new Vargas era had begun. The former dictator had demonstrated his political appeal as a democrat and "vindicated" himself in a free election. For the first and only time Vargas had reached the presidency by direct popular vote.

Vargas chose a cabinet which reflected the diverse alliance that had elected him. The PSD did best in the competition for ministries. It was awarded the ministries of foreign affairs, interior and justice, education and health, and finance. The PTB got only one ministry—labor—which went to Danton Coelho. Coelho had been a tireless PTB organizer and architect of the PTB campaign to return Vargas to power. Giving to a PTB leader the control over the vast apparatus of the Ministry of Labor would help to strengthen the PTB's campaign to gain control of the government-sponsored trade unions. Adhemar de Barros' PSP was given the Ministry of Transport and Communication (with its enormous patronage powers), and Adhemar was granted an important voice in the choice of the new president of the Bank of Brazil—a key position for São Paulo because the president of the Bank of Brazil, along with the Minister of Finance (over whose appointment Adhemar also exercised influence), determined credit and foreign-exchange policy—of vital importance to industry. Getúlio's election debts included an obligation to one state branch of the staunchly *anti-getulista* UDN. João Cleofas, leader of the UDN in Pernambuco and the unsuccessful candidate for governor, had supported Getúlio when the PSD of that state proved loyal to Machado's candidacy. Vargas therefore appointed Cleofas to the Ministry of Agriculture.[1]

In addition to his civilian cabinet, Getúlio appointed three military ministers, the most important of whom was the War Minister. For that post he selected General Estillac Leal, a respected officer who had been a tenente and a member of the Prestes column and who was now a leader of the nationalist wing in the officer corps. The Navy and Air Force Ministers, of less significance in the politics of the Brazilian military, were Admiral Renato Guilhobel and Brigadier Nero Moura.

Brazilian Society and the Question of Economic Development

As Getúlio assumed the presidency in January 1951, he faced a Brazil very different from the country he had governed as an authoritarian President from 1937 to 1945. Brazilian society presented a more clearly differentiated class structure than had existed during the Estado Nôvo, especially in its early stages. The twin processes of industrialization and urbanization had enlarged and strengthened three sectors: the industrialists, the urban working class and the urban middle class.[2]

None of these classes had, by 1950, reached a stage of self-awareness likely to produce sharply "class-oriented" politics. On the contrary, the "conciliatory" political atmosphere of patrimonial Brazil was still remarkably dominant. During the early 1950's, however, the question of economic development came increasingly to occupy the attention of politicians, who soon found that the political implications of economic policy-making could not long be ignored. It is important, therefore, to examine the attitude of the principal sectors toward economic development.

The industrialists were as yet a small group within Brazilian society. Concentrated in the south-center triangle lying roughly between São Paulo, Rio de Janeiro, and Belo Horizonte, they were timid in politics. A few followed the lead of Roberto Simonsen, the pioneering Paulista banker, industrialist, and writer, who had campaigned until his death in 1948 for a vigorous industrialization policy. The majority, however, limited their politicking to efforts to ensure favorable credit policies and a measure of government support for industry. Their political vehicle in São Paulo was primarily the PSD. But they were not a dynamic entrepreneurial sector in 1950, if measured by their influence on national politics. They were content to rely primarily upon the corporatist organizations created under government aegis during the Estado Nôvo.

The rapidly growing working class was relatively inarticulate in politics. It voted more as a mass than a class. Its aspirations were exploited by populist politicians who, instead of casting their appeals in terms of class antagonism, merely promised more services and attention. In the campaign of 1950, Vargas had occasionally struck the populist pose, but his approach remained essentially paternalistic, reflecting his own estimate of the growing but still limited political consciousness of urban workers.[3]

The position of the "middle class" was more difficult to analyze. The middle class was practically non-existent in the economically backward regions of the country, especially in the North and Northeast. Even in large cities such as Recife, with a population of over 700,000, it was difficult to identify any significant middle sector which had come to distinguish its interests from those of the archaic economy based on subsistence agriculture, inefficient cattle culture, and extractive industries. The urban groups were inextricably compromised by their familial and financial connections with the historic agrarian structure. This pattern persisted in the towns of the interior of even the most developed states such as São Paulo.

But the larger urban concentrations within the "developed triangle" had produced a self-conscious middle group composed of bureaucrats, professional people, the managerial cadres of the new industrializing society, and the commercial interests whose fate was tied to that society's growth. In numbers, this class was not large—perhaps five million out of a total population of fifty-two million in 1950. Yet it was in a powerful political position because Brazil's franchise excluded illiterates. Furthermore, the cooperation of the middle sector was crucial in administering the country and in achieving further economic development. From its ranks came the majority of the skilled managers indispensable for the functioning of the Brazilian economy.[4]

Politically, the urban middle class was an enigma. It included two main groups. The first was made up of the bureaucrats and administrators whose economic status resulted more from urbanization and the growth of federal power than from industrialization per se. Their mentality and their jobs were often an inheritance from the patrimonial world of pre-1930 Brazil. They did not, therefore, see their position as dependent on a continued transformation of Brazil's traditional role as an exporter of primary products. On the contrary, they tended to identify with the social values—and therefore with the economic system—of the planter class and the export-import merchant group which had dominated Brazilian politics since the mid-nineteenth century.[5]

The other major portion of the urban middle class was made up of managers and professional men who regarded industrialization and the spread of "modern" technical methods as indispensable for Brazil's future. Equally important, they identified themselves and their careers with this process and regarded with suspicion, although seldom hostility, the traditional values prevalent in the era before 1930. Most members of the middle class were torn between these two attitudes. At heart, they were apprehensive about their future status in a rapidly changing social and economic system. This apprehension was in turn deepened and compounded by the postwar inflation that had already set in before 1950.

The political party which wooed the urban middle class most ardently was the UDN. The UDN's devotion to anti-getulismo (especially the getulismo of the dictatorship) and the principles of liberal constitutionalism gave it a prima facie appeal to the middle class. But the UDN ought to have remembered that the middle class had been far from united in its opposition to the Estado Nôvo; nor had middle-class voters felt any instinctive antipathy for the state intervention in the economy that Vargas had accelerated. Indeed, the new bureaucratic positions created since the 1930's had given employment to many members of the middle class. Thus the natural monopoly over the middle class which the UDN appeared to enjoy at the end of the Estado Nôvo was subject to rapid erosion as the question of economic development began to occupy a central place in Brazilian politics.

These three sectors—the industrialists, the urban working class, and the urban middle class—had grown significantly since 1930. There were three other sectors whose relative weight had declined since 1930, although their influence was far from negligible in 1950: the coffee planters, the export-import merchants, and the domestic food producers.

All modern Brazilian governments have attempted, with greater or less vigor, to maximize foreign exchange earnings. Since coffee has been the largest earner of foreign exchange throughout the Republic, coffee growers have enjoyed continuous government support and protection. This support began on a state level in 1906, and was gradually taken over as a federal responsibility. The exact level and manner of coffee support varied, but the basic commitment continued after 1945. The final Dutra years saw a boom in coffee prices, beginning in 1949 and then strengthened by the general commodity price rise resulting from the Korean War.[6]

Import dealers and merchants who specialized in imported products were a powerful pressure group in Brazilian politics. They had ridden the wave of the import boom in 1946–47 which quickly exhausted the foreign exchange reserves Brazil had accumulated in the second world war. Importers thereafter had to operate under the limitations of increasingly strict exchange control, which included quotas or prohibitions on the importation of many consumer goods. These merchants were closely linked to trade associations that were well organized for political activity in major cities such as São Paulo and Rio de Janeiro. The trade associations had long been opponents of industrialization because it would ultimately displace them as middlemen for foreign sources of supply. They also opposed industrialization because short-run protectionist measures—strict import quotas and a "soft" exchange policy—would seem to make more difficult and costly, if not impossible, their import transactions. Interestingly, these commercial associations included many merchants who handled almost entirely goods that were domestically produced. Yet these merchants largely followed the lead of the anti-industrializationists. This commercial sector of the economy directly or indirectly provided the jobs for an important part of the middle class, and it was this part of the bourgeoisie which was most confused about its status in a rapidly changing Brazil.

Domestic food producers—meaning those farmers who produced a surplus for market sale (thus excluding the subsistence sector)—were a group whose basic position in the economy had never been in question even during the most interventionist period of the Estado Nôvo. Since Brazil was on a net import basis for foodstuffs, above all wheat (in 1950, 15 percent of the total value of imports was in foodstuffs), Brazilian farmers had no trouble selling what they could produce.

The class that has not been mentioned thus far is the subsistence sector of the rural economy. Politically, this sector counted for virtually nothing in 1930, and for little more in 1950. The Constitution of 1946 prohibited illiterates from voting and since the rural areas were overwhelmingly illiterate, especially in the back-country regions, the rural underprivileged had no weight in the political process. No major political figure in 1950 proposed any radical changes in the land system.

In his campaign strategy of 1950, Vargas had shown an appreciation of the several Brazils produced by the uneven economic development of the last twenty years. He had won the election by appealing to the differing and contradictory interests of these varied sectors and classes. Once in power, however, he decided to concentrate on accelerating Brazil's industrialization and the diversification of her economy. At the same time, Vargas sought in 1951 to reassure the traditional economic sectors that they had nothing to fear from stepped-up industrialization. In this strategy he was aided by the improvement in the terms of trade which began in 1949 and continued through 1951.

In his efforts to accelerate economic growth, Vargas faced a fundamental problem: what should be Brazil's strategy of development? How could Brazil move into a new stage of growth that involved the expansion of capital-goods industries and vast investments in social overhead capital such as transportation, hydroelectric power, and fuel? These needs were clearly outlined in a study published by the Economic Commission for Latin America only a few months after Vargas' inauguration. As that report emphasized, Brazil's limited capacity to import created a powerful constraint and imposed the need to establish strict priorities in economic policy-making.[7]

Given the availability of technical analyses of the principal economic problems, what would be the political basis for the strategy adopted? On what classes or economic sectors could Vargas rely for the support, leadership, and enthusiasm which adventurous and sometimes unpopular policies would require? The "spontaneous forces" were inadequate by themselves to overcome the institutional and structural barriers which now limited the growth of the economy. Brazil lacked a dynamic entrepreneurial class which could, by its own weight, seize the leadership of a drive toward industrialization. This was not to say that Brazilian industrialists could not be counted upon to expand and innovate when they were offered sufficient incentives and when the general business climate was favorable. The remarkable growth of industry in São Paulo had amply demonstrated Brazilian entrepreneurial skills.[8] By the early 1950's, however, the economy had encountered a network of bottlenecks that could be broken only by decisive government action.

The exact role of state intervention would depend on the development strategy chosen. Although the Dutra government had briefly attempted a partial return to policies of economic liberalism, the stubborn adherence to an overvalued exchange rate and the careful avoidance of any innovations in central planning had given way by 1947 to a recognition that bolder state intervention in the economy was inevitable. The exchange controls of 1947–48 and the SALTE plan were the first steps toward consciously resuming the central role which the federal government had come to play in the economy during the Vargas years. In fact, the corporatist structure imposed on the Brazilian economy by Vargas during the Estado Nôvo had been only partially dismantled in 1945–46. What remained gave the federal government some apparatus, if often unwieldy and inefficient, for directing the economy. When he returned to the presidency in 1951, Vargas, always the pragmatist, had not committed himself irrevocably to any development strategy, but he was obviously receptive to the argument that a vigorous state role would be necessary.

Formulae for Growth

The Dutra era had witnessed the beginnings of a vigorous debate over development strategy. Three principal formulae emerged: the neo-liberal, the developmentalist-nationalist, and the radical nationalist. None of these positions represented a detailed strategy. Rather, each was a combination of diagnosis and general policy recommendations.[9]

The neo-liberal formula was based on the assumption that the price mechanism should be respected as the principal determinant in the economy. Fiscal and monetary policies, as well as foreign exchange policy, should follow the orthodox principles laid down by the theoreticians and practitioners of central-banking policy in the industrialized countries. Government budgets should be balanced and the money supply tightly controlled. Foreign capital should be welcomed and encouraged as an indispensable help to a capital-poor country. Government-imposed limitations on the international movement of capital, currency, and goods should be kept at an absolute minimum. Such self-discipline would maximize the mobility of factors and relegate Brazil to its natural, inevitable, and unavoidable economic role under the inexorable law of comparative advantage. The leading spokesman for this formula was the well-known economist Eugênio Gudin. It was a view also espoused by many import merchants for whom the benefits of the law of comparative advantage were obvious. Principal newspaper chains supporting this view were *O Globo* (owned by the Marinho family which was closely linked to the large group of Portuguese importers and merchants in Rio de Janeiro), and the vast publishing empire of Assis Chateaubriand, the *Diários Associados*.[10]

The second formula was developmentalist-nationalism. It was only in a preliminary stage of formulation by 1950 and was to receive more precise definition both on the theoretical and the empirical level through the research and publications of the Economic Commission for Latin America (begun in 1949). The origins of this view in Brazil can be traced back to the economic nationalism of the tenentes and more recently to the state-directed industrialization efforts of the Estado Nôvo. Advocates of this formula began with the assumption that Brazil faced an imperative need to industrialize, but argued that the spontaneous forces which had achieved industrialization in the North Atlantic world were inadequate in Brazil. To pass through the transitional phase from an agrarian economy to a modern industrial economy required a new strategy of development. Indeed, the free operation of the price mechanism and the continued free mobility of factors would actually hamper Brazil's industrialization. The new strategy ought to aim at a mixed economy in which the private sector would be given new incentives, in proportion to an established set of investment priorities. At the same time, the state would intervene more directly by means of state enterprises and mixed public-private enterprises, in order to break bottlenecks and ensure investment in areas where the private sector lacked either the will or the resources to venture. Proponents of this formula acknowledged that private foreign capital could play an important role, but they insisted that it be accepted only if subject to careful regulation by Brazilian authorities.[11]

The developmentalist-nationalist formula was put forward by a small but varied group. Their common denominator was a strong nationalism. Many army officers, for example, thought Brazil could only become an important power if she developed industry. Furthermore, Brazil's national security demanded that the exploitation of such natural resources as fuel, water power, and mineral resources be kept out of foreign hands. This demand had been put forward by the more militant tenentes, was written into the Constitution of 1934, and then espoused in the late 1930's by nationalist army officers such as General Macedo Soares, who had served as technical director of the Volta Redonda steel works and was later to become President of the National Confederation of Industry (*Confederação Nacional de Indústria* or CNI). This formula also appealed to a younger generation of technocrats and intellectuals who thought Brazil could attain a high standard of living for all its citizens and full-fledged status as a modern nation, only if it undertook a stepped-up drive toward industrialization, thereby consciously renouncing its former role as a somnolent supplier of tropical exports for the North Atlantic world. It should be stressed again that this formula of developmentalist-nationalism was in proto-form in 1951. It was the most pragmatic of the three positions and was to become more widely disseminated and understood as the Vargas presidency continued.[12]

The third formula was radical nationalism. It deserves less attention than the other two as an economic formula, because it was put forward more in the spirit of political polemics than as a carefully reasoned strategy for development. Indeed, the radical nationalist position was based on the assumption that the existing economic and social structure was "exploitative" and demanded radical change. Radical nationalists attributed Brazil's underdevelopment to a natural alliance of private investors and capitalist governments within the industrialized world. This conspiracy sought to limit Brazil forever to a subordinate role as an exporter of primary products whose prices were kept at a minimum level, and an importer of finished goods whose prices were set at an exorbitant level by monopolistic corporations. Any industrialization program was therefore doomed to failure if based on the assumed cooperation of the developed countries. On the contrary, strategic policies to accelerate industrialization, such as maximizing the capacity to import capital equipment, could expect deliberate sabotage by the foreign conspirators. Furthermore, Brazil's state of economic underdevelopment was promoted by those domestic sectors tied to the export-import trade, aided and abetted by the Brazilians employed by foreign firms, whose investment was by nature exploitative.[13]

The radical nationalist formula was short on policy suggestions. Its aggressive polemical tone was intended to arouse passionate animosity against the existing system. Its only positive language was reserved for economic enterprises under total state control. The stridently negative tone of the radical nationalists easily led to the conclusion that at least some were primarily interested in providing the economic rationale for a strategy of political revolution. Seen from this standpoint, radical nationalism was aimed, not at revising Brazil's strategy for development, but at discrediting the political elite as a prelude to a radical reordering of the social order.

It is important to appreciate that the radical nationalist position embraced a range of opinion broader than those who were active Communists (members of the PCB) or intellectual Marxists. The "exploitation" theory of underdevelopment appealed to many Brazilians, including many intellectuals, who were not prepared to accept Marxist economics in theory or Communist Party discipline in practice. Unless the heterogeneity of the radical nationalist position is kept in mind, there is a danger that any analysis of subsequent Brazilian politics will overemphasize the influence of communism and Marxism as an explanation for the appeals of economic nationalism.

It would be a mistake to regard these three formulae as easily identifiable positions taken by large groups of Brazilians on the vital issues of economic development.[14] Rather, they were analytical positions put forward by a small number of writers and propagandists. In practice they were not even mutually exclusive. The same individual or economic sector might borrow the language of any, or more than one, of the three without making a commitment to the entire formula. It was, however, possible to identify the predominant tendencies, in terms of these formulae, of each of the major parties. The spectrum extended from the UDN, most of whose members identified with neo-liberalism,[15] through the PSD, some of whose urban leaders were supporters of developmentalist-nationalism, to the PTB, which was more solidly in favor of developmentalist-nationalism, and finally to the left wing of the PTB and the Brazilian Communist Party (illegal since 1947 although still active in politics) which adopted radical nationalism. These party positions, as was to become clear in the Vargas presidency, were far from homogeneous. Nevertheless, they represented the dominant trend within each group.

Formulae for economic development were not, of course, offered in a vacuum. They were put forward in response to the need to formulate policies that could meet the immediate problems of the Brazilian economy.[16] One problem was the need to devise and pursue an investment strategy to overcome structural bottlenecks, sectoral lags, and regional disequilibria. There were bottlenecks resulting from inadequate transportation, insufficient hydroelectric power and the lack of domestic fuel sources. Sectoral lags could be noted in areas such as chemicals and metal-working industries. Regional disequilibria, especially between the industrializing center-south and the poverty-ridden Northeast, had made Brazil a leading example of a "dual economy." To correct these disequilibria required a clearly thought-out investment policy on the part of the federal government. The logical pattern for such a policy would be to mix the promotion of state enterprises with the use of measures to coordinate and direct private investment.

Another economic problem was Brazil's balance of payments and the limitations which it imposed on her capacity to import. As we have already seen, industrialization was dependent upon the ability to purchase capital equipment and essential material abroad. This capacity in turn remained dependent on Brazil's ability to earn foreign exchange or incur foreign indebtedness. There continued to be little prospect of increasing earnings from Brazil's traditional exports—coffee, cocoa, cotton, etc.—because of the relatively inelastic demand for these products in world markets. The boom in coffee prices that began in 1949 furnished a foreign-exchange bonus, but it also served to dramatize Brazil's dependence on commodity price fluctuations over which she had little control. On the import side, almost a third of the foreign exchange had to be spent on foodstuffs and fuel, wheat and petroleum products being the most important.

The sudden increase in foreign exchange in 1949–51 gave Brazilian entrepreneurs the opportunity to import a large amount of capital equipment. The import-licensing system instituted in 1947 had put a premium on materials and equipment essential for industrialization. This increased capacity to import made possible the purchase of equipment which provided the productive capacity for a new stage of import substitution. The years 1951 and 1952 brought an import boom—merchandise imports in both years totaled 1.7 billion dollars, whereas they had barely exceeded a billion dollars in any preceding year. By 1952 the strain on the balance of payments was more severe than it had ever been in the 1940's. The improvement in Brazil's terms of trade and the sharp increase in her total foreign exchange earnings were more than canceled out by the increase in imports.

One final economic problem was the suddenly increasing rate of inflation. Brazil's price level had remained relatively stable in the immediate post-war years, partly because the large foreign-exchange reserves were available to finance an import boom which satisfied domestic demand. After 1947, however, when these reserves had been exhausted and domestic sources of supply proved inadequate, Brazil began to experience rapid price rises. In Rio de Janeiro, for example, the cost of living during 1950 rose 11 percent, whereas it had never increased more than 6 percent in any of the preceding years since 1945. It increased 11 percent again in 1951 and jumped 21 percent in 1952.

Such inflation was not without its beneficial effects. It created forced savings and helped redistribute income toward vital investment areas. But accelerating inflation also had serious disadvantages. First, it had a negative effect on the balance of payments because it made Brazil's exports more expensive in world markets, especially after the wave of currency devaluations in 1949. Since the cruzeiro was artificially maintained at the unrealistic level of 18.5 to the dollar, there was a powerful disincentive to exporters and an equivalent overincentive to those importers who could obtain the necessary licenses. The combination of domestic inflation and an overvalued exchange rate also aggravated the balance of payments problem by encouraging remittances abroad, while at the same time discouraging foreign investment in Brazil.

Economic Policy-making: Orthodoxy and Nationalism

Given these problems, what strategy of economic development did Vargas adopt in the first two years of his presidency? It would be inaccurate to say that he placed top priority on a full-fledged industrialization policy at the expense of all short-term goals. Neither Vargas' temperament, nor his political style, nor Brazilian political conditions would have permitted such a single-minded approach. Equally important, the government faced many immediate problems that often took precedence over long-term goals such as industrialization.

At times industrialization appeared to be the unconscious result rather than the rationale of government policy. Attempts to correct deficits in the balance of payments, for example, had an effect much as they had had in the 1930's and immediate postwar period: they provided a powerful stimulus to the creation of domestic productive capacity, both by limiting foreign sources of supply and by channeling the available foreign exchange into the purchase of imports essential for industrialization.

In practice, Vargas approached the short-term problems of the economy with a mixed policy. On the external side he had to worry about the balance of payments and the need to adjust the ingredients so as to avoid chronic deficits. On the internal side he faced the problem of inflation, with its resulting social tensions, and the need to devise an investment strategy that would maximize the social as well as the economic benefits of further development.

The approach of Vargas to these questions was ambivalent. The resulting "mixed" policy reflected Getúlio's estimate of the passions and interests behind the heterogeneous political forces that he sought to harness. The mixture was also a product of his own political instincts, which inclined him toward conciliation and compromise. Finally, Vargas was torn by the conflicting economic advice he received from proponents of the three formulae for economic development.

One side of Vargas' ambivalence was an economic policy which accepted the traditional rules of the international economic system and sought to operate within them. It was a pragmatic adaptation of the principles of economic liberalism and deliberately avoided any appeal to the more extreme sentiments of emotional nationalism. It was closer to developmentalist-nationalism than either of the other two formulae.

This aspect of Vargas' economic policy—the "orthodox" approach —could be seen at work on both the internal and the external aspects of Brazil's economic problems. On the internal side, Getúlio embarked on a bold new program of government-coordinated investment policies. This effort grew out of the earlier-mentioned Cooke mission, sent to Brazil by the United States in 1943, the Abbink mission sent in 1948, and the abortive SALTE program, launched in 1948. The new element in the relationship with the United States was the willingness of the American government to extend technical assistence and long-term loans for basic economic development. In December 1950 the United States government concluded an agreement with Brazil to set up the Joint Brazil-United States Economic Development Commission.[17] The Joint Commission began its work in July 1951 and submitted its final report in December 1953. The technical studies and policy suggestions of the commission were designed, in its own words, to "create conditions for and eliminate obstacles to an increase in the flow of investment, public and private, foreign and domestic, needed to promote economic development." [18]

The work of the Joint Commission gave a great impetus to the planning of investment policy. One of its first results was the creation in 1952 of a National Bank for Economic Development (*Banco Nacional do Desenvolvimento Econômico* or BNDE), which was intended to "eliminate or reduce the infra-structural deficiencies which impede the regular development of the Brazilian economy." [19] The commission also set goals and guidelines for major investment programs in the areas of transportation and power, which it had found to be two of the principal bottlenecks in the economy. The commission frankly stated that its projects were conceived so as to be "technically adapted to the requirements of foreign financing institutions, such as the Export-Import Bank, and the Bank for International Reconstruction and Development." [20] These were the principal sources of foreign financing to which Brazil immediately turned. The Vargas government cooperated fully with the efforts of the Joint Commission and welcomed the stimulus which it had given to the coordination of investment planning in Brazil. Vargas indicated in his Message to Congress in 1951 that his government would "facilitate the investment of foreign private capital, especially in association with domestic capital, as long as it does not damage the fundamental political interests of our country." [21] By its receptivity the Vargas regime had demonstrated that it was willing to cooperate with the rules of the international finance system.

The political figure who earned credit for being the architect of Brazil's new development policy was the Finance Minister, Horácio Lafer. In September 1951 Lafer announced a Five-Year Plan that called for $1 billion in new investments in basic industries and in the bottlenecked areas of transportation and power. The program became known as the "Lafer Plan," and was given a special financial basis when the Brazilian Congress authorized in late 1951 and mid-1952 an "Economic Rehabilitation Fund" (*Fundo de Reaparelhamento Econômico*) to be administered by the new National Bank for Economic Development. Assisting Lafer in the formulation and administration of the numerous new investment projects was a cadre of able young economists, engineers, and civil servants, whose varying views on the proper strategy for economic development did not prevent them from cooperating enthusiastically in the "developmentalist" drive. They included men such as Glycon de Paiva, Roberto Campos, and Romulo de Almeida.

Getúlio's moderate developmentalist approach in economic policy was also applied to the external side of Brazil's economic problems. In 1950 Brazil had enjoyed a $425 million export surplus on current account. But this surplus declined to $67 million in 1951 owing to a sharp rise in imports; and it turned into an export *deficit* of $286 million in 1952 when a decline in export earnings combined with a continuing high level of imports. By the end of 1952 it was clear that Brazil could no longer live with the complex system of exchange controls and the over-valuation of the cruzeiro. Some form of devaluation would have to be introduced.

In January 1953 the Vargas government adopted a new policy leading toward a more flexible exchange-rate policy. In essence, a multiple exchange-rate system was introduced by SUMOC (Superintendency of Money and Credit) Instruction #48 of February 1953 and Instruction #70 of October 1953. By establishing multiple categories for differing exports, imports, and capital movements, this system helped to restore Brazil's exports to a competitive price level abroad and served as a powerful instrument for channeling imports towards sectors considered essential for basic economic development.[22]

These changes also helped to convince international financial authorities and foreign investors that Brazil was prepared to maintain a measure of financial equilibrium with the outside world by the measured use of the price mechanism and free exchange rates—the classical forces emphasized by the proponents of the neo-liberal formula.

Nevertheless, the Brazilian government's need to tailor its economic policy to these external restraints was a liability in domestic politics. Whatever the facts of the case, such cooperation could appear to be "knuckling under" to foreign demands. To justify such measures, the Vargas government sometimes succumbed to the temptation to brand foreigners as the villains who had forced upon Brazil measures which, in fact, any responsible government would have had to adopt. After 1952 the pressure on the balance of payments had a negative "multiplier effect" on domestic politics. The Vargas government tried to cushion the effect of its "orthodox" economic policies by pursuing simultaneously a strategy of economic nationalism. This task Vargas embraced with enthusiasm.

When Vargas returned to the presidential palace in January 1951, he had brought with him a heritage of deep suspicion toward foreign investment. It stemmed from what was one of Getúlio's few genuine political passions: an "anti-imperialist" nationalism not uncommon in his native state of Rio Grande do Sul. It also gave him a link with the left-wing politicians and intellectuals who espoused the formula of radical nationalism. The radical nationalists, for reasons of political tactics as well as intellectual conviction, rejected any "constructive" role for foreign investment and bitterly opposed Brazil's "succumbing" to the rules of the international financial system.

When resorting to the language of economic nationalism, Getúlio greatly amplified the anti-foreign tone he had used only hesitantly during the Estado Nôvo. He now talked of "exploitation" and of Brazil's struggle against the "international trusts" which conspired to rob her of her rightful place in the world economy. During the dictatorship Vargas' government had canceled two separate iron-ore concessions previously granted to the colorful but tactless American investor Percival Farquhar. But Vargas' appeals to economic nationalism in that period were sharply muted. In the case of steel, for example, he accepted the idea of government ownership only after the United States Steel Corporation had declined to invest. And the state-sponsored national steel company, although publicly described in the language of economic nationalism, was launched with the financial support of the United States government (through the Export-Import Bank).

Now Vargas applied a new and more aggressive brand of economic nationalism to both the internal and external aspects of Brazil's economic problems. On the internal side he stressed the need for state corporations as a basic instrument of investment policy. In December 1951, he sent Congress a bill to create a mixed public-private petroleum corporation (to be called "Petrobrás"—with majority ownership in government hands) which would be given a monopoly on the drilling of oil and any new refineries, although existing refineries were to be permitted to remain under private ownership, and distribution of oil products would be in private hands. The proposal touched off a bitter campaign which divided opinion among intellectuals, military officers, businessmen, and politicians before the bill was finally passed in October 1953. A majority of opinion appeared to favor the creation of this state enterprise. But the aggressive tone of those who led the campaign suggested a passionate crusade to ensure Brazil's "emancipation" from her status as a "colonial economy." [23]

The radical nationalist position on the oil question was reinforced by the Communist Party's adoption of an aggressively anti-American policy in the early 1950's. As the cold war turned into open warfare in Korea, the PCB followed the Moscow line and concentrated its fire on the "imperialist" encroachments in Brazil. The Communists seized upon the Petrobrás proposal and attempted to outflank Vargas on the left. They attacked the idea of a mixed public-private oil corporation and launched a propaganda drive to discredit the moderate nationalists as "entreguistas" in disguise. The Communist tactic caught Vargas off guard and made it more difficult for the President to differentiate between the moderate position of developmentalist nationalism and the extremism of the radical nationalists.

International oil corporations made excellent targets for extreme nationalist propaganda. Their record of monopolistic behavior in the late nineteenth century (which helped create the need for U.S. antitrust legislation) and their record of close cooperation with unsavory politicians in the underdeveloped world, often through unscrupulous intermediaries, gave nationalists evidence for their charges that international oil concerns should not be trusted with the development of so vital a sector of the national economy. In Brazil there were constant charges of lavishly financed publicity campaigns and bribes offered by foreign oilmen to prevent the creation of a state oil-producing monopoly.

Vargas could see that majority opinion, even among the middle class, favored a "nationalist" solution to the oil question. But he preserved his detachment, leaving it to his advisers and allies on the left to use the more extreme language of radical nationalism in the Petrobrás campaign, which extended through 1952 and into 1953. Meanwhile, Getúlio preserved his own image as the master broker who could reconcile the conflicting political forces on a central issue, thereby underlining his own indispensability. At the same time, he had made himself a champion of the sentiments of economic nationalism. By 1953, debate over oil policy had seized public attention to a degree which far exceeded that of any other issue of public policy since 1945.

But the controversy developed in a way that frustrated those radical nationalists who wanted to see all basic industries in state hands. There was a willingness among moderate sectors to support the Petrobrás bill as indispensable state intervention in a unique area on the grounds that oil was different and therefore justified a different policy. These moderates did not wish to exclude foreign investment on principle. Furthermore, the campaign for Petrobrás was generating such public enthusiasm that politicians who had previously espoused doctrines of neo-liberalism suddenly became fervent adherents of a state oil monopoly. In 1953 the UDN proposed amendments to Vargas' bill which would have nationalized existing refineries, whereas Vargas' proposal permitted existing refineries to continue in private hands. The political advantage to be gained from taking a nationalist stand on oil was so great that even the anti-getulistas were trying to appear more nationalist than the President.

Seen from the standpoint of economic planning, Vargas had opted for the nationalist solution to a problem of investment policy in a bottleneck area. He proposed a similar solution for the area of electric power, which would be vastly expanded by a new corporation called Electrobrás. This was to be a state-directed effort to supplement the power-producing facilities of foreign-owned public utilities which were a traditional target for militant-nationalist attacks and popular antagonism. Electrobrás remained largely a paper creation during

Vargas' presidency, whereas the Petrobrás bill became law in October 1953. In the process of its passage, Vargas had given a new opportunity to those who wished to radicalize public opinion on the general subject of foreign private investment and rely instead on a network of state monopolies.

The Petrobrás proposal was not only an example of a "nationalist" investment policy; it was also an attempt to ease the growing strain on the balance of payments by substituting domestic sources of oil for the imported oil that was consuming scarce foreign exchange. There were other measures which revealed Getúlio's penchant for "nationalist" solutions to the balance of payments problem. One was his marked animus toward foreign firms whom he accused of "exorbitant" profit remittances to their parent firms abroad. On December 31, 1951, Vargas delivered a violent speech in support of his Petrobrás bill introduced earlier that month, warning that no one "ought to demand sacrifice and collaboration from Brazil while distributing the benefits to others." He went on to attack foreign corporations for exorbitant profit remittances.[24] During the second half of 1951, Vargas had become alarmed over the high rate of remittances which had been encouraged by Brazil's overvalued exchange rate. In 1950 profit remittances totaled $83 million (approximately the same level as the two preceding years), but in 1951 they jumped to $137 million. In late 1951 Vargas appointed a committee of financial experts to study the problem. On the basis of their report he concluded that the government must impose new controls on profit remittances. He brought this question to public debate in an impassioned speech on December 31, 1951. By calculation or instinct he had chosen to exploit sentiments of economic nationalism and popular animus towards foreign investment as justification for a policy change which could have been grounded in less emotional language.[25]

In January 1952 a decree was issued which imposed a limit of ten percent on profit remittances. The monetary authority (SUMOC) was given the power to apply this limit only when it thought it necessary because of pressure on the balance of payments. Since export prices remained buoyant in 1952, SUMOC authorities chose not to exercise this power, and the decree which had been justified in the language of crisis remained largely a dead letter. As Vargas' room for political maneuver narrowed, however, he returned to this question and repeated his attacks on profit remittances. On December 21, 1953, he complained bitterly that his plan for Petrobrás, now enacted, and his proposal for Electrobrás, still in the planning stage, were being "sabotaged" by "private enterprises" which "have in cruzeiros two hundred times the capital that they invested in dollars, so that they can send it abroad labeled as dividends. Instead of dollars producing cruzeiros, it is cruzeiros that are producing dollars and emigrating." [26]

In political terms, Vargas' problem was to maintain the delicate balance between orthodoxy and nationalism in economic policy. From 1951 through 1953 his approach was dialectical. Moderate measures had to be offset by nationalist measures. Attacks on foreign capital, for example, had to be balanced by exchange liberalization. This strategy reached its high point in October 1953, when the Petrobrás bill, the subject of a long nationalist campaign with heavy anti-foreign overtones, became law. In the same month the Vargas government issued new regulations, defining the multiple exchange rate system which would ease foreign investment and help restore Brazil's financial equilibrium with the outside world by means of the price mechanism. It was typical of Vargas' style. As 1953 continued, however, the facts of political life made this mixed policy progressively more difficult to maintain.

Foci of Opposition: The UDN and the Military

It was inevitable that Vargas' political comeback would arouse bitter feelings among the anti-getulistas. Getúlio hoped that he could, by a variety of tactics, disarm the opposition. Above all, he was determined to vindicate himself in Brazilian history by demonstrating his "democratic" vocation. In this situation Vargas enjoyed one apparent asset: a large part of the political elite was ready to cooperate in the new Vargas era. As the *Estado de São Paulo* lamented in an editorial soon after Vargas' electoral victory, "in all classes, beginning with the so-called upper classes, one notes an enormous desire to accommodate." [27]

The political scene which Vargas encountered in the early 1950's was more difficult to dominate than any he had faced in his years of rule between 1930 and 1945. Vargas now presided over a political system that was open and fluid. The votes mobilized by back-country political bosses were declining in importance as the urban electorate continued to grow rapidly. The possibilities of mass politics, first demonstrated by Adhemar de Barros in 1947, were further shown by the steady growth of the PTB.[28]

Back in the mid-1930's, Vargas had been able to count on the ultimate support of the higher military, as well as politicians of the center and right, for "emergency" measures, of which the coup of November 1937 was the logical conclusion. Now, Vargas faced a suspicious center, implacable opposition on the right, and an army which was at best neutral. In the Chamber of Deputies in 1951, he faced a complex mixture of political forces. The PSD still had the highest number of members (112), followed by the UDN (81), the PTB (51), and the PSP (24); the remaining 36 seats were divided among eight smaller parties. The majority was "centrist," uncertain over fundamental issues of policy-making but disinclined to accept radical formulae offered by either the right or the left. Getúlio's heterogeneous cabinet, appointed in January 1951, revealed a strategy designed to hold the support of as many political sectors as possible.

Vargas' most irreconcilable opponents did not wait for his inauguration to launch their attack on the newly elected President. Soon after the votes were counted in October 1950, the UDN, led by Congressman Aliomar Baleeiro, attempted to block Vargas' inauguration by arguing that a strict interpretation of the Constitution required the winning candidate to receive an absolute majority in presidential elections. The intransigent UDN leaders were joined in their protests by Carlos Lacerda, a brilliant young journalist and militant anti-getulista. By their reasoning, even Vargas' 48.7 percent of the votes had fallen short of the necessary minimum. Unfortunately for these disgruntled lawyers of the UDN, the Constitution referred only to a majority. Furthermore, the UDN had not discovered this legal ambiguity until after the defeat of their own candidate, whom they could only have expected to win by a plurality. The UDN took its appeal to the Supreme Electoral Tribunal, the body authorized to examine the election returns and proclaim the winners. Before the Tribunal met in December, the UDN and conservative organs such as the *Estado de São Paulo* filled the air with dire warnings that Vargas, if permitted to assume the presidency, was bound to attempt to impose a new dictatorship on Brazil.[29]

These Cassandras did not convince the majority of the higher Army officers, who remained stubbornly committed to "legality." President Dutra and his War Minister, General Canrobert Pereira da Costa, had announced that they would respect the decision of the Supreme Electoral Tribunal. Even that pledge was not enough for activist Generals Estillac Leal and Zenóbio da Costa, who declared flatly at a meeting of the Military Club on November 15 that Vargas had been elected. These generals were, in effect, warning the Tribunal not to honor the juridical arguments of the UDN.[30] Baleeiro then tried desperately to drive a wedge between Vargas and the officer corps by referring to the deleterious influence that the former dictator had exercised on the Army during the Estado Nôvo. Góes Monteiro angrily rejected Baleeiro's claim, and accused the UDN spokesman of invoking the prestige of the Army "when you only wish to defend the interests of the party to which you belong." Góes was in effect saying that the UDN, having failed against Vargas at the polls, could not now expect the Army to rescue it from electoral defeat.[31] The Tribunal met in December and duly declared Vargas and Café Filho the legally elected President and Vice President.

Once in power, Vargas studied his situation and decided to try the impossible. He attempted to bring his old enemies—as many as could be enticed—into the governmental fold. Here was a tactic Getúlio had often used in the past—joining forces with his former enemies. But how could he persuade the UDN to give up their *raison d'être*—antigetulismo? Throughout 1951 and the first half of 1952 he encouraged a group of "coordinators" in their overtures directed at bringing the UDN into the government. The intention was to strengthen Vargas' support among the urban middle class, which was growing in electoral importance but remained confused over the proper direction for Brazil's economic and social development.

These conciliatory moves toward the UDN, never made public by Getúlio himself, failed in their purpose. They did manage, however, to arouse the opposition of some PTB leaders, whose dissatisfaction with Vargas had become obvious in September 1951 with the resignation of the only PTB cabinet member—Labor Minister Danton Coelho. The efforts of the "coordinators" also stirred the anger of the PSD, which feared a loss of prestige and influence if the UDN should enter the government. In mid-1952 the policy of conciliation toward the UDN collapsed; thereafter Vargas lost all hope of gaining support from the party which had been created as the vehicle of anti-getulismo.[32]

If considered simply in terms of votes—either within the Congress or among the electorate—Vargas' inability to divide the UDN (and the splinter conservative parties) was hardly of crucial significance. He was fully capable of dealing with the largest single party, the PSD, to whose votes he could add his own PTB. Yet the bitterness of the anti-getulista sentiment was a poisonous element in the political atmosphere because it could easily be transformed into the kind of anti-democratic thought that had contributed to the undermining of Brazilian democracy in the 1930's. The reversal of positions was ironical. Now it was Vargas' return to power via the ballot box that had shaken the faith of the liberal constitutionalists in Brazil's new democratic order. In the view of these former champions of redemocratization, the very fact of Vargas' election meant that democracy in Brazil was not working.

This view was shared by certain junior military officers who were in contact with Lacerda and like-minded extremists within the UDN. They were opposed to Getúlio's return on any terms and in 1945 had wanted to remove the ex-dictator from *all* political activity after his deposition. But these junior officers were a minority. General Góes Monteiro, still the *éminence grise* in the politics of the higher military, gave his *imprimatur* to Getúlio's inauguration. Góes' support was indispensable because he continued to enjoy prestige among the anti-getulista officers who remembered his role in forming Vargas' departure in 1945. Furthermore, there were other prominent generals, such as Estillac Leal and Zenóbio da Costa, who openly favored Getúlio's inauguration. His return to the presidency was not, therefore, in danger of being vetoed by the Army—the ultimate power censor in the Brazilian political system.[33]

This military acquiescence was, however, far from unconditional. When Góes Monteiro had been asked about Getúlio's possible candidacy, he replied that it would be acceptable to the military as long as Vargas "respected not only the Constitution but also the inalienable rights of the military." [34] Getúlio would have to continue justifying his actions to the officer corps. Maintaining their support would be as important as maintaining the support of civilian politicians and the public. In fact, the formation of opinion within the civilian and the military sectors was closely connected because of the manner in which the Brazilian army mirrored opinions and tensions within Brazilian society.

Vargas' appointment of General Estillac Leal as his first War Minister showed that he was keenly aware of this. In 1945 Estillac had been sympathetic to the left-wing Queremistas, who campaigned to keep Vargas in the presidency while a new constitution was written. Appointing him War Minister in 1951 indicated that Vargas wished to strengthen the left-wing nationalist camp within the officer corps. But this appointment by no means ended differences of opinion in the Army about Vargas and his policies. In fact, the nationalist faction within the officer corps was not as strong as it may have appeared to Vargas in 1950. Earlier that year the elections for the Directorate (president and vice president) of the Military Club, always an important index of officer opinion, had been won by the nationalist slate of Generals Estillac Leal and Horta Barbosa. The unsuccessful candidate for president was General Cordeiro de Farias, who had emerged as a leading spokesman for the anti-Communist faction within the Army (the Military Club included only Army officers—there was a *Club Naval* for the Navy and a *Club Aeronáutica* for the Air Force).

Vargas natually looked to the nationalist wing of the Army for support as he undertook his ambitious "developmentalist" economic program. General Horta Barbosa, for example, who was a leading proponent of Petrobrás and earlier had been the first president of the largely inactive *Conselho Nacional de Petróleo* (created in 1938), represented the kind of military nationalism that Getúlio hoped to harness for his own political purposes in the 1950's, just as he had earlier capitalized on the economic nationalism of the military during the Estado Nôvo. Unfortunately for Vargas, however, the year of his election was also the year that the cold war turned into open warfare between the United States and the Communist satellite of North Korea. Once again, as in 1945, the shadow of international events fell across Getúlio's career.

The heightening of the conflict between the two world blocs had an immediate effect on the Brazilian Army. Brazil was the only Latin American country that sent troops to fight beside the Allied forces in the Second World War. The sense of ideological and personal loyalty, resulting from the close collaboration of the U.S. and Brazilian military during the war, was still strong. As a consequence, the issue of nationalism, previously limited primarily to questions of domestic economic policy, suddenly assumed a far greater political significance. The political issue was dramatized when the Brazilian Communist Party, in response to the hardening of the Moscow line in the early 1950's, adopted an aggressively anti-imperialist stance.[35] It attempted to identify economic nationalism with anti-Americanism and thereby exploit issues of economic policy for its own political purposes.

Within the Army officer corps there were some radical nationalists who partially shared the Communist Party's attitude toward the military contest between the two world blocs. In late 1950 the *Revista do Club Militar,* the Club's official publication, which had as its director an extreme nationalist major, published an article suggesting that the United States was responsible for starting the war in Korea and recommending that Brazil should preserve the strictest neutrality in the contest. There was an immediate and angry reaction from other Club members who wanted no part of a nationalism with these new geopolitical trappings. The conservative press was soon filled with letters of protest from anti-Communist officers. In early December 600 officers issued a manifesto denouncing the "Russophilic" views expressed in the *Revista* article. As the outcry increased, the Directorate of the Military Club announced in mid-December that the *Revista* had been suspended in order to ensure the officer corps "the climate of unity which it must have." [36]

In November, Estillac Leal, as president of the Club, had already tried to dissociate himself diplomatically from the anti-American views of the extremist officers, but the blow to his own prestige was nonetheless great. After becoming Vargas' War Minister in January 1951, Estillac continued to be the target of a campaign by an opposition group of officers who rejected even the moderate nationalist position represented by the War Minister. They attacked it as "Jacobinism," "false nationalism," and "emotional nationalism." These opponents also considered themselves "nationalist," but were less radical on the two issues which had recently polarized opinion within the officer corps. One was the controversy over the proper role for foreign capital in the exploitation of Brazilian mineral resources, especially oil. The second was the policy which Brazil should adopt in the cold war. That issue became urgent because of pressure from the United

States that Brazil ratify the U.S.-Brazilian military accords, which had been negotiated in 1951–52. There was also an American "suggestion" (rejected by the Vargas government) that Brazil send troops to fight in Korea.

The nationalist wing, led by Estillac Leal, strongly supported Vargas' proposal for Petrobrás, first presented to the Congress in December 1951. The nationalists also advocated a more independent line in foreign policy and argued for caution in following the United States' lead in the cold war, although most nationalist officers stopped far short of the extreme anti-American views held by their colleagues who authored the celebrated *Revista* article on the Korean War.

The controversy between the nationalists and the anti-Communists continued through 1951. By early 1952 the language of the controversy between the two factions had become abusive. The nationalist officers accused their opponents of being *entreguistas,* a favorite epithet which radical nationalists used in order to ridicule their opposition. It carried the overtone of treason. The opposition countered by accusing the nationalist wing of collaborating with "demagogues" and "agitators," who were consciously or unconsciously serving the interests of international communism.[37] The debate within the officer corps became so bitter and the opposition gained such ground that Estillac Leal was forced to resign the War Ministry in March 1952.

Part of Estillac Leal's difficulty stemmed from his deteriorating personal relations with another leading general, the outspoken anti-Communist Zenóbio da Costa. Estillac Leal had also proved unable to maintain "discipline" among the officer corps, which lacked confidence in his ability to handle satisfactorily the pressing questions of salary differentials and deficiencies in equipment. Vargas appointed as his new War Minister General Espírito Santo Cardoso, who promised to exercise a firm hand. He also soon emerged as a sharp critic of the nationalist wing in the officer corps.[38] The public struggle between the two wings of the military was far from over, however. Some younger officers of the nationalist wing convinced Estillac Leal that he should not give up without a fight. They prevailed upon him and General Horta Barbosa to accept nomination for reelection to the Directorate of the Military Club, against the opposition slate headed by Generals Alcides Etchegoyen and Nelson de Melo.[39]

Estillac Leal finally agreed, and was soon engaged in a heated campaign. Etchegoyen and de Melo were supported by the "Democratic

Crusade," a group of officers who rejected the left-wing nationalism of Estillac Leal and proposed instead a "rational nationalism" which was more uncritically receptive to foreign private investment and ready to follow American leadership in the cold war, as, for example, by readily ratifying the U.S.-Brazil military accords.[40] The supporters of Estillac Leal, on the other hand, warned that Brazil had to maintain a vigorous watch over her sovereignty both in foreign policy and in the exploitation of her natural resources.[41]

The election campaign was nation-wide. The proponents of the two slates pressed their views among the officer corps in all the principal military regions. The majority of the national press, which was anti-getulista and sharply antagonistic to radical left-wing nationalism, supported Etchegoyen and de Melo. There were reports of violence among officers and enlisted men on both sides. Preventive arrests were frequent. Estillac Leal supporters complained bitterly that nationalist officers had been systematically transferred from key commands during the Dutra era. Their complaints had a special relevance, since Estillac Leal had failed to neutralize these transfers during his thirteen months as War Minister. The "nationalists" suffered also from widespread purges and imprisonments of officers charged with being Communists and "subversives." [42]

The elections for the Directorate of the Military Club took place on May 21, 1952. Etchegoyen and de Melo received 8,288 votes, almost double the 4,489 votes for Estillac Leal and Horta Barbosa. It was a stunning defeat for the nationalist wing of the officer corps. It was also of crucial importance in Vargas' own calculations. As President, he could continue in office only as long as he maintained the support of a majority of military opinion. Nationalism in the form advanced by Estillac Leal and his supporters had been rejected by a large majority of the officers. This result reflected the political facts of life in the civilian sector, where opinion was also divided. In order to regain the presidency, Vargas had captured his votes through a combination of appeals, of which economic nationalism and the more ambiguous language of populism were only two ingredients. In neither the civilian nor the military sector was there even a near-majority of opinion supporting radical nationalism.

From Vargas' standpoint this was an important but not a decisive fact. His political strategy in mid-1952 still aimed at securing and maintaining support from as many classes and sectors as possible.

Appealing to the sentiments of nationalism which animated the left was only one of the strings to his bow. Equally important were his efforts to retain the support of the traditional political sectors represented, above all, by the PSD.

Although his political strategy was not immediately altered, there was no denying that it was not paying off. On the right the conciliatory gestures toward the UDN had aborted, while on the left the support for left-wing nationalism had proved to be limited to a minority among the military, as well as the general public. Furthermore, Getúlio was under increasingly bitter criticism from both left and right for his attempts at conciliation with the opposing extreme.

Vargas' room for political maneuver was becoming increasingly circumscribed by the need to make difficult decisions in the area of economic policy. These decisions would inevitably alienate some sectors and classes without satisfying a majority at any one time. Because Vargas had more ambitious economic goals than Dutra, the political costs of economic policy-making would inevitably be higher than they had been from 1945 to 1950. By the second half of 1952 these hard choices of economic policy-making had become inescapable.

Increasing Social Tensions

Brazil's drive toward industrialization and greater economic autonomy was bound to arouse social tensions, especially among the traditional classes tied to the export-import trade. These groups feared the loss of relative importance and status, but they were not necessarily prepared to oppose industrialization per se. They could, however, be panicked by the fear that the resulting social and economic changes would be unduly brusque, or that the existing social structure might be overthrown.

Because of this fear, emotional appeals to economic nationalism were a dangerous strategy. Such appeals tended to connect the idea of nationalism with radical views about restructuring Brazilian society. Before we can understand this connection we must look more closely at the political appeal of nationalism.[43]

Vargas had correctly sensed that nationalism, particularly on economic issues, appealed to a wide range of public opinion. Even among the most traditional political bosses of back-country Brazil, there sometimes existed a deep suspicion of foreign investment. Arthur Bernardes, for example, Brazil's President from 1922 to 1926 and a prototype of the pre-1930 politician, was an unrelenting critic of foreign mining interests. He had helped to block and finally cancel the Itabira iron-ore concession of the American investor Farquhar in the 1920's and 1930's. After 1945, as the leader of a splinter party in Minas Gerais known as the Republican Party (*Partido Republicano* or PR), he was a leading supporter of the Petrobrás bill. His passionate economic nationalism was unusual but not unique among the traditionally oriented political elite.[44]

The middle class felt an instinctive attraction for the doctrines of economic nationalism, especially those members of the middle class who identified with industrialization and modernization and felt that Brazil needed to establish control over the direction of her own economy. Naturally, the middle class would benefit greatly from this increase in autonomy. Its members would fill the managerial and technocratic posts that economic development required and created. They were also receptive to the demand that Brazil should rapidly attain political and cultural "maturity" with all that the term implied. Obviously, these nationalist sentiments were stronger among the pro-industrialization middle class than among those who identified themselves, consciously or unconsciously, with an agrarian export economy. For those observers who were not yet convinced of the strength of nationalist sentiments among the middle class, the Petrobrás campaign was convincing proof.

The class from whom nationalist appeals were most certain to find a positive response was the urban working class. The enthusiasm aroused by the Petrobrás campaign was unmistakable among urban wage earners. Indeed, the language of economic nationalism seemed easier for them to understand than the idea of domestic class conflict.

Economic nationalism, therefore, could be very useful as a means for constructing a public consensus. Nationalism was a sentiment which could draw together Brazilians of different classes and sectors and give them a sense of community. As the intellectual apologists of developmentalist nationalism argued, identification with the nation in a common effort could help to overcome the class tensions produced by a developing society.

But the strategy of economic nationalism also had its dangers. It was perilous because it could deepen political division in Brazil. If nationalism had been merely a matter of xenophobia or middle-class ambitions, the dangers of its use would not have been great. Unfortunately, however, the most active political purveyors of nationalism were also domestic revolutionaries. They were the proponents of the economic formula of radical nationalism. Some were intellectual Marxists, others were members of the Communist Party, while still others were radical leftists who did not subject themselves to any political or intellectual discipline. Their anti-foreign doctrines, directed against foreign investment in Brazil and capitalist policy toward Brazil, were part of a larger strategy which aimed at radically restructuring the economic and social system within Brazil. In other words, the anti-foreign campaign of the radical nationalists was intended to be the first stage in a process of political radicalization of which the ultimate end would be a radical redistribution of power among classes. From this standpoint the question of differing short-run tactics among radical nationalists was not important. Whether the immediate policy should be revolution or limited cooperation with the "system," the ultimate goal of radical political change remained implicit.

Center opinion, especially among the middle class, was therefore apprehensive over the ultimate purposes of a nationalist campaign. What if the working class should be roused to a deep dissatisfaction with their lot? What were the long-term purposes of "demagogues" who abused foreigners in language that could easily be employed to incite class warfare at home? Might nationalism be the stalking horse of subversion and revolution?

The propagandists and politicians of the extreme right played on these fears. This right-wing opposition was led by spokesmen for the traditional classes who opposed industrialization. They seized upon the nationalist issue in order to convert to their political ranks those confused members of the middle class who could be frightened away from support for Vagas' industrialization and development policies by the fear that Brazil was being led down the path toward class suicide. Right-wing radicalizers also played upon middle-class memories of the Estado Nôvo and on the bourgeois sense of outrage provoked by Getúlio's oft-demonstrated ability to negotiate political deals with virtually any political group. Professional anti-getulistas, such as Carlos Lacerda, attacked political nationalism as a pernicious instrument of subversion which Vargas employed to maintain in power his network of corrupt political cronies. His electoral bargain with Adhemar de Barros in 1950 furnished proof, for these critics, of Getúlio's political irresponsibility and cynicism.[45]

By appealing to sentiments of economic nationalism Vargas was therefore walking a political tightrope. He tried to combine his nationalist and orthodox approach in a complex strategy aimed at maintaining the support of different classes or parts of the same class in different moods. His mixed approach to economic policy-making was political, inspired by the need to maintain wide congressional and electoral support.

But for the problem of inflation—unlike those of the balance-of-payments deficits and structural bottlenecks—the Vargas government could not devise any mixture of orthodoxy and nationalism. Unlike the areas of investment policy and foreign trade policy, where social tensions were aroused only indirectly by the political associations of the nationalists and moderates, in wage and credit policy the immediate stake of each class was apparent.

Inflation aggravated social tensions because it dramatized shifts in the distribution of income and created uncertainties about future income shares. If forced saving was a valuable technique for facilitating investment, it might not be so benignly viewed by the sector which had been forced to forgo consumption. The constant price rises and frequent need to adjust wages and salaries focused public attention on the question of how the benefits and sacrifices of economic development were distributed.

The group suffering most from the increase in the cost of living was the urban working class. When Vargas assumed the presidency, there had been no increase in the officially decreed minimum wage since 1943. The Dutra years had, in fact, seen a loss in the real income of the wage-earning sector. In December 1951 the Vargas government decreed a new minimum wage which did little more than catch up with the more recent price rises. Labor protest over the cost of living squeeze had been blunted after 1947 by the tough policy of the Dutra government, which "intervened" in many labor unions and purged their leadership. These moves were coordinated with the suppression of the Communist Party in 1947. The Vargas government, however, purposely allowed the return to power of more radical labor leaders.

As a result, they quickly organized to press for larger wage settle-ments.[46] The middle class was also apprehensive over rises in the cost of living. The squeeze on them was more difficult to measure because their incomes were not tied to a government-decreed salary. But those who worked in the government bureaucracy suffered from persistent lags in salary adjustments. The resulting threat to their so-cial status was serious.

Domestic social tensions created by inflation were therefore grow-ing in the second and third year of Vargas' new term as President. Any attempt at anti-inflation and stabilization was likely to provoke opposition from all sectors of the economy. On the other hand, the need for anti-inflation measures had become inescapable.

1953: A New Political Strategy

This need to introduce stabilization measures was one of the factors that led Vargas to reorganize his cabinet in June-July 1953. The min-isterial changes were also a response to his own deteriorating political position. His conciliatory gestures toward the UDN had failed, and the Cabinet, aware of Getúlio's plan to alter the political complexion of his government, was demoralized and lacked any sense of cohesion. Vargas finally decided to replace his most important ministers. Two of the new ministers were old-time associates of Getúlio. José Américo de Almeida, appointed Minister of Transportation, had run for President in the abortive campaign of 1937, and in February 1945 had been one of the first to call openly for Brazil's redemocra-tization. He supported the UDN candidate in the election of 1945, although preserving an independent position thereafter. He had exten-sive contacts in the Northeast, where he had begun his career in the state of Paraíba. The new Finance Minister was Oswaldo Aranha, a fellow Riograndense whose career had been closely involved with that of Vargas since the revolution of 1930. Getúlio had once before turned to Aranha in the midst of financial difficulties—in December 1931 Aranha had replaced José Maria Whitaker as Finance Minister. He later served as Foreign Minister (1938–44) and as Brazilian rep-resentative in the United Nations (1946–47).

The other important new minister was João Goulart, a young PTB protégé of Vargas' from Rio Grande do Sul. This appointment showed that Vargas had opted for a new political tactic. Still faced with a suspicious middle class and an irreconcilable conservative opposition, Vargas decided to court more energetically the working-class vote. Up to this point, Getúlio's attitude toward the PTB had been ambivalent. The party grew rapidly between 1945 and 1950, playing an important, although not decisive, role in Getúlio's return to the presidency. Yet he had done little during the first two years of his presidency to expand or stregthen the PTB as a political instrument. This indifference earned him bitter criticism from PTB leaders such as Labor Minister Danton Coelho, who resigned in September 1951. Now, in June 1953, Vargas decided to make up for his earlier failure to cultivate the left.

His move had two explanations. First, the effectiveness of the pressure from the radical nationalists on the Petrobrás bill convinced Vargas that he had to take new steps to avoid being outflanked on the left. Furthermore, he would need political "cover" for the stabilization plan then in formulation. A vigorous pro-labor approach would help to provide this cover. Second, Vargas was already thinking about the presidential succession in 1955. The failure of his moves to conciliate the center in 1951 and 1952 had weakened his political position, which had been precarious from the outset because of the necessarily heterogeneous alliance which had elected him. His most important supporter in that campaign, Adhemar de Barros, had openly launched his own candidacy for the presidential succession. He had a claim on Getúlio's support as a return for the campaign deal in 1950. Getúlio, however, had no intention of abdicating control over his own succession. Knowing that Adhemar's strength lay with the urban wage earners, Getúlio turned to this sector and attempted to strengthen the PTB.[47]

The new Labor Minister was a young gaúcho (thirty-five years old) whose family was closely connected with the Vargas clan in the Riograndense município of São Borja. The significance of his appointment could only be understood if one considered the history of the PTB and the politics of Brazilian labor unions since 1945. For the two years between 1945 and 1947, Communist and other radical left-wing labor organizers had succeeded in gaining a number of positions of leadership in Brazilian trade unions. They were particularly active in the metal-working and dock-working unions. In 1947 the Dutra government intervened and dismissed many of these Communist and left-wing labor leaders. The Dutra government, however, made no effort to dismantle the corporatist structure of the labor unions and labor tribunals created by Vargas during the Estado Nôvo. Under this system, the Labor Ministry had vast powers to control unions through the channeling of the unions' compulsory labor dues (one day's wages a year went to the government to be distributed to the unions by the Minister of Labor). After purging the labor union leadership, the Dutra government merely exploited the Ministry of Labor's control of the union apparatus in order to prevent labor "unrest." [48]

When Vargas came into power, he appointed a PTB leader as his Minister of Labor, but the government policy toward encouraging militant union politics, either on wage issues or issues of general public policy, was cautious. Now, in June 1953, that policy was to change. Appointing João Goulart to the Labor Ministry indicated that Vargas was abandoning his cautious policy and was prepared to delegate power to a politician who had the reputation of collaborating with Communist and other militant labor leaders. Indeed, Goulart's appointment revealed Vargas' fear that he was losing control of the political situation, especially in the face of the growing leftist radicalism aroused by the Petrobrás campaign. Goulart himself, however, could hardly be described as a revolutionary or a radical. In fact, he was a comfortable member of the established political elite who was exploiting the trabalhismo of Vargas as his own political vehicle. The fact that he was a cattle-breeder from the ranch country of Rio Grande do Sul reinforced a widespread view that he cultivated the politics of labor more for electoral purposes than because of any first-hand experience with the problems of workers in an industrializing society.[49]

But whatever Goulart's own motivations, he was a suspect figure to the middle class. Because his appointment appeared to be the first step in a new campaign to court the proletariat, it alarmed industrialists, middle-class voters, and conservatively inclined military officers. In their minds Goulart was associated with the threat of a syndicalist regime, of the kind that Juan Perón had created in Argentina. Brazilians needed only to look south to see the political power of a well-manipulated labor movement. In the eyes of these anti-getulistas, Goulart was a "demagogic agitator" who, for personal political gain, would construct a working-class phalanx that might bring down the existing social order. Vargas' problem, therefore, was that any moves to mobilize the working class might panic center opinion and play into the hands of the extreme right-wing opposition. There may have been other labor ministers Vargas could have chosen for this task. Of the field, Goulart was surely the one most likely to alienate center opinion.

By his ministerial changes of June 1953, Vargas had embarked on a new political strategy, based on an effort to mobilize the working class without alienating the industrialists. This strategy would be very difficult when real stabilization measures made themselves felt. Workers were demanding wage increases to compensate for inflation, and industrialists were pressuring the government to maintain the easy credit policies which had made possible the extraordinary industrial surge between 1948 and 1952. Credit restrictions and stringent wage settlements would, therefore, undercut support among the very sectors that Vargas was courting.[50]

An Attempt at Economic Stabilization

Having reshuffled his cabinet almost completely by August 1953, Vargas launched an anti-inflation program—the absence of which had become uncomfortably obvious by mid-1953. As we have seen above, the rise in coffee prices which began in 1949 had increased Brazil's foreign exchange earnings. In 1950 there was a surplus of $106 million on current account, the first surplus since 1947. (Figures for 1946 are not available). Brazil responded by stepping up her imports, partly out of a fear that the Korean war might turn into a major war and cut off all supplies of equipment. As a result, in 1951, Brazil incurred a deficit of $468 million on current account, and in 1952 the deficit reached the alarming level of $707 million. The Brazilian government was slow to respond to this adverse turn in the balance of payments. Instead, it seemed to live on the hope that coffee prices might rise even further and thereby finance the high level of imports maintained in 1951–52. By the end of 1952, however, the short-term situation in the balance of payments had become critical. Refusing to believe that the unfavorable trend would continue, the Brazilian government had incurred large commercial arrears. The adverse balance was $612 million at the end of 1952, and by June of 1953 it totaled over $1 billion.[51]

Inflation had also reached a critical level, by the standards of the early 1950's. As noted earlier, the cost of living in Rio de Janeiro, which rose 11 percent in 1950 and 11 percent again in 1951, jumped 21 percent in 1952. Furthermore, early 1953 saw a slowdown in the rate of increase of industrial production. Vargas' first Finance Minister, Horácio Lafer, had been handicapped in his efforts to formulate a coherent stabilization program. He had attempted to limit credit expansion but he found himself working at cross purposes with the president of the Bank of Brazil, Ricardo Jafet, who insisted upon following an easy credit policy. On leaving the Finance Ministry in June 1953, Lafer lamented that often he had not even been informed about the credit policies of the Bank of Brazil.[52]

The new Finance Minister, Oswaldo Aranha, and the new president of the Bank of Brazil, Sousa Dantas, agreed on the need to attempt a thoroughgoing anti-inflation program. Vargas now recognized the need for stabilization, which could succeed only if supported both by the Finance Minister and the president of the Bank of Brazil. In explaining the policies he intended to pursue, Aranha promised to cut the large deficit in the government sector by following a policy of strict economy. He warned that Brazil had no choice but to "keep to a prudent speed the rate of industrialization," while "considering the relief or burden on the balance of payments." In other words, Brazil must accommodate herself to the unpleasant fact that there were serious external restraints on her industrial ambitions.[53]

In October 1953 the new Finance Minister unveiled his program, which became known as the "Aranha Plan." [54] First, it promised a policy of stringent credit control. Second, it provided for a new system of control over foreign exchange transactions. These new exchange controls, which had been in the making since January 1953, set up a multiple exchange system which instituted a sliding scale of de facto devaluation. It was hoped that the new measures would correct the balance of payments deficit by making Brazilian exports cheaper in world markets and by making imports more expensive while at the same time, through differential exchange rates, not unduly discouraging imports considered essential for industrialization. As 1953 ended, therefore, the Vargas government had adopted a relatively orthodox stabilization program entrusted to one of the President's most experienced collaborators.[55]

There was, however, an unexpected difficulty. Brazil's entry into difficult economic waters—deficits in the balance of payments and persistent inflation—had coincided with an increase in pressure from the United States. The Truman government, which launched the Point Four Program and had shown itself sympathetic to the financial problems of developing countries, was replaced in January 1953 by a Republican government that was openly suspicious of the need for any "special measures" to aid in the economic development of the poorer nations. The new American secretaries of treasury and state, George Humphrey and John Foster Dulles, were firm believers in the orthodox rules of international economic transactions. Furthermore, with Dulles as secretary of state, American foreign policy took on a more rigidly anti-Communist tone, especially in dealings with the "third world."

The Eisenhower government decided at the outset to reassess the high level of public assistance which had been assumed in the Truman foreign economic policy. The Republican administration stressed instead the predominant role to be played by private investment. The responsibility of foreign governments, such as Brazil, was to create the proper "climate" for private U.S. investment. Coinciding with this change in Washington's attitude was the formal termination of the Joint United States-Brazilian Economic Commission. In June 1953 the American government made clear its desire to phase out the commission. Brazilian officials found their American counterparts evasive about what the Brazilians thought had been firm commitments for the financing of projects outlined by the commission. The sudden change in the American attitude was a serious blow to the possibilities for continued moderate economic policy on the part of the Brazilian government. The effect was more psychological and political than economic, because the projects to be financed were long-term and the new American attitude did not constitute an attempt to disown the commission's work or renege on the extensive commitments already made by the Export-Import Bank. But the new policy in Washington strengthened the hand of radical nationalists who argued, sometimes to Getúlio himself, that moderation in economic policy was self-defeating. The developed capitalist countries—especially the United States—they argued, would never cooperate in Brazil's industrialization. On the contrary, they would inevitably revert to a narrow-minded policy of protecting the interests of "trusts" whose *raison d'être* was the extraction of excessive profits from the semi-developed countries.[56]

Vargas' oil policy had further dramatized the differing attitudes in Brazil and the U.S. toward economic development. The emotionally charged campaign which surrounded Vargas' efforts in support of the Petrobrás bill shocked and angered many American businessmen and bankers, who regarded the creation of the state-owned oil-producing monopoly as the triumph of irresponsible radicalism. This American reaction also strengthened the hand of the radical nationalists. Ironically, the strength of the American reaction did not reflect any long-term decision by American investors to avoid Brazil. As in the case of Mexico, foreign investors knew that oil could be a special case in an underdeveloped country's attitude to foreign investment. But the language of American indignation furnished valuable ammunition for the nationalists in Brazil.

Finally, Brazil's economic relations with the United States were strained because of the severe criticism in America over the high level of coffee prices after heavy frosts had reduced the harvest of 1953 in Brazil.

Vargas Neglects the Middle Class

The political sector which Vargas underestimated in his new calculations was the middle class. It had played a considerable role in his election of 1950. In the state of São Paulo, for example, Vargas' vote of 925,493 was almost double that of the other two principal candidates, Gomes and Machado. A good part of Vargas' vote, given the social structure of São Paulo, must have come from the middle class. After his election, however, Vargas did little to court bourgeois opinion. His overtures to the UDN were unsuccessful. His measures to speed up industrialization and move toward economic autonomy had created new jobs and new prestige for Brazil, but Vargas had not found any way to translate this into organized middle-class political support. Any attempt to narrow the political distance from the middle class was rendered more difficult by the implacable anti-getulistas on the right who constantly attacked Vargas' honesty and good faith. These political moralizers played on the middle-class weakness of conceiving of politics as a competition in the display of personal virtue.

In March 1953, a few months before Vargas adopted his new political strategy in June, an unusual election in São Paulo dramatized the depth of middle-class discontent. Jânio Quadros, a little-heralded schoolteacher-turned-politician from the interior of the state, won a smashing victory in the election for mayor in the city of São Paulo. He defeated the candidates of both the PSD and the UDN as well as the candidate of Adhemar de Barros' PSP. It was the first time since 1945 that a total outsider had won a post of this importance. Quadros, a magnetic personality on the hustings with his long black hair flying as he gesticulated, promised to return honesty to government. He attacked the "ins" and the entire system which they represented. It was an assault upon the traditional style of the political elite, couched in the populist mode which Adhemar de Barros had been the first to exploit. Whereas Adhemar had directed his appeal to the working class (although at the same time winning extensive middle-class support in the 1947 gubernatorial election), Quadros aimed his appeal primarily at the middle class. His campaign motto was "The Revolution of the penny (*tostão*) against the million (*milhão*)." This was directed toward the lower middle class who resented the economic favors which many *nouveaux riches* had received from the government, both state and federal.

Quadros was capitalizing on middle-class dissatisfaction with its share in Brazil's economic development. He also channeled their yearning for an uncorrupt political order, where the rights of the ordinary citizen would be equal to those of the man who enjoyed influence or money. This resentment had been strengthened by the increase in the rate of inflation. The middle class was being squeezed by the cost of living, and it was confused about the direction of Brazil's development. Quadros' election victory therefore underlined the discontent of the class whose importance Vargas seriously underestimated in his change of political course in June 1953.[57]

The central political fact about the middle class was the absence of any party which could represent its interests. The UDN, which began in 1944-45 as the natural home of the middle class, had allowed itself to rigidify into a defender of liberal constitutionalism in the narrow juridical sense. It had also espoused a version of economic liberalism which tended to alienate it from the nationalist sentiments of those middle-class voters who favored industrialization. Equally important, the UDN had permitted itself to become, in the more backward areas, a rival to the PSD as a spokesman for rural interests. This was true in Minas Gerais, for example, and in much of the Northeast.[58] In 1945–46 there had been a brief, short-lived attempt to form a "Democratic Left" (*Esquerda Democrática*) based on the left wing of the UDN and some representatives of small democratic socialist parties. The movement never attained any national importance. With the suppression of the Communist Party in 1947 the left of the political spectrum was inherited by the PTB and, to a lesser extent, by Adhemar de Barros' PSP. Although both the PSP and the PTB gained some middle-class voters, both had a "personalistic" image that tended to arouse middle-class suspicions of "demagoguery." Indeed, the trabalhismo of the PTB was based on a class and personal appeal that excluded the middle class.[59]

In the early 1950's the Brazilian middle class was therefore a political orphan. Given its lack of any satisfactory party expression, its opinion came to be expressed, as it had throughout the history of the Republic, by the Army. The Brazilian army officer corps, unlike its counterpart in many Spanish-American countries, was not dominated by members of the rural land-owning class. The predominant social origin was middle-class. Many officers were the sons of professional men or small businessmen and merchants. The less economically developed states produced a disproportionate share of the officers, perhaps because other avenues of social advancement were less available to them.[60]

The Army officer corps, like the middle class, was divided politically. But it had historically agreed on one idea: a devotion to the principle of legalism; above all, the preservation of constitutional processes. This conviction had grown stronger after Vargas' deposition in 1945, when the Army had been responsible for ensuring Brazil's redemocratization. Devotion to legalism meant for most officers a belief that economic and social change ought to be channeled within the existing constitutional structure, with its division of powers among executive, legislature, and judiciary.

On the other hand, many military officers believed that Brazil needed to accelerate her entry into the family of modern nations by speeding up the process of industrialization. This goal could be justified both in terms of the added material strength which this would give Brazil for the protection of her national security, and also in terms of the increased standard of living which this would bring to the many Brazilians living in misery.

This general agreement disguised a difference of opinion over how Brazil's development should take place. There were, roughly speaking, three camps within the officer corps. One was the leftist-nationalist group which had been led by Vargas' first War Minister, Estillac Leal. This group sometimes lapsed into the language of radical nationalism. Its members were fervent supporters of state-run enterprises in basic economic sectors such as iron and steel, oil, and electric power. Secondly, there was the conservative camp. They were the leaders of the Democratic Crusade which had forced Estillac Leal's resignation as War Minister in March 1952 and led the campaign to defeat him in his bid for election to the presidency of the Military Club in May 1952. This group warned against "Jacobinism" and "demagogic agitation" within the military. Their claim that the Army should remain neutral in politics masked what was in practice a sympathy with the agrarian-mercantile interests which had traditionally dominated Brazilian politics. The third group took a center position. Torn by the arguments of the right and the left, sympathetic to the need for a national (although not necessarily "nationalistic") effort toward economic development, but fearful also of the dangers of introducing class warfare into the officer corps, they were perplexed over the role which history expected of them.[61]

The defeat of Estillac Leal in May 1952 had not been an unqualified victory of the conservative faction over the nationalists. But many centrist officers had supported Etchegoyen against Estillac Leal because they feared that the nationalists were moving too fast and thereby unleashing political forces that might become uncontrollable.

This fear rested on the general assumption that, regardless of events in civilian politics, the military must preserve its own unity. This was necessary because the officer corps considered itself to be the ultimate arbiter of politics. Without internal unity it could not be certain of acting decisively in a crisis. Indeed, it was the Army's monopoly of force and its ability to deploy that force quickly throughout the

country that furnished its basis as political arbiter. Despite the ideological disagreements among officers, the commanders always took
care to make sure that at any given moment their subordinates would
respond promptly to higher commands. This, in essence, was the
meaning of the recurrent crises over "discipline." Whatever the differences among the officer corps, there was virtually unanimous loyalty
to the principle of unity vis-à-vis the civilian political sector. For this
reason, civilian politicians could cultivate their allies within the officer
corps, but if a deadlock of the civilian elite should develop into a
serious political crisis, the civilians knew they would have to face
united action by the military once the complex process of determining
majority officer opinion had been completed.

The Crisis Unfolds

In December 1953 Vargas assumed his nationalist posture more
decisively. In a speech in Curitíba he denounced excessive profit
remittances by foreign firms, and seemed to attribute Brazil's current
economic difficulties to the bad faith of foreigners. The fact was that
the President needed to carry out an unpopular and painful anti-inflation program, necessitated both by external constraints and internal
disequilibria. By attacking the foreigner, Vargas might hope to mobilize political support at home. But how could this support be translated into a willingness to cooperate in anti-inflation measures?

In a speech on January 31, 1954, Vargas reiterated the nationalist
theme. Foreign firms, he charged, were not only remitting excessive
profits, they were also committing fraud in their invoicing of ship-
ments so as to take illegal profits out of Brazil.[62] Meanwhile, Aranha's stabilization program was having heavy going. The promised
reductions in government expenditure did not materialize sufficiently
to counterbalance the constant increase in the money supply. Furthermore, Brazil's financial system was simply too primitively organized
to make feasible an orthodox stabilization program. Aranha had
hoped to reorganize the structure of the Finance Ministry in order to
increase central direction, but such reforms would take time.[63]

By January of 1954 the rise in the cost of living had provoked
worker rallies demanding wage increases. And the balance of pay-

ments problem persisted, despite the exchange reforms and a sharp cut in imports, because Brazil's stubborn insistence on maintaining a high coffee price had cost valuable foreign exchange when foreign consumers, especially in the United States, turned to other suppliers. As if to dramatize the foreign dimension of Brazil's stabilization crisis, a United States Senate committee (headed by Senator Gillette) began an investigation of Brazil's "exorbitant" coffee prices. Brazil and Vargas were enjoying the worst of all possible worlds. Brazil had set a high coffee price, thereby irritating the Americans. The Americans had retaliated with an investigation, thereby irritating the Brazilians. All this only served to strengthen nationalist sentiments in Brazil—sentiments which concentrated on the ill-will of foreigners, thereby diverting attention from the more painful question of anti-inflation measures at home. Most important, Brazil's sales of coffee to the United States had declined so much that she was actually earning *less* foreign exchange than had been the case in 1953, when lower coffee prices prevailed.

Although Aranha had not succeeded in preventing a large increase in the money supply in late 1953, there was still hope that the stabilization program might succeed if the impending revision of the minimum wage could be kept to a non-inflationary level. It was widely agreed that real wages had begun to fall in March 1953 and that an increase in the minimum wage was therefore in order. The question was the amount of the increase. Paulista businessmen, along with many economists, argued that the increase should only catch up with the increase in the cost of living since December 1951, the date of the last adjustment in the minimum wage. Any increase in *real* wages over the level established then could not be absorbed by employers, would therefore lead to new price increases, and would be certain to shock the middle class, which already entertained serious doubts about the sincerity of Vargas' stabilization efforts.[64]

Speculation about wage policy focused on the Labor Minister, João Goulart. His appointment in June of 1953 had aroused deep suspicion among the middle class. It had also given the irreconcilable anti-getulistas an invaluable target. Goulart's political opponents—above all the UDN—constantly branded him as a "demagogic" opportunist who wished to raise himself to power on a wave of "syndicalist" agitation. Goulart thus was made the focus for all the fears of the middle class, apprehensive over its possible loss of status and economic advantage in an inflation-ridden industrializing society.

Goulart had been well aware of this suspicion when he assumed office in 1953. In his first speech he pointedly announced, "I do not bring to the Ministry a program of agitation—as some political sectors claim." He promised that he would never deviate from the "democratic postulates which have always guided my public life." But he added defiantly that the anti-Goulart campaign "does not frighten me." [65]

By January 1954 Goulart was in the political crucible. Tension rose because the Labor Minister was about to make his recommendation to the President on the impending increase in the minimum wage. He deliberated amidst an atmosphere of worker protest. His own responsibility for the increasing number of strikes was difficult to assess. As Labor Minister he could have encouraged restraint. But the radical labor leaders (including some Communists), who had found success in infiltrating the unions since Vargas' return to the presidency, encountered no obstacles from the Minister of Labor. In the minds of both his supporters and his enemies, Goulart was the spokesman of an impatient working class. The anti-getulistas centered their attack on Goulart; but their real target was the President. Who were these politicians and military officers whose *raison d'être* was the liquidation of Vargas and getulismo? [66]

In the civilian sector the opposition was led by the UDN and the splinter parties of the right and center-right, such as the Republican Party, the Liberation Party, and the Christian Democratic Party. The majority of the UDN had bitterly fought Vargas' return in 1950. Born out of protest against the Vargas dictatorship, they watched in humiliation and anger as the ex-dictator returned to power by the ballot box—the instrument which they had fought to reestablish. Unable to prevent his inauguration by legal means, they were in no mood to accept Getúlio's overtures toward participation in his government in 1951 and 1952. From the moment of his return to the presidential palace, they argued that his election was a perversion of the democratic process.

Their most extreme spokesman was Carlos Lacerda, the master of political invective who founded the newspaper *Tribuna da Imprensa* as a vehicle for anti-getulista propaganda. In 1952, Lacerda argued that Brazil must declare a "State of Emergency" during which her democratic institutions would be "reformed." This was a euphemism for measures which would remove the "ins" from public office. It was based on the argument that Brazilian democracy had malfunctioned. Since the electoral machinery was bound to be manipulated (through demagoguery and bribery by the "ins"), so the argument went, Brazilian politics needed a thoroughgoing purge. This would mean the manipulation of the electoral machinery for the benefit of the "outs"—in practical terms, the assumption of power by the UDN.[67]

Many UDN politicians did not favor the extreme measures of Lacerda, because they hoped that Brazil could survive the Vargas presidency. Furthermore, these hesitant UDN members still retained some faith, however small, in their own ability to improve their national showing in elections. Although deeply worried over the state of Brazilian democracy, they were not ready to suspend it for the purge which Lacerda demanded.

The UDN opposition was supported by most of the established press, especially in Rio de Janeiro and São Paulo. The prestigious *O Estado de São Paulo,* for example, was a bitter opponent of Vargas. Two nation-wide newspaper chains, *O Globo* and *Diários Associados* (the Chateaubriand empire which included *O Jornal* in Rio de Janeiro and many provincial newspapers), were also pillars of anti-getulismo. Ever since Vargas' election they had sought a handle with which to mount a campaign against him. In 1953 they concentrated their fire on the "corruption" involved in the founding of the pro-Vargas newspaper, *Ultima Hora.*

Vargas, upon returning to the presidency in 1951, found the weight of press opinion heavily against him. He could never hope for sympathy or even objective coverage from the anti-getulista press. There were some lesser papers, such as *A Gazeta* (São Paulo), which supported him. But in order to ensure a better press, he approved a Bank of Brazil loan to Samuel Wainer to found a new pro-government newspaper chain. The paper *Ultima Hora* was launched, enjoyed success, and earned a handsome income for Wainer, who became a prestigious figure within government circles. Wainer was able to repay the loan, but Vargas' opponents seized upon the transaction as an example of the government's "cynical" misuse of public funds for partisan purposes. In June 1953 the UDN succeeded in having established a congressional tribunal to investigate Wainer's dealings with the Bank of Brazil. The resulting hearings and surrounding publicity furnished the anti-getulistas with an opportunity to exploit middle-class fears of "immorality" and "corruption" within government, fears that were widely shared in the officer corps.[68]

Vargas also had to contend with a focus of opposition within the military officer corps itself. It was difficult as of January 1954 to measure how the majority of the officers felt about Vargas. Officer attitude toward the President was a function of two factors. The first was the division among officers between the left-wing nationalist and the anti-Communist camps. This division had gone very deep in 1950, when the leftists waged a campaign to keep Brazil neutral in the Korean War and had condemned the United States for having started the war. The division between the two camps deepened during the debate in 1951 over oil policy. By the time of the resignation of Estillac Leal in March 1952, the battle lines were drawn. The subsequent election for president of the Military Club saw a decisive defeat for the nationalists.

The leaders of the Democratic Crusade, which won the election for the presidency of the Military Club, were for the most part anti-getulista, but this attitude depended upon how closely they believed Vargas to have identified himself with left-wing nationalism. Getúlio was playing an intricate game with the officer corps. Until 1953 he was able to preserve among the majority of officers at least a minimal faith in the moderation of his own intentions. But Vargas' political strategy after June 1953 raised new doubts among centrist officers and strengthened the hand of the conservative officers who were a counterpart within the military to the UDN opposition.

The leaders of the conservative officer faction based their views not so much on a conservative assessment of the need for economic change. On the contrary, many of these officers believed in industrialization because it would make Brazil stronger and furnish a larger technical and economic base on which the military could draw to defend national security. They became markedly conservative, however, in their emphasis on anti-communism. This was the issue over which the Military Club had split in 1950 when the Club's *Revista* published an article condemning United States intervention in Korea. The officers of the Democratic Crusade claimed that their nationalist opponents were the witting or unwitting collaborators of Communist infiltration in the military. The anti-Communist camp of officers was led by such figures as General Cordeiro de Farias, General Juarez Távora and Brigadier Eduardo Gomes. In the case of some of these officers, almost all politicians were considered suspect as selfish opportunists. In the case of others, such as Gomes, the identification with the UDN was complete. Most important, there was a working alliance between the anti-getulista politicians and the anti-getulista military.[69]

February 1954: Test of Power

As 1954 began, speculation increased over the level at which the new minimum wage should be set. It was widely rumored among conservative circles that Goulart was going to recommend a 100 percent increase in the minimum wage. Furthermore, he was doing nothing to discourage the wave of strikes and protest demonstrations sweeping Brazil.

In late January 1954 the *Estado de São Paulo* reported that there was a movement among junior army officers to protest their low salaries. On February 8 the junior officers presented a long memorandum to the War Minister. Details quickly leaked to the press, although the text was not published until February 20. It was a genuine case of protest moving up through the ranks. The memorandum was signed by forty-two colonels and thirty-nine lieutenant-colonels, and landed like a bombshell in the tense political atmosphere. It was a sign that Vargas could no longer afford to neglect the opinions of the officer corps.

The memorandum argued that the Army was threatened with an "undeniable crisis of authority," which might "undermine the unity of the military class, leaving it defenseless against the divisive maneuvers of the eternal promoters of disorder and those who capitalize on public unrest." It went on to specify a number of areas in which the government had conspicuously neglected the Army: failure to re-equip units, an indifference to the need for salary increases, and a lack of attention to the "inequality of opportunities for promotion" which had been produced by high-level inconsistency over the lines of hierarchy and the quota of ranks for each section of the Army. This neg-

lect, the colonels charged, had hampered recruitment both for enlisted
men and for officers and had seriously reduced the prestige of the
Army. Many officers, they explained, were leaving the Army for better-
paying civilian jobs, where "cut off from the professional interests and
problems of their class, they are not always able to keep themselves
immune from the intrigues of partisan politics."

The resulting demoralization had divided the officer corps and
made it more susceptible to "infiltration by pernicious anti-democratic
ideologies." It was implied that the Communists and radical nationalists would thereby gain adherents among the officers and enlisted men.
The implication was that the defeat of the nationalists in the Military
Club election of May 1952 might be reversed if the demoralization
continued. Such divisions within the military could be fatal to Brazil
because "with Communism always cunningly on the alert, the very
institutional structure of the nation may be threatened by violent subversion."

What was the colonels' formula for restoring unity? It was a paro-
chial answer. The government should provide more money for equipment and salaries. By becoming better equipped and better paid, the
officer corps would be able to preserve its role as the guardian of
Brazilian institutions. There were no specifically political demands in
the memorandum. There was, for example, no reference to Goulart or
to the "syndicalist threat" which the civilian anti-getulistas constantly
warned against.

Their demands did, however, reveal a strong tone of resentment
which reflected the social tensions generated by inflation, as well as
the junior officers' belief that their unique status in Brazilian society
was threatened. There was direct reference to the rapid disappearance
of salary differentials. If the rumored increase (meaning Goulart's expected recommendation of a 100 percent) in the minimum wage were
to be approved, the memorandum warned, it would mean that an un-
skilled worker would earn almost as much as a university graduate.
The nervousness over status was unmistakable. While the military
were struggling to maintain "a standard of living compatible with their
social position," the colonels complained, the government was preparing and announcing measures which would only benefit "certain
classes or groups." The target of this resentment was not only the
working class, whose wage increase was yet to be announced, but also

the businessmen and merchants who were able to protect themselves against inflation by unorthodox financial dealings. The memorandum pointedly compared the level of honesty and administrative decorum within the military to "the atmosphere of shady business deals, embezzlements and misuse of public funds" rampant in the country as a whole.[70]

This remarkable document was a warning of the utmost significance for Vargas. It was the genuine expression of discontent on the part of younger officers, many of whom had not been directly involved in the anti-getulismo of earlier years. It was also an expression of middle-class discontent transmuted into the vocabulary of the professional military. Although they expressed their fears over loss of status in the special language of the Brazilian military tradition, they were speaking for a large segment of the middle class.

The memorandum was a sign that the charges of communism and corruption constantly leveled by the civilian anti-getulistas had found an echo among the officer corps. Yet the memorandum was a remarkably provincial document. It was a cry of protest over neglect. More generous attention to the Army's technical needs and internal regulations could have answered most of the specific complaints. Although the memorandum was addressed to the top Army commanders, its wider political implications were obvious, simply because of the position of the military in the Brazilian political scene. Contrary to what newsmen believed before the memorandum was published, there was no reference to the President or his Labor Minister, or even to the frequent strikes and demands for wage increases.[71]

The memorandum came as a surprise to Vargas, who had always been careful to look after the Army's demands for pay and equipment. But the President was growing old, losing his grip. He complained to his War Minister, General Espírito Santo Cardoso, that he had not been kept informed of officer discontent: "Instead of helping, you are just creating difficulties for me." From that moment it was merely a matter of time until Vargas found a new War Minister.[72]

Meanwhile, Goulart was preparing his report on minimum wages. Finally, on February 22, he submitted his recommendation, which called for 100 percent increase in the minimum wage (from 1,200 to 2,400 cruzeiros per month), which applied primarily to commercial and industrial employees in the urban sector. In his covering letter

Goulart offered his explanation of inflation: "It is not wages which raise the cost of living; on the contrary, it is the rise in the cost of living which requires higher wages." He went on to attack "those who exploit popular misery" by raising prices and earning "excessive and anti-social profits." If enacted, Goulart's recommendation would have led to a sharp increase in real wages, considerably above the level of the last adjustment in December 1951.[73]

The date of Goulart's recommendation was also the date of his resignation. In an effort to recover political ground he had lost with the middle class and among the officer corps, Vargas decided to replace both his War Minister and his Labor Minister. Although the colonels' memorandum of February 8 had not mentioned Goulart by name, Vargas had received repeated warnings from the conservative military that the first step toward restoring the faith of the officer corps in the President would be the dismissal of the Labor Minister. Goulart's departure, especially in view of his recommendation for wage policy, would also reassure those at home and abroad who were suspicious about Vargas' real commitment to the Aranha stabilization plan.

In January the *Estado de São Paulo* had asked rhetorically if Goulart would be the Jafet (the President of the Bank of Brazil whose easy credit policies undermined the stabilization efforts of Aranha's predecessor in the Finance Ministry) of the Aranha period. A week before Goulart's resignation, the same paper called him the "alter ego" of Vargas and "the chief of Brazilian Peronism." On February 2, the *Estado* succinctly expressed the views of the anti-getulistas by calling Vargas the "caudilho" who was fomenting a crisis in order to "justify to the people and the armed forces his beloved continuist coup." In early February the UDN had issued a manifesto denouncing Goulart's "subversive" activities among the working class. The anti-getulista opposition was in full cry. Emboldened by the colonels' memorandum, they stepped up their pressure on Vargas.[74]

The ministerial changes of February 22 represented an important concession by the President. More significant, they were a sign of political weakness. Goulart had been the key to Vargas' new political strategy, undertaken with the Labor Minister's appointment in June 1953. Surrendering him now, in the face of the growing phalanx of civilian and miltiary opposition, was a symptom of Getúlio's loss of control over the political situation. Goulart was replaced by an acting minister, Hugo de Farias, who was little more than a senior bureaucrat in the Ministry of Labor.

The War Minister, Espírito Santo Cardoso, was replaced by General Zenóbio da Costa, known for his outspoken opposition to Communist infiltration in the armed forces. Zenóbio was also known as the "Hero of Monte Cassino," the site of the Brazilian Army's most valorous action during the 1945 campaign in Italy. Furthermore, he had been a leading military supporter of Getúlio's inauguration after the election of 1950. He was generally considered a decisive figure, and Vargas hoped that his new War Minister could reestablish the authority over the officer corps which Santo Cardoso had so conspicuously lost.

Equivocation and Polarization

Although Vargas had been forced to pay greater attention to the opposition within the officer corps, he was still capable of riding two horses at once. On February 21, the eve of Goulart's dismissal, Getúlio spoke to a rally of workers at the Volta Redonda steel mill. He declared that his goal was to maintain the democratic process. He assured the workers that "the government is looking out for your interests. The unremitting battle which I am waging against the oppressors and exploiters is equalled only by my unceasing struggle to defend the disadvantaged and exploited." [75] Then he proceeded to dismiss Goulart, and gave the impression that he had no intention of carrying out his former Labor Minister's recommended doubling of the minimum wage. The new wage level, he led a reporter to believe, was more likely to be around 1,700 cruzeiros, a 42 percent increase in money wages, rather than 2,400 cruzeiros, Goulart's 100 percent increase.

On March 15 Getúlio submitted his annual message to Congress. It was more nationalistic than the message of a year earlier. Now he emphasized the structural disadvantages under which Brazil labored in foreign trade. In his speeches of December 20, 1953, and January 31, 1954, he had attacked foreign investors for their pernicious role in exacerbating the balance of payments; he now reported to the Congress that the "free exchange market has proved itself an inadequate instrument for achieving the objectives which led to its creation: it has not led to an expansion of exports, nor stimulated the inflow of capital." He went on to explain that the disequilibrium in the balance of payments was neither "transitory nor superficial," but the symptom of "a profound structural crisis in the area of our relations with the foreigner—with grave repercussions on the internal economy of the country." [76]

In April Vargas continued his nationalist course by presenting to the Congress a bill to create Electrobrás, a federally operated electric power enterprise which could fill the gap in power production left by the foreign-owned (primarily U.S. and Canadian) public utilities. These companies, whose rates and service were a constant target for Brazilian criticism, were hesitant to expand their capacity because of uncertainties over rate regulations and possible expropriation. Meanwhile, the pressure became greater to settle the minimum wage question.

With Goulart gone, the anti-getulista opposition had lost their favorite target for attack within the Cabinet. Instead, they concentrated their fire on Vargas himself, claiming that the President still nurtured hopes of a coup to keep himself in power after the expiration of his term in January 1956. Immediately after the ministerial changes of February 22, an UDN leader, Olavo Bilac Pinto, placed the blame for the crisis on the very fact that Vargas was President. He reviewed the "scandals" of the Vargas administration such as the government favors for the creation of *Última Hora* and the irregular loan policies of President Ricardo Jafet of the Bank of Brazil.[77] There is little doubt that influence peddling had grown alarmingly in the shadow of the personally honest but increasingly tired Vargas. Having succeeded in forcing Goulart's dismissal, the opposition now hoped to remove the President from office.

On April 4 the opposition was given a new opportunity. João Neves da Fontoura, the Foreign Minister from 1951 until he was replaced at the time of the cabinet shift of June-July 1953, published a sensational press interview in Rio. Neves da Fontoura charged that Vargas had been secretly negotiating with President Perón of Argentina to sign an agreement among the ABC powers (Argentina, Brazil and Chile) to form a block against the United States in the Western Hemisphere. These negotiations, alleged the former Foreign Minister, had been carried out by Vargas and Goulart, without the knowledge of the Foreign Ministry. The immediate occasion for Neves da Fontoura's revelations was his claim that Perón had recently complained bitterly in a speech to a group of Argentine Army officers that Vargas had not kept his promises in the negotiations. The Argentine government quickly denied that Perón had given any such speech. But the uproar in Brazil was immediate.[78]

Here was an ideal issue for the anti-getulistas. Vargas' own ex-Foreign Minister had given new evidence to substantiate the charge that the President harbored hopes for a "syndicalist" state on Peronista lines. Furthermore, the Neves da Fontoura charges raised the ideological question of Brazil's foreign policy in a new form. The anti-Americanism of the alleged ABC pact infuriated those anti-getulistas who identified Brazil's fortunes with a prudent following of the United States' lead in foreign policy. Such a view was typical, for example, of General Cordeiro de Farias and the officers of the Democratic Crusade who had vigorously opposed the nationalist faction.

The UDN decided to attempt the President's removal by legal methods. It introduced impeachment proceedings in the Congress. But Getúlio's support was still too strong. The PTB vigorously supported the President. The PSD, although it had no party or ideological loyalty to Vargas, was not prepared to trade its own position of strength in the government for an unknown situation where the UDN might gain increased influence. Furthermore, Getúlio could still count on the personal loyalty of many PSD leaders such as Gustavo Capanema and Benedito Valadares, who had helped to ease Goulart out in February. The UDN could not summon enough votes against the PSD-PTB majority, and the impeachment attempt failed.[79] Vargas could now only be deposed, under present political conditions, by direct intervention of the Army. The majority of the officer corps, however, was not yet convinced that the legally elected President constituted a threat to democratic institutions in Brazil, nor that the civilian political conflict justified arbitration by the military.

Although Getúlio had dismissed Goulart in February, he had not during March or April made public his decision about the minimum wage increase. On May 1, the international socialist holiday that Vargas always reserved for "trabalhista" pronouncements, the President made public his decision. In an aggressive speech in Petrópolis he announced that the increase in the minimum wage would be 100 percent. He pointedly praised the work of his former Minister of Labor, João Goulart, an "indefatigable friend and defender of the workers." Vargas reviewed the steps he himself had taken during his career to protect the lot of the working man. And he ended with one of the boldest appeals he had ever made for working-class support: "With your votes you can not only defend your interests, but you can influence the very destiny of the nation. As citizens your views will bear weight at the polls. As a class, you can make your ballots the decisive numerical force. You constitute the majority. Today you are with the government. Tomorrow you will be the government." [80]

The 100 percent increase in the minimum wage was inflationary in the sense that it represented an increase in *real* wages over the level of the last minimum wage decree (Dec. 1951). Workers gained what a United Nations source estimated as at least a 54 percent increase in real wages. Although the new minimum wage was still low compared to developed countries, it caused alarm among employers, who knew they could not absorb the increase without passing on large price increases, and among the middle class, which felt neglected and threatened. The colonels' memorandum in February had already expressed their concern over the cost-of-living squeeze.

Vargas had decided on the 100 percent increase against the counsel of virtually every economic adviser he consulted. The National Economic Council (*Conselho Nacional de Economia*), for example, recommended scaling down Goulart's suggested 100 percent increase to 40 percent. The fact was that Getúlio had decided to court working-class political support by means of a handsome increase in real wages, regardless of the consequences on other sectors of opinion. It was a sign that Vargas had lost his well-tested sense of control. His new strategy was reckless, given the facts of Brazilian political life, since the alienated groups—industrialists, middle class, military officers— were in a much stronger position to mobilize their opposition than were the workers to mobilize their support.

The outcry of protest against Vargas' wage decree of May 1 was immediate. The opposition *Correio da Manhã* thundered: "For Getúlio Vargas, who has already fallen into irremediable political decay, the worse it gets the better. If the economic and social structure of the country begins to collapse, shaken by unsettling agitation and protest, he will attempt to come forward as its 'saviour' with a new regime." Should he fail, "what does it matter? After him the deluge. . . ." [81] The extreme anti-getulista UDN leaders were hard at work in public speeches and private conferences mobilizing support for their offensive against the President.

Their counterparts in the military had gone even farther: they were mounting a conspiracy to depose the President, by force if necessary. One of Vargas' former personal secretaries, Luiz Vergara, visited Rio de Janeiro in early May and was shocked to discover an anti-Vargas conspiracy actively operating among junior Air Force officers at the Galeão air base near Rio. He hurried to inform his former chief and was amazed when the President replied that this information merely confirmed what he had heard from other sources. Incredulous, Vergara asked why the President did not dismiss his Minister of the Air Force, who, Vargas readily explained, had done nothing to quell the conspiracy. "Send him away and put someone else in his place," Vergara implored; "this situation can't continue." Vargas, who looked tired and preoccupied, replied to his former companion of the Estado Nôvo, "Don't worry. . . . Remember that together we surmounted similar or worse situations than this and in the end everything was resolved without irreparable damage." [82] Vargas continued to follow his long-established routine of conferring with each minister on his appointed day of the week. There were no indications that he was making significant efforts to organize the working class to which he had dramatically appealed on May 1.

The economic situation was worsening, not improving, moreover. Employers fought the minimum wage decree through the courts, where it was finally declared legal by the Brazilian Supreme Court, deliberating under the threat of a general strike. Finance Minister Aranha's attempt at credit control aroused protests from São Paulo businessmen, who petitioned the minister in July to protest the large money reserves which the Bank of Brazil had accumulated from the profits of its auction sale of foreign exchange under the regulations introduced the preceding October.[83]

Coupled with the domestic tensions over wage, credit, and exchange policies was a disastrous decline in dollar earnings abroad. Coffee prices had reached record levels in early 1954, rising as high as

97 cents a pound in the New York market in April. But Brazilian coffee had gotten a smaller than customary share of the New York market because the Brazilian government insisted on maintaining a price above even the rising market level. Emboldened by the buoyancy of world demand, on June 3 the government set a minimum price of 87 cents a pound. This tactic had the worst possible effect. The American market boycotted Brazilian coffee, sending Brazil's dollar earnings even lower. In August, Brazil exported only 145,000 sacks of coffee, earning $14 million, as compared to the same month a year earlier (1953), which had seen 860,000 sacks, exported for a value of $66 million. This disastrous failure to maximize dollar earnings from Brazil's most important export reinforced the country's dependence on short-term financing to cover the deficit in the balance of payments, often carrying most disadvantageous terms. It also reinforced the extreme nationalists, who blamed Brazil's entire financial disequilibrium on foreign ill-will.[84]

From Assassination to Suicide

As July ended, the President was in an extremely vulnerable position.[85] Although the stabilization plan had yet to show any benefits, it had succeeded in alienating almost every economic sector, including the working class, which Vargas had kept waiting many months for its wage increase, now finally set to take effect in early July. Furthermore, under Brazil's constitution, the incumbent President could hope to enjoy only two or three years of political predominance. After that time, because the Constitution forbade the incumbent's reelection, the President was bound to find attention centering on the negotiations over the rival candidates for his succession. As the popular saying had it: "Brazil is governed for only half a presidential term. The other half is spent electing the next President." Adhemar de Barros' launching of his own presidential campaign in 1953 helped force Vargas to embark on the new political strategy initiated by the ministerial changes in June and July of that year.

The opposition to Vargas had gathered momentum since the beginning of the year. The UDN leaders gained many military converts to their position after the colonels' memorandum of February. The anti-getulista press kept up a drumfire of attack on the "immorality" and corruption (which had indeed become rampant) within the "caudilho's" entourage. Brazilian democracy was "sick" and needed a "purgative."

Against this formidable opposition, which rested on a growing coalition of civilian and military anti-getulistas, Vargas' political strategy was proving ineffective. His minimum wage decree was aimed at the working class. Yet Vargas had done remarkably little to mobilize working-class support. He had made no strenuous efforts to strengthen the PTB in preparation for the congressional elections in October. This was all the more important since there were few extra-party working-class political organizations to which he could turn. The labor unions, for example, continued to be instruments of the Minister of Labor, and that post, since Goulart's departure in February, was not occupied by a dynamic political figure. The fact was that Getúlio's strategy of relying on working-class support rested on little more than a threat. Having cultivated the image of "the father of the poor," the President could not expect to find spontaneous support from his unorganized "children." The passive political mentality of the working class to which Vargas had contributed was now a serious liability.

The best-organized independent political force on the left, the Brazilian Communist Party, assumed an equivocal attitude toward Vargas. On the one hand, the PCB, in line with the cold-war position adopted after 1949, was violently opposed to Vargas' willingness to enter into military accords with the United States and to follow the American lead in preparations for hemispheric defense. On the other hand, the party had begun cooperating informally with the Vargas followers in the labor movement, where the Communists had lost ground since the height of their influence during the immediate post-war years. But Vargas regarded the Communists with suspicion, knowing that they could offer him no significant support at this stage in his career.

Although Vargas' strategy of relying upon the working class produced small returns, it was overt enough to erode confidence among the middle class. The colonels' memorandum of February and the UDN's vindictive and inflammatory campaign had undermined the minimum of middle-class support which the President needed. His unsuccessful economic policy further contributed to the growing discontent, not only of the middle class, but also of industrialists.

Throughout his career Vargas had always been able to rely on his own talents of persuasion and manipulation. Now, however, his friends began to notice that he seemed to have grown old and tired. He was seventy-two and showed the effects of his years of attention to administrative detail during the Estado Nôvo. He was slow to react to the warnings of his intimate supporters. The vigorous action necessary to restore the confidence of the officer corps—which was becoming the key to the solution of the political deadlock—appeared to be beyond his powers.

Several of Vargas' intimates and supporters observed with anguish the deterioration of the President's political position. The leading edge of the opposition's attacks, they agreed, was the belligerent journalist Carlos Lacerda. If only he could be "removed" from the scene, the situation might be saved. These Vargas supporters decided to take matters into their own hands. General Mendes de Moraes and Congressional Deputy Euvaldo Lodi suggested to Gregório Fortunato, Chief of the Presidential Palace Guard, that it was his duty to "take care of" Lacerda. Fortunato, an illiterate Riograndense Negro who had faithfully served Vargas for more than thirty years, saw an opportunity to render the President his greatest service. He arranged, unbeknownst to Vargas, for a professional gunman to assassinate Lacerda.

Lacerda knew that there were plots against his life and was taking precautions. Guarded day and night by a volunteer contingent of junior Air Force officers, he had already escaped several attacks. At 12:45 a.m. on August 5 a gunman, acting on indirect instructions from Fortunato, opened fire on Lacerda as he approached the door to his apartment building on Rua Toneleros in the Rio de Janeiro district of Copacabana. Lacerda was only slightly wounded, but his companion, Air Force Major Rubens Florentino Vaz, was killed. Lacerda returned fire as the assailant escaped.[86]

The political impact of the shooting could hardly have been greater. Vargas is reported to have said, "That shot was not aimed at Lacerda, but at me." Since the "honor" of the officer corps was at stake, the military had now been drawn directly into the political quarrel between the President and the anti-getulistas. Air Brigadier Eduardo Gomes, chief of staff of the Air Force and a long-time personal enemy of Vargas, warned, "For the honor of the nation, we trust that this crime will not go unpunished."

Although an investigation was immediately ordered by the Minister of Justice, the Air Force began its own inquiry. The President's remaining authority began to melt away almost visibly. Vargas was booed in public, and the congressional campaign posters of his son, Luthero, were defaced and destroyed. After an intensive man-hunt the assassin was captured, and under interrogation revealed his connection with palace officials. On August 10, Vargas agreed to dissolve the presidential guard, but the momentum of military protest increased inexorably. On the same day, the anti-getulista officers, led by Eduardo Gomes and Juarez Távora, demanded that the War Minister, General Zenóbio da Costa, request the President's resignation. The War Minister refused, thus underlining the division of opinion within the officer corps.

The President's position worsened as the results of the police and Air Force investigations were leaked to the public. There were lurid reports of large-scale corruption among the presidential staff, involving the granting of favors to many prominent public figures. Fortunato, the President's loyal aide, besides having arranged for Lacerda's death, was found to have had close connections with many professional criminals and to have amassed a large fortune by exploiting his official position. Shocked by the revelations, Vargas remarked despondently, "I have the feeling I am standing in a sea of mud." [87]

The phrase was soon on everyone's lips. Lacerda was in his element. The editorials in his *Tribuna da Imprensa* became daily more violent, now dramatized in the public mind by the author's near martyrdom. Lacerda was on the radio nightly, inventing new invectives to describe the getulistas and their deeds. With each attack the aging Vargas seemed to recoil visibly.

To the rising chorus of demands for his resignation, Vargas replied in a speech in Belo Horizonte on August 12 that he would not "flee my duty" which he promised to "fulfill to the end." He promised to maintain "constitutional guarantees" and to carry out the October elections "in a climate of order and tranquility." He disdained the "lies and calumnies" directed at him, and he appealed for confidence in "the healthy reaction of public opinion and the sentiments of patriotism and discipline in our armed forces." The latter group was crucial, as Vargas knew, and he ended by stressing the issue which many officers, including the War Minister, still considered central—the legality of the President's position: "Being in the government, I represent the principle of constitutional legality which it is my responsibility to preserve and defend. I shall not deviate from it and I warn the perennial fomenters of provocation and disorder that I shall know how to resist any and all attempts to disturb the peace and public tranquility." [88] Despite the brave rhetoric, Vargas returned to Rio and virtually withdrew into the presidential palace, where his true friends were difficult to distinguish in the "sea of mud."

Meanwhile, the officer corps of the three services were meeting in constant consultation and debate over the political crisis. General Zenóbio da Costa, Vargas' faithful War Minister, reiterated publicly his pledge that "the legally constituted powers" would be respected. But his references to the need to maintain "discipline" and "unity" within the armed forces were an unmistakable sign that the anti-getulista officers were making great inroads in their campaign for military intervention against Getúlio.

On August 21 Vice President Café Filho, who was a special target for the UDN attempt to foment a split within the government, suggested to Vargas that they both resign, allowing the Congress to elect an interim successor for the remainder of the presidential term. Vargas refused, telling Café Filho that he would never leave the palace before the end of his term except "dead." Later, on August 23, Café Filho broke openly with the President by revealing the proposal in a speech to the Congress.[89]

The sensational revelations of corruption within the presidential palace had given the anti-getulista military officers new evidence with which to convince their "legalist" colleagues of the need to depose Vargas. On August 22 a group of Air Force officers, led by Eduardo Gomes, issued a manifesto demanding the President's resignation. It was endorsed by several key Army commanders and transmitted to Vargas at the palace by Marshal Mascarenhas de Morais, the commander of Brazil's Expeditionary Force to Europe in the Second World War and now a supporter of the Air Force officers' ultimatum. Again Vargas refused to resign. "I will only leave here dead," he told his caller. "I am too old to be intimidated and I have no reason to fear death." [90]

Vargas' last hope was the loyalists within the Army. Zenóbio da Costa remained confident that he retained the control of the lines of command, despite the defections of some anti-getulista officers. In fact, the situation was much worse than he wished to admit. On August 23 his opponents within the higher ranks of the Army outflanked him.

Twenty-seven Army generals, led by familiar anti-getulistas such as Generals Canrobert Pereira da Costa and Juarez Távora, but including also more centrist generals such as Pery Constant Bevilacqua and Machado Lopes, as well as generals who were later to earn the title of "nationalist" such as Henrique Lott, issued a "Manifesto to the Nation" that demanded Vargas' resignation. It declared that the "criminal corruption" around the President had compromised "the indispensable moral authority" of his office, and that the "continuation of the present politico-military crisis is bringing irreparable damage to the country's economic situation," and may "culminate in grave internal disturbances." [91]

The military had spoken. Vargas had been given an ultimatum from the Army command for the second time in his life. In the early morning hours of August 24 Vargas called together his cabinet for a somber meeting. After consulting his ministers he agreed to take a leave of absence, although it was understood that the President would not offer a definitive resignation. He concluded on a defiant note, warning that "if you come to depose me you will find my body." [92] The War Minister, Zenóbio da Costa, was still intent on organizing resistance against the "rebellious" generals, who now represented near-unanimity among the Air Force and Navy, and a large majority within the Army. Upon conferring with the opposition Army generals, the War Minister finally realized that Vargas' leave of absence must be permanent. Word of the final military ultimatum, now endorsed by the War Minister himself, was relayed to the presidential palace where Vargas was informed shortly after eight o'clock on the morning of August 24.

Vargas now proved true to his word. Never hesitating over his final defense against his enemies, he carefully aimed a pistol at his heart and fired one shot. His family and aides rushed to his room to find the President dead. Oswaldo Aranha, the companion from so many battles of the past, burst into tears.

An inflammatory suicide letter, allegedly left by Vargas, was immediately released to the press. It charged that "a subterranean campaign of international groups joined with national groups" had tried to block "workers' guarantees," limits on excess profits, and the proposals to create Petrobrás and Electrobrás. "Profits of foreign enterprises reached 500 percent yearly," he claimed, while Brazilian measures to defend her coffee exports provoked "violent pressure upon our economy to the point of being obliged to surrender." The letter left little doubt how the President's suicide was to be interpreted: "I offer my life in the holocaust. I choose this means to be with you always." The message concluded: "I gave you my life. Now I offer my death. Nothing remains. Serenely I take the first step on the road to eternity as I leave life to enter history." [93]

Whether the letter was authentic or not, it was immediately accepted as such by the general public. It had ended Vargas' indecisive alternation between an orthodox and a nationalist policy. His suicide message was the strongest nationalist appeal he had ever made.

The public reaction caught his opponents unawares. A wave of sympathy for Getúlio engulfed the country. Lacerda, the crusading journalist whose courage had galvanized the opposition, went into hiding, and soon fled the country until the furor could subside. Delivery trucks of the opposition newspaper, *O Globo,* were burned by angry crowds, which went on to assault American diplomatic buildings. Throughout their campaign, the anti-getulistas had centered their fire on the person of the President. By his final act of self-sacrifice Vargas neutralized the political and psychological advantage his opponents had accumulated. In death, as in life, Vargas' action was well designed to yield maximum political effect.

IV

GOVERNMENT BY CARETAKER: 1954–1956

Politics Without Vargas

The sensational denouement of the political crisis of August had disarmed the anti-getulistas and robbed them of clear-cut victory. The street riots and public protests against Vargas' tormentors gave the former President's popularity new life. Unlike his departure from power in 1945, Vargas' disappearance in 1954 produced a psychological trauma which prevented the liberal constitutionalists from eradicating the system that they associated with Vargas. There was, therefore, little prospect that the bitter division between getulistas and anti-getulistas could soon be overcome.

Vice President Café Filho was sworn in as President immediately after Vargas' suicide. He was a leader of Adhemar de Barros' PSP party and had gone on the ballot in 1950 as part of the electoral deal between Vargas and Adhemar. He was known to be more conservative than Vargas and had openly split with the President during the August crisis. Upon assuming office he assured the country that he would give "the humble the protection which Vargas always gave them." [1] He organized a new cabinet which included several leading figures identified with the UDN. The Finance Minister was Eugênio Gudin, a prominent professor of economics who often spoke and wrote (newspapers, magazines) in favor of orthodox financial policies. In the last years of the Estado Nôvo Gudin had been an outspoken opponent of the industrialization proposals of Roberto Simonsen. Several other civilian ministers were distinguished public figures of moderately conservative views such as Candido Mota Filho, the new Minister of Education, and Raul Fernandes (a well-known and aging UDN politician), the new Minister of Foreign Affairs. The ministries of Air and Navy went to prominent anti-getulistas, Brigadier General Eduardo Gomes and Admiral Amorim do Vale. Both had been leaders in the conspiracy to force Vargas' resignation. The new War Minister was General Lott, who had the reputation of being a centrist officer not tied to any of the political factions within the Army, unlike Generals Juarez Távora and Canrobert Pereira da Costa (linked to the militant anti-getulistas) who were also considered for the War Ministry. The Labor Ministry went to Colonel Napoleão de Alencastro Guimarães, a former associate of Vargas but now a dissident leader of the PTB, which forbade its members to participate in the new administration. The appointment of Alencastro Guimarães showed that the interim government felt it needed to make some political gesture to the left.

Although UDN politicians and anti-getulista military were prominent in the new government, there was no prospect of an anti-Vargas purge on the lines previously urged by extremists such as Lacerda. Café Filho was known to have a strong devotion to the principles of "legality." From the outset he made clear that he regarded his government as an interim regime, which had a prime responsibility to pursue economic stabilization and preside over the elections that would produce a constitutional successor. The first test of the President's resolve came on the question of holding the congressional elections scheduled for October 1954. Many UDN leaders, fearful of the psychological impact of Vargas' suicide, demanded that the elections be postponed. The PTB leaders dismissed their proposals as disguised pleas for the suspension of constitutional government.

The elections were held, as scheduled, on October 3.[2] The results revealed, surprisingly enough, how little the political crisis had affected voter opinion. The PTB did not make significant gains (56 seats in the Chamber of Deputies as against 51 seats in the previous Congress), although Vargas' son Luthero was reelected to the Congress. João Goulart was decisively defeated in his attempt to become a PTB senator from his home state of Rio Grande do Sul. His failure was all the more striking since his campaign was based directly on an appeal to the memory of his recently "martyred" mentor and fellow gaúcho, Vargas. The UDN lost ground in the election, declining from 81 seats to 74, although Lacerda was elected to the Chamber of Deputies. The PSD, the party least clearly marked in the recent conflict, increased its number slightly, from 112 to 114 seats. There was a marked tendency for candidates to run on "coalition" tickets, which combined party labels. Nevertheless, the election results indicated that whoever was elected President in 1955 would confront a Congress of substantially the same political complexion as Vargas had faced.[3]

Café Filho began 1955 by reaffirming his government's intention to hold the presidential election, as scheduled, in October. He endorsed the suggestion of the higher military—led by the anti-getulistas—that the electorate should be offered a "national union" candidate. No such figure could be found, however. The PSD was the first party to choose its own candidate. At a convention in February the party unanimously nominated Governor Juscelino Kubitschek of Minas Gerais. Kubitschek, a former physician and grandson of a Czechoslovakian immigrant, had risen through the PSD ranks in Minas and was therefore an heir on one side of the Vargas political system. His nomination set the scene for subsequent maneuvering among the politicians.[4]

The anti-getulistas nervously sought a candidate who could attract votes in the center. But the nomination of Kubitschek had provided the occasion for the revival of the most passionate anti-getulista feelings. Their concern centered on the reports of preliminary negotiations between the PSD and the PTB. It was rumored that the PSD would put João Goulart, chief target of the anti-getulistas, on their ticket as candidate for Vice President. Military officers who had led the campaign forcing Vargas to dismiss Goulart only a year earlier, now saw their enemy aiming for even higher office. The press was alive with rumors about alleged "warnings" by the military, including War Minister Lott, of the dangers involved in the Goulart candidacy. In April the electoral alliance was sealed—Kubitschek for President and João Goulart for Vice President. It would be the electoral power of the PSD's rural machine combined with the PTB power in the cities.

Also in April, a dissident faction of the PSD held its own convention in protest against the nomination of Kubitschek, whom they thought to be moving too far left. This conservative PSD group nominated as their candidate former Governor Etelvino Lins of Pernambuco, a politician with little national appeal. He was subsequently endorsed by the UDN, which had been at a loss for a candidate since the failure of its efforts in January to find a "unity" candidate with sufficient electoral appeal to ward off the return of the Vargas forces.

In May, Adhemar de Barros added his hat to the ring, undaunted by his defeat for Governor of São Paulo at the hands of Jânio Quadros the previous October. Adhemar still eyed the presidential palace, which he felt had been promised him in the electoral bargain with Vargas in 1950. Adhemar was expected to draw working-class votes away from Kubitschek and thereby improve the chances of the UDN candidate.

In June the UDN became worried over the lack of appeal of their candidate, Lins, and withdrew his nomination, replacing him with General Juarez Távora. He had once been a leading tenente and an important ally of Vargas in the Revolution of 1930, serving as the virtual viceroy of the Northeast in 1931. In 1937 Távora virtually broke with the Vargas regime, leaving the country to become military attaché in Chile. After 1945, however, he became closely identified with the anti-Vargas military. He was active in the Democratic Crusade that defeated the nationalist faction within the officer corps in the early 1950's and was a commander of the Higher War College, an important center for anti-Vargas military opinion. Having been a principal conspirator in the events leading to Getúlio's suicide in 1954, Távora was rewarded by being appointed chief of the military household in the Café Filho government. He had already been nominated by the Christian Democratic Party in May and was hoping to present a moderate centrist image under the banner of Christian Democracy. His endorsement by the UDN belied that party's fear that its own label lacked sufficient appeal in a national election.

The Presidential Election of 1955: Return of the "Ins"

As the campaign began, speculation hinged on estimates of how well Kubitschek could hold together the two elements of his alliance. Speeches which pleased the back-country PSD political bosses would hardly appeal to the PTB voters in the cities. On the other hand, Kubitschek could not appeal to nationalist sentiments among the urban electorate without running the danger of provoking the anti-getulista military to the point where the incumbent government might think it necessary to postpone the election. Kubitschek's strength with the urban electorate, especially in São Paulo, was further threatened by Adhemar's candidacy.

Kubitschek's chances looked certain enough to alarm the anti-Vargas forces. The PSD candidate had no sooner been nominated in February than Carlos Lacerda, architect of Vargas' demise, attacked the idea of holding a free election. He called Kubitschek the "catalyst of national treachery [*canalhice*]" and called for a reform of Brazilian democracy "in order to install legitimate legality." Lacerda envisioned an emergency government that would prevent getulistas from reaching power. In effect, Lacerda was already conceding the election and therefore arguing that it should not be held. Others on the right shared Lacerda's pessimism. F. Rodrigues Alves Filho, a member of the Paulista political clan prominent throughout the Republic, argued for an immediate military coup because only the military "have the force to silence the riotous confusion of our political habits." Elections? "The vote does not resolve anything because the people are not given the means to choose decent individuals." [5]

Most of the UDN was willing to wait for the results of the election, although pessimism ran high in party circles. At the national convention in July, for example, the UDN leader, João Agripino, painted a lugubrious picture of the misuse of liberty in "free" Brazil—it was liberty to "corrupt" and "steal," and he suggested that "it would be better to live cleanly in jail than to be free in this rottenness." He held out a thread of hope, however: "We have confidence in the Brazilian people's capacity to react and to recuperate morally." [6]

Afonso Arinos, a moderate UDN leader, typified the attempt to soften the image of the party and thereby widen its appeal. But his language itself showed how remote were the chances for success. The UDN was not "a retrograde party," he argued. "We harbor no hate and we are ready to extend a brotherly hand to those who join with us in the necessary national union, based on an agreement to reject crime and rottenness." There was no response.[7]

Távora's campaign emphasized the familiar moralistic appeals of the UDN, but the candidate adopted a different approach to economic and social problems than had Eduardo Gomes in the election campaigns of 1945 and 1950. Távora promised to retain the social welfare laws, whereas in 1950 Gomes had seemed to advocate repeal of the minimum wage law. But Távora's approach to economic policy was timid. "The principal activity of a government is fiscalizing [*fiscalizadora*]," he emphasized, explaining that the government must aim at "the equilibrium necessary for the progress of the nation." [8]

The contrast with Kubitschek's campaign was striking. Instead of talking in terms of "equilibrium," the PSD-PTB candidate urged a speedup in Brazil's industrialization. The effort would require the maximum participation of both the private and the public sectors, he argued, urging massive public investment in the areas where bottlenecks had long been evident—power and transportation. He also appealed to the democratic sentiments of those middle-class voters (including many military officers) who were anxious that Brazil remain on the constitutional path after the trauma of Vargas' fall.[9]

The Café Filho government was determined to proceed with the elections, despite the open demands by the "golpistas" (those favoring a *golpe* or coup) that only a suspension of the elections could keep the "Vargas gang" from returning to power.[10] On September 5, President Café Filho confessed that his government had made no attempt to be popular but had intended only to carry out a few essential short-term measures. Undoubtedly economic stabilization was uppermost in his mind. He explained that his government had not had the time to attack the basic problems. That would have to be left to the new government to be elected on October 3. Café Filho pleaded for optimism. As if to refute the golpistas he declared, "Fear and pessimism build nothing." He made explicit his government's pledge to transfer power to its legally elected successors: "The government exhorts the electorate to join in meetings and to march to the polls on October 3 in the certainty that respect will be shown for the verdict of this national judgment in which the only judge will be the people." He repeated this pledge in equally unequivocal language on October 1. Equally important, Café Filho's War Minister, General Lott, was known to favor "legality" and was an important barrier to the campaign efforts of those military officers who favored a coup.[11]

On October 3 the voters went to the polls and elected Kubitschek and Goulart. The vote itself was relatively close. Kubitschek received 36 percent of the vote, while Juarez Távora received 30 percent, Adhemar de Barros 26 percent and Plínio Salgado, the also-ran fascist candidate, 8 percent. Juscelino had a clear plurality, but his vote was little more than a third of the total national vote. He ran breathtakingly well in Minas Gerais, where the PSD machine performed with its expected efficiency. In Minas Kubitschek won 713,113 votes, as compared to Vargas' mere 418,194 votes in 1950 (when the total vote in Minas was actually larger than in 1955). Kubitschek's performance in other major states was less impressive. In São Paulo, for example, he gained only 240,940 votes, slightly more than one-eighth of the total vote in that state, which had given 867,320 to Adhemar de Barros and 626,627 to Juarez Távora. The electoral pact with the PTB had given Kubitschek minimal help in São Paulo and Rio de Janeiro. Elsewhere in the country the PSD produced the votes which gave Kubitschek a national plurality.

João Goulart won the vice presidency with a larger vote than Kubitschek. His total was 3,591,409, as against Kubitschek's 3,077,411. But Goulart's margin of victory over Milton Campos, Juarez Távora's running mate, was only slightly over 200,000, whereas Kubitschek's margin over Távora was almost 470,000.[12]

Kubitschek was a minority President-elect. His percentage of the total vote (36 percent) was significantly lower than Vargas' in 1950 (49 percent) or Dutra's in 1945 (55 percent). Even his total vote of 3,077,411, in spite of the growth of the electorate, was less than Vargas' in 1950 (3,849,040), or even Dutra's in 1945 (3,251,507). It was clear that Adhemar de Barros' candidacy had cut deeply into Kubitschek's expected vote, especially in São Paulo.

Inauguration or Coup?

The advocates of a coup took up the cry as the results began to come in. Carlos Lacerda appealed to "those who have in their hands the power to decide the question. It is enough for them to listen to the voice of their patriotism and not to those who talk about legality in order to deliver Brazil to the law-breakers and those who commit the worst of all crimes which is to deceive the people with the money robbed from them." It was the Communists who had elected Kubitschek and Goulart, Lacerda claimed.[13] The "Brazilian Anti-Communist Crusade" ran newspaper advertisements demanding that Juscelino and Jango must be deprived of the fruits of the election. It was essential they not be permitted to assume positions for which they were "not duly elected" because, in addition to being supported by the Communists and lacking an absolute majority, their votes came from an electorate "made up of an ignorant, suffering, disillusioned mass, wrought up by the most sordid demagoguery and poisoned by the destructive propaganda of the Communist Party." The "Movement of August 24," as the statement put it frankly, "had failed." [14]

The key figure, as everyone now recognized, was General Lott, the War Minister. On October 8, Lott made it known that he would abide by the Constitution and endorse the inauguration of the elected candidates.[15] The UDN voted to take the issue to the Electoral Tribunal, arguing that under the Constitution the winning candidates needed an absolute majority of the vote. But this protest had proved ineffective after Vargas' election in 1950 and offered little promise of greater success now. The Congress was equally useless as an escape for the anti-getulistas. In September it had defeated a proposed Constitutional amendment which would have thrown the presidential election into the Chamber of Deputies if no candidate received an absolute majority. The anti-Vargas leaders fell into deep despair. At the end of October, Octávio Mangabeira gave an interview in which he reviewed the functioning of Brazilian democracy since Getúlio's deposition in 1945, concluding that the country's "weakened institutions" could not "handle crises of all the kinds which they are expected to survive." [16]

Extremists such as Lacerda had already given up faith in "legal" means to block the return of the getulistas. Lacerda was in contact with a group of junior military officers who hoped to push the higher military into intervening directly. First they tried publishing a document (the "Brandi" letter) purporting to prove that Goulart had bought arms from Perón in 1953 in order to equip workers' militia. An Army probe found the letter to be a forgery. Furthermore, Perón himself had been overthrown in Argentina in mid-September, thus reducing the scare value of charges of "Peronism."

On November 1 one of the leaders of the military conspiracy made a public appeal to his colleagues to intervene. It signaled the beginning of a new and more critical phase in the struggle between the golpistas and the pro-legality camp. In his funeral oration at the burial of General Canrobert Pereira da Costa, Colonel Mamede, one of the signatories of the colonel's memorandum of February 1954, praised in extravagant terms the dead general's courage in having led the movement against Vargas in August 1954.[17] He attacked the politicians who use "immoral and corrupt pseudo-legality" to justify "their appetites for power and command." Leaving no doubt about the current situation, he suggested pointedly that it would be "an indisputable democratic lie" if a presidential regime, which has "the enormous sum of power that is concentrated in the hands of the Executive," should allow "a victory of the minority" in the "inauguration of the highest official of the Nation." [18]

The speech angered General Lott. Mamede had gone too far; he must be disciplined. This step was all the more necessary from Lott's viewpoint because only two weeks earlier he had forced the resignation of General Zenóbio da Costa, who had publicly demanded the inauguration of the elected candidates. To let Mamede's pronouncement go unpunished would therefore undermine Lott's effort to prevent *any* political statements by Army officers. But the War Minister had a difficulty: Mamede was on the staff of the Higher War College (*Escola Superior de Guerra*) and was subject to the direct authority of the President, not the War Minister. Lott telephoned the military aides of the President asking that Mamede be disciplined.[19]

At the same time, Lott and the other military ministers tried to demonstrate their impartiality by requesting the President to suppress the "Communist press" because of its "provocations and continuous insults directed at the Armed Forces." [20] The President consulted his Justice Minister, Prado Kelly, who confirmed Café Filho's own judgment that such a measure would be unconstitutional. The ideas of Lott and Café Filho on how to preserve "legality" were already diverging. There was good reason to believe, however, that they could have continued to work together, as they had since early 1955, to ensure the peaceful transfer of the presidency and vice presidency to the two men who had won the elections. That possibility was cut short by the President's weak heart.

On the morning of November 3, Café Filho suffered a cardiovascular attack and entered the hospital; the doctors prescribed complete rest. Members of the Cabinet continued to consult the President in his hospital room, but it soon became clear that Café Filho would have to delegate his presidential powers, at least temporarily. On November

8, Carlos Luz, president of the Chamber of Deputies (and therefore next in succession under the Constitution), assumed power as Acting President. Luz was known as a less neutral figure than Café Filho, and had been a leader of the dissident PSD faction which had opposed Kubitschek's nomination in February. He was also said to enjoy poor relations with General Lott, whose request for the disciplining of Colonel Mamede still awaited action.[21]

On November 9, Carlos Luz held his first cabinet meeting. When Lott indicated that he wished to speak, presumably about the Mamede case, Luz dismissed the meeting and drew the War Minister aside to discuss the matter in private. When Luz refused to accede to Lott's demand for Mamede's transfer, the War Minister resigned in protest. On November 10, Luz replaced Lott with General Fiuza de Castro, who reportedly began drawing up a long list of military commanders to be transferred.[22]

At this point subsequent events become comprehensible only if one remembers the political atmosphere in which this seemingly minor administrative struggle took place. Since Kubitschek's nomination by the PSD in February, there had been a campaign to suspend the Constitution, cancel the elections, and launch what Carlos Lacerda called an "Emergency Regime." The campaign was led by the intransigent anti-getulistas who considered Vargas' fall in 1954 as the beginning of a "revolution" (the "Movement of August 24") which would purge Brazil of the "malefactors," meaning the politicians who had remained influential despite Vargas' deposition in 1945 and who had boldly returned to power in 1950. In effect, it was an argument in favor of excluding from power the PSD and PTB, which could command the majority of the vote in national elections. The obvious beneficiary would be the UDN.[23]

The UDN leadership did not publicly favor a coup to prevent the inauguration of Kubitschek and Goulart. Their attitude was equivocal. Officially, the party followed the strategy which it had used after Vargas' election in 1950: an attempt to argue before the Supreme Electoral Tribunal (which would meet in December to certify the winners) that the election was invalid because no candidates had received an absolute majority. No one, including the UDN leaders, had any illusions about the success of this tactic. In reality, they knew that

Lacerda was right: the only means of blocking the inauguration of Kubitschek and Goulart was a military coup.[24]

Yet a military coup would be the negation of the liberal tradition in whose defense the UDN had been founded. Politicians such as Octávio Mangabeira, one of the UDN's founders and now a member of the splinter right-wing *Partido Libertador,* and Afonso Arinos de Melo Franco, a distinguished constitutional lawyer from the UDN, found themselves in a moral dilemma: depressed by the thought of another presidential term for the PTB-PSD coalition and all it represented, they were also repelled by the crudity of the pro-coup advocates. If Lacerda's language was exhilarating, its ultimate implications were disturbing. The dilemma of the UDN was another chapter in the history of the anguished relationship between the liberal constitutionalists and the military. When was the suspension of the democratic process justified in the defense of democracy, as *they* understood it? And would reliance on military intervention infect Brazil with the disease of "caudillismo" from which her Spanish American neighbors had suffered for so long? [25]

As the tension intensified after the election, the UDN's equivocal position became increasingly obvious. In late October the UDN was the only major party which did not make a public statement opposing a coup. It also did not choose to follow the lead of its defeated candidate, Juarez Távora, who issued a statement wishing success to the victors and renouncing the idea of a coup. After the Mamede speech, Lacerda grew bolder. On November 4 he published a lead editorial in his newspaper *Tribuna da Imprensa* with the unmistakable signal: "This is the hour of decision for the Armed Forces." On November 9, at the moment of Lott's confrontation with Carlos Luz, the *Tribuna da Imprensa* announced the political death knell of Kubitschek and Goulart: "These men cannot take office, they should not take office, they will not take office." [26] Rio de Janeiro was alive with rumors of connections between Acting President Luz and the golpistas led by Lacerda and junior officers such as Mamede. In this atmosphere Lott's replacement was immediately interpreted as a sign that Luz's dedication to "legality" was weaker than that of Café Filho.

Lott himself was resentful over his departure from the War Ministry. He had tried hard to control the extremists on both sides—the Communists on the left and the anti-democrats on the right. He had wanted to suppress the Communist press and discipline Mamede. Both measures depended on the President; neither had been carried out.

But it was not the Communists who were the real target of the golpistas. As Lacerda explained in late October, "What we fear is that General Lott will deliver power to Jango Goulart, so that Jango Goulart can govern this country with a fifth column." [27] On the propriety of Goulart's assuming high office, Lott, along with other centrist officers, had mixed feelings. Lott had been uneasy about Goulart's nomination in April, knowing the strong opposition to the former Labor Minister, especially at the level of the colonels. But the War Minister was a stubborn devotee of the principle of legality. Goulart was a legally nominated candidate, and Lott repeatedly guaranteed to preserve the Army's "non-political" role. His promise had rapidly become, in effect, a pledge to *enforce* the election results.[28]

Furthermore, Lott was receptive to the arguments of Kubitschek supporters, both in and out of the officer corps, who pointed out that the President-elect's fate was tied to that of Goulart, since both were "minority" victors. It was both or neither; there could be no "selective" veto. Since Kubitschek was patently a political moderate and a "getulista" only by very general association, this argument carried weight with the pro-legality military, who were loosely organized into a *Movimento Militar Constitucionalista*.[29]

There was also a personal dimension to Lott's agony of decision. Although he prided himself on promoting the Army's "non-political" role, Lott was a proud general, not impervious to suggestions that he was the man to save Brazilian democracy in a moment of peril.

The Military Intervenes: A Coup for "Legality"

Convinced that Acting President Luz was in league with the conspirators, Lott decided to stage his own "preventive coup." On November 10, the day his replacement was made public, the former War Minister hurriedly mobilized the Army command in Rio de Janeiro. On November 11, Army units occupied all principal government buildings, radio stations, and newspapers. It was a military coup in the classic style.[30]

Having deposed the Acting President, General Lott immediately announced that the president of the Congress and the president of the Supreme Court had declared their "solidarity with the movement intended to return the situation to that of a normal constitutional regime." [31] Although Lott had the support of the Army in Rio and the neighboring commands, the Navy and Air Force Ministers denounced his action as "illegal and subversive." Their resistance proved half-hearted, however, when Army units surrounded the dissident air and naval bases.

The target of the coup—Acting President Luz—fled from the Army's grasp onto a rebel cruiser, the "Tamandaré," which hurriedly steamed out of Rio carrying a curious collection that included several government ministers as well as erstwhile leading golpistas such as Lacerda. The cruiser escaped unscathed from the fire of shore batteries as it left port and headed for Santos, evidently with the intention of setting up a government in São Paulo. While Luz and his entourage cruised at sea, broadcasting back dispatches asserting their right to remain as the legal government, General Lott moved quickly to legitimize Luz's deposition.[32]

The Congress went into session immediately. On November 11 the Chamber of Deputies voted 185–72 to install in the presidency Nereu Ramos, the speaker of the Senate and next in line for succession under the Constitution. The vote followed strictly party lines: the PSD and PTB supporting the measure and the UDN opposing.[33] The congressional action had a number of interesting features.

First, the narrow party lines of the vote emphasized the partisan character of the conflict. Although expressed as legalism versus "golpismo," the issue reduced itself in the vote to a victory of the majority coalition over the embittered minority. Second, the military intervention gave the UDN defenders of Café Filho and Carlos Luz (neither of whom was, ironically enough, from the UDN—Café Filho being of the PSP and Carlos Luz of the PSD) the opportunity to turn the tables: it was the "legalists" who had staged a "brutal" coup against the legitimate President. With the worrisome question of the presidential succession settled beyond doubt—the full prestige of the Army was now committed to the inauguration of Kubitschek and Goulart—the anti-Vargas forces could vent their frustrations in bitter complaints against the "unjustified" interruption of the legal process.[34]

Third, the constitutionality of the "preventive" coup remained murky. The Congress voted to recognize Nereu Ramos as the new President but did not vote to impeach Carlos Luz, who therefore remained president of the Chamber of Deputies. Furthermore, the Congress did not vote any sanctions against Luz, Café Filho or any of their ministers. In short, there was no attempt to establish proof that either Luz or Café Filho or any of their ministers were guilty of the plot whose prevention was the justification of Lott's coup. The Congress voted to recognize without fully legitimizing a transfer of power imposed by the military. The result was a legacy of bitterness among the anti-getulistas over the ambiguous legal "cover" which the two majority parties had voted.

In the judgment of General Lott and a majority of the higher military, there had been on November 9–10 a grave danger that the Acting President was in league with the golpistas and planned to block the inauguration of Kubitschek and Goulart.[35] Given the braggadocio of Lacerda and the boldness of his allies among the military, it was not easy to assess the real danger. At the minimum, Luz made no effort to dispel the rumors of a coup. Furthermore, it was a grave error on Luz's part to allow the War Minister to resign over the case of Colonel Mamede. On the other hand, Lott and his fellow generals made no effort to prove their charges of an imminent coup against Kubitschek and Goulart. Perhaps they feared the inevitable political embroilment in trying to document the golpistas' intentions. In any case, assertion was not replaced by evidence. As a result there was long argument over the shaky legal foundation for their "preventive" coup to preserve legality.

The deposed Acting President took advantage of the ambiguous legal situation to defend himself and his ministers. On November 14, Carlos Luz, fresh from his brief voyage on the "Tamandaré," spoke in the Chamber of Deputies. He vigorously denied that there had been any justification for Lott's charges that the Mamede case offered proof of designs for a coup within government circles. Luz bowed to the logic of events, however, by resigning as speaker of the Chamber, although he retained his seat as deputy.[36]

One week later the succession crisis erupted anew. On November 21 Café Filho emerged from the hospital and announced that he intended to resume the presidential powers which had been taken from his interim successor. The constitutional issue was once again forced. The Army again surrounded government buildings; the sequence of November 11 was repeated. The Chamber of Deputies responded on November 22 by voting to disqualify Café Filho from office and confirming Nereu Ramos as President until Kubitschek's inauguration in January. Two days later the Congress voted to approve a request from the military ministers for a 30-day state of siege—a modified form of martial law. In late December the state of siege was extended for another month.

After the furor over the conspiracies and counter-coups of November died down, Kubitschek and Goulart sought to reassure centrist opinion that their enemies' fears were ungrounded. Goulart denied any ties with Communists, a sin of which he was perennially accused. The Labor Party leadership emphasized the party's democratic nature and repudiated the suggestion that Communist Party endorsement of the Kubitschek-Goulart ticket had involved any electoral bargain.

The state of siege powers were exercised discreetly, with irregular press censorship continuing until the inauguration of Kubitschek and Goulart on January 31, 1956. Lacerda, the fearless advocate of strong measures before November 11, had disembarked from the voyage of the "Tamandaré" to take up immediate asylum in the Cuban embassy. He thence retreated into a year of exile, during which he continued his attacks on the "corrupters" and "malefactors" whose return he had been unable to prevent. Lacerda and the conspiring anti-getulistas were able to provoke a coup; but it was a coup against them. They had succeeded in proving one significant point: Brazilian democracy was not yet able, after the political trauma of Vargas' last year in office, to transfer power—the ultimate test of the system's viability under strain—by normal constitutional processes.

In terms of political conflict, the lessons of November were striking. The liberal opposition, which had seemingly gained so much with Vargas' death in August 1954, lost any short-term possibility of an extra-legal path to power. The military had tried to pull back from the temptation to pass their own judgment on the politicians. Lott's intention was to underwrite the rules of the electoral process. But the irony of his devotion to "legality" lay in the fact that "legality" had to be guaranteed by the arbitrary act of a military coup. The result was the creation of a new division within the officer corps: the division between the "Movement of August 24" and the "group of November 11." The contrast between the two was sharpened by their respective civilian apologists. The anti-getulista civilians promoted the August 24 group as their military arm; the PTB and PSD militants, as well as the left, championed Lott as the leader of the November 11 group. The total effect was to deepen the uneasiness among centrist officers about their proper role as the "non-political" guardians of Brazilian democracy.

The interim between Vargas' death and Kubitschek's inauguration had dramatized several features of Brazilian politics. First, the election of October had shown again the inability of the liberal opposition (identified, above all, with the UDN) to win a national election, even when their enemies were divided. This electoral weakness strengthened the hands of those among their ranks who favored a coup. Second, the higher military, although suspicious of the new populist style, were not prepared to hand over power to the anti-getulistas. This was demonstrated in November 1955. Third, the presence of Adhemar de Barros in the election had brought the PSD and the PTB together more closely, thereby reinforcing the curious alliance of the "ins" created by Vargas. The effect was to preclude any remaining chance, however slight, that the PTB might develop into an independent leftist party. Instead, it became increasingly the manipulable collection of "ins" among the organized working class and their government-appointed leaders.

Attacking Inflation: Accomplishments and Limitations

The Café Filho regime inherited the difficult economic situation which had caused Vargas to fluctuate more and more frantically between a moderate and an extreme policy. Vargas had in effect given up any attempt at stabilization by his wage decree of May 1, 1954. Furthermore, the boycott of Brazilian coffee in the New York market in response to Brazil's high minimum price had exacerbated the balance of payments problem in the last three months. In August Vargas' government finally ended its unrealistic minimum coffee price policy in an effort to regain its dollar earnings. The new government of Café Filho therefore inherited a financial crisis of alarming proportions. It should be emphasized that industrial production, both of capital goods and consumer goods, had continued to rise rapidly in the early 1950's. The problems that had proved to be beyond Vargas' ability to solve, and thereby contributed to the political crisis that cost him his life, were inflation at home and payments deficits abroad. It was these two problems in the area of economic policy—essentially financial problems—that the caretaker government of Café Filho set out to tackle.[37]

Café Filho's first Finance Minister was Eugênio Gudin, a long-time critic of the Brazilian government's unwillingness to undertake rigorous anti-inflation measures. In his maiden speech as minister, Gudin promised to carry out the Aranha stabilization plan which Vargas had scuttled for lack of political support. Gudin painted a grim picture of the financial tangle left by Vargas. He pledged to cut the government deficits, to which he attributed major responsibility for inflation.[38] His anti-inflation team included as director of the monetary authority (SUMOC), Octávio Govêa de Bulhões.[39] Gudin knew that the success of his efforts would depend in part upon the attitude of the U.S. government and the International Monetary Fund. In September, soon after Café Filho formed his Cabinet, the new Finance Minister traveled to Washington for the annual meetings of the World Bank and the IMF (Gudin was a member of the IMF's board of governors). Although he denied that his trip would include any negotiations with IMF authorities on Brazil's financial plight, Gudin undoubtedly used the opportunity to impress upon his colleagues in Washington the seriousness of the anti-inflation program he was about to launch at home.

"Nationalist" critics in Brazil seized upon his trip to attack Gudin viciously for his "begging" mission, charging that his orthodox monetarist policies would result in economic stagnation. Whatever may have been Gudin's own expectations, he did not in fact apply measures that constricted the economy to the degree his detractors on the left predicted. Gudin himself complained that he was saddled with a disastrously expensive coffee support program that canceled the savings from his cuts in other areas of public expenditure. Soon after taking office, Gudin tightened the money supply sharply by raising the minimum cash balance required of commercial banks and by requiring, further, that half of all their new deposits had to be deposited with SUMOC, the national monetary authority. The effects were immediate and painful. In November 1954 two banks in São Paulo closed their doors, and the Bank of Brazil had to make special advances to other São Paulo banks to allay the incipient panic. By early 1955 the Governor of São Paulo, Jânio Quadros, was negotiating with Café Filho for a change in the tight credit policy that had caused a serious slowdown in the capital goods industries centered in São Paulo. Fearful that the President's commitment to the anti-inflation program was weakening, Gudin resigned in protest in April 1955, along with the president of the Bank of Brazil, Clemente Mariani.[40]

The new Finance Minister was José Maria Whitaker, an ancient Paulista politician who had been Getúlio Vargas' first Finance Minister after the Revolution of 1930. Whitaker immediately eased the monetary policy by no longer requiring banks to deposit half of their own new deposits with SUMOC. This change in credit policy led to the departure in May 1955 of the last member of Gudin's anti-inflation team, Bulhões, who resigned in protest from his position as director of SUMOC. Whitaker hoped to balance the effects of his easier credit policy by his suspension in April of the coffee purchase program. But that action, taken in his first month as minister, had provoked violent protests from coffee growers. Whitaker planned to mollify them by instituting a radically simplified exchange policy which would eliminate the "exchange confiscation" (*confisco cambial*) that gave coffee brokers (and thus coffee growers) a lower cruzeiro return for their coffee than the equivalent free dollar rate.

Whitaker's exchange reform, introduced at the end of September 1955, was never approved, however. Café Filho was hesitant to endorse the surrender of what had proved to be a very powerful instrument (i.e., "exchange confiscation") for the allocation of foreign exchange. Indeed, this device was the closest Brazil had come to a state export monopoly and it had turned out to be a useful method of diverting part of the exchange earnings from Brazil's principal export into areas of high-priority investment as determined by the government. The Treasury also gained considerable revenue by the premium earned from the system introduced in 1953 of auctioning off foreign exchange. Thus the Café Filho regime found persuasive reasons for caution in scrapping the exchange system that Finance Minister Whitaker and the IMF (which had worked carefully with Whitaker in drafting the reform proposed in September 1955) wished to simplify drastically.

Café Filho explained to his Finance Minister that the Congress would have to be consulted. Pressed hard by Whitaker, the President had put the matter to his cabinet and ended by endorsing the view of his military ministers, who considered "inopportune a measure of such significance in the last days of a transitional government." Whitaker promptly resigned and was replaced by Mário Câmara, a high bureaucrat in the Brazilian Treasury.[41]

Câmara continued the easier monetary policy of Whitaker, and by the end of 1955 industrial production had recovered from the mild decline earlier in the year. Consumer goods production had suffered relatively little, and the recovery in the capital goods industries helped to bring about a total increase of about 4 percent in the industrial sector, as contrasted with an increase of about 10 percent in 1954.

In the area of price stability the Café Filho government had been able to demonstrate relatively little immediate success. The cost of living in Rio de Janeiro increased 26 percent in 1954 and 19 percent in 1955. The inflationary pressure continued because wages and government deficits continued to rise. The fact was that the interim regime was not prepared to pursue the severely constrictionist monetary policies that might have slowed down price increases but would also probably have caused a serious drop in levels of production. Café Filho saw his government as a transitional government that lacked authority and time to carry out any vast changes in economic policy.

Furthermore, the Finance Ministry simply did not have under its control total government expenditure (there were semi-autonomous government agencies whose budgets could not be cut back by the Finance Minister on short notice). In fact, current government expenditure in 1955 was even higher than it had been in 1954. And there were previous decisions of the Vargas presidency that seriously limited the Café Filho government's room for maneuver during its short life. The wage increase of May 1, 1954, for example, could not be revoked, and it encouraged other wage earners to press their demands. Also, the introduction of the auction system to allocate foreign exchange in 1953 caused producers to pay a premium for imported goods, both raw materials and equipment, thus raising domestic costs and necessitating further price increases.

On the balance of payments front the caretaker government was able to show more impressive results. In 1954, which had been a bad year because of difficulties in coffee marketing, Brazil ended with a deficit on current account of $230 million. In 1955, however, Brazil virtually balanced her current account, while at the same time liquidating more than $200 million of short-term indebtedness. This was achieved in spite of a fall in coffee and cotton prices. The method chosen was the draconian step of sharply cutting imports, which in 1955 dropped by $409 million, or almost 30 percent from the previous year. This was a policy which could not long be pursued without seriously damaging the country's economic development. Nevertheless, it offered the opportunity to interrupt Brazil's recent record of steadily rising indebtedness.

The Café Filho government proved that it was not afraid to make one far-reaching decision on economic policy. In early 1955 the financial authorities issued a decree (SUMOC Instruction #113) favoring foreign investors who would agree to import industrial equipment for the production of goods given a priority classification by the government. This overture to foreign capital was the result of Finance Minister Gudin's firm belief, often stated in the past, that Brazil badly needed foreign investment and must be willing to give it special incentives. This SUMOC directive, along with Gudin's willingness to cooperate with the IMF in a stabilization program, angered the economic nationalists, who had become steadily more vocal since Vargas' election campaign in 1950.[42]

V

Years of Confidence: The Kubitschek Era

Few Brazilian presidents have taken office under less auspicious political circumstances than Juscelino Kubitschek. Although he had been legally elected, his inauguration had to be guaranteed by a "preventive" coup. The political divisions left by the fall of Vargas and the ensuing crisis extended far into the military, where an apparent minority of anti-getulista officers were known to be bitter over General Lott's coup. Yet Kubitschek became one of the two presidents since 1945 to have served a full term. How did he succeed, when failure seemed so certain? [1]

Juscelino Kubitschek was born in Diamantina, one of the most traditional towns of Minas Gerais. His mother was the granddaughter of a Bohemian immigrant who migrated to Brazil in the middle of the nineteenth century. Juscelino was trained as a doctor and pursued his profession briefly in the state militia of Minas Gerais. His real vocation, however, was politics. From the outset of his political career he was intimately associated with the closely knit political elite of Minas Gerais. One of his chief patrons was Benedito Valladares, long-time associate of Getúlio Vargas and a founder of the PSD. With Valladares' support, Kubitschek became Mayor of Belo Horizonte in 1940, a post he retained until the purge of mayors following Vargas' deposition in October 1945. The same election which brought Vargas back to the presidency made Kubitschek Governor of Minas Gerais. As Governor he gained a reputation as a builder, completing an impressive number of projects in the area of transport facilities and power-generating capacity. It was from the governorship that Kubitschek launched his successful bid for the presidential nomination.[2]

Governing Minas Gerais was excellent preparation for the greater task of governing Brazil. As the most important state which did not border on the seacoast, Minas offered in microcosm many of the problems (stemming from inadequate social capital) that were characteristic of Brazil as a whole. Furthermore, Kubitschek was able to bring to the presidency the solid backing of one of the most cohesive political forces in Brazil, the PSD of Minas Gerais.

The Economics of Confidence

The Kubitschek period became known for its economic accomplishments, and it is there that one must begin in analyzing the presidency. The ebullient President promised "fifty years' progress in five," and there can be little doubt that from 1956 to 1961 Brazil did record remarkable real economic growth. The basis for the surge was an extraordinary expansion of industrial output. Between 1955 and 1961 industrial production grew 80 percent (in constant prices), with even higher percentages recorded by the steel industry (100 percent), mechanical industries (125 percent), electrical and communications industries (380 percent), and the transportation equipment industries (600 percent). From 1957 to 1961 the real rate of growth was seven percent per year, and nearly 4 percent per capita. For the decade of the 1950's, Brazil's per capita real growth was approximately three times that of the rest of Latin America.[3]

How was this high rate of growth achieved? In part it was the result of favorable basic economic circumstances: a large domestic market, more capacity in key areas such as iron and steel production than any other Latin American country, and a readiness of foreign businessmen to invest in Brazil. Yet it was the dynamic role of the Kubitschek government that served to stimulate and channel the forces of economic growth.

In terms of the three formulae of economic development differentiated earlier, the Kubitschek government embraced a policy of developmentalist nationalism. It was a pragmatic approach to an already mixed economy, aimed at achieving the most rapid rate of growth possible by encouraging expansion in both the private and the public sectors. The guiding emphasis was on basic industries. In essence, this was a new phase of the process of import substitution which began around the turn of the century, accelerated in the 1930's, and had produced virtual self-sufficiency in light consumer goods by the mid-1950's.

The later Dutra years had seen a new phase of the process of "spontaneous" industrialization. During the truncated Vargas presidency there emerged a development *policy* intended to direct and guide the further industrialization made possible by the exchange policy and the favorable turn in the terms of trade after 1949. During the Kubitschek years import substitution would have to enter yet another phase, with greater emphasis on the creation of capital goods industries.

Kubitschek had outlined his strategy of economic development during the campaign. Even before his inauguration, the President-elect published a preview of his "National Plan for Development," which had been drafted by a group of young technocrats on whom the candidate relied for advice during the campaign.[4] Once in office, Kubitschek announced his strategy clearly and frequently.

First, he made a direct appeal to private investors, both domestic and foreign. For Brazilian businessmen his government offered liberal credit policies and the promise to maintain a high level of domestic demand, thereby assuring profitable markets. In order to guide private investment in basic industries, the government established "executive groups" in industries such as automobiles and electrical goods, which saw to it that government regulations aided and did not hinder rapid expansion of capacity.[5]

Foreign firms were given a special incentive to invest in Brazilian industry. In order to encourage foreign firms to bring into Brazil badly needed industrial equipment, the government made liberal use of SUMOC Directive #113, issued during the Café Filho government. This regulation exempted foreign firms from the need to provide foreign exchange "cover" for importing machinery, as long as the firms were associated with Brazilian enterprises—an advantage not enjoyed by all-Brazilian firms. The Kubitschek government also made repeated assurances of fair treatment in matters such as profit remittances and taxes. The appeal to private investors, foreign and domestic, was very successful, especially in key industries such as vehicle production, where virtual self-sufficiency was achieved in only five years, with production reaching 100,000 vehicles a year by the end of the Kubitschek presidency. In sum, the Kubitschek government's appeal to the private sector was amply rewarded.[6]

The Kubitschek strategy by no means relied exclusively on the private sector, however. The government undertook a stepped-up program of public investment aimed at overcoming structural bottlenecks in the areas of transportation and power production. Here the government was able to capitalize on a set of projects and institutions which it had inherited from the early 1950's. The Joint United States-Brazil Commission of 1951–53 had outlined a program of public investment, which had been only partially enacted during the Vargas presidency and had been slowed down further during the stabilization efforts of the Café Filho interlude. There were also the technical studies of the Joint Working Group, made up of representatives from the Economic Commission for Latin America and the National Bank for Economic Development. The latter institution was an excellent vehicle for increased public investment, since it enjoyed certain privileged sources of tax revenue earmarked for expanding electric power production and highway capacity. Furthermore, the Kubitschek government could look to expanding sources of public funds abroad, such as the United States government and international lending agencies. These sources were important because they helped to provide a balance in Brazil's use of foreign funds. While Brazil gained foreign private investment for her domestic private sector, she also obtained foreign public investment for her domestic public sector.[7]

Guiding the entire Kubitschek strategy of economic development was a set of overall production "targets," spelled out formally in 1958. This was not a full-fledged plan, but rather a set of goals toward which the designated sectors were to aim. In implementing its program the government was pragmatic, emphasizing the growth of basic industries, and choosing virtually to ignore such areas as agriculture and education, which had been nominally included in the Target Program.[8]

Symbols and Strategies

The Kubitschek strategy deserves the label "developmentalist nationalism" rather than simply "developmentalism," because of the manner in which it was presented to the Brazilian public. Underlying the government's statements and actions was an appeal to a sense of nationalism. It was Brazil's "destiny" to undertake a "drive to development." The solution to Brazil's underdevelopment, with all its social injustice and political tension, must be rapid industrialization.

The success of Kubitschek's economic policy was a direct result of his success in maintaining political stability. He was able to do so only by a political *tour de force*. The secret lay in Kubitschek's remarkable ability to find something for everyone, while avoiding any direct conflict with his enemies. This political style involved no fundamental changes; instead, Kubitschek exploited the system itself in order to win support for—or in many cases to buy off opposition to—his programs. This turned out to mean capitalizing on the network of getulista alliances without the authoritarianism or populism to which Vargas had resorted at various stages in his career.[9]

The essence of Kubitschek's style was improvisation. Enthusiasm was his principal weapon, reflecting an infectious confidence in Brazil's future as a great power. His basic strategy was to press for rapid industrialization, attempting to convince each power group that they had something to gain, or at least nothing to lose. This required a delicate political balancing act.

First, Kubitschek endeavored to generate a sense of self-confidence among Brazilians. Equally important, he stressed a faith in the democratic process. He was both a narrowly elected minority President seeking to broaden his political support, and an ambitious leader attempting to secure his place in history by seizing the leadership of Brazil's drive to industrialize—a role first claimed by Vargas.[10]

The symbol which Kubitschek chose was the new inland capital of Brasília. During the election campaign he had promised to carry out the provision for the new capital which had been written into the Constitution of 1891. Discussed for over a century, the project was usually dismissed as utopian or prohibitively expensive. When the new President put the matter to the Congress for direct vote in 1956, however, the project was readily approved, almost to the disbelief of the Congress itself. Kubitschek plunged into the construction with indefatigable enthusiasm, commissioning a world-renowned Brazilian architect, Oscar Niemeyer, and an equally famous Brazilian city planner, Lucio Costa. Work proceeded at a break-neck pace, generating a sense of excitement among all classes of Brazilians, who looked upon the construction of a new capital in the neglected interior as the sign of Brazil's coming of age. It gave the rest of Kubitschek's economic program, the details of which remained unknown to much of the public, an immediately understandable symbol.[11]

The building of Brasília served other functions as well. It diverted attention from many difficult social and economic problems, such as reform of the agrarian system and the universities. In both cases, optimists in the Kubitschek regime argued that the mere construction of the new capital would have side effects leading to the solution of the problems in question. In the agrarian sector, for example, it was argued that the construction of new roads leading to Brasília would open up previously uncultivated lands and ease the burden on the inefficient system of food distribution. In the educational sphere, enthusiasts of Brasília argued that the radically new university to be founded there would serve as a model for educational reform throughout the country. Invariably the emphasis was on transforming the approach to old problems by beginning afresh on the desolate site of the new capital.

Kubitschek carefully adapted his developmentalist nationalism to gain maximum sympathy from each class. Among the industrialists he could expect to find keen support. The beginning of his presidency coincided with the emergence of a group of more self-consciously political businessmen in São Paulo. In June of 1957 the National Confederation of Industry began publishing a monthly magazine which vigorously endorsed the industrialization program. These businessmen were the spiritual heirs of Roberto Simonsen, the pioneer Paulista industrialist; their support indicated that, although Kubitschek had earned relatively few votes in São Paulo, he could count on the "national bourgeoisie" of that state.[12] His government offered businessmen easy credit and continued protection from foreign imports, thus promising them large profits in a rapidly growing domestic market. Some businessmen resented the favors granted foreign investors, especially their advantage in importing equipment. But this dissatisfaction was relatively small, and was partially undercut by the legal requirement that foreign firms needed Brazilian partners.[13]

Brazilian landowners did not offer any major problem for Kubitschek's strategy. Coffee growers were treated to continuous government support, including new measures, largely unsuccessful, to arrest the decline in world coffee prices. Dissatisfaction caused by the system of "exchange confiscation" was allayed by periodic increases in the "bonus" paid to exporters.[14] As for other landowners, they had little reason to fear significant changes in Brazil's archaic pattern of land tenure. On the contrary, Kubitschek, like Vargas before him, never raised the land question in a way other than to suggest politically innocuous measures such as the expansion of rural credit, or the improvement of food distribution through the construction of new storage facilities. Having been trained in the political school of the PSD in Minas Gerais, Kubitschek was hardly inclined to tamper with the existing system of rural property.[15]

Toward the working class, Kubitschek adopted a cautious policy of generous wage settlements (dictated through the government labor tribunals set up by Vargas) and continued government stewardship of the labor union structure. In dealing with organized labor Kubitschek was able to rely upon his Vice President, João Goulart—the young populist politician who, as leader of the PTB, had regained much of the control over the labor union apparatus which he had first been given by Vargas. After his election as Vice President in 1955 (as running mate of Kubitschek), Goulart was able to resume his links with the Labor Ministry from which his resignation had been forced in 1954 by the Army. Insofar as Kubitschek himself resorted to a populist appeal to the mass voter, at least until 1959, it was on non-ideological issues such as Brasília.

The urban middle class was the sector Kubitschek had most difficulty in courting. His free-wheeling "developmentalism" seemed to carry with it many of the unsavory features of the Vargas era—corruption and political favoritism—that middle-class voters censured. They were torn between a sense of satisfaction with Brazil's economic progress, and a sense of shame over the "waste" and "corruption" that Kubitschek's UDN detractors claimed was a side product of monumental projects such as Brasília.[16] In general, however, there was little in Kubitschek's policies that threatened the status of the average middle-class city dweller, at least until inflation stepped up after 1959. Most important, Kubitschek's brand of nationalism was based on the Brazilian entrepreneurial and administrative elite, not on any mass movement. Kubitschek had made no attempt to merge leftist populism and developmentalist nationalism, a move which might be expected to unite the middle class and the military in opposition.

Finally, the President chose to make a special appeal to the intellectuals. The traditionalist intellectuals—those who at heart opposed all attempts to transform Brazil's agrarian-dominated export economy—were beyond the reach of any appeal Kubitschek might make. But many nationalist-minded intellectuals were attracted by the President's enthusiastic confidence in Brazil's future and his willingness to experiment in accelerating the process of economic change. There was a federally financed institute—Higher Institute of Brazilian Studies (*Instituto Superior de Estudos Brasileiros* or ISEB)—which became a mecca for research and teaching on Brazil's problems as conceived from the broad position of developmentalist-nationalism. The institute published a stream of books and lectures offering a rationale for industrialization and explaining the cause and effect of underdevelopment in every sector of the country's society and economy. The hundreds of younger Brazilians who attended the one-year course at the institute were profoundly influenced by the "developmentalist" mystique. Radical leftist intellectuals who were attracted to the economic formula of radical nationalism, on the other hand, were unsympathetic in principle to the Kubitschek policies; but their opposition was undercut, at least in the first three years of his presidency, by the evident success of his policies.[17]

Support and Opposition

In choosing his political strategy, Kubitschek had to concern himself with more than merely selling his strategy of economic development. He had also to worry about the continuing political feud between the heirs of Vargas and the anti-getulistas. Lott's preventive coup of November had insured Kubitschek's inauguration, but it also created a legacy of bitterness among the Vargas enemies who had despaired over the "failure" of the "Movement of August 24." In late January 1956, the Congress voted to continue the state of siege through the first month of the new administration.

Although Kubitschek appealed to his opponents to express their opposition by democratic means, within the first two weeks of his term a military revolt broke out. A group of right-wing Air Force officers established a rebel outpost at the remote Amazon air base of Jacareacanga. The collapse of the revolt at the end of February gave the President the occasion to declare an amnesty for all officers charged with "revolutionary acts" since the coup of the previous November.[18]

Throughout his Presidency Kubitschek courted the military with a variety of wiles. He was attentive to their demands for pay increases and modern equipment. In December 1956 he purchased for the Navy's amusement a cast-off British aircraft carrier which was refitted at considerable expense. The Navy, which, along with the Air Force, harbored more conservative political views than the Army, was delighted to receive the new ship. Unfortunately, it soon led to an eight-year feud with the Air Force over which service had the right to land on its deck. (The Navy's case was weakened by lack of any appropriate aircraft.) Throughout his term, until Lott's resignation to run for President himself, Kubitschek was aided in his efforts to maintain support within the armed forces by his strong-minded "pro-legality" War Minister.[19]

Kubitschek also sought to reassure the staunch anti-Communists among the military by his repeated anti-Communist declarations and his orthodox foreign policy. He did not deviate, for example, from the traditional Brazilian support for Portugal, and he was receptive to following the American lead in hemispheric diplomacy, at least on the anti-Communist issue, thereby reassuring anti-gestulista generals such as Cordeiro de Farias and Juarez Távora, who were deeply suspicious of "nationalist" adventures in foreign policy. The President, in fact, geared his nationalism to center opinion among the officer corps. There was no element of anti-Americanism, no attacks on "imperialism." It was a language of nationalism on which the maximum number of officers could agree. Accelerated industrialization, expansion of power and transport facilities, and the construction of an inland capital all matched the idea of development entertained by a wide range of officer opinion.[20]

And Kubitschek did not limit his anti-Communism to mere statements. In June 1956, for example, he ordered the closing of the Dock Workers Union of Rio and the National Emancipation League, both Communist-manipulated. However, as if to balance this repression on the left, in August of the same year the government seized the extreme right-wing newspaper, *Tribuna da Imprensa,* which had printed a manifesto from its self-exiled publisher, Carlos Lacerda, charging that the Kubitschek government bowed to Communists and was dominated by "traitors." These measures to suppress the political extremes were intended to convince center opinion in the officer corps and in the country at large that the Kubitschek government would not allow radicals of the left or right to drag Brazil off its democratic course.

There is one aspect of Kubitschek's handling of the military which remains difficult to explain. That is the relative ease with which anti-getulista officers reconciled themselves to the tenure of their former enemy, João Goulart, in the vice presidency. As part of the electoral bargain between Kubitschek's PSD and Goulart's PTB, Kubitschek gave Goulart a free hand in the choice of the Minister of Labor. Goulart contributed his part by advertising strenuously his anti-Communist beliefs. In May 1956 he visited the United States, where he repeatedly reassured the Americans of his democratic views. In October 1957 he explained that "pragmatic nationalism" was the guiding light of the Labor Party, and in the congressional elections of October 1958 he again denied charges of cooperation between Communists and the Labor Party.[21]

Goulart also succeeded, throughout this period, in making no moves in the labor area which could alarm those officers for whom the idea of a syndicalist Republic was anathema. In other words, Goulart successfully avoided giving any substantial evidence for the perennial charge that he was a would-be Perón.[22]

In dealing with Congress, Kubitschek relied upon an alliance between the two parties which had nominated him. The PSD-PTB coalition proved a reliable vehicle, although it frequently voted more federal expenditures and higher wage settlements than the President wanted. The hostile politicians, especially of the UDN, were in a minority in the Congress. Despite their strongly "legalist" tradition, their only hope of success seemed to lie in a coup against the government. But this, in turn, required a radicalization of opinion among the middle class and the military against which Kubitschek's non-ideological, undogmatic style successfully protected him. By his success he revealed himself an able pupil of Vargas, while being free of Vargas' one insuperable liability—his authoritarian past from the Estado Nôvo.

Kubitschek was, in any case, a master at handling recalcitrant politicians by means of liberal patronage. Whatever larger purposes the overnight construction of Brasília served, it gave the President an unprecedented amount of leverage in dealing with opponents susceptible to the attractions of profitable participation in the new enterprise. And the accompanying program of road construction meant that the possibilities extended far beyond the confines of the new Federal District.

Kubitschek was also effective in dealing with the state governors, who were less powerful than in the days of the Old Republic but who continued to be important public opinion-makers. The President cooperated effectively, for example, with the ambitious Governor of São Paulo (1955–9), Jânio Quadros, whose supporters cast him in the mold of anti-getulismo—thus trying in vain to push him into active opposition to the President.

There was another area of politics where Kubitschek was equally active: relations with the United States. From the outset he calculated that the success of his industrialization drive would depend upon close cooperation with the United States government and American private investors. He therefore made every effort to sell his programs to American public and private authorities. His government pursued public relations in New York and Washington as had no other Brazilian regime. Fortunately for the new President, 1956 and 1957 were relatively calm in hemispheric diplomacy. The CIA-sponsored overthrow of the Arbenz regime in Guatemala in 1954 and the emergence of Fidel Castro in Cuba in 1959 were equally distant. In May 1958, however, Vice President Nixon visited South America and ran into an ugly reception from hostile students. Kubitschek sought to capitalize on the ensuing American worry over its Latin American policy.

In a dramatic letter to President Eisenhower, the Brazilian President proposed an ambitious new program, "Operation Pan-America," which would bring together the United States and Latin America in a long-term multilateral program of economic development. The real purpose was to ensure American support for the attainment of Latin America's ambitious economic goals. It would include agreement on measures such as commodity agreements and long-term public loans.

Politically, such a commitment would give progressive democratic governments (in Brazil the position could be described as "developmentalist nationalism") an invaluable source of foreign support against their domestic opponents on both the right and left who sought to sabotage any economic development under democratic auspices.[23]

Kubitschek's idea of Operation Pan America was given a conspicuously perfunctory reception in the Washington of Eisenhower and Dulles. It was not until the disastrous turn in relations with Fidel Castro's Cuba that the United States in 1960 hurriedly launched an early version of the Alliance for Progress, a multilateral program essentially similar to what Kubitschek had proposed.[24]

Inflation Again

The ambitious economic program of Kubitschek had an Achilles' heel: financing. It had been hoped in 1956 that sufficient funds could be obtained from public and private sources abroad and from Brazilian export earnings. Although the former source proved satisfactory, the sharp deterioration in Brazil's terms of trade, under way since 1955, continued, thereby eroding her export earnings.[25] Because the government refused to compromise its ambitious plans for industrialization, the symptoms of financial disequilibrium soon appeared. In 1957 the balance of payments showed a deficit of $286 million on current account, whereas the figures for 1955 and 1956 had resulted in the current account being nearly balanced. The government worried also over the signs of domestic inflation. The price increases, although still modest (the cost of living rose only 13 percent in Rio de Janeiro during 1957, the lowest increase since 1951), began accelerating the first half of 1958. Between January and August of 1958 the cost of living climbed 10 percent in Rio de Janeiro. In June Finance Minister José Maria Alkmin resigned amidst bitter criticism that he had failed to gain sufficient new international financing or to arrest the rate of inflation and the growing deficit in the balance of payments. He was replaced by Lucas Lopes, a well-known engineer from Minas Gerais who had been Kubitschek's first Director of the National Economic Development Bank (BNDE).

Unfortunately, the Kubitschek government's realization of the urgent need for an anti-inflation program coincided with the congressional elections scheduled for October 1958. Kubitschek decided to wait and see how voter opinion was running. The elections produced no real surprises. The positions of two of the three major parties—the PSD and the UDN—were virtually unchanged, while the PTB gained ten seats (from 56 to 66), largely at the expense of the PSP (from 32 to 25) of Adhemar de Barros, who was again defeated for the governorship of São Paulo (his victorious opponent in 1954 had been Jânio Quadros, and in 1958 was Carvalho Pinto, the candidate endorsed by Quadros). A number of radical leftist candidates were defeated, to the surprise of many observers who thought that inflation might already have strengthened the hand of the extremists.[26]

With the election safely past, the Kubitschek government announced an elaborate economic stabilization program, designed to "allow the development of the country to proceed under conditions of economic equilibrium and social stability by means of the pursuit of monetary stabilization." The program was divided into two phases: (1) from October 1958 to the end of 1959 would be a "phase of transition and readjustment" during which the government would "reduce drastically the rate of price increase" while at the same time reducing the distortions in investment and improving real wages; (2) beginning in 1960, with price stability achieved, the subsequent expansion of the means of payment would be limited strictly to the amount necessary to cover the increment in real product. All of this was to be achieved without in any way sacrificing the Target Program, which was "perfectly compatible" with the stabilization program.[27]

In his covering letter endorsing the program, Kubitschek exuded his usual optimism ("Brazil's basic economic situation does not offer the occasion for any lack of confidence"), and he announced his government's goal of slowing the increase in the cost of living to a level of 5 percent in 1959.[28]

This stabilization program was drafted by the Finance Minister, Lucas Lopes, and the director of the National Bank for Economic Development, Roberto Campos. Beneath the confident language and detailed charts, a question remained: how were the apparently contradictory goals of maintaining a high level of investment and achieving price stability to be reconciled? The "structuralists" in economic circles argued that a measure of inflation (perhaps as much as 20 percent) was inevitable during the industrialization of an underdeveloped country and that price stability could be achieved only at the cost of stagnation. Campos and Lopes, well aware of the danger of stagnation, hoped to achieve stabilization gradually—rather than by the shock treatment often urged by the International Monetary Fund and then currently being attempted in Argentina and Chile.

The financial disequilibrium had two causes about which the government could do little in the short run—the terms of trade, and bottlenecks in the structure of the domestic economy. Commodity agreements might eventually alleviate the former, while only long-term public investment could overcome the latter. But a high level of public investment was itself a further stimulant to inflation because it produced large deficits in the federal budgets. In 1957, for example, the federal deficit jumped to 4 percent of the Gross National Product from slightly over 2 percent in 1956, and less than 1 percent in 1954 and 1955.[29] The conflict between the Target Program and stabilization was therefore inevitable.

The Kubitschek government's decision to pursue an anti-inflation program was taken in response to pressure, both domestic and foreign. As the Program itself noted, inflation was beginning to have negative effects by distorting the pattern of investment and offering a growing disincentive to private saving.[30] There were also social tensions resulting from the scramble of every class and sector to adjust its income in the face of rising prices. The foreign pressure came from the swelling ranks of creditors, who wanted evidence that their client was taking steps to make possible the speedy repayment of her debts. The chief indicator of foreign opinion was the International Monetary Fund, whose approval of any stabilization plan was crucial. The IMF had a central role not because of the funds it could release, which were relatively small, but because its imprimatur was the precondition for the further cooperation of the principal creditors, such as North American and European private banks and the United States government.

The Brazilian government consulted the IMF in the drafting of the Lopes-Campos stabilization plan, on which the IMF adopted a wait-and-see attitude. The IMF, well known for its advocacy of the "shock treatment" approach to stabilization, insisted that the Brazilians should simplify their nightmarishly complicated exchange regulations (which included substantial subsidies on the import of wheat and oil) and approximate more closely to a balanced budget. American approval of the Brazilian request for a $300 million loan hinged on IMF approval. Brazil's every action in the area of economic policy was now under the scrutiny of her foreign creditors.

Kubitschek finally learned, to his growing discomfort, the political costs of an anti-inflation program. The social attitudes engendered by long-term inflation had created a formidable political obstacle to any attempts to enforce the restrictive wage, credit, and public expenditure policies needed to arrest a deeply rooted inflationary process. Every class and sector wanted the burden to be borne by some other group first—"just one more adjustment and then we can cooperate" was the inevitable reaction to calls for "sacrifice." This was the situation as the Kubitschek government attempted stabilization while promising to avoid the least hint of stagnation.[31]

Attempts to restrict industrial credit brought protests from São Paulo businessmen, who angrily pointed out that credit for the public sector was conspicuously more available than for the private sector. The president of the Bank of Brazil, Sebastião Pais de Almeida, proved responsive to these complaints. In December 1958 Pais de Almeida's refusal to cut back credit to industry made obvious the Finance Minister's inability to enforce an overall anti-inflation program. The situation was similar to the disagreement between Ricardo Jafet and Horácio Lafer in 1952–53: a Finance Minister bent upon stabilization, but a president of the Bank of Brazil who would not refuse industry the essential working capital that they could obtain nowhere else.

São Paulo had been the focus of an earlier clash over coffee policy. The Kubitschek government had committed itself to a costly program of purchasing surplus coffee stocks in the face of the continuing fall in world coffee prices. These purchases could only be financed by issuing additional currency, which in turn added to the inflationary pressure generated by other deficits in the public sector. When in September 1958 Finance Minister Lopes substituted a more limited program of coffee support for the previous blanket purchase policy, there was an anguished outcry from the Paulista coffee growers. In October Lopes had to ask the Army to block the coffee growers' plan to sponsor a two-thousand-car motorcade to protest the new policy.

On the wage front, a new minimum wage was announced on January 1, 1959, following a 30 percent salary increase for civil servants and military personnel. This did little more than catch up with the cost of living increase since the last wage adjustment, except to provide employers with proof of the need for further price increases.

Public expenditure was the area where the President was most reluctant to sanction any attempts at real austerity measures. He would not compromise his Target Program. Deeply committed to his goal of accelerating industrialization and overcoming structural bottlenecks, he continued to declare that it would be compatible with stabilization, as he had promised when the Lopes-Campos proposals were launched in October 1958. Nevertheless, in January 1959 the President announced that the federal budget would be reduced to the bare essentials.

As the early months of 1959 passed, the government experimented more and more desperately with the differential exchange rate system. New bonuses were awarded to exporters, and the subsidies on imports such as oil and wheat were lowered. But the demand for Brazil's exports did not increase significantly, and the trade gap remained, requiring more short-term financing. The cut in import subsidies caused domestic prices to increase, especially on conspicuous items such as bread (made from imported wheat) and bus fares (reflecting costlier imported oil). Still, the government did not reform the exchange system drastically enough or restrict the increase of the money supply sharply enough to satisfy the IMF. The $300 million loan from the United States hung in abeyance. Kubitschek had pursued stabilization long enough to suffer from its political disadvantages—social unrest resulting from demands for new wage increases stepped up during early 1959—but not long enough to find evidence that it had achieved its objective. The exchange rate adjustments and wage increases had, as the economic advisers warned they would, exacerbated price instability in the short run. Furthermore, credit restrictions threatened to prevent fulfillment of the targets, especially in industrial production.

Nationalism and Development: The Troubled Dialogue

The first half of 1959 also witnessed a sharp growth in the political opposition to the Kubitschek government. The presidential succession question was already in the air. Who would be the candidate of the "ins" to succeed Kubitschek? Would he be saddled with an unpopular anti-inflation program during his campaign?

Kubitschek began to feel the sting of organized attacks from the left. Advocates of radical nationalism, always ready to argue that Brazil's industrialization was threatened with "strangulation" by capitalist foreigners, now found a wider audience for their arguments. The IMF became the symbol for what they claimed was the willful incomprehension of Brazil's special problems by the capitalist powers. The United States government and the IMF became the scapegoats for the painful stabilization measures the Kubitschek government had begun. The Communist press, for example, branded Finance Minister Lopes and chief adviser Roberto Campos as stooges of Wall Street who were compliantly carrying out an IMF plot to sabotage Brazil's development. The constant trips to Washington by Brazilian officials, as well as the frequent visits to Brazil of U.S. and IMF officials, served to dramatize the international dimension of Brazil's inflationary crisis.[32]

The Kubitschek government was actually divided on the proper course to follow. Lopes and Campos argued that the anti-inflation program must be intensified, and were struggling to convince the IMF and the American government that their views would carry the day with Kubitschek. But the President was equivocating. His unwillingness to endorse strongly enough all the Lopes-Campos proposals, especially on credit policy, wage policy, and budget matters, clearly indicated his own doubts about the political viability of any government that carried through the kind of anti-inflation program to which he had committed himself the previous October. In fact, it was difficult to measure the public's comprehension of the complex issues involved in the stabilization crisis.

Although the extreme version of radical nationalism did not represent the views of most Brazilians, the resentment against "foreign pressure" was widespread. Augusto Frederico Schmidt, whom Kubitschek sent to Washington in late 1958 to help in the negotiations for additional financing and who was by no stretch of the imagination a leftist (he strongly favored foreign private investment, for example), bitterly attacked the "unrealistic" requirements of the IMF. Among some Kubitschek advisers there was a strong resentment at the failure of the United States government to respond to Operation Pan-

America, proposed a year earlier. It had been, after all, a suggestion aimed at heading off just the kind of mutual misunderstanding now apparent between Brazil and the United States. Yet the Americans were indifferent, talking only in terms of austerity measures which the developmentalists thought would hobble Brazil's long-term development. This anti-American view was widely shared in the Brazilian press, including elements not otherwise known for their "nationalism." In May 1959, Vice President Goulart blamed Brazil's economic problems on the excessive profits of foreign-owned firms, thereby giving new prestige within the PTB to the extreme nationalist position that Vargas had often endorsed during his own anti-inflation crisis.[33]

The controversy over stabilization soon widened into a more general debate over the proper strategy for Brazil's development. The proponents of the three formulae—radical nationalism, developmentalist-nationalism and neo-liberalism—propounded their views with full confidence that the problems highlighted by the crisis over anti-inflation policies only confirmed the correctness of *their* respective views. Believers in radical nationalism, drawing their strength from the far left, thought they saw their chance. Seizing on the stabilization controversy, they tried to inflame public opinion over more basic questions, such as the role of foreign capital and the entire economic and political relationship with the United States. They attacked Kubitschek as a traitor who had sold out to foreign investors and was now surrendering the final shreds of economic sovereignty to the foreign bankers and the IMF.[34]

More moderate voices tended to be drowned out in the shrill chorus of political hysteria. The bitter controversy extended to the intellectual circles which had succeeded in constructing a consensus in support of Kubitschek's developmentalist-nationalism. ISEB, the institute where "developmentalist" intellectuals had gathered, was racked by a bitter quarrel between moderates and extreme leftists. The intellectual consensus supporting developmentalist-nationalism collapsed as the language of public discussion deteriorated into abusive polemics. Moderates such as Hélio Jaguaribe were labeled *entreguistas* by the left, while the right called them "communo-nationalists." Most significantly, the mutual good faith, on which the very process of democratic discussion rested, was undermined. Disagreement was labeled treason as rational dialogue became steadily more difficult.[35]

In June 1959, Kubitschek made his choice. Amidst the heated political atmosphere, he instructed his representatives in Washington to break off negotiations with the IMF. Faced with a choice between continuing the drive to fulfill his targets and the need to constrict the domestic economy to satisfy foreign creditors and Brazilian anti-inflationists, Kubitschek opted for the former. He had decided that it was too late in his presidency, now already beginning to be overshadowed by the succession question, to carry out the stabilization plan outlined in 1958. He refused to accept the arguments of Lopes and Campos that the economy was about to enjoy the fruits of previous stabilization measures.[36] Instead, he chose to break dramatically with the foreigners, thereby hoping to divert domestic opinion from the increased level of inflation bound to result from the jettisoning of the Lopes-Campos program. Brazil would therefore have a chance of fulfilling the targets laid out in 1956–57, and the resulting dislocations could be blamed on foreign ill-will. It was a bold strategy, resorted to by a political leader anxious to preserve his own reputation and thereby, perhaps, pave the way for his return to the presidency in the election of 1965. He would leave the problems of inflation and foreign indebtedness for his successor. His new strategy was also a response to the more passionate brand of nationalism which his own efforts at building national self-confidence had indirectly helped foster.[37]

The President tried to make maximum political capital out of his break with the IMF. In late June he spoke before the Military Club, scene of many bitter controversies over Brazilian nationalism. The President delivered a defiant message: "Brazil has come of age. We are no longer poor relatives obliged to stay in the kitchen and forbidden to enter the living room. We ask only collaboration of other nations. By making greater sacrifices we can attain political and principally economic independence without the help of others." [38]

Telegrams of congratulation poured into the presidential palace from all over Brazil. The satisfaction seemed even greater than if Brazil had actually received the $300 million loan which had been hanging fire for so long. Brazilians were given the sensation of successfully defying the foreign authorities to whom their Argentine and Chilean neighbors had recently bowed. It was an exercise in political brinkmanship, the final consequences of which no one could foresee.[39]

In August 1959 Kubitschek replaced the advisers who had planned the stabilization program. Lucas Lopes, the incumbent Finance Minister who had been seriously ill for several months, was replaced by Sebastião Pais de Almeida. Lúcio Meira replaced Roberto Campos as the president of the National Bank for Economic Development, and Marcos de Souza Dantas replaced José Garrido Torres as the director of the Monetary Authority. Left-wing nationalists celebrated the departure of the "entreguistas." [40]

The ministerial changes which sealed Kubitschek's rejection of the stabilization program were closely related to the maneuvering for the presidential election campaign.[41] The controversy over stabilization raised again many of the questions which had plagued Vargas and toward which Kubitschek had adopted a strictly pragmatic attitude. What should be the roles of the private and the public sector? In which industries should there be state monopolies? To what extent could Brazil rely on native entrepreneurial talent for innovation and management? What should be the source of badly needed capital? How much foreign investment would be consistent with the widely felt desire to maintain control of the Brazilian economy in the hands of Brazilians? Given the need for foreign capital, what should be the balance of private and public foreign investment? Finally, how should national and regional planning be used? These questions involved not only the technical considerations of economic analysis; they were also policy matters for the politicians to debate and negotiate. And because such questions aroused increasingly deep social divisions as well as sharp ideological differences, they would not be easy to resolve. High expectations of future economic growth had been aroused, and conflicting formulae for its achievement had been proposed. The hybrid political system, despite Kubitschek's resourceful policy of improvisation, was beginning to strain under the pressures of economic decision-making.

The Limits of Improvisation

It would be too strong to conclude that Kubitschek's political style could not possibly have been continued. In fact, there was no candidate in 1960 capable of the attempt. The essence of Kubitschek's success had been his ability to maneuver within the presidential system. Like

Vargas, he had chosen not to depend on any single party or movement. Indeed, the parties had remained loosely organized, passive instruments, seldom initiating action on important policy issues. Kubitschek's success as a resourceful manipulator had reinforced the ad hoc nature of the system itself, without providing any institutional continuity for the future. As the campaign of 1960 approached, the PSD and PTB renewed their electoral alliance, but there was no Kubitschek to be found.

But even if the "ins" of the Kubitschek era had discovered another "grand improviser," he would have faced an exceedingly difficult task. It was doubtful if the policy of political brokerage, based on the assumption that most sectors stood to gain and none to lose (at least in absolute terms), could have been continued on the same terms.[42] Brazilian society had undergone sufficient development for its social conflicts to have rendered this approach less promising. The populist politicians of the left, best represented by Leonel Brizola (elected Governor of Rio Grande do Sul in 1958), had begun to threaten the equilibrium of the political balance so carefully maintained by Kubitschek.[43] Along with the radical nationalist intellectuals, they were having success in identifying nationalism and populism in the public mind. This was the identification which Kubitschek had gone to pains to avoid in his own political style.[44]

The increasingly important phenomenon of the populist politician deserves closer examination. By definition, his appeal was directed to the mass voter. The economic prosperity of the cities had enlarged the urban masses. Although this brought an increase in labor union membership, their leadership was for the most part lacking in political initiative, preferring to enjoy their privileged ties with the government. This did not, on the other hand, prevent these leaders from being carefully watched by the military, many of whom could not forgive Kubitschek's continued use of the union apparatus for his limited political purposes. But populist politicians such as Brizola were far less inhibited than Kubitschek. They were prepared to promise the urban masses a larger share in economic prosperity (larger wage settlements) and a more nationalist economic policy (stricter regulation of foreign investment, if not actual confiscation, and a more aggressive stance toward foreign creditors' demands for stabilization). Furthermore, their language often implied radical changes in the political power structure. Their growing following seemed to duplicate the radicalization which Brazilian politics had undergone from 1932 to 1937, but with an important difference—there was no corresponding mass movement on the right.

The Kubitschek presidency also witnessed the beginnings of political radicalization in the countryside. The extent of activity among the peasantry since the late 1950's has undoubtedly been exaggerated by outside observers. Such activity was nonetheless significant because it called attention to a huge but previously quiescent sector. It was not the exact size of the following of leaders such as Francisco Julião—nor the sincerity of their motives—which mattered, but the potential threat which the peasant demands for land and higher wages (for seasonal labor) represented to the rural landowner. This was especially true in the more highly organized areas of plantation agriculture such as Pernambuco.[45]

Taken together, the signs of awakening mass politics in the urban and rural sectors were bound to frighten those groups which had most to lose if the power equilibrium should be disturbed by the populist politicians: the rural landowners, never before threatened, even in Vargas' populist phase; the urban middle class, still linked by many personal ties to the rural landowners and deeply uncertain over their future status in a period of rapid change; and the military officer class, whose distaste for populism stemmed partly from a fear of losing their position as supreme political arbiter, and partly from their own disagreements over the proper strategy for Brazil's economic development.

It is important not to overestimate as of 1960 the extent of the conflict between the proprietors of the established political order and the masses for whose allegiance the populist politicians of the left were bidding. It was far more a potential clash, whose possible outlines were only beginning to emerge. As will become clear later, the coming confrontation was further muted by the character of the presidential campaign of 1960.

There were two fundamental issues, both suggested previously, which helped to speed the process of political radicalization. One was the question of how far the political system ought to be opened to wider public participation. Should illiterates be granted the franchise?

Such an extension of the electorate might radically alter the political balance. The second issue was economic policy. Advocates of conflicting economic formulae propounded their respective prescriptions, but none had close attachments to the varying social sectors which were as yet only sporadically capable of political self-consciousness on issues of economic policy. (A possible exception were the commercial groups, whose endorsement of neo-liberal views reflected a long-standing and deep commitment.)

The Kubitschek presidency demonstrated the limits of a policy of improvisation not only in economic policy and in political style, but also in institutional life. As part of his policy of shunning conflict, Kubitschek had seldom attempted to abolish or radically alter existing administrative institutions. He preferred the more practical course of creating a new organ to meet a new problem. SUDENE, the new development authority for the Northeast, was a striking example. Kubitschek bypassed the largely ineffective Anti-Drought Agency (DNOCS), captive of a corrupt and obsolete mentality, and created a new authority, supplying it with a level of leadership and money that the old agency had never enjoyed.[46] This tactic was even easier to follow in the case of Brasília, where a new agency (NOVACAP) was given generous authority and financing. If this approach helped to get things done quickly, it also made more difficult the maintenance of central control over the sprawling government apparatus. Such proliferation of ad hoc agencies meant that future policy changes at the highest national level would become increasingly difficult to implement because they would only slowly reach the operating level of administration, if at all.

The existing political institutions of representative government constituted another area where improvisation had begun to reach its limits. Brazilian society had become divided into more self-conscious sectors with conflicting interests. Yet these interests were very imperfectly represented in the new party system. Many congressmen, for example, still conceived their task in terms of the political world of pre-1930. They saw their role as one of dividing up the spoils and gaining favors for their associates. This was the "clientelistic" style, so typical of traditional back-country politics, which persisted in the habits of many politicians elected even from the more developed states.

The coming presidential election would only accentuate the gap between the national polity and the majority of constituencies represented in the Congress. Congressional representation was determined on the basis of population, and yet the electorate was limited to literates. The agrarian oligarchies which dominated the primarily rural states, therefore, were overrepresented in relation to the developed areas. Through their congressmen, who were masters of the congressional machinery, they could obstruct measures which were favored by the developed regions. Their advantage was lost, however, in a presidential election, where it was the total national vote that mattered. There was a natural tendency, therefore, for a presidential candidate to assume a position to the left of a majority of the Congress because of the difference in the composition of their respective constituencies. Thus, the Brazilian constitutional structure, like other federal systems combining a popularly elected President with a legislature that weighted heavily regional representation, exhibited an inability to respond quickly to the need for rapid economic and social change.[47]

Examples of comparable obsolescence could be found in many other important areas, such as education where there was a desperate shortage of public secondary schools.[48] The gap between the rapidly changing society and the responsiveness of the political system was made all the more serious by the widely assumed need for continued rapid economic growth. Any slowdown would imperil the gains which had come to be generally expected since the second Vargas presidency. By a *tour de force* of improvisation in every field, Kubitschek had realized the ultimate potential of the system he inherited from Vargas. But a new degree of social tension and conflict, as yet inadequately reflected within the formal political process, had now forced a large number of fundamental questions into the arena of national attention.[49]

VI

JÂNIO QUADROS: AGONIZING INTERLUDE

The Rise of the Outsider

It was amidst these grave doubts about the old political alignments, the adequacy of the constitutional and administrative system, and the direction of economic policy, that Jânio Quadros emerged as a political figure of national stature. Quadros had come onto the political scene as the outsider par excellence. Because he was not definitively identified as an anti-Vargas leader (although no one would ever have considered him a *getulista*), he appeared to be a figure capable of trancending the established lines of political conflict. This seemed all the more possible because of his charismatic electoral appeal.

Throughout his career, Quadros had been an unorthodox politician. Beginning as a schoolteacher in São Paulo, he first ran for alderman, continuing up the ladder to become mayor of the city of São Paulo in 1953; the next year he was elected governor of the state of São Paulo, defeating that redoubtable vote getter, Adhemar de Barros. Jânio's appeal was based on his image as the "anti-politician," the honest amateur who offered a radical change from the old style office holders who clung to their pre-1930 habits and could not adapt to the needs of a modern, urban Brazil. It was hardly coincidental that he had achieved his success in São Paulo, economically the most developed state. Quadros' electoral success was so great that he could afford to treat the parties cavalierly. He began under the banner of the Christian Democrats (*Partido Democrata Cristão* or PDC), but broke with the party in 1954. Along with his electoral triumphs in São Paulo, Quadros achieved an impressive record as an efficient administrator. He seemed to incarnate the hopes of the middle class, who wanted dynamic but honest government; at the same time he preserved an appeal for the working class, who found him a charismatic leader with an evident concern for spreading the economic benefits to those at the bottom. As if to underline his contempt for party labels, he won election as a PTB candidate for federal deputy from the neighboring state of Paraná in 1958. His real goal was the presidency, however, and he never bothered to appear in the Congress. By 1959 Quadros had emerged as a legendary figure from the new Brazil of São Paulo: the politician who could direct effective government of a rapidly growing economy while reconciling the social conflicts which it produced.[1]

Was Quadros a populist? The difficulties in answering that question reveal a great deal about the lines of Brazilian conflict and Quadros' relationship to them. In his Paulista career up to 1959, Quadros exhibited certain features of the populist style: he was, for example, a colorful, dynamic campaigner who urged the public to trust in *him*. He was thus offering the atomized individual of the urban electorate the hope of radical change through the redemptive force of a single leader's personality. Like Adhemar de Barros, whom he defeated for the governorship in 1954, he promised to rise *above* the conventional party structure, dominated at the national level by the UDN, PSD, and PTB. But the content of Quadros' message before 1959 made him less clearly classifiable as a populist. He directed his appeal to the middle and lower middle-class voter, for whom his record of honest and efficient administration in São Paulo seemed well-nigh miraculous. His attractiveness for the working-class voter depended more on defying middle-class standards in dress (he wore open-necked shirts and often appeared unkempt) and his dramatic demonstrations of personal independence than on promises of extended social welfare or emotional appeals to sentiments of economic nationalism. He also gained lower-class support by maintaining the reputation, as mayor and governor, of always being accessible to the complaints of the most humble citizen.[2]

Yet Quadros' opposition to the "system" became broad-based enough to have an appeal for elements in all classes. After 1959 he took a growing interest in efforts to reform the labor union structure. By 1960 he was actively backing his own reform candidates for key posts against the professional labor politicians (primarily of the PTB). This effort to transform the Vargas paternalistic legacy in the area of labor organization was a counterpart to Quadros' attack on the inefficiency of the Vargas legacy in the field of state administration. In both cases, Quadros promised a more positive transformation than the conventional anti-getulistas or even populists such as Adhemar de Barros or Brizola offered, but it was exceedingly dependent on Jânio's personal control. Growing from success to success, Quadros intensified his personalistic style, casually sloughing off those movements which grew up in the wake of his meteoric rise.

There was a further complication in assessing Quadros' political career. He made his reputation in São Paulo as an outsider who fought the "system"—which meant essentially the Vargas legacy—but he was never willing to associate himself unequivocally with the anti-Vargas forces. As Mayor of São Paulo in 1953–54 and an obvious candidate for the governorship in 1954, for example, he preserved an ambiguous position on Getúlio, even in the moments of Vargas' gravest peril.[3] In 1955 he was directly responsible for the resignation of Finance Minister Gudin, who feared that President Café Filho's apparent political negotiations with Quadros were undermining the tight credit policy that Gudin considered essential to his anti-inflation program. Gudin's replacement, José Maria Whitaker, was named expressly on Quadros' recommendation, and the easier credit policy that followed was a violation of the austerity ideas that many anti-getulistas demanded.[4] Quadros also did not encourage Carlos Luz in his quixotic attempt to maintain a separate government in Santos after the coup of November 1955. Quadros was, therefore, far from enjoying impeccable credentials as an anti-getulista.

Presidential Election: Defeat of the "Ins"

As the time for nominating candidates for the presidential campaign for the 1960 election drew near, the "ins" could find no candidate; nevertheless, the PSD and the PTB decided to continue the uneasy electoral alliance of 1955. For lack of any civilian figure capable of continuing the Kubitschek style, the alliance turned to Marshal Lott, the architect of the "preventive" coup of November 1955. Lott had a prima facie attraction for nationalists on the left. He had, for example, embraced several "nationalist" causes—such as granting illiterates the vote and sharply limiting profit remittances sent abroad by foreign firms. Most important, he had crushed the conspiracy led by the anti-getulistas after Kubitschek's election. His "legalism" was therefore a highly useful weapon against the right, especially among the officer corps. Lott was, however, a weak candidate, inexperienced in politics and lacking any personal appeal—a fact which the old-line PSD and PTB politicians, as well as the nationalist intellectuals, soon realized.

The excitement of the pre-campaign maneuvering centered on the probable candidate of the "outs." Quardros' formidable reputation in São Paulo made him an irresistible figure to the frustrated liberal opposition led by the UDN. They now saw their chance. Although Quadros was hardly a loyal UDN member, he was the party's one hope of reversing its unbroken record of defeat in presidential elections. For them, Quadros loomed as the charismatic leader who could overthrow the oligarchy of "ins" and achieve for the party what their own electoral weakness had failed to do. At the UDN convention in November 1959, Lacerda delivered an impassioned plea to "go with the people" by endorsing Quadros' candidacy. Any other course, such as the nomination of Juracy Magalhães, the leading contender from within the party's own ranks, would be conceding defeat, warned Lacerda.[5]

The overwhelming majority of the UDN, sick of failure and attracted by Quadros' oratory and record in São Paulo, followed Lacerda's advice. Quadros accepted the nomination but announced that he would consider his independence uncompromised by party endorsements. A month later he demonstrated his resolve. In December 1959 he resigned the UDN nomination in protest at a squabble between the UDN and the Christian Democratic Party (both had nominated Quadros for President but each had its own vice presidential nominee— Milton Campos for the UDN and Fernando Ferrari for the Christian Democrats) over which vice presidential nominee would appear at the first campaign rally. Quadros resumed his candidacy only after public reassurance by the endorsing parties—most important of which was the UDN—that he was in no way bound by their support. This incident again demonstrated how completely the UDN was dependent upon Quadros; it further dramatized Quadros' political independence for those voters who had come to view the whole party structure with contempt.[6] Quadros' slender loyalty to the UDN, and the PDC as well, was also demonstrated by his tolerance of the local "Jan-Jan" committees that urged voters to split their ballots, choosing Jânio Quadros for President and João Goulart for Vice President.

Despite Quadros' aloof attitude, the liberal opposition still considered him to be *their* candidate against the Vargas system. Quadros, on the other hand, based his campaign on a wider appeal than the traditional UDN position. He promised honesty and extolled democracy, as they always had, but he also pledged to maintain a rapid rate of economic development which would reach previously neglected areas such as agriculture, education, and public health. All this was to be done while controlling inflation and preserving Brazil's independence as a sovereign nation. On the controversial question of how "nationalist" Brazil's strategy of economic development ought to be, Quadros came close to the neo-liberal formula. He endorsed a balanced budget and stressed the need to create favorable conditions for foreign investors. There was, for example, no talk of a systematic set of targets, such as Kubitschek had outlined in the campaign of 1955.[7]

But Quadros did modify his earlier stand against Petrobrás; now he even opposed the participation of foreign firms in Brazilian oil production. His dynamic campaign style convinced many, including even some nominal Lott supporters who were advocates of developmentalist-nationalism, that his orthodox views on economics were inherited ideological baggage which he would soon jettison. Once in office, they suspected, he would see that an ambitious President had no alternative but to follow a "developmentalist" policy—in other words, the country must continue its drive to industrialize, even if that meant a dose of inflation.

It was in the area of foreign policy that Quadros most clearly revealed a drift away from his UDN sponsors. In March 1960 he visited Fidel Castro's Cuba. He left the impression that he was sympathetic to Fidel's socialist experiment, although he protested the misuse which he claimed the Cuban regime had made of his public statements. Both his UDN supporters and his PTB-PSD opponents suspected "demagoguery." But why did the candidate consider such gestures necessary? It seemed an interesting question, but hardly of overriding importance. Jânio had never been an orthodox political figure.[8]

As the campaign continued, Quadros succeeded in generating a wide enthusiasm among the electorate, although surveys showed that his appeal was strongest among the upper classes (graded by occupa‹

tion). In the eyes of his followers, Quadros seemed to assume miraculous powers. For every problem there was the answer of Jânio's dynamic personality, symbolized by the slogan which preceded him on the campaign circuit: "Jânio's coming!" Quadros' appeal went far beyond the conventional political popularity of Kubitschek. Whereas Juscelino had pleased and inspired many Brazilians by his policies, he had depended on familiar tactics of democratic leadership. Quadros possessed the rarer quality of charisma.[9]

When the ballots were counted in October 1960, the UDN strategists who had urged Quadros' nomination were proved right. For the first time since 1945, the candidate of the "outs" won a presidential election. Jânio, the political outsider, the leader free of entangling alliances, was decisively elected. He received 48 percent of the 11.7 million votes cast for President. Unlike 1950 and 1955, the UDN and Lacerda now saw nothing irregular in the winning candidate's lacking an absolute majority. The candidate of the "ins," Henrique Lott, won only 28 percent of the vote, running only slightly better than Adhemar de Barros, the perennial candidate, whose total was 23 percent. Jânio's drawing power among all classes was shown by his impressive vote in his home state of São Paulo, where his vote of 1,588,593 was almost double the total of his *paulista* rival de Barros, who gained 855,093 votes. The results also showed how rapidly the electorate had grown in the four presidential elections since 1945: it had been 5.9 million in 1945, 7.9 million in 1950, 8.6 million in 1955, and now 11.7 million in 1960.[10]

Quadros' dramatic election victory had for the moment obscured some fundamental questions inherent in Brazilian political development. Instead of debating the limits of Kubitschek's record of improvisation, the victorious candidate had campaigned on a moralistic critique of bureaucratic inefficiency and social injustice which he promised to sweep away (his campaign symbol was a broom) by the force of his personality. There had been little explanation of how the institutional limits of previous policies could be overcome. And a surprisingly large number of observers (including some traditional supporters of the PTB) who had previously emphasized the importance of these problems were carried away by the momentum of Quadros' campaign. Finally, the election result had obscured the potential conflict, also carefully avoided during Kubitschek's presidency, between the populist leaders and the power establishment.

For those who studied the returns a little more carefully, however, that conflict was apparent. The new Vice President was João Goulart, the running mate of defeated presidential candidate Lott. Goulart had won by a narrow plurality over the UDN candidate, Milton Campos, and a third nominee, Fernando Ferrari. (The Brazilian electoral law permitted voters to split their ballot in voting for President and Vice President.)

What had been obscured by Quadros' candidacy therefore became clear in the vote for Vice President. Milton Campos was a distinguished lawyer, a former Governor of Minas Gerais, and an outstanding representative of Brazil's traditional political elite. The UDN could hardly have nominated a more respectable and responsible leader. For the second time in a row, however, he lost to João Goulart —a populist of modest talents. This result was all the more striking because in 1960 Campos could count on a strong third candidate (PTB break-away Fernando Ferrari) to take many votes away from Goulart, whereas in 1955 a similar third candidate, Danton Coelho, had been a less formidable rival for the PTB vote. Even with the charismatic Quadros at the head of their ticket, the UDN had been unable to capture the Vice Presidency.

Economic Policy: Stabilization and Development? It was characteristic of Jânio Quadros that during the three months between his election and his inauguration he should have remained delphically uncommunicative about what he would do as President. He took a trip to Europe, deliberately turning his back on speculation about his forthcoming appointments and programs. His supporters complained that his continued absence crippled all efforts to plan an attack on the economic chaos which Kubitschek's lame-duck policies aggravated. The President-elect's dramatic withdrawal was typical of his idiosyncratic political style. It would, of course, serve to make his entrance onto the presidential stage all the more dramatic.

The new ministers named by Quadros in January 1961 were a mixture of UDN figures and leaders of smaller parties whose *raison d'être* had been anti-getulismo. The important post of Finance Minister went to Clemente Mariani, an UDN leader from Bahia, who had served as president of the Bank of Brazil in 1954–55, and had cooperated fully in the stabilization efforts of Finance Minister Gudin. The new Foreign Minister was Afonso Arinos de Melo Franco, scion of the UDN clan from Minas Gerais and a veteran anti-getulista who had been in the forefront of the assault on Vargas in 1954 and a leader in denouncing Lott's coup of November 1955. The former "ins," the PSD and the PTB, were denied any posts except for the Ministry of Transport, which was given to a PSD figure, Clovis Pestana. Also conspicuously absent were the leaders of the non-party citizens' movement (*Movimento Popular Jânio Quadros*) which had played a prominent role in the campaign. As an ad hoc organization, strictly loyal to the person of Quadros, it might have formed the nucleus of a new extra-party movement which the new President could use to mobilize public opinion. But he made no effort to encourage such a development. As for the military ministers, Quadros retained the incumbent Minister of War, General Odílio Denys, and he appointed new Ministers of Navy and Air Force.

Even in the first several months after Quadros entered office, the impression persisted that the real direction of his presidency was yet to be determined. This "equivocal" or "ambiguous" quality is the one aspect of the Quadros presidency on which his critics agreed. The two issues which Quadros emphasized in his inauguration speech on January 31 were government inefficiency and the financial crisis (domestic inflation and an alarming burden of foreign indebtedness). The tone of the speech alternated between defiance and despair. He scored "false nationalism" and the "new imperialism" which had infiltrated some classes, especially the intellectuals. The financial situation was described as "terrible"—$2 billion of foreign debt due in the new presidential term and over $600 million payable within the first year. Quadros lamented, "all this money, spent with so much publicity, we must now raise, bitterly, patiently, dollar by dollar and cruzeiro by cruzeiro. We have spent, drawing on our future to a greater extent than the imagination dares to contemplate." He attacked the Kubitschek administration for "favoritism and nepotism in administrative appointments" and berated his predecessor for the huge federal deficit in prospect for 1961.[11]

The Quadros government quickly launched an anti-inflation program more thoroughgoing than any attempted since 1954–55. In March, Quadros announced a reform of the exchange rate system, simplifying the multiple rates and effectively devaluing the cruzeiro by 100 percent. There was a drastic lowering of the subsidy on essential imports such as wheat and oil, thereby doubling the retail price of bread and sharply increasing bus fares and other transportation costs. The President promised to cut the government deficit, and also make new investments in the export sector in order to help overcome Brazil's "chronic insufficiency of exports." These exchange reforms earned the IMF's tentative approval, thereby giving Quadros the prerequisite for debt renegotiation which Kubitschek had failed to gain. The new President had now begun to carry out his campaign pledge: a painful financial retrenchment in order to lay the basis for another "developmental" drive later. Although the credit squeeze, wage freeze, and cut in import subsidies were bound to prove unpopular, that political risk seemed manageable in the euphoria which engulfed the Quadros camp in early 1961.[12]

In May and June the Quadros government was able to report brilliant success in its dealings with foreign creditors. A total package of more than $2 billion was announced, including over $300 million in new financing, along with the consolidation and stretching out of the large burden of short-term debt to United States and European (the "Hague Club") banks, as well as international financial authorities. The government's stabilization efforts at home had earned it full marks abroad. The terms of the new agreements were, considering Brazil's weak credit position, remarkably favorable. Politically, of course, Brazil's financial "weakness" also served as an asset. The Brazilian negotiators knew full well how badly the new Kennedy government wanted the Quadros regime to succeed in Brazil. The American communiqué announcing the loan arrangements emphasized that Brazil's future was vital to the future of the hemisphere and that the maintenance of free government in Latin America was dependent upon the success of Brazil's economic development.[13]

After the three-year frustration of increasingly acrimonious negotiations with the Kubitschek government, Brazil's creditors felt great relief at the prospect of a serious stabilization program which promised to return equilibrium to Brazil's foreign accounts. At home, Brazilians began to hope that Jânio's courage might bring a halt to the constant price increases which had become part of the Brazilian way of life. Already, however, there were the inevitable complaints from businessmen, workers, and consumers, all of whom, although they did not disapprove of stabilization in principle, thought the particular sacrifices imposed on *them* were unfair.

Furthermore, Quadros soon began to have doubts about the rigorous anti-inflation program to which he was committed. In the early months of the new administration, Finance Minister Mariani encountered little difficulty in convincing the President that such measures were necessary. But the immediate protest over unpopular steps such as the exchange reforms that doubled the price of wheat and oil brought home to Quadros the political costs of fighting inflation. He was therefore receptive to the advice of "developmentalist" intellectuals, who began to win his ear in March and April. They argued that measures to fight inflation, although clearly necessary, were inadequate alone, because the deeper causes of inflation lay in the structural disequilibria of the Brazilian economy. Any stabilization program would, therefore, prove self-defeating if it were not part of a larger plan for continued industrialization and increased public investment.[14]

By August, Quadros had been convinced by the developmentalists that he needed a powerful staff (directly responsible to the President) that could oversee economic planning. He had spent the early months of his presidency virtually without a staff, especially in the area of economic policy-making. The contrast with the aggressive cadre that had surrounded Kubitschek (they were often more important than the ministers in economic decision-making) was painfully obvious. On August 5, Quadros announced the creation of a National Planning Commission (*Comisão Nacional de Planejamento*), which was to be a new version of the Council of Development (*Conselho do Desenvolvimento*) which had been a rallying point for Kubitschek's principal economic planners, but which Quadros had allowed to languish after his inauguration. Also in preparation was a Five-Year Plan (*Primeiro Plano Quinquenal*) that would become Quadros' successor to Kubitschek's target program. Here, too, the early months of the Quadros presidency had revealed a total lack of any long-term planning. Instead, there was a preoccupation with the immediate tasks of stabilization and foreign debt renegotiation.[15]

Finally, Quadros' resolve to continue his "austerity" credit policies had weakened by August. The IMF and the U.S. government had been impressed by the swiftness and decisiveness with which exchange liberalization had been instituted (especially SUMOC Instruction #204 in March). But credit restrictions were a more difficult matter. By August the monetary authorities were exceeding the limits on the increase in the money supply that had been set earlier in the year. Already the alarm signals were beginning to sound for the IMF officials who had given strong approval to the Brazilian anti-inflation program in May and June.[16]

In his first six months as President, Quadros had begun by endorsing a tough, orthodox anti-inflation program, but had then been attracted to a "developmentalist" strategy. This shift in economic policy attitudes was hardly evident to the public by August, however, and was only beginning to become apparent to the politicians. It was in other areas that Quadros' policies had provoked the widest political debate.

Unorthodox Policies and Uncertain Support

The other principal feature of Quadros' domestic policy was his attack upon corruption and inefficiency in public administration. The bureaucratic ineptness which Quadros had so relentlessly attacked in the presidential campaign of 1960 had two causes. The first was the backwardness of administration in a developing country. Many civil servants continued to look upon their government job as one among several ill-paying occupations. But there were institutional problems which made the improvement of government service difficult. These problems constituted the second factor behind the inefficiency—the ad hoc administrative approach used so frequently by Juscelino Kubitschek. The result was to reinforce the helter-skelter structure of Brazilian public administration and to impede the establishing of responsibility in areas where multiple agencies existed.

Quadros attacked the bureaucratic inefficiency by issuing presidential *bilhetinhos*. The President sent off his hand-written decrees in every direction. He seemed to fancy himself a latter-day Napoleon, dominating the entire apparatus of government by the sheer force of his personality. Unlike Napoleon, however, Quadros dissipated much of his energy on unimportant matters. Along with decrees to tighten up administrative regulations in executive departments went directives outlawing perfume bombs at Carnival time (Quadros' bad eye was said to have been caused by an accident with such a bomb) and prohibiting bikinis on the Rio beaches.

These expressions of the President's personal impatience with federal inefficiency could never overcome the basic institutional limitations. They were negative moves, while the question of the President's larger designs remained unanswered. What would be the purpose of a more efficient government apparatus and how would morale be maintained in the midst of a moralistic campaign which discredited honest as well as dishonest employees? Both anti-inflation and anti-corruption were laudable programs, given the Brazilian situation in 1961. They did not, however, add up to a program which could maintain political appeal and mobilize social effort for the developmental tasks upon which Quadros had begun to focus in his presidential campaign.[17]

There was another, more political, aspect of the drive against corruption and inefficiency. Quadros' attacks could not fail to serve as an instrument by which the former "outs"—especially the UDN—could gain a partisan advantage over the former "ins"—especially the PSD and the PTB. Soon after his election Quadros launched a flurry of investigations into financial scandals involving government money. In May a report was released which linked Vice President Goulart to irregularities in the use of state pension funds. Goulart's protest that the investigations were made public merely for political reasons was angrily rejected by Quadros. The PSD-PTB majority in Congress, disturbed by the political threat to themselves, voted to investigate the President's investigators.[18]

In the short run Quadros could hope to gain prestige with the middle-class public by his crusade for honesty and efficiency in government. But in the long run he would still have to deal with the Congress. He would need to leave the door open for compromise with the politicians of the opposition whom he was now fearlessly "exposing." This was all the more true since Quadros was doing so little to maintain the UDN's support. After a month and a half in office he had held only two cabinet meetings and was acting virtually without consulting the congressional leadership of the UDN. As Quadros began to listen to his new set of "developmentalist" advisers after March, the UDN politicians became even more worried.

Once the euphoria of Jânio's first months in office wore off, how would he govern? Where would he find his political base? As an "anti-politician" in his earlier career, Quadros had been effective because politics in São Paulo, both in the city and the state, were well adapted to his approach: extremely fluid party lines and a relative wealth of non-partisan administrative talent ready to work for a "reform" leader. Neither condition existed to nearly the same extent in Brasília.

Quadros' ambivalence toward his most ardent campaign supporters became even more evident in the area of foreign affairs. With the full cooperation of his Foreign Minister, Afonso Arinos de Melo Franco, the President moved Brazil toward an "independent foreign policy." It was the Brazilian response to what had become a post-cold-war trend in the "third world." During the election campaign, there had already been hints that Quadros was considering a more adventurous foreign policy; and between his election and his inauguration Quadros traveled around the world—the first such tour ever undertaken by a Brazilian President. He was impressed with the attempt of many developing countries, such as Egypt, to find a "middle course" between the Western and Communist paths to development. His reluctance to agree with the American demands for a boycott of Cuba, and his visit to that island, indicated that he was prepared to follow a less straightforwardly pro-American policy than any Brazilian President since the Second World War.[19]

Such a policy had a certain obvious rationale. In the economic sphere, for example, Quadros hoped to ease Brazil's financial ills by simultaneous negotiations with three power centers: the United States, West Europe, and the Soviet bloc. Walter Moreira Salles was sent to Washington, Roberto Campos to Europe, while the Brazilian Foreign Ministry drafted a trade accord with the eastern bloc. But it was an awkward moment to launch an "independent" policy in the western hemisphere. The cold war had become hot in the Caribbean, where the fiasco of the Bay of Pigs invasion made the United States government all the more intent upon ensuring the diplomatic isolation of Cuba. The Kennedy administration made every possible effort not to let the growing diplomatic friction endanger the financial negotiations with Brazil. Yet there remained the obvious question from the American standpoint: why, in the face of such understanding and assistance from a Democratic administration in Washington, was the Quadros government pursuing a quixotic policy toward the Communist world?

Many observers felt that Quadros' foreign policy might be an elaborate cover to divert domestic attention from an unpopular economic stabilization program. This opinion was shared by some American officials who felt that they had to swallow Quadros' unorthodox position of Cuba (an unswerving devotion to a strictly legalistic interpretation of the principle of non-interference) as the price for seeing Quadros impose the prescribed medicine of the International Monetary Fund at home. This adventurousness in foreign policy, however, was itself bound to stir up domestic dissent. This domestic reaction to the "independent" foreign policy was simply a reflection of the fact that Quadros could not hope to placate the nationalist left on foreign policy, without at the same time irritating important conservative and center elements.

The government repeatedly denied that Brazil was turning "neutralist," but gestures such as support for the UN debate over the seating of Communist China and the announcement that Brazil was studying the resumption of relations with the Soviet Union (severed since 1947), aroused the indignation of Brazilian conservatives such as Cardinal Jaime de Barros Câmara of Rio de Janeiro and Admiral Pena Boto, president of the "Brazilian Anti-Communist Campaign." There were also a number of unpleasant incidents with United States representatives—emissaries kept waiting, routine courtesies omitted. The deeper purpose of these gestures—if any—remained unclear.[20]

Quadros Resigns

It is difficult to determine how much of the reaction to Quadros' foreign policy was a genuine concern over the question of Cuba and Communist infiltration, and the extent to which it merely provided an issue on which to attack Quadros himself. The point is crucial because on it turns any interpretation of the sincerity of the opposition which Quadros had aroused by July of 1961.

Carlos Lacerda, the destroyer of presidents and now Governor of Guanabara (greater Rio de Janeiro), led the attack.[21] Disturbed by Quadros' drift away from any semblance of UDN control, Lacerda tried to discredit the President in the eyes of the middle class and the military. It was the same technique he had used against Vargas and had repeatedly attempted against Kubitschek. Against those two he had been able to use the issue of corruption; against Quadros he now used the issue of the President's "independent" foreign policy. Lacerda launched into radio and television attacks in an attempt to draw Quadros into a direct clash. The controversy began over Quadros' sudden award of the Cruzeiro do Sul Order to Cuba's Che Guevara. Lacerda went to Brasília to consult with the President, and there ensued a comic-opera incident, involving a mix-up with Lacerda's baggage (was it to have been delivered to the presidential palace or to a hotel?) and the alleged refusal of Quadros to meet with his visitor. With any other politician, this incident might have passed unnoticed; in the case of Lacerda, it was mounted into a major challenge to the President because of Lacerda's access to mass media and the huge audience which he could always command.

On the night of August 24, Lacerda delivered a blistering radio attack, alleging that the Justice Minister, Oscar Pedroso D'Horta, was planning a coup which Lacerda had been invited to join. Having previously threatened to resign as governor of Guanabara, Lacerda now vowed to remain "so that my country will not leave the path which its founders mapped out." [22] Pedroso D'Horta heatedly denied Lacerda's charge, but confidants of Quadros later revealed that the President had been seriously discussing the possibility of a "Gaullist" solution for Brazil. One congressional supporter warned Quadros to forget about being a De Gaulle "because the Brazilian Congress will never give you such power." [23]

The larger significance of Lacerda's challenge to Quadros in August 1961 lay in the manner in which foreign policy questions had intruded into domestic politics. By his independent foreign policy, Quadros had begun to identify himself with the "nationalist" position, which contradicted the views of most of the UDN, as well as the "anti-Communist" officers among the military. This "nationalist" position was in turn identified with anti-Americanism, particularly on the Cuban question. By concentrating his fire on Quadros' foreign policy, Lacerda was thereby attempting to identify the President in the minds of the middle class and higher military with a nationalist position usually associated with populist politicians of the left. What remains in doubt is the extent to which this confrontation over foreign policy was a disguised confrontation over domestic political issues. An assessment of the domestic political crisis is all the more difficult because

Quadros cut it short. On August 25, in a moment of grave miscalculation, he submitted his resignation to the Congress, which quickly accepted it.

It is worth asking why the Congress might have been prepared to acquiesce so readily in the President's departure.[24] Quadros, the political outsider, had aroused such uncertainty and fear among the professional politicians of all parties in Brasília that they were relieved to see him surrender power. They were also caught unawares because Quadros' opposition, which had begun to form in the early months of 1961, had not yet crystallized. It is clear, however, that a number of powerful groups had already found reason to worry over the Quadros presidency.

First, there were the traditional politicians. Quadros had announced a series of investigations into political corruption. These could not fail to touch politicians of every party. Perhaps the group most affected would be the PSD, the traditional "ins," whose political compromises had made possible the relative stability of Brazilian government and public administration since the Second World War. Second, there was the huge apparatus of government bureaucracy. Government workers, including many important officials, had reason to worry about Quadros' emphasis on the improving of government efficiency. Third, there were the industrialists and merchants who worried about the stabilization program and its possible effects of economic stagnation. Fourth, there were the labor leaders and the left-wing intellectuals who were upset by the unequal social sacrifice involved in the continuing stabilization program and the failure to establish clearcut priorities for further economic development.[25] Fifth, there were the UDN politicians, once eager in their support of Quadros, but now harboring serious doubts that they could ever control him while in office. As always, Lacerda was their most unabashed spokesman. Finally, there were the military officers who grew increasingly disturbed over the implications of Quadros' foreign policy innovations. Their uneasiness in this area, as well as their alarm over the President's erratic personal behavior, made them suspicious of Quadros' plans. He was thus unable to count on full support from his military ministers. This became important, for example, when the War Minister refused to replace the Army commander in Rio de Janeiro who had not fulfilled Quadros' order to use the national communications regulations to ban Carlos Lacerda's speeches from the air.

The August crisis has remained difficult to analyze because the lines of conflict in domestic politics were obscured by the personal eccentricities of the President. Close observers, including Quadros' personal aides, agreed that the President found it difficult to make basic decisions and was prone to lapse into long periods of isolation, aided by a private cinema and generous quantities of alcohol. There was a genuine fear that the entire process of government, so dependent upon presidential decisions, might break down. Quadros, for example, had been unable to decide upon nominees for several critical posts. These personality defects were an open secret in Brasília, especially among the higher military and the Congress, into whose hands the succession question was suddenly thrown in 1961. Many former Quadros supporters had grown worried that the President, despite his great talents, lacked the judgment and stamina to govern Brazil. Regardless of their views on his particular policies, therefore, they were prepared to doubt that he could remain President. These personality defects may also have affected Quadros' own judgment about his resignation. Perhaps he was exhibiting the behavior of a man who had risen too high and too fast for his abilities. Could some self-destructive urge, or was it a self-protective instinct, have driven him to flee the gargantuan tasks he had laid out for himself?

If the August crisis is viewed as part of a growing confrontation between the traditional power arbiters and a President who had come to realize that his election had not broken a deadlock in Brazilian politics, how then did Quadros think he might emerge from such a contest? Evidently he hoped he could assume wide new presidential powers. Undoubtedly Quadros was seriously overestimating his own political popularity and believed that the Congress and the military would have no choice but to request that he remain as President on his own terms. This presupposes that Quadros was prepared to mobilize public opinion; in fact, he had made no effort since his election to create any new political movement which could furnish support in a crisis. He failed even to use the existing *Movimento Popular Jânio Quadros*.[26] If his resignation was intended as a challenge to the professional politicians and the higher military, it was an empty challenge, because Quadros proved unwilling and perhaps unable to organize his popular support.

Quadros may have overestimated another factor: the presence of João Goulart as his Vice President. Many of the higher military would undoubtedly view with alarm the succession of Goulart to the presidency—the legal consequence if Quadros' resignation should be accepted. At the moment of Quadros' resignation, Goulart was on a good-will tour of Communist China—a fact which could not fail to dramatize his unacceptability to the anti-Communist military. If Quadros assumed that the politicians and higher military would not dare accept his resignation, he could not have been more wrong. They quickly ratified the resignation, taking it at face value. They were prepared to treat the problem of Quadros' successor as a separate question.

Goulart was, in fact, a man with whom the politicians of the PSD—the most powerful single group in Brasília—had always been able to deal. He had been the running mate of Kubitschek in 1955 and Marshal Lott in 1960 on a PSD-PTB ticket. Despite his populist background and connections, Goulart was a more integral part of the political system in Brazil than Quadros had ever been. The question of Goulart's unacceptability to the military would have to be settled at a subsequent stage. But the resignation of Quadros must be accepted and ratified first. That was quickly done by the PSD politicians who controlled the Congress. The ensuing crisis over whether or not João Goulart, the heir apparent to the Vargas political tradition, should be permitted to occupy the Alvorada Palace in Brasília was soon to become the first chapter in the troubled history of the Goulart era.

VII

GOULART IN POWER: THE DEADLOCK PROLONGED

From Janio to Jango: A Military Veto?

The Constitution of 1946 left little doubt about the procedure to be followed if the presidency should fall vacant. Article 79 stated simply that "the Vice President succeeds." Despite this unambiguous provision, the question of Goulart's succession immediately aroused a bitter debate. Only after a ten-day crisis, which included the threat of civil war and a constitutional amendment establishing a parliamentary government, was the Vice President installed in the presidential palace. That ten-day crisis illustrated important features of the relationship between society and the political system, as well as the balance of political forces.[1]

Jânio Quadros wrote his resignation on the morning of August 25, apparently in consultation with his Justice Minister, Pedroso d'Horta. The President peremptorily informed the stunned military ministers of his decision, hardly waiting to hear their reactions to his insistence that Brazil could only be governed with emergency powers. His strategy, if such impulsiveness merited that description, was set. The resignation was not to be transmitted to the Congress by the Justice Minister until three in the afternoon. By 11:00 a.m. the President and family had left Brasília, flying in the direction of São Paulo.[2]

The Quadros party landed at Cumbica, an airport in the state of São Paulo commanded by a personal friend of the now-former President. Upon arrival, Quadros told a group of governors gathered to meet him that his resignation was irrevocable. This statement only compounded the bewilderment over Quadros' motives. If he was waiting to be called back to Brasília to be invested with greater powers, why was he now closing the door?

Quadros' resignation letter was read to the Congress at the appointed hour of 3:00 p.m. It came with so little warning that there were present only thirty-four deputies (out of a total membership of three hundred and twenty-six) in the Chamber at the time. "I have performed my duty," said the letter, "but I have been frustrated in my efforts to lead this nation onto the path of its true political and economic liberation, the only path that would bring the effective progress and social justice which its noble people deserve." The tone of self-pity was startling: "I feel crushed. Terrible forces have risen up against me, intriguing against me and defaming me, sometimes under the guise of collaboration. If I remained I would not maintain the confidence and calm, now shattered, which are indispensable in the exercise of my authority. I believe that I could not even maintain civil order." [3] Despite the speculation over his possible tactical motives, the suspicion grew that the whirlwind from São Paulo had lost his nerve.

The deputies listened to the letter in amazement and disbelief. The corridors were suddenly alive with wild rumors and hurried conferences. At a dramatic evening session, Jânio's Minister of Mines and Energy, João Agripino, expressed the shock and disappointment of the deserted *janistas:* "After six months in the Ministry I return to my House [the Chamber of Deputies] where I spent more than fifteen years. Never, in Brazil, was there a President so free, with so many possibilities to carry out and build all that we, at least of my generation, wanted and want." The surprise caused by Quadros' sudden action could hardly have been greater. [4]

Although the Constitution provided that if the President should be impeded from exercising his office, the Vice President would succeed, it also provided that in the absence of the Vice President, the president of the Chamber of Deputies was the next in line of succession. João Goulart was indeed absent—abroad heading a special economic mission to Communist China. Therefore the president of the Chamber of Deputies, Ranieri Mazzilli, was sworn in as the Provisional President of Brazil. On the night of August 25 the situation was as follows: Jânio Quadros had left Brasília and a temporary President had been sworn in. Effective power was held by the three military ministers— General Odílio Denys, the Minister of War; Brigadier Moss, Air Minister; and Admiral Sílvio Heck, Minister of the Navy. They quickly declared *de facto* marshal law in an attempt to prevent public demonstrations.

The immediate political question was whether there would be any significant movement demanding Quadros' return to the presidency. It was difficult to discern the lines of political conflict. Quadros had risen in politics as an independent; he had been at pains to avoid close association with any party or movement. In this he was like Getúlio Vargas in the period from 1930 to 1943. Unlike Vargas, however, Quadros declined to cooperate with the politicians whose "clientelistic" style was still common in the Brazil of 1961. Quadros' asset was his enormous public following, but there were several factors which undermined any attempt to demonstrate that support now. First, Quadros had precluded it by the seeming finality of his resignation and by the subsequent statement at Cumbica. Secondly, he was under heavy guard and either did not wish to, or was not permitted to make any further public statements. Thirdly, his popular support had never been institutionalized; he had failed to build any organizations which could mobilize and direct public demonstrations in support of his government. Finally, many of the "popular forces" which might be expected to demonstrate for Quadros were torn in two directions. On the one hand, they were tempted to support Quadros because they were attracted by his foreign policy and by the promise of greater independence from his conservative supporters in domestic policy; on the other hand, they were attracted by the prospect of having an historic populist—João Goulart—as their new President.

In any event, the popular demonstrations during the first three days after the resignation proved relatively unimpressive. On August 26 a group of labor leaders in Rio de Janeiro issued a statement, appealing to Quadros to return to power and vowing to crush the *golpistas* whom they identified as the *éminences grises* of the crises. There were also scattered student demonstrations in Recife and Rio de Janeiro, and a statement by the governors who had met Quadros at Cumbica, imploring him to return to power and asking the Congress to reject his resignation. This group included Governors Magalhães Pinto of Minas Gerais and Carvalho Pinto of São Paulo, historically the two most important states in modern Brazilian politics. And there ended the serious efforts to bring about his return.

In the subsequent nine days, from August 26 to September 4, there ensued a struggle between the military ministers, who were opposed to Goulart's succession, and the supporters of "legality"—composed of those military, politicians, and public figures who felt that the legal successor *whoever he might be* must be allowed to take office immediately. Constitutionally, if João Goulart could be prevented from acceding to the presidency, elections would be necessary within sixty days to elect a new President. In the interim, Mazzilli would remain the temporary President. This was the objective of the military ministers, who were backed by a small but vocal group of civilians. The *Estado de São Paulo,* for example, viewed Goulart's succession with alarm—the clock of history suddenly seemed to be turned back to 1950: "We would return to the situation in which Brazil found itself when, in a flagrant perversion of the principles which inspired the revolution of October 29, 1945, the dictator Getúlio Vargas, under the constitutional cloak, returned to climb the steps of power." What the anti-getulistas had won by the Army's intervention in 1945, lost in Vargas' election in 1950, won by the military again in 1954, lost in 1955 (both by the election and Lott's coup), and apparently won by the ballot box in 1960, was now again lost.[5]

The key to understanding the subsequent struggle over Goulart's succession lies in an analysis of the political sentiments within the Army. Quadros had chosen to retain the military ministers whom he had inherited from Kubitschek. Most important among them was War Minister Denys, who had been appointed to replace Marshal Lott when the latter was nominated for President in the campaign of 1960. Denys was a vigorous opponent of the Vargas legacy in domestic politics and was prepared, with his like-minded colleagues Moss and Heck, to impose these views after Quadros presented his resignation.

On August 28, Acting President Mazzilli sent a short message informing the Congress that the military ministers regarded the return of Goulart to Brazil as inadmissible "for reasons of national security." The military ministers hoped to force the Congress to act as it had acted earlier, in November of 1955. At that time, in response to Marshal Lott's preventive coup, the Congress followed the wishes of the War Minister and voted the removal of Acting President Carlos Luz (who was temporarily in office during Café Filho's illness) and elected to the presidency his constitutional successor, the vice president of the Senate, Nereu Ramos. The military ministers now hoped the Congress would simply ratify by a formal vote the absence of the Vice President and his ineligibility to hold the office, and thereby continue the interim presidency of Mazzilli, pending the elections to be held within sixty days.[6]

The Congress, however, declined to rubber-stamp the veto of Goulart's succession. Instead, the Congressional Commission, empowered to consider the question, recommended the creation of a parliamentary system. The politicians refused to abdicate, but they were prepared to compromise. The military ministers were not appeased; on August 29 they issued a manifesto, spelling out their reasons for continuing to regard the return of Goulart as unacceptable on grounds of national security. Their manifesto went farther than the language used by colonels in February 1954 when they forced Goulart's dismissal as Vargas' Labor Minister. It accused Goulart of being a notorious agitator in labor circles and of having granted key positions in unions to "agents of international Communism," as well as having extolled the success of popular communes during his recent visit to Communist China. The manifesto ended by charging that a Goulart presidency might promote infiltration of the armed forces, thus transforming them into "simple Communist militias." It was a symptom of the constant fear on the part of the military that a "syndicalist" labor movement might displace the armed forces as the most powerful group in Brazilian politics.[7]

Opinion within the Army was not, however, unanimous. Immediately after Quadros' resignation, Marshal Lott, by this time merely a retired general, issued a manifesto urging that Goulart be permitted to accede to the presidency as provided in the Constitution. It failed to rally even the "pro-legality" faction among the officer corps. Lott was no longer War Minister, and the presidential aspirant was not Kubitschek but João Goulart, long-time anathema to the conservative officers. Lott was promptly arrested on the orders of the War Minister. But the exact balance of opinion within the military—above all, the Army —at this moment was difficult to assess because the struggles were in private.[8]

Suddenly the split broke into the open. General Machado Lopes, the commander of the Third Army, which was centered in Goulart's home state of Rio Grande do Sul, announced his total support for Goulart. His unequivocal statement seemed to threaten civil war. Without this defection by a regional commander, the "legalist front" could probably not have countered the veto of the military ministers. Goulart owed his new prospect of succession, therefore, to the officers who dissented from the implacable opposition of the military ministers.

The period from August 28 to September 4 saw an elaborate process of military sparring.[9] This shadow struggle among commanders verged on warfare, as the political compromise demanded by the threat of violence seemed beyond reach. Unlike the political crises in which the military had previously intervened directly—October 1945, August 1954, and November 1955—the War Minister this time had failed to ensure the loyalty of all major commands. Rio Grande do Sul was ready to do battle. Furthermore, the commander of the Third Army enjoyed the support of Leonel Brizola, the Governor of Rio Grande do Sul, who was also, significantly, Goulart's brother-in-law. Brizola was an aggressive left-wing populist with ambitions in national politics. He saw immediately the crucial position of his state in the succession crisis. Indeed, he had pushed General Lopes into taking his rebellious stand by organizing the pro-Goulart officers around him. Brizola was also quick to organize mass demonstrations in Pôrto Alegre in support of fellow Riograndense Goulart. A chain of pro-Goulart radio stations labeled the "voice of legality" was immediately organized, to galvanize opinion in the rest of Brazil. When the naval ministry in Rio de Janeiro announced that it was sending a battle force south, Brizola ordered several ships to be sunk in order to block the entrance to the port of Pôrto Alegre.

Rio Grande do Sul's militant stand gave General Lopes the opportunity to present Marshal Denys and his colleagues in Brasília with the prospect of armed resistance to their attempted veto. The military ministers had committed a serious error in their calculations. They had overestimated the loyalty of their regional commanders—and other commanders were now wavering toward support of the Third Army position.

Quadros' resignation was so unexpected that it had caught the anti-getulista military off balance. They were not prepared for the test of power posed by the sudden prospect of Goulart's succession to the presidency. Intervention by the Army, if it were to be based on widespread agreement within the officer corps, required a long process of debate, in order to overcome the *prima facie* devotion to legality felt by most officers. Unlike 1954, or even 1955, the political crisis arose so suddenly that the "democratic" process of opinion formation within the officer corps was foreclosed. The result was that the War Minister overreached his base of support within the Army and was forced to retreat to a compromise position. To his dismay, he discovered that his announced veto did not have the weight of a sufficient majority of his own officers behind it. United, the armed forces might be able to impose an unpopular political solution. Divided, they could never succeed.

Compromise Solution: Parliamentary President

As the military split over Goulart's succession, a growing body of civilian opinion demanded that the Constitution be observed and Goulart installed as the legal successor. This "legalist" opinion represented a broad front. First, it included the "popular forces," led by left-wing students, labor leaders, and intellectuals. Although these groups attempted to organize protest demonstrations against the military ministers, they were not the decisive group in the final test of power. More important was the wide spectrum of opinion in the center—prominent figures such as governors and church leaders, as well as much of the middle class, who saw the issue as one of faith in democratic procedures and constitutional principles. Goulart had been elected Vice President in the 1960 election by defeating Quadros' running mate, Milton Campos. The fact that so many voters had been willing to split their ballot, voting for the nominee of one party for President and that of another for Vice President, indicated that Goulart's election was no accident. To disallow Goulart's succession to the presidency would be to renounce the principle of free elections, and to repudiate the millions of Brazilian voters who had put Goulart in the position from which he was now constitutionally entitled to assume the presidency. In essence, the "legalists" thought Goulart should be given his chance as President; his opponents must not be allowed to exclude him on the basis of charges about what he *might* do when in office.[10]

It is important to remember, however, that center opinion was supporting João Goulart "on probation." Many still harbored a suspicion that Goulart might sooner or later attempt a Peronist solution. They were unwilling to sacrifice from the outset Brazil's tradition of legality, but from this moment on "legality" was riding on Goulart's ability to serve out his presidency without upsetting the political equilibrium.

On September 2, the Congress adopted an amendment establishing a modified parliamentary system. The military ministers now realized they could not overcome the division within the ranks of the Army and could no longer ignore the widespread public reaction to their attempted veto. On September 4 the three service ministers indicated through a letter of Acting President Mazzilli to the Congress their willingness to accept the parliamentary compromise. On September 5, 1961, Goulart arrived in Brasília.

It was a circuitous route which had brought Goulart back to Brasília. From Communist China he had gone to Singapore when the crisis erupted. Hesitating to return to Brazil until some compromise solution had been worked out, he flew from Singapore to Paris, where he conferred with a hastily dispatched congressional delegation. During this conference he had agreed to accept a parliamentary solution. From Paris he flew to New York, thence down the west coast of South America, stopping in Montevideo. From Montevideo he went to his own state, the center of the opposition to the military ministers. It was from Rio Grande do Sul that Goulart made his way to the presidency in Brasília. On September 7, 1961, the one hundred and thirty-ninth anniversary of Brazilian independence, João Goulart was sworn in as President.

Recourse to a parliamentary system as the solution to the political crisis was the product of the long-time campaign by a small group of devotees of the parliamentary system. They were led by Raul Pilla, a tireless constitutional reformer. Pilla had long attributed Brazil's ills to the "vicious" presidential system, which in his view was a disastrous deviation from the parliamentary tradition of the Empire. But the sudden congressional approval of parliamentarism (a cabinet of ministers nominated by the President but serving at the pleasure of the Chamber of Deputies) was a little more than a desperate search for some compromise solution to the crisis produced by the military ministers' veto of Goulart's succession.[11]

The crisis from August 25 to September 5 dramatized several features of the Brazilian political scene. First, it was now apparent that Jânio Quadros' electoral victory had given him political power which was more apparent than real. He had channeled center opinion and middle-class aspirations as no politician before; but these hopes rested on a naive understanding of the political process. Quadros could not bring the weight of his popular following to bear within national politics unless he could somehow institutionalize it. In a word, he needed a broadly based party or movement to sustain him in what was bound to be a period of severe political strife. The only other path open to the new President was to exploit his charisma in order to impose some form of authoritarian rule, perhaps on the Gaullist model.[12] If he chose to remain within the constitutional system, his lack of an institutionalized following would have doomed his presidency to increasing ineffectiveness.

Second, the succession crisis demonstrated that in moments of breakdown in the civilian political process, the balance of opinion within the military would be decisive. If the military had been united against Goulart's accession, it is doubtful that he would ever have become President.

Third, the moderate military reflected the opinion of a large number of civilians, who were committed to the legal process in Brazil and who recoiled at the thought of renouncing a popularly elected politician because his views were *thought* to be unacceptable. For the moment, at any rate, the Brazilian political system had remained flexible enough to accommodate the conflict between the traditional arbiters of power and the new populist politicians, of which Goulart was an example.

Fourth, it was clear that the problems bequeathed by the Kubitschek government would require a strong government and a reasonable measure of public consent. But could a President "on probation" maintain the political equilibrium necessary to undertake a vigorous attack upon the range of problems facing Brazil in September 1961?

Finally, the "popular forces" which had vigorously supported Goulart's succession to the presidency may have drawn misleading conclusions from the August-September crisis. If they thought they had been responsible for preventing the military ministers' vetoing Goulart's succession, they were mistaken. Goulart became President, not because of pressure from the left, but because of a division within the military combined with a broad base of center opinion anxious to secure the observance of constitutional processes.

Who was João Goulart, the new President of Brazil? For one thing he was the political heir of Getúlio Vargas and therefore inescapably caught in the getulista-anti-getulista dichotomy which to some extent Kubitschek and particularly Quadros had seemed to offer hope of superseding. Suddenly, Brazil had returned to the divisions of 1954. Goulart was now in the presidency, although with limited powers, whereas in 1954 his opponents were able to force him out of the Labor Ministry in eight months.[13]

Goulart was the leader of Brazil's fastest growing major party, the PTB. Indeed, he was the only figure of national stature that party could offer. The PTB had conspicuously failed to develop a cadre of outstanding leaders. Like many parties of the left, it seemed to drive its best men into sterile dissent, soon leaving the party to lose their voices in well-meaning but ineffectual attempts to found "reform" labor movements. Two talented gaúchos, Danton Coelho and Fernando Ferrari, had left the PTB this way.[14] It was as if the party repelled its most talented and sensitive leaders, leaving the hacks and the opportunists to enjoy the political stewardship of the growing working-class vote and the benefits of the government-run labor unions. Among these undistinguished ranks, João Goulart excelled as a master in short-term political intrigue. Goulart had sought his political fortunes almost entirely on the national scale. Although military and civilian support in his home state of Rio Grande do Sul made possible his succession to the presidency, he was by no means a regional figure. On the contrary, he built his career upon the federally created system of labor unions and labor tribunals. It was this system which he had inherited from Getúlio Vargas and whose power the military deeply distrusted.

A wealthy rancher, he had moved almost by reflex into the political world of the PTB in Rio Grande do Sul. The great strength of the party in that state may have seemed paradoxical, since one would hardly have expected ranches to produce leaders of a party which claimed to represent the working class. Yet Rio Grande do Sul had given Rio de Janeiro many a radical in the Revolution of 1930; furthermore, Vargas had carefully nurtured the new PTB in his home state during his "exile" from 1945 to 1950. Given an indispensable boost by Getúlio in early 1950, Jango was the natural heir (in more ways than one, suggested his detractors) to the PTB leadership after his mentor's suicide in 1954. The party chose him as its vice presidential candidate in the alliance with the PSD which had won the presidency in 1955. Although this alliance lost to Quadros in 1960, Goulart managed to survive as Vice President. His victory reflected the apparent schizophrenia of the Brazilian electorate in 1960, choosing an independent as President, and as Vice President a representative of the system which the President-elect had made the target of his campaign.[15]

Despite the fears of his opponents and the claims of his supporters, Goulart lacked long-term political vision and was not an impressive vote-getter. He probably had less voter appeal than any President elected since 1945 with the exception of Dutra. In both 1955 and 1960 he had won the vice presidency only by a narrow margin against Milton Campos, a conventional UDN candidate. In 1954 he had even been defeated in an attempt to win election as senator from Rio Grande do Sul.

The prospects for Goulart's presidency depended upon two factors. What would be the policies of the new President and where would he seek his political support? It is worth noting that Quadros had not yet answered these questions for his own presidency when he resigned on August 25, 1961. Goulart could construct a strong political base only by cultivating the center and at the same time maintaining support from the left. The situation was further complicated by the divergence between Goulart's populism and the new forces on the left. His established contacts lay with the oft-corrupt officials of labor unions and social security institutes, as well as with traditional, non-ideological local politicians. But there had emerged a more radical position on the left, whose spokesmen viewed Goulart's traditional "labor" politics with scorn.[16] He would need, therefore, to bridge a growing division within the left, as well as between the left and the center. Goulart needed to find and retain an operating political base—a delicate political balancing act in itself—within a newly created parliamentary system, and in the face of increasing radicalization at either end of the political spectrum.

Marking Time

In the fourteen months from September 1961 to January 1963, Goulart maneuvered carefully to regain full presidential powers by winning popular approval in a plebiscite for the rejection of the Additional Act that had established the parliamentary system. There were, however, many obstacles on that path. First, the new President had to prove his "respectability" to the traditional arbiters of power. He began by attempting to disarm his most powerful opponents, especially the anti-getulista military who had forced his dismissal as Labor Minister in 1954 and who had tried to prevent his accession to the presidency in 1961. They had failed only because the officer corps was split and because civilian opinion in the center preferred a "legal" solution to the crisis.

Goulart's problem with the opposition military was far greater than that of Kubitschek in 1956. Kubitschek had to isolate a minority of extremist officers, but Goulart faced a more entrenched and widespread opposition that had already succeeded in shearing him of his full presidential powers.[17] Goulart was President in a parliamentary system. His authority had been diluted by the elevation of cabinet ministers who could be legally forced from office only by congressional disapproval.[18]

The first cabinet included a balanced representation of the major parties. The PSD, still the largest party in the Congress, received four ministries, including the Prime Ministership. The latter went to Tancredo Neves, who had been Vargas' last Minister of Justice in 1954, when he favored a last-ditch battle against the ultimatum of the military. The PTB was given two ministries, including the Foreign Ministry (San Tiago Dantas), and two posts went to UDN leaders, one of whom was the well-known economic nationalist from Minas Gerais, Congressman Gabriel de Rezende Passos. The all-important portfolio of War Minister passed from Marshal Denys to General João de Segadas Vianna, who had acted as a mediator between the intransigently anti-Goulart military ministers and the "pro-legality" Army officers during the succession crisis.[19]

In the first six months of his parliamentary presidency, Goulart labored to consolidate his political position. He stressed his anti-Communist principles and his devotion to the democratic process.[20] Given the continued financial crisis, which Quadros had only begun to attack, Goulart knew that he would have to convince the United States and the international monetary authorities of his serious intent. He partially succeeded in doing this by a trip to Washington in April of 1962. His visit included a speech to a joint session of the American Congress and lengthy conversations with President Kennedy and other officials. Although Goulart's trip was essentially a good will mission, both sides made concrete gestures. Goulart assured the Congress that Brazil was an independent but not a neutral nation, and declared his opposition to the totalitarian regime of Castro. The United States government in turn completed negotiations for $131 million in aid funds for the Northeast, which had been held up because of American insistence on controlling its expenditure. The two Presidents also issued a joint communiqué reaffirming the principles of the Inter-American system and pledging support for the Latin American Free Trade Association. During the informal conversations in Washington, Goulart had given "indications of reasonable treatment" of foreign-owned public utilities, whose expropriation had become a burning political issue in Brazil. But he proved relatively unresponsive to American urgings for a more cooperative attitude toward the Alliance for Progress in Brazil and was unimpressed by American worries over Communist infiltration in the labor union movement. Although the visit produced limited results, it appeared to mark the beginning of what might prove to be more fruitful cooperation between the Goulart government and the United States. But the IMF and Brazil's other principal creditors had returned to their wait-and-see attitude of the later Kubitschek years. They were skeptical that Goulart had either the will or the power to continue the tough anti-inflation program launched by Quadros.[21]

At home, Goulart's trip, which included a stop in Mexico, had earned him new respect from middle-class voters and conservative opponents. But Goulart now began to worry about where the balance of power actually lay in the Brazilian political system. How many votes did the radical populists such as his brother-in-law Brizola represent? How far had the fiasco of Jânio's resignation radicalized public opinion? In what direction? The congressional elections scheduled for October, 1962, might settle some of these questions. In the meantime, Goulart thought he needed to cultivate the left. Bored and confused by briefings over the financial crisis, the solution of which promised little but political unpopularity, he was attracted to the growing campaign in favor of "basic reforms." The idea of such reforms, which were often left disconcertingly vague, appeared to offer Jango the opportunity of making an historical reputation for himself and also a way of building his own political following. Kubitschek had gone into history as the industrializer and the builder of Brasília; Quadros had launched a crusade to purge Brazil of political and financial corruption; Goulart would now bring "basic reforms." In a speech on May Day 1962, he began by calling for agrarian reform, demanding an amendment to the constitutional provision requiring that owners of expropriated land be paid in cash.[22]

Goulart's tactic of appealing to the left had one grave weakness: the left itself was divided. As if to recognize this fact, Brazilians often referred to "the lefts" (*as esquerdas*), which included two principal groups. One was the moderate left (or "positive left"), represented by San Tiago Dantas, a PTB politician-lawyer from Minas (and a former *Integralista*), and by the young technocrats such as Celso Furtado, who shunned party labels but were important nonetheless. This group was respected by the center for the seriousness of its intentions. The radical left (or "negative left"), on the other hand, represented by Leonel Brizola, was more violent in its language and appeared ready to go beyond constitutional processes.[23] In his speech of May Day and another on May 13, Goulart's *language* seemed to be close to the positive left, but his *tone* sounded closer to the negative left. The President had taken up the campaign for reforms, but he had also aroused the suspicions of the center about his ultimate motives.

Goulart's attitude toward the left became more ambiguous in June when Tancredo Neves, the first Prime Minister under the parliamentary system, resigned.[24] In fact, Neves and Goulart had pursued a plan aimed at deliberately demonstrating the "unworkability" of the parliamentary system. Their objective was to strengthen the campaign for a return to the presidential system. Goulart nominated as his successor San Tiago Dantas. (As Foreign Minister in the Tancredo Neves cabinet, Dantas had defended Brazil's neutrality on Cuba, thereby provoking the ire of the right.)[25] The UDN bitterly attacked Dantas, and as the Chamber of Deputies balked at his nomination, it appeared there would be a test of power between the two extremes: on the left, the National Confederation of Industrial Workers (CNTI), threatening to strike in support of Dantas' nomination; on the right, anti-getulista military officers, campaigning to discredit Dantas and prevent his confirmation. The Chamber rejected Dantas' nomination by a decisive vote (174–110). Skeptics suggested that his nomination was merely a tactic by Goulart to dramatize the difficulties of working with a Congress dominated by the conservative majority.

The key to the congressional deadlock was the PSD. It had worked in a loose alliance with Goulart's PTB ever since the beginning of the Kubitschek presidency. But the more conservative PSD members were now alarmed over Goulart's tack toward the left, especially on land reform. After consulting the congressional leadership, Goulart out-flanked the PSD by simply nominating Senate President Moura Andrade, a PSD leader, as Prime Minister. It was rumored, however, that Goulart had extracted in advance an undated but signed letter of resignation from Andrade. Within forty-eight hours the new Prime Minister did indeed announce his resignation, ostensibly over Goulart's refusal to approve his ministerial appointments.

The political wrangling in Brasília had reached the point of maximum confusion. Goulart had tried nominating a prominent PTB and a prominent PSD nominee, resulting only in a stalemate with the Congress. The Army fretted over the politicians' inability to produce even a modicum of political stability in the face of the inflationary spiral. With the announcement of Moura Andrade's resignation, the armed forces went on alert.

There was ample reason for such precautions. The CNTI called a general strike, paralyzing public transportation in the leading cities. Food riots broke out, and hundreds were injured in the looting of food supplies in Duque de Caxias, an industrial suburb of Rio de Janeiro. Shopkeepers in Rio shuttered their windows in panic. Labor leaders responsible for the general strike flew the same day to Brasília, where the President convinced them to end the walkout. Here was an innovation in Brazilian politics: the President negotiating with labor leaders who themselves depended on the government-collected labor dues and the approval of the Ministry of Labor for their positions. Was Goulart moving to allay *genuine* pressure on the left or was it pressure of his own making? [26]

Goulart seized on the strikes and riots as proof that he needed full executive powers to govern Brazil. His die-hard opponents charged that he was deliberately condoning social unrest for political purposes. Goulart now tried again to find a Prime Minister acceptable to the Chamber of Deputies. He nominated Brochado da Rocha, a PSD deputy from Rio Grande do Sul who had been Governor Brizola's Secretary of Interior and Justice. He had also been a close adviser during the expropriation of the International Telephone and Telegraph subsidiary the preceding February. Brochado da Rocha proved less controversial to the Chamber than Dantas, perhaps because he was a PSD member and also a less well-known figure in national politics.

Goulart Wins Full Presidential Powers

A new cabinet was agreed upon and approved by the Chamber. It included Moreira Salles, an eminently respectable banker who remained from the previous cabinet as Finance Minister, and José Ermírio de Morais, a PTB leader and "nationalist" industrialist, as Minister of Trade and Industry. The new Prime Minister promised an emergency program to fight inflation and food shortages; he also pledged to continue Brazil's "independent" foreign policy. The latter was ensured by the return of Afonso Arinos de Melo Franco as Foreign Minister, to replace Santiago Dantas, who had succeeded Afonso Arinos after Quadros' resignation a year earlier.

Most significant, Brochado da Rocha called for an early plebiscite on the question of continuing the parliamentary system. The amendment of September 1961 had provided for a plebiscite in early 1965, but opinion was now growing in the center and left that the decision ought to come sooner. By August Brochado da Rocha was requesting special powers, including authority for the Cabinet to legislate by decree. Weren't these the powers Quadros had claimed he needed to govern Brazil? The Congress, especially the PSD and the UDN, balked at Brochado da Rocha's request. The Prime Minister introduced a bill to hold the plebiscite in December, more than two years before the date set in the Additional Act of September 1961. Conflict now centered on that question.

On the right came attacks from Lacerda and the extreme UDN. Goulart's regime was tied to the Communists and was plotting a coup, they charged; to give the President full powers or his ministers emergency authority would only aid their "subversive" purposes. On the left there was the voice of Brizola, who threatened the Congress with armed intervention if it did not pass the bill providing for a plebiscite in December.

There was wide support among the center as well as the left for an early return to the presidential system.[27] Almost all observers, regardless of political opinion, agreed that Brazil needed a strong federal executive. This had been the lesson of the period since 1930. The lines of authority in the Brazilian executive were sufficiently tangled without requiring direct ministerial responsibility to the Congress. Even some of Goulart's die-hard political enemies backed the return of the presidential system in the belief that any President could be held accountable only if he possessed full authority.

Furthermore, the prospects for effective government under the hybrid parliamentary regime were poor because the President and his political allies did not really want the system to work, especially after early 1962. They hoped instead to capitalize on its apparent ineffectiveness, to which they were contributing, in order to hasten the plebiscite. This tactic had its allies within the PSD. Kubitschek, for example, urged Goulart not to content himself with his "castrated" powers under the parliamentary system. Kubitschek's strong approval of the campaign for the early plebiscite was undoubtedly linked to his own ambitions to run for the presidency again in 1965.

But the essential support necessary for wider presidential powers had to come from the military. Goulart succeeded in gaining their support by a shrewd policy of promotions and transfers. He promoted more "nationalist" generals into key command positions. Military friction over the question of a plebiscite reached its height in August and September of 1962. In August the three military ministers issued a manifesto supporting a plebiscite, and the Congress subsequently set the deadline of April 1963 for the national vote on the question. But Goulart wanted the question of parliamentarism vs. presidentialism put on the ballot in the congressional elections of October 7, 1962. In September, the commander of the Third Army (Rio Grande do Sul), General Dantas Ribeiro, telegraphed the President, the Prime Minister, and the War Minister, informing them that he could not guarantee to maintain order "if the people revolt over a Congressional refusal to hold the plebiscite before, or at least simultaneously with, the October elections." War Minister Nelson de Melo indignantly rejected Dantas Ribeiro's threat.[28]

General de Melo had also been, however, a firm supporter of an early plebiscite. His reaction to Dantas Ribeiro was more a matter of military discipline than of disagreement over the issue, although there were many officers, probably a minority, who opposed an early plebiscite. The War Minister was irritated that the atmosphere of deliberation in Brasília, already heated by the military ministers' pro-plebiscite manifesto of August, should now be poisoned by the threat of civil war from the commanding general in Rio Grande do Sul. For a centrist officer such as General de Melo, the incident was doubly irritating because Brizola was Governor of Rio Grande do Sul and was undoubtedly instrumental in Dantas Ribeiro's sending his ultimatum, as he had been in General Machado Lopes' threatened revolt during Goulart's succession crisis a year earlier.

In early September the Brochado da Rocha cabinet resigned because of disagreement over strategy on the plebiscite bill. The new Prime Minister was Hermes Lima, a well-known socialist who supported the plebiscite. (Lima was not formally confirmed by the Chamber until late November.) One of the new government's first acts was to replace War Minister Nelson de Melo with General Amaury Kruel, a close personal friend of Goulart. This move further ensured the President's strength among the military. Goulart failed to get the plebiscite on the October ballot, but in the closing months of 1962 he had been able to find strong military backing for his demand that the Congress set an early date. A few days after Brochado's resignation, the Congress finally acceded, and the date of the plebiscite was set for January 6, 1963.

Amid charges that he had neglected the basic economic and social problems, Goulart named Celso Furtado, the noted economist and architect of the Northeast Development Authority (SUDENE), to draw up a plan for national economic development. Furtado had a large order: to prescribe a formula for insuring rapid economic growth combined with reasonable price stability. With the plebiscite set for January, however, it was unlikely that any bold new policies would be adopted before the end of 1962. Goulart was not yet ready to commit himself to a clearly defined policy or to opt for any single base of political support. That was only to occur after he regained full presidential powers.

The elections in October gave a new indication of political sentiment in the country. First, the ghost of Jânio Quadros was laid to rest in the election for Governor of São Paulo. Three days after his resignation, Quadros had left Brazil on a round-the-world trip, punctuated by frequent promises that he would return and resume his political crusade. Remarkably enough, Quadros remained a popular figure in Brazil, and this became more evident as the new parliamentary system proved unwieldy and unworkable in its first months. In March 1962, Quadros landed in Brazil and gave a much-heralded speech purporting to explain the reasons for his resignation. The speech was a total anti-climax, and many of the Quadros followers who had remained faithful finally began to waver.[29]

The Christian Democratic Party refused to nominate him as its candidate for governor of São Paulo in the upcoming election of October 1962. Undaunted, Quadros announced that he would run as an independent. His opponents were Adhemar de Barros, the well-tested Paulista populist, and José Bonifácio, a former protégé of Quadros and now the candidate of incumbent Governor, Carvalho Pinto. Jânio was defeated, although narrowly (1,249,414 to 1,125,941), by Adhemar de Barros, who gained crucial last-minute support from panicked followers of Carvalho Pinto, who realized that José Bonifácio (who got 722,823 votes) stood virtually no chance of election. This defeat greatly diminished the lingering legend of Quadros and cleared an important barrier to Goulart's campaign for a return to presidentialism.[30]

The congressional elections of October 1962, as well as the elections for governor in eleven states, confirmed the strength of the center. The Congress retained its relatively non-ideological character, and the middle positions in most parties continued to hold the balance of power within the two chambers.[31] On January 6, 1963, the Brazilian public voted five to one to scrap the parliamentary system and return to the presidential system. Goulart could now enter history as a full-fledged President in his own right.

The Political Spectrum and the Extremists

What political situation did Goulart face as he began this new period of his presidency? [32] Most important, the politics of compromise were becoming steadily more difficult. Goulart, now on the verge of attempting to prove that he deserved his new powers, was about to reap the harvest of the prolonged political deadlock. At either end of the spectrum, political extremists were urging anti-democratic solutions in the common belief that each stood to gain most from a breakdown of democratic politics. It is important to distinguish among the varying groups that were now attracted to the arguments of the "radicalizers." [33]

The first important group was to be found among the traditional anti-getulistas. Stunned by Quadros' sudden resignation in 1961 but unable to prevent Goulart's succession or his gaining of full presidential powers in January 1963, they lapsed into a despair reminiscent of their mood after Kubitschek's election in October 1955. But they were now better organized and more resolute. Goulart's tactics in maneuvering to get an earlier date for the plebiscite—especially the evident condoning of the general strike in July 1962—convinced them that they were dealing with the same Goulart whose resignation the colonels had forced in February 1954. In early 1962 these anti-Goulart leaders had begun conspiring to overthrow the President. They were represented among the military, for example, by former War Minister Denys and former Navy Minister Heck, as well as by generals such as Cordeiro de Farias and Nelson de Melo. Their chief civilian contact was Júlio de Mesquita Filho, owner of the influential newspaper, *O Estado de São Paulo*. In 1962 these conspirators were already exchanging ideas on the nature of the "discretionary" regime that would need to follow Goulart's overthrow.[34]

The anti-Goulart radicalizers had a familiar inventory of anti-democratic doctrine to draw upon. As had been argued in 1950 and 1955, they claimed that the Brazilian electorate could not be trusted. Only under careful tutelage could the public be prevented from succumbing to the wiles of "demagogic" politicians. Morality and anti-communism were the watchwords of these radicalizers. The difference after 1961, however, was that among the intransigent anti-Goulart forces there were some elements that wanted to experiment with their own techniques of mobilizing the electorate before they were willing to succumb to the idea of an armed conspiracy.

There was, for example, a "Civil-Military Patriotic Front" (*Frente Patriótica Civil-Militar*) that constituted the "left wing" of the anti-government conspiracy. These anti-Goulart leaders sought to compete with Goulart's efforts at mobilization of the masses and thereby produce a more "authentic" movement of their own. Their objective was to replace the "corrupt" Vargas "system" by organizing, for example, labor unions free of government supervision. These efforts, which had hardly begun by January 1963, were a continuation, in a new form, of Jânio Quadros' brief attempt at backing left-wing reformers within the labor movement in 1960.[35]

In addition to the *Frente Patriótica,* the anti-Goulart militants could count on a new and well-financed Paulista businessmen's movement, centered in the Institute of Social Research and Study (*Instituto de Pesquisas e Estudos Sociais* or IPES), founded in 1961. This group began with the objective, in the words of one of its founders, of mobilizing "democratic public feeling" against the "leftists" around Goulart. By late 1962, however, there was serious consideration of more direct methods. One Paulista industrialist who was a member of IPES expressed the mood when he organized vigilantes to silence leftist hecklers at anti-Communist meetings with "intellectual methods— like a kick in the head." [36]

On the left, the radicalizers sought to capitalize on any political crisis in order to bring about an abrupt transfer of power. Their aim was to influence public opinion to such an extent that the established arbiters of power would become discredited or outmaneuvered. Organizations taking a radical left-wing position were, for example, labor groups such as the *Comando Geral de Greve,* the *Pacto Sindical de Unidade e Ação* (PUA, railroad and port workers), and the *Comando Geral dos Trabalhadores* (CGT).[37] Prominent also were the Peasant Leagues and the *Frente Parlamentar Nacionalista* (FPN), an interparty pact of left-wing congressmen.[38] The National Union of Students (UNE) was controlled by students who often espoused this position.[39] The Brazilian Communist Party (*Partido Communista Brasileiro*) was working to force a more "nationalist and democratic" government within the existing structure. The pro-Chinese splinter Communist Party of Brazil (*Partido Communista do Brasil*) spoke more uncompromisingly, but constituted a very small group, having been formed only in 1962.

The most prominent political leader within the radical left was Leonel Brizola, now PTB federal deputy from Guanabara. Brizola was given to violent language against his enemies, often threatening extra-parliamentary action against the Congress, as he did in the crisis of September 1962 over advancing the date for the plebiscite on the return to the presidential system.

The important feature to note here about these radicalizers on the left is their emphasis on *direct* methods to fight the "golpistas," "entreguistas," and "reactionaries." None of these groups was frankly revolutionary by late 1962, but the radical left was, nonetheless, demonstrating grave doubts about the possibility of satisfying their desire for radical change within the existing constitutional structure.

The pressure from the radical left was, however, far from homogeneous. On the one hand, there were the confident but amateurish leftists, sometimes described as "Jacobins," who scorned the discipline of the PCB and were impatient over the strategy of cooperating with the "national bourgeoisie." Brizola was certainly in this category, as were many radical nationalist student leaders from groups such as *Ação Popular* (an outgrowth of the youth movement sponsored by the Roman Catholic Church), and certain labor leaders who were not consistent in their loyalty either to the PCB-dominated leadership of the CGT or the government-manipulated Ministry of Labor. Very active among the "Jacobins"—meaning non-Communist radical nationalist left—were intellectuals and writers such as Franklin de Oliveira, an adviser to Brizola during his governorship of Rio Grande do Sul (1959–63).[40] The Prestes-led Communist Party (PCB), on the other hand, was a voice for caution, warning against any strategy that overestimated the true strength of the "popular forces."[41] These divisions within the radical nationalist left were to become crucial in the last fifteen months of the Goulart presidency.

Despite the growth of extremist opinion, in early 1963 the majority of Brazilians was still to be found in the center. Pro-democratic, they favored a mixed economy which would make use of foreign capital under careful national control. Center opinion believed in opening the political system, but only with caution. Its social basis was primarily the urban middle class, which retained its belief in liberal constitutionalism, but also recognized the need for industrialization while resisting any clear-cut ideological approach to that process. But these middle-of-the road views were not clearly formulated, and in fact contained their own spectrum of opinion—from the "positive left," which favored large measures of government control, to the "enlightened industrialists," who wanted government interference to be carefully restricted.[42]

In the last nine months of Goulart's "parliamentary" presidency, however, the extremists had seemed to gain ground. Certainly their views were receiving more public attention. Two issues, neither of which lent itself easily to the politics of compromise, were largely responsible for this. The first was the role of foreign capital. In November 1961 a stringent profit remittances law was passed by the Chamber of Deputies. The most controversial provision dealt with the treatment of reinvested profits, essentially excluding such reinvestments from the definition of the capital base on which profit remittances could be calculated. Vargas had criticized bitterly the inclusion of reinvested profits in the capital base, and the ending of this practice had been thereafter the principal goal of the nationalist congressmen, led by PTB Deputy Sérgio Magalhães, who guided the bill through the lower house. The bill's opponents, who included UDN leaders such as Senator Mem de Sá, the foreign business community, and United States Ambassador Lincoln Gordon, argued strenuously that reinvested profits *should* be counted along with original investment as part of the base on which remittances could be sent abroad.

The Senate amended the Chamber's bill, softening the provisions on reinvestment in a compromise version. The Chamber, however, which had the power to pass its own version the second time around, rejected the compromise bill and reinserted the tougher provisions on reinvestment. Although the nationalists per se were a minority of the Chamber, they were able to organize a majority by drawing on the widespread suspicion toward foreign investors that permeated otherwise middle-of-the-road deputies. The bill had aroused a storm of debate among economists and businessmen, and its passage, along with the continuing inflation and unstable political situation, caused foreign investors to delay further commitments in Brazil.[43]

Goulart's reaction to the final bill was typical. Confused by the detailed arguments but aware of the grave political implications, he found himself caught between the nationalist wing of his own PTB and his Finance Minister, Miguel Calmon, who recommended that he veto the bill. He finally decided to sign the bill on the understanding that he would support a Senate-initiated bill amending the provision on reinvested profits. When the time came, however, and the Senate sent its amending bill to the Chamber, Goulart lost his nerve and failed to bring pressure to bear against the nationalists in support of the amendment. Meanwhile, the division between nationalists and the advocates of more orthodox policies had deepened and become more bitter.[44]

There was another issue involving foreign capital that also exacerbated the divisions. In February 1962, Leonel Brizola, as Governor of Rio Grande do Sul, had expropriated a local telephone company which was a subsidiary of the International Telephone and Telegraph Company.[45] This incident, a foreboding of expropriations contemplated by other governors, aroused feverish diplomatic negotiations between the United States and Brazil. Carlos Lacerda, the militantly anti-Goulart governor of Guanabara, decided to court nationalist opinion in his own fashion; he announced that he would expropriate the telephone company in Rio de Janeiro, owned by Canadian interests. In an effort to forestall further such unilateral actions by local politicians, the federal government speeded up its efforts to negotiate an overall settlement with foreign owners of utilities.

Political radicalization was also increasingly evident in a second sphere: the rural land structure. In November of 1961, a national Peasants' Congress was held in Belo Horizonte, with Francisco Julião the most prominent figure. Earlier in 1961, Julião and one hundred peasant leaders had visited Cuba for the May Day celebrations. Following the Peasants' Congress in November 1961, violence became more frequent in the countryside, with squatters fighting off land speculators who attempted to expel them from rural properties over which they had established de facto ownership. Violence became frequent in Minas Gerais, the state of Rio de Janeiro, and several Northeastern states.[46] The once-quiescent countryside was awakening politically. Such a development was bound to send a shock wave through national politics, since many national politicians owed their existence to the backward political systems of areas still manipulated by landowners.[47]

Beyond these two issues—the role of foreign capital and the question of land structures—was the perennial problem of Brazil's inflation and deficits in the balance of payments. The latter disequilibrium required that Brazil submit to "financial discipline," thus appearing to follow the dictates of the developed countries and the international monetary authorities. This situation, as usual, offered ready arguments to political radicalizers of both right and left.

Party Lines

What was the pattern of party politics when Goulart gained full presidential powers in January 1963? It is often asserted that political parties per se meant relatively little in postwar Brazil because of the great regional variations within each party. Such a conclusion can be misleading if it is not based on a careful consideration of the general character of each party *within* which the variations occurred. Furthermore, party loyalty, however illogical it may have seemed in terms of the principles at stake (in economic policy, for example), was still a powerful force among politicians. This was all the more true since the President, now enjoying full powers, was a self-proclaimed heir of the Vargas "system"—and it was the beneficiaries and opponents of this "system" who had first organized the three major parties.

Nevertheless, there was evidence that, on the local level, party lines had become steadily more blurred since the creation of the new party system in 1945. This development was best illustrated by the increasing predominance of coalition tickets in congressional elections. Of the 409 members elected to the Chamber of Deputies in November 1962, only 216 ran on single-party tickets. The other 193 were elected on coalition tickets—alliances brought together for immediate election purposes and without any implications for a coherent party or multi-party position in subsequent legislative action. The increasing reliance on election coalitions prevented the electorate, presuming that it had sufficient consciousness and motivation, from demanding of their congressmen any accountability along party lines.[48]

The practical result of this lack of definition of party lines was to make of each party, although with significantly different weightings, a microcosm of the national political spectrum. The UDN, born in 1945 out of liberal democratic opposition to Vargas, represented primarily the urban middle and upper classes of the center-south regions who had already gathered the fruits of Brazil's limited industrial development. But a left-wing group, known as the "Bossa Nova," akin to the more liberal position of Governor Magalhães Pinto of Minas Gerais (elected in 1960), made impossible simple ideological or class categorization of the party as a whole. The PSD was preeminently the "clientelistic" party accustomed to enjoying power and its fruits under Vargas and Kubitschek. But it had its left-wing "aggressives," who had little in common with the much more numerous representatives of the large rural landowners. The third major party, the PTB, although designed by Vargas to channel for his benefit the growing working-class vote, contained a number of members from backward states, representing more conservative positions than the leftist members of the PSD or the UDN. The PTB also has its *grupo compacto,* which sought a new, more radically left-wing, ideological identity for the party.[49]

Although the elections of November 1962 did little to change the apparent party strengths in the Congress, there were several individual contests, both for governor and for Congress, that gave evidence of the growing polarization of opinion.[50] The key states of Minas Gerais and Guanabara had been captured two years earlier by the UDN. Magalhães Pinto, who won in 1960 in Minas, was a moderate opponent of Goulart, while Carlos Lacerda—the incumbent Governor of Guanabara—was violently anti-Goulart. In 1962 the governorship of Rio Grande do Sul went to Ildo Meneghetti, an uninspired and avuncular PSD politician, who defeated the PTB nominee backed by outgoing radical leftist Governor Leonel Brizola. (There was also a third candidate in the field: independent Laborite Fernando Ferrari.) In São Paulo the gubernatorial election in 1962 was won by Adhemar de Barros, the ever-resourceful campaigner, who defeated both Jânio Quadros and the hand-picked candidate (José Bonifácio) of retiring Governor Carvalho Pinto. Both Meneghetti and Adhemar de Barros, although not yet outspoken opponents of Goulart, were victors who owed nothing directly to the "popular forces" Goulart longed to harness. In not a single one of the eleven gubernatorial contests in 1962 was there an alliance between the PSD and the PTB—the alliance on which both Vargas and Kubitschek had based their party support. It is interesting to note that in 1960 there had been eight such alliances in the eleven elections for state governor.

The 1962 elections in Guanabara, on the other hand, seemed to indicate a swing to the left. The election for vice-governor went to Eloy Dutra, an outspoken opponent of Lacerda, the incumbent anti-Goulart governor. In the congressional election Leonel Brizola won a sensational victory, amassing a total vote of 269,000, the highest ever given to a congressional candidate in Brazil. His victory was all the more impressive because he had no connection with Guanabara. His appeal seemed to be highly personal, however, and he was not able to transfer his electoral magic to his designated candidate for Governor of Rio Grande do Sul. Indeed, his heavy vote in Guanabara was in part due to his drawing votes away from other left-wing PTB Congressional candidates. But this personal victory reinforced Brizola's limitless ambitions for power within the PTB by strengthening his claim that he represented its most dynamic element.

Pernambuco also offered evidence of a trend to the left. The winning candidate for Governor was Miguel Arraes, who was supported by a coalition of left-wing parties, including the small Communist Party. Arraes' election represented the first clear-cut victory of a leftist-oriented urban electorate in a state that was relatively backward economically. Arraes had succeeded in mobilizing the seasonal sugarcane workers on the coastal strip (literate enough to qualify for the franchise), and had thereby overcome the electoral dominance of the traditional political oligarchy which had begun to lose its grip in the previous gubernatorial election (1958). Also elected in Pernambuco was a "nationalist" industrialist from São Paulo, José Ermírio de Morais, who won a seat in the federal Senate. He ran under the PTB label and gave generous financing to Arraes' campaign in return for endorsement in Pernambuco.

There was another feature of the 1962 elections that signified a new stage in the development of political activity: the lavish financing of campaigns. The Goulart government made available extensive sums for leftist candidates through the use of the facilities of federal institutes and patronage. The Goulart opponents were also well-financed. Brazilian businessmen (and foreign businessmen, according to leftist critics) contributed to an electoral war chest administered by a new extra-party organization, the Brazilian Institute of Democratic Action (*Instituto Brasileiro de Ação Democrática* or IBAD). This group was a counterpart on the electoral level to anti-leftist organizations such as IPES, the Paulista businessmen's movement.[51]

What conclusions could be drawn from the elections of 1962 about the relative party strengths? First, there was no clear-cut trend either to the left or to the right on a national level. The growing influence of the radicalizers could be seen in several individual contests, but the respective gains of the extreme right and left seemed to have canceled each other out. Brizola ran well in Guanabara but lost his control in

Rio Grande do Sul. Lacerda continued to catalyze anti-Goulart opinion in the nation but saw his electoral base in Guanabara weakened. Within the left the trends were ambiguous. The PTB increased its membership in the Chamber of Deputies sharply, rising from 66 to 104 seats. Yet this did not seem to strengthen the position of Goulart, the party's titular head. Goulart was caught between the two wings of his own party. On the left there was his brother-in-law, Brizola, flushed with victory in Guanabara and demanding radical action. The "positive left" within the PTB was represented by San Tiago Dantas, the brilliant PTB deputy from Minas Gerais, who was Goulart's Finance-Minister-designate in the new Cabinet named after the plebiscite in January 1963. But Dantas had received only 35,000 votes in his reelection as deputy from Minas Gerais, significantly less than PSD candidates such as Sebastião Paes de Almeida and Gilberto Faria. This was significant in view of the fact that in mid-1962 Dantas' abortive nomination as Prime Minister under the parliamentary system had occasioned threats of a general strike from the left-wing labor leaders, who now preferred the radical language of Brizola.

The most ominous fact evident in the pattern of party politics was the absence of any effective party representation of center opinion. The UDN was split between its moderate wing, led by Governor Magalhães Pinto (Minas Gerais) and Senator Afonso Arinos, and its intransigent wing, led by Carlos Lacerda (who was nonetheless running an efficient and progressive administration as Governor of the state of Guanabara) and Deputy Bilac Pinto. The latter were the custodians of the tradition of the anti-Vargas crusades. In national politics their interest was in radicalizing public opinion against the new beneficiaries of the Vargas "system," not in joining forces to accelerate economic development or achieve social reform. Their approach was totally partisan, since for them the essential question was: how could the heirs of Vargas be overthrown?

But this militant attitude did not match the mood of the center as of January 1963. Although the violent demands for radical change by leftists such as Brizola frightened many centrist voters, there was widespread sympathy within the center for the idea of social reform. Evidence of this mood could be found, for example, in the work of the progressive wing of the Catholic Church, which made clear its rejection of extremist views, whether of the right or left, while also endorsing the need to overhaul Brazil's archaic structure in areas such as agriculture and education. Unfortunately, however, this legalist, democratic, reform-minded center opinion could find no party refuge.[52]

Their position was close to that of San Tiago Dantas within the PTB, but Dantas was far from controlling the PTB, whose rank and file followed the uninspired leadership of such stereotyped would-be Vargas-heirs as Doutel de Andrade, a deputy who lacked any ability to inspire confidence among the center.[53] Within the UDN the center views were close to Magalhães Pinto, but he was losing ground within the party to radicalizers like Lacerda, for whom the confrontation with the party's historic enemies, such as Goulart, was the essence of politics. And the PSD was essentially passive in the face of this radicalization of opinion. As a group, the party seemed to be waiting in the wings, enjoying a measure of participation in the government and hoping that Goulart could survive his term so that Kubitschek could return to power. Furthermore, the PSD was hardly a likely vehicle for centrist aspirations for reform, especially in the area of agriculture.

At the same time that center opinion could find no true party home, it was increasingly subject to panic at the prospect of seeing the stewardship of reform pass into the hands of the extremists on the left—radical populists such as Brizola and leaders of groups such as the militant dockworkers' and metalworkers' unions. In short, the search for a party base capable of sustaining effective government was a race against time: could a centrist regime achieve results before the extremists undermined any possibility of democratic politics?

Goulart inherited, therefore, a party structure which promised little success for his program, whether in its short-run aim of economic stabilization, or its long-range ambition for structural reform. Without a radically reconstituted party system, how could the President hope to carry out an ambitious program in either the short run or the long run? One lesson of the Quadros interlude was the impossibility of reform by presidential fiat, within Brazil's existing constitutional framework. There was no avoiding the need for much new legislation. But how could congressmen be made to act in a coherent, consistent way, given the fact that party lines so inadequately reflected the predominance and mood of center opinion? Despite this obvious inadequacy of the party system, there existed no ready alternative to organization of national political action on party lines.

A Five-Month Experiment: Development and Reform

From January to June of 1963, João Goulart engaged in his most serious attempt to attack the nation's problems within the context of the existing framework. This "positive phase" was the work of several prominent representatives of the moderate left, who were among the ministers Goulart included in his first presidential government after the plebiscite of January 1963. One was Celso Furtado, a holdover from the last parliamentary cabinet (Hermes Lima: September 1962-January 1963) continuing as minister without portfolio (for economic planning). Furtado had emerged as a leader of a younger generation (he was born in 1920) that wanted rapid change in Brazil's outmoded structures. His directorship of SUDENE, the Northeast development agency, had earned him international attention as a dynamic technocrat supervising a crash effort to reverse the cycle of human misery in the largest backward area of Brazil.[54] Now he had been chosen to map an attack on inflation and to establish a new set of economic priorities. His ideas were spelled out in a Three-Year Plan aimed at maintaining economic growth while also reducing the rate of inflation. A summary of the plan was published on December 30, 1962, a few days before the plebiscite. Once Goulart regained full powers, the Three-Year Plan became central in Goulart's five-month experiment with the "positive left." [55]

The other leading representative of the moderate left was San Tiago Dantas, the new Minister of Finance. Dantas had accumulated a private fortune as a highly successful lawyer and, as a member of Brazil's financial and intellectual elite, was attempting to bridge the gap between the untutored and undisciplined new political forces on the left, over which Goulart had uncertain control, and the older power establishment. Gifted with a brilliant mind and inexhaustible ingenuity in political negotiation, Dantas had earlier been rejected by the Chamber of Deputies as Goulart's nominee for prime minister in June of 1962. A leading young *Integralista* intellectual in the 1930's and now a member of the moderate left wing of the PTB, he was determined to carry out a vigorous stabilization policy as the prerequisite for further economic development.[56]

Neither Furtado nor Dantas, however, had a strong political base. Furtado had never entered the world of party politics, preferring, like other outstanding Brazilian modernizers of his generation, to exert his influence by remaining a technocrat and intellectual. But this left him without any party base as the battle *within* the left accentuated during the Goulart presidency. Dantas was different. He had chosen to enter the PTB (from Minas Gerais) and was struggling to gain influence within the national party. But he was still a minority figure. Even in Minas Gerais he had failed to gain an impressive vote in his reelection as federal deputy in November 1962. Intellectually, Dantas was admirably fitted to represent center and moderate left opinion; personally, however, he lacked the political skills that could have made him either a popular leader with the public or a successful manipulator of other politicians. The leaders of what Dantas called the "positive left" were, therefore, not in command of party forces and were thus unable to mobilize support in the moments of peril soon to come.

Goulart's first presidential cabinet also included an important representative of the radical left—Almino Afonso, the Labor Minister—known for tolerating radical leftist and Communist infiltration of the trade-union movement. Afonso's presence indicated that Goulart intended to pursue a double political game. On the one hand he could endorse the programs of Furtado and Dantas, negotiating to gain the support of the center. This policy would be based on a resumption of the stabilization efforts pursued by Quadros in 1961, although even more ambitious because it also included a program of "basic reform." On the other hand, Afonso's appointment as Labor Minister was evidence that Goulart intended to strengthen the trade union power structure (*dispositivo sindical*) on whose loyalty he had learned to rely.

Military support (*cobertura militar*) was essential for any government in Brazil, and Goulart appeared to have it as he began the new phase of his presidency. General Amaury Kruel, a respected officer of moderate political views, remained in the first presidential cabinet as War Minister. There was also evidence, however, that Goulart wanted to build up more active military backing (*dispositivo militar*) by appointing conspicuously pro-Goulart officers to posts of importance. Prominent among the pro-Goulart officers were General Osvino Alves, commander of the First Army (headquartered in Rio de Janeiro), and General Jair Dantas Ribeiro, commander of the Third Army (Rio Grande do Sul). Goulart's cultivation of the *dispositivo sindical* and the *dispositivo militar* was taken as evidence by his long-time enemies that he was planning their use as a source of support for a presidential attempt to maneuver toward the leadership of extra-congressional forces. This possibiilty lurked in the background as Goulart began his experiment with the positive left.

The Dantas-Furtado program had been mapped out in the Three-Year Plan. This document, written largely by Furtado in late 1962, outlined a set of objectives based on an analysis of Brazil's postwar economic growth and the evident impasse that it had reached by 1962.[57] The Plan acknowledged that the rate of inflation (52 percent for 1962) had exceeded tolerable levels, both from the standpoint of its effect on investment and further growth and its exacerbation of social tensions. But the diagnosis emphasized that any anti-inflation measures must form part of an overall policy to resume high growth levels, explaining that "a decline in the rate of growth would be, from the social point of view, considerably more negative than the present development with all its deficiencies." [58] The Plan therefore proposed a simultaneous program to fight inflation and regain a high rate of growth. The goal was to reduce the rate of inflation over a three-year period to a level of 10 percent in 1965, while maintaining an annual real rate of growth of 7 percent, and at the same time introducing reforms that would eliminate institutional barriers (educational, agrarian, administrative) to further growth and also alleviate glaring income inequalities among classes and regions. The Goulart government had therefore committed itself to the most ambitious program of any postwar Brazilian regime: it would maintain a growth rate at the level of the best Kubitschek years (7 percent) while reducing price increases to a level never equalled since Dutra (10 percent); and at the same time undertake "basic reforms"—on the character or purpose of which there was as yet no clear consensus, either on the left or the center.

From the beginning of his presidency in 1961 Goulart had stressed Brazil's need for "structural reforms." He mentioned several areas in need of reform—such as education and housing—but argued most insistently for changes in the tax system and the land structure. The latter area, he suggested, would need a constitutional amendment, since the Constitution of 1946 required that expropriation of land be covered by "prompt and adequate compensation" in advance—in other words, compensation must be in cash in advance.

What was the exact purpose of the reforms which Goulart after January of 1963 began to push more vigorously? There were three aims which such reforms might accomplish:

(1) Reforms might be intended primarily to eliminate a new set of "bottlenecks" in the process of economic development.[59] Land reform, for example, could be advocated on the grounds that an archaic system of rural tenure blocked any further increase in agricultural production. It also restricted the spread of the money economy—and, therefore, the market for manufactured goods—into the rural sector. The "bottleneck" explanation could be applied to other proposed reforms—administrative, tax, and financial. The emphasis in this rationale for reforms was on the relevance for further economic growth, rather than redistribution of income.[60]

(2) Reforms could also be urged on the grounds that the fruits of economic growth already achieved must be distributed more equitably. Land or tax changes that hit the wealthiest sectors, for example, could be aimed at regaining from the "privileged" sector their "antisocial" profits. The same rationale might justify rural education or other increased public investment as a means of aiding the least advantaged citizens.

(3) Reforms might be intended primarily to alter the political balance, a task Kubitschek never attempted and Quadros only began to consider during his brief presidency. The vote for illiterates (or mass literacy programs) or the granting of political rights to enlisted military men might radically change the electoral balance of voters and thereby open the way to other profound changes in social structure.

Goulart talked primarily about the second purpose, although the Three-Year Plan stressed the first while acknowledging the importance of the second. What was dangerous was the President's continual emphasis upon the need for "reforms" without calming the growing suspicions of the center about the third purpose. By arousing deep fears on the part of established social sectors and classes, such a strategy played into the hands of the extremists on the right who had opposed Goulart's succession to the presidency and were now conspiring to depose him. It also strengthened the hand of the extremists on the left who scorned Goulart's "conciliatory half-measures" and conspired to pull him to the left or, if necessary, outflank him in the process of radicalizing opinion to make possible extra-Congressional action. Furthermore, Goulart aroused suspicion within Congress by continually claiming that the Congress would never approve reforms when he had not really exerted himself to line up congressional votes on specific measures. Allowing the drive for reforms to appear as a mere tactic in the service of some unspecified ultimate purpose was therefore perilous.

In the Three-Year Plan, Furtado focused on two immediate prerequisites for the success of any program aimed at resuming growth while reducing inflation: (1) The inflationary pressure produced by deficits in the public sector must be sharply reduced by financing a continued high level of public investment (considered essential for further growth) through non-inflationary means, unlike the generous emission policies of the last decade. This would require new taxes aimed at the wealthier sectors, as well as a reduction in the subsidies that produced huge deficits in the government-owned shipping and rail industries.[61] (2) The capacity to import (also considered essential for further growth) would have to be maintained by an immediate refinancing of Brazil's foreign debt, now concentrated in medium and short-term obligations. In 1962, the Plan estimated that debt repayments and profit remittances reached $564 million, or 45 percent of the value of all Brazil's exports in that year. The first step must be to refinance the foreign debt. But it would have to be combined with a more aggressive export program for items such as manufactured goods and iron ore, thereby ensuring the foreign exchange to cover the level of imports necessary for continued industrialization.[62]

These two prerequisites required resolute action by the Goulart government both at home and abroad. The two areas were in fact but the new version of the internal and external problems in economic policy-making faced by Vargas between 1951 and 1954. In many respects the Three-Year Plan was a relatively "orthodox" approach to the perennial problem of inflation. Its novelty, as compared to the Lopes-Campos plan of 1958 or the Quadros program of 1961 (never elaborated in the comprehensive manner of the other two), was its greater emphasis on viewing anti-inflation measures as part of an *overall* program of economic and social planning.[63]

Fighting Inflation

Both Dantas and Furtado knew that the ambitious Three-Year Plan would be difficult to implement. The early phase would require unpopular measures to reduce deficits in the public sector, as well as pursuit of a firm wage policy. They hoped to alleviate the sacrifice imposed on the lower-income sectors by increasing the tax burden of the wealthy. The first step was implementation of a tax reform bill passed by the Congress in late 1962.[64]

The next step in economic policy was similar to the first move of the Quadros government in 1961: an attempt to make exchange rates more uniform. The subsidies on wheat and oil imports were ended, in January 1963, by abolishing the preferential rate that had been allowed to creep back in since Quadros ended the subsidies in 1961. Because oil products and wheat exercised such a strategic influence on the cost of living (directly affecting the cost of transport and bread) there was a continuous temptation to subsidize their import. But the Goulart government appeared ready to risk the popular repercussions such as those the Quadros government had encountered after a similar move in 1961. The Goulart regime went even farther toward a realistic exchange rate in April 1963 by devaluing the "official" rate by 30 percent (from 460 cruzeiros per U.S. dollar to 600 per dollar). This move brought the official rate close to the black market rate and thereby temporarily restored confidence in the Brazilian government's determination to fight inflation.

Although these adjustments in the official exchange rate were undoubtedly essential in order to regain equilibrium in the balance of payments, they contributed to an immediate increase in the cost of living by raising the cruzeiro cost of the import component in domestic consumption. The dilemma in the case of wheat and oil subsidies was especially cruel: the inflationary effect of the public deficit previously incurred in order to finance the subsidies, was replaced by the inflationary effect of the increased prices that consumers had to pay for non-subsidized bread and bus fares. In February it was estimated that ending the subsidies would increase transport costs by 40 percent and the price of wheat and bread by 177 percent.[65] The Goulart government was learning the unpleasant lesson brought home to every government that had attempted an anti-inflation program since 1950

—Vargas in 1953–54, Café Filho in 1954–55, Kubitschek in 1958–59, and Quadros in 1961. The lesson was that the introduction of "realistic" exchange rates, which were necessary to approximate equilibrium in the international balance of payments and to gain IMF approval for further financing (unified and nondiscriminatory exchange rates were a specific commitment in the Charter of the IMF), was in the short run bound to increase domestic prices even more.

In March 1963 Dantas undertook the journey to Washington that was an indispensable step in any stabilization program. He planned to argue for immediate and massive United States aid and to lay the groundwork for discussions on the renegotiation of Brazil's foreign obligations. Armed with Furtado's Three-Year Plan, Dantas could point out that Brazil had finally met the requirements of economic planning and social reform called for in the Alliance for Progress.

Dantas would have preferred to arrive in Washington after having achieved more progress in the attack on inflation at home. But Brazil's economic plight was desperate. Dantas needed some immediate proof of the cooperation of foreign creditors. In fact, he had laid out a three-stage plan for securing foreign help in rescuing Brazil from impending economic disaster. The first step was the negotiation of a large aid package from the United States government. The second was to be the renegotiation of Brazil's indebtedness to her European creditors. The third was a set of trade and financing agreements with the Soviet Union and the eastern bloc. For tactical reasons, Dantas felt he could not begin serious work on steps two and three before he had made his Washington trip. This weakened his position within the left in Brazil because it exposed him to the immediate charge that he had "sold out" to the North Americans.[66]

Dantas pursued protracted negotiations in Washington, including lengthy conversations with President Kennedy. In the end he succeeded in gaining a $398.5 million agreement with the United States government. Only $84 million, however, was earmarked for immediate use. The rest remained contingent upon Brazil's carrying out a reform and stabilization program spelled out in a joint communiqué between Dantas and David Bell, director of USAID.[67]

Dantas was deeply disappointed with the caution displayed by both the U.S. government and the IMF. He felt he needed a more dramatic gesture of support from abroad in order to disarm his political enemies at home. From the nationalists on the left he knew he would face charges of having been too "soft" with the uncomprehending bankers in Washington. Indeed, he was at pains to explain to the American authorities the danger from the extreme left in Brazil.[68] As the discussions bogged down amidst American skepticism conditioned by disillusionment with previous Brazilian promises, especially since Quadros' resignation, Dantas and Roberto Campos, the Brazilian ambassador in Washington, actually considered breaking off the negotiations and attempting to surmount the economic crisis by mobilizing nationalist opinion in support of a go-it-alone policy that would temporarily forgo foreign aid. They were tempted by the course of action Kubitschek had chosen in similar circumstances in 1959. But Dantas and Campos concluded that Brazil could not risk relying on her own resources alone because the government lacked "sufficient cohesion," and because Brazilian nationalism was too shallow to generate the necessary political support for the resulting austerity. In effect, they were admitting to themselves the severe political limitations that Brazilian democracy placed on the mobilization of *domestic* resources for economic development. They also feared that such a policy might bring to power the "negative left" of Brizola, "as corrupt as it was inefficient," in the words of Campos.[69] So Dantas returned to Rio de Janeiro with the first installment of an aid package, whose balance was dependent upon the enactment, by the Congress, of a program including measures aimed at achieving both economic stabilization and social reform. Most important in the short run was the wage policy: a proposed increase in the salaries of civil servants and the military awaited approval.[70]

The American government had decided to keep the Brazilians on a "short leash," and release further aid and refinancing only in return for specific anti-inflation steps that would gain the approval of the IMF mission scheduled to visit Brazil in May. April and May would be the critical months.

When Dantas arrived back in Brazil at the end of March, he found the inevitable repercussions of the anti-inflation measures were subjecting the Goulart regime to fire on several fronts. The anti-inflation battle was centered on four areas: credit policy, exchange policy, federal budget policy, and wage policy.

In the area of credit policy, Dantas was having his most conspicuous success. Although there were complaints from industrialists, especially the vehicle manufacturers in São Paulo, the government had succeeded in keeping the increase in the money supply within the limits projected in January. Unfortunately, this also caused a mild recession in the auto and construction industries and led Dantas to have to assure businessmen that the situation would become more normal in the second half of the year.[71]

On exchange policy, however, the government's resolve was already faltering. When the official dollar exchange rate was devalued to 600 cruzeiros to the dollar on April 22, the rate for oil and wheat imports was kept at the old level of 460 cruzeiros to the dollar, thus reintroducing a consumer subsidy on these vital items. The promised cuts in public expenditure were difficult to assess at this stage, although the spectacular increases in suburban commuter train fares (five-fold; they had not been raised for twenty years) assured a reduction in the public sector deficit.

It had become apparent that prices were continuing to rise faster than had been forseen in the Three-Year Plan, which provided for a 25 percent increase in all of 1963. In March alone the price level rose nine percent, bringing the increase for the first three months to 16 percent. This rise reflected the "anti-inflationary" measures taken earlier (exchange reform), as well as the pressure of inflationary momentum inherited from 1962. Nevertheless, the rapid price rises weakened the government's case as it braced itself for the struggle over wage policy.[72]

Wage policy presented the Dantas-Furtado anti-inflation program with a severe test. The issue was a pending salary increase for civil servants and the military, the minimum wage for other sectors having already been raised by the Labor Minister in November 1962.[73] Setting the pay increase for civil servants and military was politically more awkward than the minimum wage, since the former had to be approved by Congress, whereas the minimum non-government wage was fixed by decree of the Labor Minister. During the March negotiations in Washington, Dantas had virtually promised that the government would recommend a salary increase of no more than 40 percent. But the civil servants and military officers were angered by this figure. They wanted at least 60 percent and were pressing for 70 percent. In mid-April the government presented to Congress its bill, calling for increases ranging from 40 percent to 56 percent for the civil servants, and from 25 percent to 55 percent for the military.

By early May there was intense pressure for an even higher figure. Politically, the issue was perilous for Goulart and his ministers because they were dealing with the vital interests of Brazil's most powerful group: the military. The officer corps was once again unhappy over the erosion of salary differentials. Their ominous discontent sounded like an echo of the colonels' memorandum of February 1954. Late in May a group of officers sent Goulart a detailed message protesting the low level of officers' salaries, pointing out, for example, that a second lieutenant in the Army received only as much as a cook's aide in the Merchant Marine.[74] (This wage issue was not finally settled until July, after Dantas' resignation, but already in mid-May the Cabinet, in contradiction to Dantas' policy, agreed to a 70 percent increase in civil service and military salaries.)

This military pressure on Goulart was especially significant because he was in a difficult position vis-à-vis the Army command. As in 1951–52 and in 1955, there were deep political disagreements within the officer corps. Radical nationalist views had gained support among some non-commissioned officers in the First Army (whose area included Rio de Janeiro) under the command of General Osvino Alves, who was actively courting leftist groups, such as the student group UNE, and labor leaders, such as Dante Pelacani. At a rally in early May, a sergeant violently attacked the IMF and the other "imperialist forces" that obstructed Brazil's development and the achievement of "basic reforms." War Minister Kruel, representing a centrist position within the officer corps, ordered immediate disciplinary action against the sergeant. His move might have passed as simply another incident in the familiar struggle of war ministers to maintain "discipline" within the Army. But the evident sympathy of a senior commander (Osvino Alves) for the views of the disciplined sergeant, dramatized the dispute as an apparent test of power among the political camps within the officer corps. Goulart called the commanders of all four military zones together for a "peace lunch," and the conflict was surmounted without changing any of the higher command.[75]

Divisive Issues: Foreign Capital and Agrarian Reform

This disagreement among the higher military paralleled the political tension which had arisen in the civilian sector. Conflict was bitter not only over the "sacrifices" required by the anti-inflation program, but also over two other issues which had become central in Goulart's experiment with the leadership of the positive left. The first was the Dantas policy on the purchase of foreign-owned public utilities. This aspect of foreign investment touched the rawest nerve of nationalist opinion. During Goulart's visit to the United States in April 1962 he had discussed with President Kennedy the purchase of U.S.-owned public utilities in Brazil, with the funds from the sale to be invested in specified manufacturing industries in Brazil. It was hoped that this formula would allow American investors to withdraw from investments considered politically ultra-sensitive as well unpromising financially, without depriving Brazil of foreign capital, which could be very useful to the Brazilian economy as well as profitable to its American owners. This discussion was in response to the need to head off incidents such as Governor Leonel Brizola's expropriation of a subsidiary of International Telephone and Telegraph Company in Rio Grande do Sul in early 1962.

The bitter controversy on this issue exacerbated the inevitable political conflict over stabilization in a manner remarkably similar to the way in which Roberto Campos' equivocal statements about Petrobrás helped inflame nationalist opposition to the stabilization attempt of 1958–59. Dantas had firm views on the question of nationalizing foreign-owned public utilities. Immediately after assuming the Finance Ministry in January 1963 he announced that these firms would be nationalized only with full guarantees assuring the reinvestment of the purchase price in other enterprises in Brazil.[76] This formula had been used to settle the case of the IT&T subsidiary in Rio Grande do Sul in 1962. Negotiations were now underway for a similar settlement with the largest single foreign-owned public utility system in Brazil—the American and Foreign Power Company, which valued its Brazilian holdings at well over $100 million.

Dantas evidently felt that a decisive settlement with this huge firm would deprive the extreme nationalists of a favorite issue and at the same time strengthen his hand with the United States government. It was clear that Ambassador Lincoln Gordon was a strong advocate of such a solution, and the United States Government was under pressure from the Congress, which had attached a rider (the Hickenlooper Amendment) to the 1962 Foreign Aid Bill obligating the government to suspend aid to any country that confiscated American-owned property without demonstrating within six months that it was prepared to pay "just and prompt compensation."

In late April the American and Foreign Power Company (AMFORP) and the Brazilian government announced an agreement providing for the purchase of the Brazilian holding at a price of $135 million, 75 percent of which was to be reinvested in non-utility enterprises in Brazil, the remaining 25 percent to be paid in dollars. There were understandable reasons for the Brazilian government's desire to reach a settlement as quickly as possible. AMFORP had been negotiating an agreement for over a year, spurred on by the fact that three of its Brazilian subsidiaries had already been the target of expropriation by state governments.[77] Furthermore, Goulart had reached an understanding for a settlement along these lines during his visit to the United States in April 1962. But Dantas had chosen a singularly bad time to announce the AMFORP agreement. It had nothing directly to do with the anti-inflation program, yet it came in the midst of the April battle over the bill on civil service and military salaries. The AMFORP settlement—more than generous to the company from the Brazilian standpoint—furnished excellent ammunition for the extremists of right and left who devoutly desired the failure of Goulart's experiment with the "positive left."

Brizola led the attack from the extreme left, charging that Dantas had engaged in a "sellout." In violent language the President's brother-in-law warned that consummation of the AMFORP agreement would constitute an irrevocable break with the radical left. At the same time, Carlos Lacerda, now alert to the potential political mileage in the widespread nationalist sentiment on this issue, attacked from the right. He criticized the planned purchase of the foreign-owned telephone company in his state of Guanabara, claiming that its equipment (labeled "junk" or *ferro velho*) was obsolete and grossly overvalued.

Dantas angrily defended his nationalization policy. He attempted to rally center and moderate left support against the abuse of Brizola (who was also arguing that the salary adjustment before the Congress should be at least 70 percent). Dantas was now suffering from the ambiguous political situation made evident by the congressional election of October 1962: although the center undoubtedly represented the majority of opinion among the electorate, it lacked any clear party expression. The possible support for an unpopular anti-inflation program was already battered by a political issue—foreign capital—that raised the most incompatible ideological arguments.[78]

There was a second issue that served to polarize political opinion during the Dantas-Furtado ministry: agrarian reform. Following Goulart's avowed commitment to "basic reform," agrarian reform had been made an important part of the Three-Year Plan, both as a measure of social justice and as a step to facilitate further productivity and consumer demand in the rural sector. For Goulart, the campaign seemed to offer a means of consolidating his hold over the "popular forces" and undercutting his critics on the left, who were attacking him for having surrendered to the "reactionaries" at home and abroad in his economic policy.

In March Goulart had submitted an agrarian reform bill to the Congress providing for compensation in government bonds rather than cash; it therefore required an amendment to Article 141 of the Constitution. But a constitutional amendment needed a two-thirds vote of the Congress, even more unlikely in the midst of the tense political atmosphere. Opposition to the bill rapidly formed in the Chamber of Deputies, where the over-representation of rural districts gave landholders great influence because the literacy requirement and strong local machines prevented most peasants and rural workers from voting. The bill was immediately attacked by the ultra-conservative *Ação Democrática Parlamentar,* an inter-party alliance of right-wing deputies primarily from the UDN and PSD.

Goulart was accused by the center and right of "demagogic gestures" designed only to arouse opinion in support of a bill which was insufficiently prepared. No such bill could possibly have had an easy passage through Congress. Jânio Quadros, for example, would have been in a stronger position, because of his enormous popular mandate, to demand such a bill from the Congress in 1961. But he never attempted to introduce one. His successor was more vulnerable. The traditional distrust of Goulart on the right had now come to be shared by large elements of the center. There were many congressmen who felt uneasy about the existing agrarian structure and who were prepared to consider possible changes. But they had become so suspicious of Goulart's ultimate political aims that they declined to consider seriously a measure which would give the Executive such enormous power.[79]

The radical left, led by Brizola, profited by this clash and warned Goulart that it was typical of the result he could expect if he continued to attempt to work within the existing political framework. It was the inevitable failure inherent in the "half-measures" of the positive left, they argued. Meanwhile, the bill provoked splits within the two parties which had comprised the former PSD-PTB alliance. The PSD, heavily influenced by its predominantly agrarian supporters, opposed the bill; interestingly enough Kubitschek, the PSD's most famous member, was now anxious to strengthen his electoral prospects for the presidential election in 1965, and sought to reverse the party's stand. The PTB was badly split, while the UDN was almost united in its opposition to the bill. The issue had, however, spread far beyond the halls of Congress. It was a subject for heated debate within the Roman Catholic Church, with opinion spread from warm support to violent opposition.[80]

The social sector least touched by the industrialization and political change since 1930 had become too important to be ignored any longer. The disenfranchised rural sector began to be mobilized by Peasant Leagues and shaken by spontaneous land invasions. But the prospects for any constitutional solution were poor, as long as the majority of Congress wanted to restrict Goulart's power at all costs. And Goulart was unlikely to increase his efforts to conciliate the center, since he was clearly upset by the charges of the radical left and showed signs of disenchantment over his experiment with the moderate left.

In May a committee of the Chamber of Deputies rejected the agrarian reform bill by a vote of seven to four. Brizola, a member of the defeated minority on the committee, responded by demanding that the Army "take up arms" to support social reform. Dantas had included agrarian reform in his joint communiqué from Washington in March as an essential part of his aid agreement; now the political deadlock had made any such reforms highly unlikely.

The Failure of Presidential Nerve

By late May the Dantas-Furtado experiment was in grave jeopardy. Rumors of a cabinet change had been current since late April, when the salary bill and the AMFORP agreement ran into heavy opposition. The critical issue in the short run was the anti-inflation program. The IMF mission arrived in the second week of May and was studying the Goulart government's attack upon inflation. The conclusions of the mission were crucial, since both the American and European creditors were awaiting the IMF's decision before embarking on further refinancing of Brazil's enormous short-term debt.[81]

One of the policy decisions at which the IMF mission looked hardest was the salary bill before the Congress. On the eve of the mission's arrival, Dantas confidently announced that it would be impressed by the anti-inflation steps already taken. Only a week thereafter, however, the Cabinet agreed to a 70 percent salary increase for civil servants and military. A few days later Dantas extracted a vote of confidence from the cabinet; it was undeniable, however, that he had lost control over a major policy decision. He was hardly in the best position to assert his views. While vigorously defending the stabilization and public utility nationalization proposals in April, Dantas had fallen victim to lung cancer and was sub-par physically in the intragovernmental struggle. Furtado, who had played a less prominent political role in defending the government program, was absent for an ECLA meeting during the period when the position on the salary bill was decided. The principal leaders of the "positive left" had lost influence within the presidential circle.

Goulart's natural inclination to see the April-May struggle in the narrowest political terms was strengthened by the growing influence of the extremists. Within the UDN, for example, the moderates suffered a serious blow when a UDN convention in the State of Paraná chose Carlos Lacerda as their candidate in the presidential election that was still two years away. This boost for Lacerda strengthened the UDN's right wing, which wanted at all costs to discredit Goulart's entire program, above all, the reforms. Lacerda gained ground at the expense of his chief UDN rival—moderate Governor Magalhães Pinto, who represented the emerging but still disorganized center-to-moderate left. Indeed, Dantas had been cultivating Magalhães Pinto by letting the banks of his state (Minas Gerais) exceed the credit limits established under the anti-inflation program. But Dantas now found that his enemies on the right were as anxious for him to fail as were his opponents on the left. Typical of their irresponsible attacks was a column by David Nasser in the mass circulation magazine *O Cruzeiro;* it likened Dantas to a famous woman of easy virtue in eighteenth-century Brazil.[82] These long-time enemies of the "Vargas system" could not bear the thought that anything could be achieved under Goulart's aegis. His failure was their surest guarantee of greater electoral strength in 1965. They were, therefore, hardly a "loyal opposition"; on the contrary, they turned to the Cassandras who warned that the President's *real* motive was to subvert the constitutional order.

Goulart himself was most concerned about the attack from the left. Here the personal aspect was important, because the self-proclaimed leader of the radical left was Brizola, the President's brother-in-law. Because of this family connection (which made Brizola ineligible to run for President in 1965), Goulart seemed to become associated with Brizola's extreme views on stabilization (larger wage settlements), foreign capital (confiscation with minimal, if any, compensation), and reform (radical change with or without the Congress). During the April-May political crisis Brizola took center stage. He was everywhere, attacking the "entreguistas" around the President, the "reactionaries" in the Congress, the "gorillas" in the Army, and the "imperialists" in the American Embassy and the IMF.

The replies to Brizola's invective were frequent and indignant. Dantas branded him a member of the "negative left," which had no real interest in achieving non-inflationary economic growth. João Calmon, a conservative congressman and executive in the Chateaubriand newspaper and TV chain, attacked Brizola as the stalking horse of subversion. Centrist congressmen demanded that the President repudiate his brother-in-law's attacks upon the Congress. Moderate Army commanders led by War Minister Kruel warned Goulart against such denunciations of conservative officers as Brizola had made of General Murici in Natal in May. They also cautioned Goulart against Brizola's collusion with radical leftist organizers among the non-commissioned ranks. Even the American ambassador offered his contribution to the debate. He characterized the anti-foreign-capital campaign of the Brizolistas as the technique of the "big lie" first perfected by Joseph Goebbels.[83]

As had happened in the political crisis surrounding the stabilization effort of 1958–59, the language of political discourse seriously deteriorated. With the government under the strain of simultaneously attempting reform, stabilization and economic development, the extremists reaped their harvest of discord—thus promoting, so they believed, their own prospects for ultimate power.

There was another personal aspect to Goulart's political dilemma. Having become President under such unfavorable circumstances in 1961, and having gained full presidential powers only at the start of the third year of his five-year presidential term, Goulart was acutely conscious of how little time he had left. Ineligible for reelection, he viewed with envy the emergence of Dantas, who was the most dynamic figure within the government. It was Dantas, not the President, who met the attacks from left and right. The Finance Minister appeared frequently on television to appeal for public understanding of the sacrifices required by an anti-inflation program. Not only was he becoming the leading public spokesman for the government, but he was also a potential contender for the leadership of the PTB (then held by Goulart). He was even mentioned as a presidential possibility for 1965. The experiment of the positive left was further undermined by personal friction between Furtado and Dantas, resulting in Furtado's virtual abandonment of the Three-Year Plan by May, when he realized that there was little hope of its projections being fulfilled, or of any sympathetic consideration of its revision by the President.

Through the bitter political conflict of April and May Goulart had tried to measure the impact of his ministers' measures. Unable to comprehend the intricacies of anti-inflation policy, he could understand only the political dimension: he was losing ground on the left while strengthening his opponents on the right. He preferred to believe that the *real* issue at stake was social reform, not the control of inflation. In political terms, this option had an obvious logic. As of late May there was no political group vigorously supporting anti-inflation measures. But there was a vocal constituency demanding social reforms, especially agrarian reform. Most important, there was no political force that could be readily mobilized by Dantas and Furtado in order to bring pressure upon either the Congress *or* the wavering President. In other words, Dantas could not present Goulart with the ultimatum that even if *he* were dismissed, the President would have no alternative, given the line-up of party forces, but to follow the desires of the center and moderate left on both stabilization and reform.

By early June the Three-Year Plan and the Dantas-Furtado program were beyond rescue. The cabinet, under intense pressure from the military and the civil service, agreed to a 70 percent salary increase. The IMF mission, which Dantas had greeted so optimistically in early May, left Rio with a low opinion of the government's determination to fight inflation. The essential prerequisite for further aid and refinancing from both the U.S. and Europe was therefore missing. Dantas' gamble that he could gain quick and large-scale cooperation from Brazil's foreign creditors had failed. The projections of the Three-Year Plan had already been rendered obsolete by the accelerated inflation, which reached 25 percent in the first five months of 1963—the level Furtado had set for the entire year. The new salary bill would undoubtedly be financed by greatly increasing the money supply, because the bill's "self-financing" provision for a compulsory increase in the income tax was unlikely to produce the necessary revenue through a collection system that was notoriously leaky and already burdened with other recently approved tax increases.[84]

Caught between the extremists of right and left but unwilling to stake his presidency on the Dantas-Furtado programs, Goulart cast about for an undramatic manner in which to change his principal ministers. By mid-June he had succeeded. Dantas, seriously ill with lung cancer but nevertheless attempting to hold his post, was forced to resign as Finance Minister. Celso Furtado had earlier left the new Planning Ministry, which was now dissolved, although technically Furtado remained a minister without portfolio. Goulart could not bring himself to replace the "positive left" with the "negative left," so he also replaced his Labor Minister Almino Afonso. All three military ministers were replaced, but the new War Minister did not turn out to be, as some had expected, General Osvino Alves, "the people's general." Instead, Kruel's successor was General Jair Dantas Ribeiro, the commander of the Third Army (Rio Grande do Sul). Although in September 1962 Dantas Ribeiro had warned that he could not guarantee public order if the Congress did not approve an early date for the plebiscite on presidentialism, he was a respected officer and a more neutral political figure than Osvino Alves.

Almino Afonso's replacement as Labor Minister was a political unknown—Senator Amauri Silva. Most important, the new Finance Minister was Carvalho Pinto, the former Governor of São Paulo and a leading spokesman for centrist opinion. He had entered politics as state Finance Minister during Jânio Quadros' governorship of São Paulo, and was now a leader of the progressive wing of the small but rapidly growing Christian Democratic Party. Carvalho Pinto's appointment reassured Goulart's critics both at home and abroad, but there was little reason to expect that the new Finance Minister could find a party base or a steady presidential nerve where his predecessor had failed so conspicuously.

VIII

Brazilian Democracy Breaks Down: 1963–1964

Mobilization and the Loss of Consensus

During the five months from January to June 1963 political conflict continued to polarize around the extremes. Since 1945, national politics, which had been largely the private game of a limited elite, had begun to be invaded by populist leaders. Adhemar de Barros, Getúlio Vargas, Jânio Quadros, João Goulart, Leonel Brizola—their success was based on increasing, if ill-organized, popular participation in politics. Although social classes were only occasionally and incompletely self-conscious about their political role, direct appeals to class and sectoral interests became more frequent after the beginning of Vargas' presidency in 1951. The rapid growth of the electorate and the increase in political participation decreased the scope for the elitist manipulation. But the rules of the emerging mass politics were unclear. Goulart, for example, had to play a very cautious game in order to gain full presidential powers. After the plebiscite he faced a dilemma. Could he continue a moderate line, or was he fated to fulfill the role of the dynamic populist in which his past had cast him?

The political battles over the Dantas-Furtado program of stabilization and reform gave the extremists an opportunity to recruit new adherents. The significant factor was the manner in which this recruitment occurred. It was a process of mobilization wider than any political participation previously seen in the history of the Republic. One might almost have concluded that Brazil was experiencing the awakening (*tomada de consciência*) that the ideologues of nationalism had preached since the early 1950's. The fact that the mobilization was often undertaken by the extremists simply reflected the gravity of the issues and their far-reaching social consequences.

On the left, radical student organizations such as UNE and *Ação Popular,* undertook an ambitious program of political organization. If the movement for basic education (*Movimento de Educação de Base,* which was sponsored in part by the Ministry of Education) were to attain its goal of mass literacy, it would add millions of voters to the Brazilian electorate. The organizers of the literacy campaign could be expected to attempt to mobilize these new voters in support of populist politicians, perhaps of the radical nationalist camp.[1]

In the countryside the growth of the Peasant Leagues and the increasing land invasions indicated that the backward agrarian sector had finally come to life. The controversy over the reform bill emboldened the organizers of agrarian revolt, who included both radical leftists and reform-minded centrists such as the progressive clergy in the Northeast. This mobilization of peasants and rural workers was still in a primitive stage by mid-1963, but its further growth could only alarm the center and at the same time lead Goulart to think the strength of the "popular forces" justified an even greater commitment to agrarian reform.[2]

The traditional patrons of the agrarian sector did not view with indifference the nascent mobilization of the agrarian masses. In Minas Gerais, Rio de Janeiro (state), and the Northeast, landowners increased their stock of arms and at the same time strengthened their opposition to the agrarian reform measures already proposed by Goulart.

Other anti-Goulart mobilizers also stepped up their activities. The military conspirators had redoubled their efforts, capitalizing on the "disciplinary" incidents involving Generals Kruel and Osvino Alves in order to convince pro-legality officers that Goulart must be opposed more actively. These conspirators had civilian counterparts. UDN politicians such as Bilac Pinto had long believed that Goulart would sooner or later have to be deposed. The Paulista opposition movements, led by Júlio Mesquita Filho and the businessmen's group (IPES), represented a wider mobilization than the earlier anti-getulista movement, such as Lacerda's small and eccentric "Lantern Club" (named after Diogenes who carried a lantern in search of one honest man) that had been organized to fight the getulista heirs after Vargas' suicide in 1954.[3] There were also signs that the large body of center opinion which had favored a constitutional solution to the Quadros resignation crisis was becoming frightened by the rapidly increasing inflation and by Goulart's apparent unwillingness to pursue a stabilization program. They viewed with apprehension the political mobilization of the urban and rural masses. Goulart's experiment with the "positive left" had only served to exacerbate this simultaneous process of mobilization and polarization. A weak figure caught in a maelstrom, the President had acted indecisively and thereby exposed himself to attacks from both right and left.

The public consensus in Brazil was disintegrating. Increasingly vocal groups at either extreme proclaimed their loss of faith in democratic politics. The limits of improvisation, obvious by the end of the Kubitschek presidency, were now again apparent. The interlude of the Quadros presidency and the fifteen months of Goulart's parliamentary period had solved nothing. Indeed, throughout Goulart's campaign to regain full presidential powers there was a general feeling that the essential issues had been postponed. Once Goulart obtained full powers and attempted a coherent economic policy, the fragility of the public consensus became clear.

The failure of Goulart's positive phase also pointed up the importance of the President's own motives. João Goulart had the reputation of being a weak man. He had seemed perfectly cast in the role of Vice President, proving irresolute in the crisis of August-September 1961, when he had to be urged on by Brizola and General Lopes, commander of the Third Army in Rio Grande do Sul. Goulart's apparent weakness made it difficult for his conspiring enemies within the military to convince their skeptical colleagues as well as center opinion that he was an anti-democrat who was promoting chaos in order to justify his own assumption of authoritarian powers. Many officers and middle-class civilians had a low opinion of Goulart's abilities and his ultimate political goals, but they still hoped that Brazil could survive the remainder of his presidency, which would end with the inauguration of a new President to be elected in 1965. Since the Brazilian constitution excluded the incumbent from running, the "accident" of the Goulart presidency would thereby come to an end.

Goulart was usually dismissed by both left and right as incapable of governing. Yet the belief became more widespread, as Goulart changed his government in June 1963, that the President himself had lost faith in constitutional processes. This view was common not only among his long-time opponents on the right who were conspiring to stage a coup, but also among radical nationalists on the left. Brizola feared that the ministerial changes of June might be the prelude to an attempt by Goulart to remain in power beyond the end of his legal mandate. Mid-1963, therefore, saw the Brazilian political scene characterized by increasingly strident calls for extra-legal action from both right and left, while the President's own goals remained undefined, thereby strengthening the hands of the extremists.

Lessons of the Dantas-Furtado Phase

The conspicuous failure of the Dantas-Furtado program was only temporarily disguised by Goulart's appointment of Carvalho Pinto, a widely-respected moderate, as his new Finance Minister. The abandonment of any coherent policy combining development and an attack on inflation soon became evident in the fate of the planning apparatus. Furtado's Planning Ministry had officially disappeared in June. It was to be replaced by a new body, created by decree on July 11, called the "Coordination of National Planning" (*Coordenação do Planejamento Nacional*) that was to continue the implementation of the Three-Year Plan. Among the signatories of the decree was Furtado, who remained nominally a minister but had lost any role within the Goulart government.[4]

Planning was virtually impossible, however, given the collapse of anti-inflation policy. The salary increase for the civil service and military was a good example. Although the cabinet agreed to a 70 percent raise before the ministerial changes of June, the Congress still had not passed the bill by the beginning of July. The anger of the military spilled over. Two thousand officer-members of the Military Club endorsed an ultimatum to the Congress demanding passage of the 70 percent bill within ten days. The president of the Military Club, retired Marshal Augusto Maggessi Pereira, and several other officers violently criticized Congress and Goulart at the club meeting and as a result were given a ten-day "disciplinary" sentence by War Minister Dantas Ribeiro. The Congress, however, complied with the military ultimatum (set to expire on July 14) and passed the bill on July 11. Since the accompanying provision for a compulsory income tax increase to finance the salary raise could be expected to work slowly, if at all, the money supply was increased almost immediately.[5]

The rate of inflation continued to rise. The cost of living in Rio de Janeiro increased 31 percent in the first six months of 1963, as compared to an increase of 18 percent for the same period of 1962. The inflation rate for 1962 had reached 52 percent; it was obviously headed for a level of at least 75 percent by the end of 1963.

Finance Minister Carvalho Pinto found the situation on the balance of payments equally depressing. He reported to the new Cabinet on July 4 that Brazil's foreign indebtedness totaled about $3 billion and that amortization and interest payments already scheduled for the years 1963–65 would amount to $1.8 billion, or about 43 percent of the expected export revenue for that period.[6] There was little doubt that this figure was well beyond the country's capacity to pay. In June, after the veto by the IMF mission, there was active consideration of a plan for Brazil to declare a unilateral debt moratorium, suspending all payments until 1965. The idea was that thereafter a fixed percentage of exchange earnings would be set aside to pay off amortization and interest by 1977, instead of the current scheduled date of 1981. The plan never passed beyond the stage of rumor.

The question of foreign refinancing was further complicated by issue of the purchase of the American-owned public utilities. The radical nationalist opposition to the AMFORP settlement had frightened Goulart. He announced that, despite the announcement in April, the Brazilian government had not yet committed itself on the exact price to be paid. The issue was referred to a series of study commissions that were to render their judgment on a "fair" valuation. President Kennedy was irritated by this delay on what he thought was an issue already settled. The profit remittances law of 1962, for which the enacting decree was still to be issued, was another irritant to foreign creditors whose willingness to discuss refinancing was now dampened by their anxiety over the Brazilian government's weakness in the face of its own nationalist opposition.

This interaction of the internal and external sides of the financial crisis had long been a fundamental feature of Brazilian history. Ever since attaining their political independence in 1822, Brazilians have had to tailor their political decisions to the constraints imposed by their debts abroad. Before the International Monetary Fund existed

Brazilian governments were having to convince European bankers of the "soundness" of their financial policies.[7] Only once in the history of the Republic did the government enjoy any considerable margin for maneuver in financial matters—the years immediately after World War II. But that opportunity was squandered when the large currency reserves accumulated during the war were dissipated, with little thought for the priorities of economic development. As a result, the high level of imports necessary for Brazil's spectacular industrialization of the 1950's could be maintained only by incurring a heavy burden of foreign indebtedness. This adverse trend was reinforced by the disastrous decline in Brazil's terms of trade since 1954, thereby depriving her of the possibility of adequately financing essential imports through the earnings from traditional agricultural exports.

Given this debtor role, no domestic economic policy could fail to be heavily influenced by the need to consider how any measure would affect currency reserves, Brazil's trade position, and, not least important, the attitude of her foreign creditors. This necessity of paying constant heed to European and North American financial circles, often of the most orthodox type, had been a political liability to many governments. It gave the economic nationalists (including some São Paulo industrialists as well as left-wing intellectuals) ready ammunition with which to attack Goulart as he faced the unavoidable necessity of pursuing an anti-inflation program. The political stakes grew higher as Brazil's foreign debts mounted and her prospects for repaying them grew dimmer. Abandoning the attempt at stabilization, on the other hand, could only mean the slide toward a radical political solution involving unilateral renunciation of foreign debts and possibly even confiscation of foreign investments in Brazil. Moreover, this prospect suited the strategy of the radical left, which focused its propaganda on the "injustice" of Brazil's economic relations with the "capitalist" world.

The lesson of the political costs of stabilization had not been lost on Goulart. He had alienated, only temporarily he hoped, the very groups from which he expected to gain his basic following. These were the more highly organized workers whose ostensible leaders made up his *dispositivo sindical*. They were also the civil servants who manned the apparatus of public administration and were an important element among the political "ins." Goulart's historic alliance with the

PSD was based in part upon his willingness to nurture this *estado car-torial*. It was no coincidence that the pay raise for civil servants and the military was one of the issues on which the Dantas stabilization policy foundered. The difficulty was that although most Brazilians wanted to avoid hyperinflation, no group—businessmen, labor, civil servants, or military officers—wanted to begin stabilization by cutting *their* particular claims. The Dantas-Bell agreements had tied further aid and loans to Brazil's implementation of a tough anti-inflation program. This requirement put the Goulart government at a pressure point between her foreign creditors and the domestic pressure groups, none of which was ready to forego its short-run interests for the sake of an uncertain long-term gain. It was the familiar problem of breaking the vicious circle of inflation psychology.

In August, new rumors of a unilateral debt moratorium by the Brazilians provoked a stern warning from the *New York Times* that Brazil would "merit help, whether through aid or a revision of its schedule for payment of foreign debts" only after "it gives concrete evidence that it is living up to its pledge to restrain inflation." Carvalho Pinto replied by reaffirming his commitment to a gradual attack on inflation, which he argued was Brazil's only hope of avoiding "unemployment and misery." [8]

The failure of the Dantas-Furtado experiment dramatized another aspect of the deepening economic difficulties. Stabilization had a dual purpose. First, it was needed in order to correct the dislocations and social tensions that inflation was producing in the domestic economy. Second, it was necessary in order to gain foreign creditors' cooperation in helping to meet Brazil's immediate balance of payments pressure. In the longer run, however, the desperate need for foreign exchange could be met only by increasing and diversifying Brazilian exports, as well as by finding domestic sources of supply for the massive imports of wheat and oil, which in 1962 totaled $380 million, more than a quarter of the value of all imports for the year. During the experiment of January to June 1963 there had been little time to begin on these longer-run tasks.[9]

Rehearsal for Defeat

After the ministerial changes of June it became clear that Goulart had lost interest in the central problems of stabilization and continued economic growth. Having halfheartedly supported a policy aimed at achieving development without inflation, he had only achieved inflation without development. There was one other goal of the Dantas-Furtado program that predated their ministerial tenure and to which the President now turned his limited powers of concentration: reform.

Furtado had included reforms in the Three-Year Plan as essential both for their role in removing institutional barriers to further economic growth and for their contribution to social justice. The reforms fell into four categories: administrative, financial, tax, and agrarian. It was the last issue that Goulart now stressed most. Yet his tactics were self-defeating. Instead of using his political skill to mobilize the reform-minded center, he preferred to berate the Congress for its short-sighted opposition. Obviously a measure with such profound social implications as agrarian reform was bound to arouse passionate feelings. Rural property owners, for example, were attempting to convince middle-class voters in the cities that a constitutional amendment allowing compensation in bonds rather than cash for expropriated land would be an attack on the entire principle of private property. Goulart could have done much to line up party support for a PSD-sponsored constitutional amendment in July. But by failing to assert his own leadership of the disorganized PTB, he allowed Brizola and the extreme leftists to gain ground within his own party. This, in turn, helped to push the PSD toward the militantly anti-Goulart UDN, and thus undermine the PSD-PTB alliance that was Goulart's only hope of congressional support for reforms. He was now preaching the inevitability of reform without any coherent base of political support.

In September and October there occurred a series of political crises which deepened the general uneasiness. On September 12, several hundred noncommissioned officers and enlisted men of the Marines, Air Force, and Navy staged a revolt in Brasília, attempting to seize control of the government. They succeeded in holding prisoner the president of the Chamber of Deputies and a Supreme Court justice. The rebels, who were quickly subdued, claimed that their action was intended only to dramatize the plight of noncommissioned officers whom a lower Court (just upheld by the Supreme Court) had ruled ineligible to run for elective office.[10]

The revolt had far-reaching implications. First, it came as a shock to many congressmen to see how easily and effectively they could be isolated in Brasília. A few hundred soldiers had surrounded the principal government buildings, cutting them off from all radio and telephonic communication with the rest of the country. A delegation of UDN congressmen arriving for a morning session, for example, found themselves ingloriously detoured by a contingent of enlisted men. This experience deeply impressed the conservative congressmen who were drafting proposals to impeach Goulart. If an ill-coordinated sergeants' revolt could be so effective, what if a military coup should be directed from the highest level?

Second, the revolt signaled an attack on military discipline from below, made all the more significant because the rebel sergeants had been in contact with the radical leftist labor leaders of the CGT (*Comando Geral dos Trabalhadores*). Equally important, Goulart responded by taking a neutral stand, refusing to defend or attack the rebels. He thus increased the growing suspicion among higher officers that he might someday capitalize upon a demoralized military in order to stage his own coup against constitutional processes.

The first week of October saw a strange series of presidential moves that deepened this fear and led directly to the rapid growth of the military conspiracy aimed at deposing the President. On October 4, Goulart sent Congress a message urgently requesting approval for rule by state of siege for 30 days—the martial law powers that had been used between November 1955 and February 1956 and much more frequently in the pre-war history of the Republic. Goulart was pressed to recommend this measure by his military ministers, who were worried over the mounting wave of strikes and incidents of politically-motivated violence, especially in the countryside. They were also outraged over an interview that Governor Lacerda had given to an American newspaper correspondent in late September. Lacerda allegedly labeled his long-time enemy Goulart as "inept" and "pro-Communist" and suggested that he was still in office only because the military hesitated to remove him. Lacerda had been violently criticizing the federal government ever since 1961, but now he had impugned the courage of the armed forces.[11]

The military ministers wanted rapid congressional approval in order to forestall new demonstrations and protests. The Congress, however, proved obstinate. At first the PTB in the Chamber of Deputies pledged unanimous support, but then changed its stand after well-nigh the entire left condemned the proposal. It suddenly seemed that every political sector feared that *it* would be the target of the emergency powers that the executive would exercise through the military. The outcry from the left extended all the way from the extremist groups— such as UNE (university students), the CGT (labor alliance) and nationalist congressmen such as Sérgio Magalhães—to San Tiago Dantas, who worriedly advised Goulart that the emergency powers might easily become an instrument for repressing the working class.[12] The UDN denounced the proposal, which was also opposed by the centrist Governor of Minas Gerais (Magalhães Pinto), the leftist Governor of Pernambuco (Miguel Arraes), and the militantly anti-Goulart Governors of São Paulo (Adhemar de Barros) and Guanabara (Carlos Lacerda).

Buffeted by this negative reaction, the congressional leaders procrastinated. On October 7, only three days after his original request, Goulart withdrew the proposal on the grounds of "new circumstances" which he said had been explained to him by his Justice Minister and his three military ministers. The situation was, if anything, more tense than it had been three days earlier. The day of Goulart's new message to the Congress saw an outbreak of violence (resulting in six deaths) during a demonstration at a steel mill in Minas Gerais. The protracted bank employees' strikes throughout the country had provoked recurrent bank runs and necessitated a series of heavy bank note issues, thus further feeding the flames of inflation.

The truth was that Goulart had again lost his nerve. In the April-May stabilization struggles he failed to support his ministers of the "positive left." The fluid political situation had permitted the President to follow a policy of drift for several months thereafter. But the increasing mobilization of the extremists alarmed the military ministers who convinced Goulart to put his prestige on the line in a new manner. They wanted him to preside over an emergency regime resting primarily on the Army. The resulting rule might actually have to be anti-party in character, a realization that undoubtedly led the PTB in the Chamber to change its stand on the proposal. Government by state of siege would inevitably mean clamping the lid on the new mobilization, especially on the left. Yet the Army's natural desire to maintain its diminishing monopoly over the instruments of violence also made it suspicious of the arms build-up on the right. In the message that the military ministers enclosed along with Goulart's withdrawal of the state-of-siege request, they explained that their original request had been motivated by concern over "the extensive traffic in arms conducted by clandestine organizations throughout the entire country." [13]

Stranger than the state-of-siege request was the abortive attempt, made at the same time, to arrest Lacerda himself. The plot, apparently directed from the presidential palace, called for a small unit of paratroopers to seize Lacerda at a public dedication ceremony. Not only did the force arrive too late (because of a traffic delay!), but the Governor had been warned by some officers who had refused the order to carry out the plot. Lacerda and the dissenting officers immediately denounced the plot. The ensuing publicity, predictably exploited by Lacerda, diverted attention from what had been a simultaneous plan to depose Miguel Arraes, the leftist Governor of Pernambuco. Goulart's objective was to remove at one stroke the two governors who symbolized the mobilization on the left and right, thereby giving his bid for emergency powers a politically "neutral" character. He would also be removing two of the leading candidates for the presidential election of 1965. The plan seemed ominously similar to Vargas' preparations for the coup of 1937. Preparations in Pernambuco were even more rudimentary than in Guanabara, however, and the whole plot came to nothing.

Goulart's abortive moves might have passed as little more than another act in the history of his feud with Lacerda. Instead, the President chose to be decisive on a fatally important matter. In November he insisted on disciplinary action against the paratroop officer (Colonel Boaventura Cavalcanti) who had refused the order to take part in the action against Lacerda and was now denouncing the government for its "subversive" aims.

Presidential Options and Conspiratorial Opposition

This move confirmed the fears of many senior Army officers who had previously been reluctant to join the network of military conspiracies aimed at overthrowing Goulart. For the last decade there had been a small group of "hard line" military, anxious to intervene in the political process. They succeeded only when a majority of the officers normally devoted to "legality" became convinced that constitutional processes were breaking down, as in 1954 and 1955 (but not in 1961).

Now, in October 1963, a large number of senior officers began to organize a conspiracy they considered "defensive." They were not prepared to initiate action against the President, but they were determined to "contain" and "resist" such possible inroads upon the constitution as the closing of the Congress. Their leader was the recently appointed (September 1963) Army Chief of Staff, General Castello Branco—a representative of the moderate majority, uneasy about Goulart's motives but unwilling to intervene in the democratic game until the President made a clear attempt to change the rules.[14]

What had brought the moderates closer to the militant officers who had been advocating a coup against Goulart since 1962? It was the events of September and October, which raised the question of military discipline. In the end, both the state-of-siege request and the abortive arrest of Lacerda were anti-climactic. They weakened Goulart's position because they reinforced the suspicion that the President was experimenting with anti-democratic solutions to the political deadlock, which had only worsened since the ministerial changes of June. Furthermore, he now appeared ready to tamper with discipline in the Army; the moderate majority began to consider seriously the charge leveled by their more extreme colleagues that Goulart was veering toward the radical leftist position of his brother-in-law and would drag Brazil into a social convulsion. If he were able to neutralize the Army, he might then follow any course he wished.

What about the "nationalists" within the officer corps? They were again being outmaneuvered and outnumbered. The familiar battle lines from the early 1950's could be discerned. In early December, for example, Goulart appointed a radical leftist, Admiral Candido Aragão, to the command of the Naval Fusiliers Corps. The appointment provoked a public protest from twenty-six conservative Navy officers.

The protesters were briefly arrested, but this disciplinary action could not conceal the predominantly conservative opinion among the Navy officer corps.

A similar event occurred in November with the removal of the commander of the Second Army (São Paulo), General Pery Bevilacqua, who, despite his moderately leftist views, had joined Governor Adhemar de Barros in taking a tough line toward the unsuccessful industrial strike attempted under the leadership of the radical leftist CGT. Bevilacqua was replaced in the command of the Second Army by former War Minister Kruel, a moderate. But the impression persisted that Bevilacqua had been removed because of his repeated denunciation of the CGT leaders, who were now in frequent contact with the President.[15]

Did Goulart realize the cost of his abortive moves of October? He had allowed his military ministers to go down the line for a state-of-siege request, only to undercut them days later. As a Brazilian President, he must have known that the balance of opinion within the Army would be crucial in any contest of power. Yet he did not seem to realize that his *dispositivo militar* was disintegrating. His illusions on this score were nurtured by the War Minister, Dantas Ribeiro, and the chief of the Military Household, Assis Brasil, who continued to give him confident guarantees of military backing.

None of these political and military maneuverings had changed the fact that Brazil found herself in a deep financial crisis for which the government had lacked any coherent policy since the dismissal of Furtado and Dantas in June. In late November 1963 Goulart gave a long magazine interview in which he depicted the financial situation with a curious mixture of pessimism and detachment. "Inflation, accompanied by a structural recession, threatens to devour us shortly," he warned. "I have not the slightest doubt that the dizzying inflationary process to which we are now submitted will drag the country to bankruptcy, with all the sinister consequences of a social disaster of catastrophic proportions." In the same interview he despaired of Brazil's deteriorating terms of trade except for which, he explained, "Brazil would now have no international debt to pay." [16]

The Goulart government's irritated reaction to the growing financial pressure presented by Brazil's foreign economic relations was revealed in Goulart's independent attitude at the second annual meeting of the Inter-American Economic and Social Council, held in São Paulo in November 1963. The principal order of business was a proposal for a new Inter-American Committee to coordinate and "multilateralize" the administration of the Alliance for Progress. Goulart chose to call instead for a common Latin American front in trade policy vis-à-vis the developed nations. His tone indicated a distinct lack of interest in trying to satisfy Brazilian foreign creditors.[17]

In December, Goulart made a series of conciliatory gestures to Brizola, who had stepped up his campaign to discredit any measures short of the sweeping ones proposed by the radical left. Rumors were widespread that Brizola was about to replace Carvalho Pinto, whose authority as Finance Minister had been steadily undercut by radical leftist advisers around the President. This would have signified, at last, a decisive turn toward the negative left.

Such a turn was but one of three possible courses of action Goulart could have followed after his rejection of the "positive left" became obvious in the months following the ministerial changes in June. The first course would have been to play off the radical left and the reactionary right against each other—dramatizing the political deadlock in the Congress and relying upon his own trade union and military *dispositivos* to assure him the emergency powers necessary to govern. This appeared to be the idea behind the state-of-siege request to Congress in early October. But that option contained an obvious contradiction: no Brazilian President, above all Goulart, could turn to a *combination* of the unions and the military, to the exclusion of all other political forces. The unions were very weak, compared to the military which were the strongest force in Brazil. Goulart was therefore proposing to give himself emergency powers that might very well be used by the military to suppress the labor structure on which he had based his entire career. This was undoubtedly the point explained so forcefully to the President by the CGT leaders immediately after the state-of-siege request. His maladroit withdrawal of the request removed this line of strategy from further consideration.

The second course of action would have been to pursue an innocuous role of administering without actually governing the country. This would have confirmed the image of Goulart as the perpetual Vice President who lacked the courage to follow an active policy of his own. Goulart could have continued his zig-zag style, neutralizing each concession to the radical left with a concession to the center. This course, which many observers expected of Goulart, was made more difficult by the deteriorating financial situation and the growing pressure from the political extremists. It also failed to satisfy the President's own ambitions. For all his indecisiveness, João Goulart was possessed by a desire to enter Brazilian history as a *leader*—a President whose record could stand comparison with his mentor, Getúlio Vargas. But he was racked with doubt over how he could fulfill that role. One answer would have been his third possible option: a clear turn to the radical left. But by so doing he would risk losing leadership of the "popular forces" to a more dynamic leader with greater talent for the ruthless infighting certain to follow—Brizola was his most obvious rival.

Carvalho Pinto did resign in December 1963 after a calculated insult by a recent appointee of Goulart's, but Brizola did not turn out to be his replacement.[18] Goulart chose as his new Finance Minister Ney Galvão, a minor Riograndense politician serving as the director of the Bank of Brazil. Goulart seemed, therefore, to have maintained his indecisive course, although few expected Galvão to last long in his new post. At the least, this appointment made possible another attempt at cultivating the battered PSD-PTB coalition in the Congress.[19]

Financial Pressure: No Exit

The replacement of Carvalho Pinto by the colorless bureaucrat Ney Galvão laid bare Goulart's lack of new ideas on the economic and financial front. In truth, he had exhausted without really trying what the moderate left and their technicians could offer. The Dantas-Furtado policy was dropped for lack of will as soon as it became a short-run political liability. Carvalho Pinto, the sober Paulista professor, soon found the presidential palace an equally unreliable source of support.

Pinto had tried to adapt the Three-Year Plan to the hard political realities made evident by the April-May 1963 crisis. It was now clear that however "structural" factors were contributing to rising prices, only a firm control over the money supply could arrest the alarming increase in the rate of inflation. Some non-inflationary means of financing wage increases and federal deficits had to be found. The "compulsory loan" attached to the 70 percent wage increase of July 1963 for civil servants and military was ineffective, for example, because of the "leakage" in collection. Some more direct method of commandeering the means of payment was necessary.

The staff of Carvalho Pinto, led by the Paulista administrator, Diogo Gaspar, contemplated the problem and proposed an ingenious new scheme by which the Bank of Brazil would sell Treasury certificates whose purchase would be required by private banks exceeding their government-authorized credit limits. By altering the level of compulsory government bond purchases, the federal monetary authorities would be able at the same time to finance the federal deficit and control the availability of credit to the private sector. Equally important, this far-reaching new policy could be instituted by the Finance Minister, SUMOC, and the Bank of Brazil without requiring any congressional action.

The purpose behind the plan was to capture private savings, which could then in part be invested in developmental projects given high priority by the directors of the National Investment Fund. If carried out, the compulsory bond scheme would give the federal government control over investment allocations by means of the monetary system —something which the inefficient tax collection system could never make possible.[20]

The implications of the new plan, launched by SUMOC Instruction #255 in October 1963, soon became clear to private bankers, who immediately protested. Nonetheless, Carvalho Pinto went ahead. The bonds began trading at a high discount, confirming the pessimistic forecasts of the plan's opponents. The death-knell for the scheme sounded when Carvalho Pinto lost his post as Finance Minister in late December. One of his successor's first acts was to acquiesce in the revocation of the October SUMOC Instruction. The last device for financing the moribund Three-Year Plan had been surrendered.[21]

In his six months as Finance Minister, Carvalho Pinto had also struggled in vain to renegotiate Brazil's foreign debt. New terms from foreign creditors depended upon evidence of success in domestic stabilization. Since Quadros' resignation the internal and external sides of Brazil's financial deterioration had acted to reinforce each other. Dantas' Washington mission, in March 1963, was intended to be the overture to what he hoped would be an extensive renegotiation of the foreign debt along the lines laid down in June 1961, but never carried out because of the political uncertainty following Jânio's departure. Near the end of his term, Carvalho Pinto succeeded in negotiating a delay on several short-term loans from the IMF and the U.S. Treasury that came due in September and October, but the repayment was merely postponed until 1964, thereby leaving the remaining part of the $1.928 billion due to be settled before the end of 1965. Such a sum was far beyond Brazil's ability to pay. Carvalho Pinto could do little more toward renegotiation than deny the persistent rumors that Brazil was about to declare a unilateral moratorium.[22]

As the incoming Finance Minister in December 1963, Ney Galvão found the situation even worse than had Carvalho Pinto when he succeeded Dantas in June. Inflation had continued to accelerate, with the cost of living (for Guanabara) rising 81 percent in 1963, an alarming increase over the rise of 55 percent recorded for 1962. The budget deficit was out of control, the figure for 1963 (504.6 billion cruzeiros, more than a third of total expenditure) exceeding even the most pessimistic forecasts.

Out of desperation the Goulart government turned to direct controls. In February and March 1964 the President issued decrees setting up new agencies to control pricing of essential consumer goods such as clothing, shoes, and drugs. Food prices were to be controlled by the National Supply Agency (SUNAB). Goulart's Justice Minister, Abelardo Jurema, promised to prosecute promptly anyone violating the complex regulations being issued to control rents.[23] Along with the welter of direct controls came a torrent of moral injunction against "profiteers." Although the poor undoubtedly suffered most, everyone was squeezed in the confusion of constantly rising prices and wages. Recourse to unenforceable direct controls was a desperate measure that gave the government the illusion of activity. In fact, the Goulart regime had come close to losing the last remnants of control in the battle against inflation.

The pressure produced by the deficit in the balance of payments also continued to be intense. In February 1964 the government moved to reform the bewilderingly complex exchange rate structure.[24] It was essentially a simplification, and therefore a gesture in the direction of IMF orthodoxy. In principle, all imports and exports were to be transacted at the free rate (about 1200 cruzeiros to the dollar). But the exceptions were significant. The Bank of Brazil was given a monopoly over all foreign exchange earned by coffee and sugar exports, for which the previous dollar rate of 600 cruzeiros was maintained. This meant that the "exchange confiscation," so long practiced on coffee, had been extended to sugar. On the import side, wheat, petroleum, and equipment for the domestic petroleum industry were to be subsidized at the rate of 620 cruzeiros to the dollar. Once again, the expensive subsidy of wheat and oil imports had been continued at a level contributing significantly to the inflationary federal deficit.

The Brazilian government talked bravely in early 1964 about rescheduling the foreign debt. Negotiations with the IMF were resumed after a suspension during the Carvalho Pinto period. Talks with European creditors were scheduled for March. The optimism expressed by Goulart in his February 19 speech (when the exchange reforms were announced) was apparently based on an overestimate of the significance of a favorable turn in the terms of trade in 1963, as coffee prices rose rapidly from 33¢ a pound (for the pace-setting grade known as "New York Spot Santos No. 4") to 44.8¢ a pound in January 1964. Brazil's foreign trade balance had improved sharply in 1963, producing a surplus of approximately $100 million, but the balance of payments picture was still gloomy because of the heavy interest and capital payments falling due.[25]

Goulart also pointed confidently in his February 19 speech to the attitude of Japanese and European investors. The German government had just announced a $50 million long-term loan to Brazil, and Japanese importers of Brazilian iron ore had offered a $220 million credit against ore to be purchased from the state-owned Rio Doce Valley mining company. But the fact was that these isolated agreements, long under negotiation, did not represent any sudden brightening in the foreign payments crisis. Prospects for rescheduling were, if anything, worse. The United States government, which held the key to the debt refinancing, was growing visibly more concerned over the leftward trend of the Goulart government. Since the abortive state-of-siege request in October 1963, and especially since the first of the New Year, the State Department, through its exceptionally well-informed Embassy in Rio de Janeiro, knew that the conspiratorial opposition to Goulart was gaining strength rapidly. With the political atmosphere in Brazil so embittered, the American government preferred to follow a waiting game, conceding small short-term renegotiations, but giving no encouragement to Brazilian overtures for large-scale refinancing. If the U.S. had been chary with Dantas a year earlier, their caution was many times greater now.[26]

The American attitude was further complicated by the ill-starred AMFORP case. Goulart had lost his nerve under nationalist attack in 1963, and referred the disputed matter of the value of the AMFORP properties to a newly appointed evaluation board. Meanwhile, the American government took this delay as a sign of bad faith and implied that any large-scale payment refinancing would depend upon satisfactory settlement of the AMFORP case.

The profit remittances law was another irritant in Brazil's relations with her foreign creditors. In January 1964, Goulart finally issued the regulation that rendered operative the profit remittances law passed by the Congress in September 1962. His decree settled unequivocally the question, which the law had not made completely clear, of the definition of the capital base on which remittances could be computed. Reinvested profits were to be counted as "national capital," not foreign capital, therefore running directly contrary to the oft-stated views of foreign investors and the United States government (the American ambassador had been an outspoken critic of the 1962 bill).[27]

In December 1963 the Goulart government had taken another step with far-reaching implications for foreign investors. A decree was issued ordering a complete review of all government concessions in the mining industry. At the same time, Goulart announced his intention to cancel all concessions not exercised during the past twenty years. Here was another point of maximum conflict between U.S. investors and Brazilian nationalists. Mining concessions had been a political hot potato in Brazil for more than forty years, going back to the bitter controversy that began in the early 1920's over Percival Farquhar's abortive Itabira iron ore concession.

The current focus of conflict was the São João del Rei concession (formerly held by an English consortium) now owned by the Hanna Corporation, a large American firm known for its clumsy public relations and notorious insensitivity to the political dimension of mining operations by foreign investors in Brazil. Hanna's unfortunate image was reinforced by the fact that the firm was headed by Eisenhower's ultraconservative former Secretary of the Treasury, George Humphrey, and by its sending to Brazil as consultants Herbert Hoover, Jr., and the son (J. W. F. Dulles) of John Foster Dulles, both obvious *bêtes noires* to the nationalists. Hanna's clumsiness contrasted sharply with the notable success of other U.S. firms, such as Bethlehem Steel, which had wisely entered into partnership with a Brazilian firm, Antunes. The latter held 51 percent ownership (to 49 percent for Bethlehem) in the highly productive and profitable manganese-mining concession (ICOMI) in the northern state of Amapá. Bethlehem had left the delicate matter of relations with the Brazilian government, insofar as possible, to its Brazilian partner. Cool-headed Brazilians pointed to this and other successful foreign concessions as proof that there was no difficulty in principle for foreign investors; but the December decree immediately led to the rumor that the Hanna concession was about to be canceled.[28]

In this as in practically every other principal area of economic policy, Goulart had managed to irritate everyone and please almost no one. Like Vargas in 1951–54, Goulart was attempting to combine nationalist and orthodox measures. The result was confusion.

The nationalists, for example, railed against his caution. They attacked the foreign exchange reform of February (SUMOC Instruction #263) as a near-surrender to the IMF, and demanded immediate cancellation of the Hanna concession and confiscation of the AMFORP properties. They denounced the impending debt renegotiations in Europe and called instead for a unilateral moratorium.

The center and the conservatives, on the other hand, along with Brazil's foreign creditors, could see only Goulart's caving in to the pressure from the left. Delay on the AMFORP case, enactment of the profit remittances law, virtual abandonment of a coherent anti-inflation program—these moves to appease the radicals for whom Brizola claimed to speak—strengthened the belief that Goulart was, wittingly or unwittingly, losing control of economic policy. The conspirators among the opposition went even farther: they took it as proof that the President was deliberately promoting economic chaos in order to prepare the way for his own "continuist" coup.[29]

Presidential Hopefuls: Support for Democratic Politics

Late 1963 and early 1964 saw the political conflict intensify in an atmosphere loaded with charges of planned coups and counter-coups. But there were many leading politicians who hoped that Goulart would be able to finish his presidential term. None held any special brief for Goulart; indeed, several were his sworn enemy. But each had staked his political future on the electoral process, and each feared that some reversion to extra-legal methods might drastically alter the rules of the democratic game. Presidential fever was in the air, and those whom it afflicted were, by the logic of their position, natural opponents of a coup.[30]

The first leading presidential hopeful was the perennial candidate, Adhemar de Barros. Narrowly elected governor of São Paulo in 1962, this old-style populist was an anomalous figure in the midst of the deepening political crisis. Although he had based his career on welfare promises, having first become governor with Communist support in 1947, he had lined up against the radical left in the ideological clash since mid-1963. Barros, for example, was taking a tough line in late 1963 toward Communist infiltration in Paulista labor unions, and was even encouraging strikebreaking by force. His presidential ambitions rested upon his personal party—the PSP—which, because it was restricted primarily to São Paulo, could only carry him to victory as a plurality winner. In February 1964 the PSP held their national convention and nominated Adhemar for President in the election (October 1965) that was still a year and a half away. His designated running mate was João Calmon, a violently anti-Brizola congressman (he changed his party from PSD to PSP to get the nomination) and executive in the Chateaubriand TV-newspaper-magazine empire. Adhemar had a dwindling hard-core political support. As governor of São Paulo he was able to rely on the best trained and equipped state militia in Brazil; in case of a showdown, however, it would have to face the larger and much better equipped federal Second Army, headquartered in São Paulo and commanded by General Kruel, a close personal friend of Goulart.

The second presidential hopeful was Juscelino Kubitschek, who had been planning for the 1965 election even before he left office in 1961. The PSD, also sensing the need to dramatize its faith in the continued existence of open politics in Brazil, held its convention in March, nominating, to no one's surprise, Kubitschek. Having formalized that step in his long-pursued plan to return to power, Juscelino was now desperately seeking to preserve the alliance with the PTB that had previously won him the presidency. He worried that Goulart's flirtation with the radical left might open a permanent schism in the PSD-PTB alliance; more important, he feared that the President's ineptness might lead to financial chaos and civil war. Kubitschek therefore tried to act as a moderating influence on Goulart while at the same time urging the PSD to be more receptive to the President's plea for "basic reforms." Kubitschek's hope for a return to power depended on Goulart's remaining committed to what the radical left contemptuously labeled the "politics of conciliation." Kubitschek at this time was a senator, and therefore had control over no military forces of any kind in case of a showdown.[31]

The third presidential hopeful was Carlos Lacerda. His position was the most anomalous. He had been a leading advocate of a coup in 1950, 1954, and 1955, when his political ambitions were dependent upon military intervention. By 1961, however, Lacerda believed that his career lay in the electoral arena. He had been a federal deputy, but his election to the governorship of Guanabara in 1960 had given him a new base from which to launch a bid for presidential nomination. Long a brilliant polemicist in politics, Lacerda was now proving an able administrator. As Goulart veered farther toward the radical left, Lacerda's campaign for the presidential nomination of the UDN gained strength. Many center voters, cruelly disappointed over the Quadros fiasco, were now attracted by Lacerda's intransigent anti-getulismo. Speaking-visits throughout the country in late 1963 and early 1964 gave evidence that Lacerda's following was growing not only among middle-class voters in the cities, but also among worried landowners in the countryside. His greatest asset was the continued presidency of Goulart, because the lack of any anti-inflation program and the flirtation with the radical left tipped wavering center voters toward Lacerda. The UDN convention was set for April, and Lacerda loomed as the probable nominee.[32]

There were two other factors which made Lacerda less in favor of a coup than ever before. The first was his rivalry with other leaders within the UDN. By early 1964 Bilac Pinto, for example, was openly preaching the need for "extraordinary measures" to counter the "revolutionary war" which he alleged Goulart had already unleashed.[33] But if a coup were staged against Goulart, what would happen to Lacerda's presidential hopes? There might well be no election. Second, Lacerda was in an exposed position if it should come to a test of power with the federal government in his state of Guanabara. He had only a small police force, which had been seriously depleted by mass transfers to federal service in late 1963. Since the First Army was headquartered in Rio, Lacerda's forces could be easily overcome in a civil war.

The fourth politician with a major stake in the 1965 presidential election was Governor Magalhães Pinto of Minas Gerais, Lacerda's chief rival for the UDN nomination. A prosperous banker, Magalhães Pinto was busily cultivating the center-left. Until February of 1964 he sought an "opening to the left" and was an important contact in San Tiago Dantas' efforts to construct a united front in early 1964. Magalhães Pinto had made himself the chief spokesman for the liberal wing of the UDN, but he had steadily lost ground within the party to Lacerda, who was more effective in gaining the support of local and state UDN organizations. Nevertheless, he retained hopes of increasing his support and, therefore, had his own reasons for wanting to continue the democratic game. In contrast to Lacerda, Magalhães Pinto commanded a large state militia, which put him in a strong position should he change his mind about a test of force. It was in fact larger than the federal forces stationed in Minas Gerais, which were only a part of the First Army.[34]

The fifth presidential hopeful was the leading leftist Governor, Miguel Arraes of Pernambuco.[35] With Goulart and Brizola ineligible to run for President in 1965, Arraes was the principal contender on the left. Unlike Brizola, Arraes appeared prepared for the long process of organizing the mass vote nationally on the lines which had proved successful in Pernambuco. Such efforts might not bear fruit by 1965, but Arraes hoped that time was on his side. What he feared most was that some ill-judged move by Goulart might provoke a coup which would set back indefinitely efforts to organize the vote on the left. Furthermore, Arraes rightly feared that Goulart might stage his own "preventive coup," removing prominent governors of both right and left. In October 1963, at the time of the abortive attempt to arrest

Lacerda, troops of the Fourth Army, headquartered in Recife, occupied the heart of the city and surrounded the governor's palace in what the commander, General Justino Alves Bastos, termed "maneuvers."

There was an even stranger incident in February 1964, when the employers of Recife staged a lockout that the federal government apparently condoned (they would not send in troops), thus helping to prolong an acute conflict between the traditionally powerful landowners now allied with commercial elements against the Arraes government. Arraes would be very vulnerable in a test of power with the federal government, since Pernambuco (like the other northern states) had virtually no state militia to pit against the Fourth Army. Arraes was walking a tightrope between his declared enemies on the right and his competitors on the left. His future could only depend upon the electoral process. He had no forces for a revolt of his own, and he had reason to believe that a *golpe* of either the right or the left would make his removal a primary aim.[36]

Of these five leading politicians, three finally became conspirators. The other two became victims of the repression that accompanied and followed Goulart's deposition.

The Left: Divided and Overconfident

Since the end of 1961, Goulart had focused his political message on the need for "basic reforms." Action in this area could attract simultaneous support from the center and left as long as the issues remained vague. When it came to the hard reality of detail, however, significant action became extremely difficult. Goulart's indecision and ineffectual leadership in 1963 had left the center and moderate-left demoralized and discredited in the eyes of the anti-reformists on the right.

Having followed a policy of drift in late 1963, Goulart adopted a more strident tone as 1964 began. In his New Year's speech he attributed Brazil's economic crisis to obstinate politicians who refused to cooperate in the fundamental social changes that alone could save the constitutional process.[37] Agrarian reform was again the keynote, combined with a more aggressive attitude toward foreign capital. By signing in January 1964 the decree finally implementing the stringent profit remittance law passed in September 1962, Goulart was acting on an issue that was a touchstone for the radical left. The more he turned to the foreign-exploitation theory as an explanation of Brazil's economic crisis, however, the more irretrievably the President turned his back on the moderate left and center. There was hope for center support as long as Goulart turned no farther left than the reformist position of Dantas and Furtado. He could never carry the center if he should turn to the Brizola position.[38] Indeed, the essence of Brizola's radical nationalism was a repudiation of any reform within the existing structure.

The idea of Goulart "turning to" Brizola, as the President's enemies charged was imminent, showed how the rhetoric had oversimplified the actual situation. Goulart's political dilemma was far more cruel. There was no clear-cut alternative to the left of the moderates, whom Goulart had discarded in June 1963. Instead, there was a bewildering variety of ill-disciplined, overconfident ad hoc groups dominated by political amateurs. Brazilian political journalists spoke of the "lefts," rather than the "left." [39] As the Goulart presidency continued, the "lefts" grew more and more convinced that the disorganization of the traditional political elite was preparing the way for radical changes in Brazil's political structure. In the flush of their self-confidence they failed to appreciate that they were even more seriously divided than their enemies.[40]

A factor complicating the calculations of all factions on the left was the attitude of Goulart. He had become President by an act of miscalculation on the part of his predecessor. 1963—the first year that Goulart enjoyed full powers—had seen the President adopt and soon discard the policies of the moderate left. Now the pressure of the financial crisis and the political impasse seemed to be driving him farther left. The radicals concluded that an unexpected turn of events had delivered the President into their hands. They also led themselves to believe that this apparent development was the inevitable result of their efforts. On the contrary, the trend was the result of Goulart's own frustrated and miscalculating search for a heroic role, abetted by the temporary demoralization and confusion of the center forces among the military and the middle class.

Who were the groups and leaders on the radical left? One might begin by reviewing Dantas' desperate effort, begun in December 1963, to prevent an irrevocable split within the fragmented left. Dantas' abortive tenure as Finance Minister had made painfully clear the lack of a mobilizable political base for the moderate left. After his dismissal in June 1963, Dantas grew concerned over the radicals' increased influence.

Bravely ignoring his mortal illness, he negotiated feverishly to construct a united front on the left. His plan was to maintain the dominance of the moderates by controlling the radicals within a coalition. If free on their own, radical leftists such as the Communist leaders of the CGT might succeed in leading Goulart to overestimate their real political strength. Domesticated by a popular front, however, the moderates might be able to maintain dominance. Dantas therefore proposed a united front to include everything from the Brazilian Communist Party to the PSD. By his patient negotiation Dantas hoped to bridge the growing chasm between the positive left, which he had represented in power a year earlier, and the radical nationalists, who now smelled blood. Dantas, as a renegade member of the political elite, had not forgotten the facts of power. He knew that the conspirators on the right were benefiting most from the growing political impasse because they could, in any ultimate test, count on the support of the military.[41]

Dantas' proposal met almost universal hostility among the groups to whom it was directed. One of the few to view it favorably, albeit with reservations, was the Brazilian Communist Party (PCB).[42] This Moscow-oriented party, still led by the venerable Luís Carlos Prestes, liked Dantas' proposal to legalize the party—a gesture that Dantas thought would isolate the PCB and thereby reduce its effectiveness as a disruptive force. The PCB was in fact a voice for caution compared to the intransigent radicals who spurned the "politics of conciliation" symbolized by the Dantas approach. But Prestes remembered the disaster of 1935 and was too experienced a student of Brazilian political reality to over-estimate the revolutionary potential of 1964. The "democratic and nationalist" government he sought on behalf of the PCB would represent a phase of continued cooperation with "bourgeois" politicians.[43] What most concerned him was the danger that the reckless tactics of the amateurs on the left might provoke a premature test of force that the left was bound to lose. Prestes was hardly the dominant figure within the radical left, however. The younger generation of radicals dismissed him as the tired bureaucratic manipulator of an obsolete apparatus, comparable in mentality to the "bankrupt" elite of the center and right.[44]

Among the older generation, Prestes' cautious policies had aroused the opposition of a group of old-line PCB leaders such as João Amazonas and Maurício Grabois who broke away to form a pro-Chinese splinter party (*Partido Comunista do Brasil* or PC do B) in 1962. They angrily rejected the united front of Dantas, calling instead for revolutionary organization of the peasants. The PC do B was very small, numbering only a few hundred members. It was burdened by a rigidly dogmatic position and had succeeded in gaining no significant adherents among the labor movement or the student organizations, the centers of radical leftist organization.[45]

The most significant force on the left was also the newest and the least experienced. It was the heterogeneous spectrum of militant organizations often described as the "Jacobin" or "Fidelista" left. These groups frequently used the language of Marxism, but they were far from accepting the discipline of the PCB or the PC do B. They were militantly nationalist, concentrating their fire on the United States as the leading agent of "imperialism" in Brazil. Their vision for Brazil was romantically revolutionary; their attention was focused on what they thought was the immediate struggle for power.[46]

What made these "Jacobin" militants different and important was their effort at popular mobilization. Groups such as *Ação Popular* (AP), the Roman Catholic student movement, had succeeded in gaining control of the mass literacy programs being launched by the Ministry of Education. *Ação Popular* had grown out of the earlier *Juventude Universitária Católica* (JUC) and was the youthful, militant representation of the socially-conscious progressive wing of the Catholic Church. It was one of the fastest growing and most unpredictable elements within the independent radical left. Its leadership included a minority of Communists who competed with independents for the control of AP.[47]

Another student organization on the radical left was the official National Union of Students (*União Nacional de Estudantes* or UNE). This group was a product of the corporatist structure bequeathed to postwar Brazil by Vargas' Estado Nôvo. UNE was financed by a subsidy from the Ministry of Education, and also enjoyed extensive income in unofficial funds from Petrobrás and Goulart's own presidential office. Since the 1950's, UNE had been effectively infiltrated by the Communists, who now competed with AP members for the control of the UNE apparatus. By early 1964, UNE, as a separate organization, was more bureaucratized than *Ação Popular*.[48]

Elsewhere on the "Jacobin" left there were the labor groups such as CGT *(Comando Geral dos Trabalhadores)* and the PUA *(Pacto da Unidade e Ação)*, more impressive on paper than in fact. The CGT was led by several old-line Communists, such as Oswaldo Pacheco (who had been a PCB member of the Congress elected in December 1945). These labor leaders, whose salaries came directly from the Ministry of Labor under the corporatist labor union structure created by Vargas, had achieved influence with Goulart during the previous struggles of his presidency, calling strikes during the ministerial crisis of July 1962 and the crisis over the plebiscite in September 1962. They had helped dissuade Goulart from carrying through his state-of-siege request in October 1963. By early 1964 they seemed convinced that they had at their command a union apparatus that could provide the basis for a syndicalist regime. They were therefore unreceptive to Dantas' proposal of a united front, believing that their direct access to the President rendered such political stratagems unnecessary.[49]

In the rural sector there were signs that Brazil might at last be experiencing the protest movement that her archaic land system, especially in the Northeast, seemed to make inevitable. The Peasant Leagues (*Ligas Camponesas*) of Pernambuco, led by Francisco Julião, were the best-known example. By early 1964, however, Julião had virtually faded from sight, distracted by the pleasures of Rio de Janeiro and Brasília, and his followers had been overshadowed by other, newer movements. The legislation authorizing rural syndicates in 1963 had proved a great stimulus to organizing efforts, which coincided with spontaneous peasant land invasions in the states of Minas Gerais and Rio de Janeiro, as well as in the Northeast. The rural organizers were beyond the reach of Dantas' united front efforts, unless through the medium of the Church, whose priests in the Northeast were competing with Julião and the PCB to organize the rural syndicates that would gain official recognition by the federal government.

Finally, there were the independent figures on the left: Brizola and

Arraes. From Goulart's standpoint, Brizola was the most danger-ous.[50] His career was a history of electoral triumphs culminating in his election as federal deputy from Guanabara (despite the fact he was a Gaúcho) with a record-breaking total of 269,000 votes. Brizola had what only one other politician of national stature, Quadros, could claim: an electrifying campaign presence. He could translate the rhet-oric of radical nationalism into the language of the street. Overbearing and vulgar, he was given to brawling with his political enemies on the floor of Congress or in airport waiting rooms, his courage reinforced by several armed bodyguards. This crudely virile side of Brizola in-creased his lower-class following at the same time it outraged the mid-dle class and the "respectable" political elite. In short, Brizola was the most dynamic left-wing populist.[51]

He was also an isolated figure on the left. Quarrelsome and arro-gant, Brizola could hardly hope to assume the leadership of the left; at best he might aspire to seize it. Those radical leftists, such as Con-gressmen Sérgio Magalhães and Marco Antônio, who thought in terms of careful long-term organizational efforts, feared that Brizola's reckless ambition endangered the prospects for the entire left. They, along with many other personally honest leftists, were also contemptu-ous of Brizola's ostentatiously luxurious private life. For a large part of the "Jacobin" left, Brizola was a figure commanding fear, but not respect.

In 1963 Brizola attempted to institutionalize his following. He gained control of a chain of radio stations (Mayrink Veiga) and began organizing armed political cells called "groups of eleven." In early 1964 he launched his own weekly newspaper, *O Panfleto,* thereby adding to the welter of dailies and weeklies on the left.[52] Fortified by his own radio and newspaper, Brizola had a wider audience as he urged radical measures (foreign debt moratorium, a Constituent As-sembly in place of the Congress) on his brother-in-law, the President. At the same time he could pass on instructions and exhortations to the "groups of eleven," which *Panfleto* claimed would reach the announced goal of 100,000 groups by June.[53] These attempts to organize his own power apparatus reflected Brizola's realization that, like Dantas, he could not trust the President to adopt his policies as a matter of course. His failure to win the Finance Ministry at the time of Car-valho Pinto's departure in December 1963 angered Brizola and convinced him that he must redouble his efforts to mobilize popular pressure on the government, since that now seemed the only way to force his way into the highest circles of the Executive.[54]

As might be expected, Brizola had nothing but scorn for Dantas' efforts to form a coalition. Dantas symbolized for Brizola everything that had to be destroyed if Brizola was to emerge victorious from the power struggle on the left. Having helped to cut short the Dantas-Furtado experiment of January-June 1963, Brizola now ridiculed Dantas as a self-seeking "entreguista." *Panfleto* lampooned the united front and ran a smear campaign alleging that Dantas had profited personally from surplus wheat agreements signed with the United States during his ministry.[55] Dantas replied with a libel suit.

The only other independent leftist of national prominence was Governor Miguel Arraes of Pernambuco, who had been the first populist politician to capture a governorship in the Northeast. He won in 1962 in a campaign which mobilized the working-class vote of Recife along with the rural-worker vote of the coastal sugar cane country. Arraes, as noted earlier, was deeply committed to the democratic process. In his first year as Governor, he had significantly consolidated his political following by leading the coastal agricultural wage laborers (just organized under the rural syndicate legislation passed by the Congress in 1963) to demand wage increases that would close the huge gap between their income and that of the urban workers, who enjoyed the protection of the federal minimum wage regulations.[56]

Arraes was even more isolated on the left than Brizola, however. Despite his striking success in Pernambuco, he retained the image of a provincial Northeasterner whose political style seemed out of place in the industrializing world of the center-south. Although he had gained the interest and admiration of some left-wing nationalist intellectuals in Rio de Janeiro, his small following within the PTB was overshadowed by Goulart and Brizola, who stood at the center of national politics. Arraes' power position had been further neutralized in early 1964 by Goulart's collusion with the lock-out staged in Pernambuco by the landowners and commercial class. In short, Arraes' honest, democratic style did not match the mood of the radicals on the left, who liked his language but found him too cautious.

Thus the radical left was deeply divided. To refer to "Communist" infiltration in order to explain the new life on the left was seriously misleading. The PCB (the Moscow-line party led by Prestes) was being swept along in the events of early 1964, fearful of the reckless bravado of the Brizolistas, and counseling continued cooperation with the "bourgeois" politicians. The Chinese-oriented PC do B was an insignificant influence. The real push on the left came from the "Jacobins." Some of their organizations (UNE, AP, the industrial unions) were PCB-infiltrated but the PCB itself was hardly a well-disciplined organization. Was Oswaldo Pacheco, a CGT leader and former PCB member of Congress (elected in 1945), for example, following Prestes' instructions as he urged his syndicalist design on Goulart? Brizola, on the other hand, openly boasted that he knew perfectly well how to outwit the Communists in the coming struggle for power.

The romantic Jacobins on the left were torn between their visions of a vast popular mobilization in support of a radical nationalist policy, and their hope that such a policy might miraculously emerge from on high, i.e., that Goulart was transforming his "reformist, bourgeois" regime into an instrument of radical change. Committed to efforts at widespread mobilization of the "popular forces," they were also tempted to believe that Goulart might save them the trouble of mobilization by imposing their policies from the top down.

In this jungle of maneuver and counter-maneuver on the left, Dantas' efforts were doomed to failure. Any plan to "domesticate" the Jacobins was hopeless because the moderate elements, such as the "positive" left, were seeking unity out of their own weakness. It was the same reason that led Prestes' PCB to support the idea of a united front. But the radical nationalists had little time for unity, because they were growing steadily more certain that they stood to gain most from the approaching breakdown of democratic politics.

The hapless Goulart, adrift toward the left, clung to the tactic on which he had so long relied: the playing off of one group against another. Now the tactic was applied to his maneuvers *within* the left. In December, he fed Brizola's hopes of becoming Finance Minister, then appointed Galvão. In February, he collaborated with the local conservatives and the Fourth Army in their efforts to intimidate Arraes in Pernambuco, then pulled back. Goulart's ambiguous policy with the "lefts" was a caricature of the Machiavellian style of his mentor, Vargas. Whereas Getúlio had an instinct for retaining potential allies throughout his byzantine moves, Goulart increasingly narrowed his range of support as he cast about in the quicksand of the deepening political impasse. But his fate was tied to his success with the left, since he had (in early October 1963) already tried and then discarded the idea of a "non-political" emergency regime underwritten by the military. That request for a state of siege, vigorously opposed at the time by all the "lefts," had reinforced their suspicions about Goulart's ultimate intentions. Despite their ebullient optimism, therefore, the "lefts" had their own grounds for mistrusting the President, who was now the target of an active conspiracy on the right.

A President's Fate: Friday the Thirteenth

It is at this point that one must focus upon the personality and motives of Goulart himself. Everyone agreed that the President was an enigmatic personality. "A veritable sphinx," his Justice Minister later called him. Like Quadros, he was ridden by complexes that distorted his political judgment. He could hardly fail to know, for example, that rumors of his beautiful wife's amatory adventures made him the subject of endless popular jokes. This reflection on his manhood was an important political liability in a Latin country. His sense of personal confidence, always undermined by self-consciousness over his slightly paralyzed leg, suffered a further blow in July 1963 when his mother died. Friends reported that she had been a powerful moderating influence on her son, and had warned him especially against the machinations of his "atheistic" brother-in-law, Brizola. Always the understudy, twice Vice President, Goulart had never been certain about how to conduct himself in the Presidency. Haunted by the shadow of the political genius who had first sponsored him, Goulart now found events closing in.

If the President came to appreciate his lack of a base of political support, he never drew the obvious conclusions. He made no serious efforts to reorganize the party structure. After the end of the Dantas-Furtado experiment in 1963, he played the role of a broker, shuffling the rival, ill-defined party and extra-party groups. His attitude toward the structure of Brazilian politics remained essentially passive. But time was running out on this zig-zag policy. Impatience on the far left, disillusionment among the moderate left, alarm in the center, conspiracy on the right—it added up to a volatile political cauldron.

The confused situation was further complicated by the conflicting currents within the presidential palace. His circle of advisers included relatively orthodox politicians such as the Justice Minister, Abelardo Jurema—A PSD member and former leader of the government majority in the Chamber of Deputies during the Kubitschek regime—who was a voice in favor of continuing a dialogue with the center. There were also labor union leaders such as Oswaldo Pacheco, Dante Pelacani, and Hercules Correia, who were urging the President to present the Congress with an ultimatum demanding enactment of radical leftist reforms, backed by the threat of mass strikes. These leaders headed a government-supported trade union hierarchy whose power to mobilize mass support was essentially untested. Yet they had intoxicated themselves with their own rhetoric about mass mobilization. Goulart was especially susceptible to their arguments because they were the manipulators of the union movement on which he had come to rely as a historical reflex.[57]

Also influential within the presidential circle were the War Minister, General Dantas Ribeiro, and the chief of the Military Household, General Assis Brasil.[58] Both proved unimpressed by the repeated warnings of the growing military conspiracy against the President. Dantas Ribeiro could not believe that centrist officers such as Castello Branco would desert their traditional role of political neutrality, despite warnings from Castello Branco himself; and the War Minister trusted in the long-standing friendship between Goulart and General Kruel, commander of the Second Army (São Paulo) and Dantas Ribeiro's predecessor as War Minister, to ensure the loyalty of that key command.[59] Assis Brasil went even farther in nurturing Goulart's illusion that he enjoyed a comfortable margin of support among the officer corps. The President should have noticed that Assis Brasil's weakness for alcohol made him an unreliable informant as well as someone who commanded less than wide respect among his fellow officers.[60]

Among occasional but influential Goulart advisers was Samuel Wainer, publisher of the pro-government newspaper chain, *Última Hora*. Wainer encouraged Goulart's flirtation with the idea of assuming emergency powers as a way out of the political crisis. Finally, the President had come to rely heavily upon the advice of two ambitious political amateurs. One was Raul Riff, the presidential press secretary, and the other was Darcy Ribeiro, chief of the Civil Household, a former anthropologist and vice rector of the University of Brasília, who had left higher education for the presidential palace. Both men had assumed wide authority and were pressing the President to take radical action.[61]

The radical advisers around Goulart had long tried to convince him that his conciliatory half-measures were the source of his political troubles. Their view ran along the following lines: all Brazil's major economic problems—balance of payments, inflation, lagging agricultural production—were related symptoms of Brazil's "exploitation" by an alliance of domestic and foreign enemies. Brazil was the victim of the "occult forces" that Vargas had denounced in his suicide note of August 1954, and to which Quadros had alluded in his resignation letter of August 1961. Efforts to conciliate these enemies could only weaken the government's position. Goulart's only course, therefore, was to take an unequivocal stand. He must rally the "popular forces," a majority of Brazilians, against the selfish elite that was so practiced in the manipulation of democratic politics. Goulart could only hope to regain economic growth and achieve basic social change in Brazil by rousing the latent majority. Structural reform was impossible without constitutional reform. But if the opposition would not vote the former, why would they possibly vote the latter, a far more serious matter? What hope was there that the Congress would amend the constitution to grant the vote to illiterates (thus benefiting primarily the agrarian poor) when it would not even consider agrarian reform? The Congress must therefore either be intimidated or bypassed.

The radical-leftist "explanation" became steadily more comforting to the harassed President. Each new symptom of economic chaos and political intransigence strengthened the hand of those who assured Goulart that all he needed was a blueprint for new lines of political action. They finally convinced him to opt for their strategy.

The President was to preside over a series of mass rallies in the major cities to mobilize what the radicals assured him was an overwhelming majority in favor of "basic reforms." While demonstrating this massive support, Goulart would begin to carry out reforms by decree. The idea was to bypass the Congress through the Executive powers that, his advisers told Goulart, he had yet to exploit. When the congressional opposition protested, the President could resort to plebiscites to demonstrate his popular support. This new phase of the presidency was set to begin on Friday, March 13, in Rio de Janeiro, the stronghold of Goulart's arch-enemy, Carlos Lacerda.

The President's radical advisers laid plans for a massive rally to be held that day in the Praça da Republica.[62] The scale of preparations indicated that this would be no routine political gathering. The presidential palace announced that the speakers would address the throng from the very same wooden structure which had been built for Getúlio Vargas' more famous appearances, and since remained stored and unused. The carefully chosen site was the huge square in front of Rio de Janeiro's principal railroad station. For weeks in advance the government organized participants for the rally. Petrobrás workers from refineries in the state of Rio de Janeiro and labor union cadres from São Paulo were to be brought in at government expense. The political significance of the occasion was to be heightened by the fact that it was being held in the city governed by Brazil's most adamantly anti-Goulart figure, Carlos Lacerda. The President took the precaution of ordering heavy Army protection for the rally. Lacerda countered by decreeing a holiday for all employees of the state of Guanabara, in the hope that the cariocas would take a long weekend and thereby reduce Goulart's crowd.

As the hour for the rally approached, tension mounted throughout the country. Until the speakers ascended the platform, few knew for certain who would speak. Would Goulart's rivals, Brizola and Arraes, appear at his side? On Friday evening 150,000 people crowded into the square. They bore a sea of banners demanding agrarian reform and legalization of the Communist Party. Cadres of white-helmeted Army police, brandishing machine guns, kept the festive crowd in check. The scene, carried into middle-class homes throughout the country by television, repeated a similar rally in Rio de Janeiro the previous August on the anniversary of Vargas' suicide. Now, however, the rhetoric was to be transformed into action.

As the hour for his appearance approached, Goulart grew nervous. He wanted to arrive at the rally toward the end of the long list of speakers who were to precede him. He wanted especially to avoid being present for Brizola's speech. After repeated delays, however, his aides told him he must start for the rally, and he reached the Praça da República in time to hear his brother-in-law electrify the crowd with a call for a Constituent Assembly in place of the Congress.[63]

Finally came the President's turn. Perspiring intensely in the humid
carioca night, he approached the speaker's platform with his beautiful
and stylishly dressed wife at his side (highly unusual in Brazilian politics).[64] His speech did not disappoint the crowd. Fortified by the
presence of his civilian and military advisers, Darcy Ribeiro and Assis
Brasil, he dramatically signed two decrees, whose promulgation had
been rumored for months. The first nationalized all private oil refineries. These facilities were owned by Brazilians but had become a target for the radical nationalists, who argued that all petroleum-process-
ing should be in the hands of Petrobrás, the federal monopoly. The
second was the SUPRA decree which declared subject to expropriation all "under-utilized" properties of over twelve hundred acres situ-
ated within six miles of federal highways or railways, and lands of
over seventy acres located within six miles of federal dams, irrigation
or drainage projects.

In his speech Goulart began by thanking the "syndical organizations" that had "mobilized their members" for "this great manifesta-
tion." He went on to attack those who "exploit [the people's] Christian beliefs by mystifying them with anticommunism." Goulart then
moved immediately to the central question of his speech: the need for
agrarian reform. "I am not afraid of being called a subversive for
proclaiming the necessity of revising the present Constitution, which
no longer conforms to the wishes of our people. It is antiquated because it legalizes an economic structure that is already obsolete, un-
just and inhuman." He invoked the authority of Pope John XXIII and
General MacArthur in support of the idea of a thoroughgoing reorganization of the rural land structure, which was also needed to "enlarge
and improve the internal market." The SUPRA decree, he explained,
was only "a step forward on the path of the great structural reforms."

Goulart invoked the memory of Vargas, "the great and immortal
patriot," to justify the other decree—nationalizing the privately-
owned oil refineries. He warned that nationalist enterprises such as
Petrobrás were so passionately supported that "the people will always
appear in the streets and public squares to honor [prestigiar] the government that is enacting measures such as these in order to show the
reactionary forces that the people must continue their march."

Goulart concluded by announcing the other areas in which he was
either planning to issue decrees (rent control), or propose legislation

to the Congress (tax reform, vote for illiterates and enlisted service-men) in the annual message due on March 15. The President ended on a confident, even a defiant note: "To all citizens I want to say, finally, that no force will be capable of preventing the government from continuing to assure absolute liberty to the Brazilian people, that no force will prevent the people from demonstrating freely and demo-cratically, and for this purpose we can say with pride that we are able to count on the patriotism of the brave and glorious Armed Forces of this nation." Sustained applause greeted his concluding pledge that the government would "fight with all its strength" for further reforms "at the people's side for the progress of Brazil." [65]

The significance of the March 13 rally was unmistakable. Goulart had finally turned to the radical left for his policies. He had begun by attacking the principle of private ownership in both the industrial and the rural sectors. The decree on oil refineries, however, had little obvious economic logic. The refineries' operation did not hinder Petrobrás, and they represented a less significant private effort than the distribution of petroleum products, which was completely in pri-vate hands, including foreign firms such as Standard Oil and Shell. Their expropriation was not even an attack upon foreign capitalists, because the refineries were Brazilian-owned.[66] The agrarian decree was more significant. It was an oblique attack upon the most difficult and controversial problem of Brazilian social structure, and therefore of domestic politics. Having failed to convince the Congress of the need for a change in the rural land structure, Goulart was proceeding unilaterally by decree. Since there had been no amendment to the congressional provision requiring prior payment in cash for govern-ment land-taking, Goulart would have to find enormous sums in his deficit-ridden Treasury. That was a virtual impossibility, as the rural landowners knew. The next step, they charged, would be outright con-fiscation.[67]

The two decrees of March 13, relatively modest in their immediate effects, represented the victory of the radicals around the President. Throughout the Executive there were a number of increasingly active centers of left-wing pressure, such as the Ministry of Education, which was subsidizing a mass literacy program with heavy political overtones—evidently part of a long-range effort (possibly meant to bear fruit in the elections of 1965) to create the base of mass support the regime notably lacked. Petrobrás, the government oil-monopoly, was engaging in politics, diverting funds to the National Union of Students, operating a radio station, and furnishing workers to be transported in Petrobrás trucks to support Goulart at the March 13 rally. It was clear that these dynamic elements were gaining increasing control over the actual policy of the government. They were no longer merely mobilizing political pressure against the opposition *within* the existing constitutional structure. Indeed, they aimed at displacing the allegedly obsolete institutions. There was, for example, a large-scale attack on the private secondary schools, directed by interconnected elements in the Ministry of Education, the government-subsidized National Student Union, and ad hoc student groups, financed by undisclosed (but probably federal) sources.

It is difficult to unravel the exact character of the policies which Goulart chose to endorse on March 13, because of the many crosscurrents within the presidential palace. It was reported that the Rio rally was to be but the first of a series of rallies throughout Brazil—Belo Horizonte, Bahia, Recife—ending with a climactic rally in São Paulo on May 1, the day Getúlio had always reserved for his most dramatic gestures to the left. At each rally there were to be new decrees, in line with Goulart's decision to govern without the Congress, if need be. What was the underlying rationale of these measures?

That question can be partially answered by examining the "Introduction to the Annual Presidential Message to Congress," dated March 15. In that document Goulart explained: "I have chosen to fight the privileged and to assume the initiative for basic reforms, which will make possible the replacement of the structures and institutions that are inadequate for the peaceful continuation of our progress and for the establishment of a complete and effective democratic community." He endorsed a "bottleneck" rationale for reforms that would accelerate "the transformation of an archaic society into a truly democratic, free, and modern nation."

The document went on to outline an ambitious program of increased public investment to be financed without the difficulties of the recent past, "thanks to the rescheduling of our foreign commitments and to the consolidation of Brazil's position with her creditors." In fact, these negotiations were just beginning in Paris, and Goulart was overconfidently predicting the end of Brazil's foreign trade gap.

The final section of the "Introduction" laid out the "Brazilian road"—an agenda of basic reforms, including agrarian reform (constitutional amendment to permit state-supervised redistribution of land without prior compensation in cash), political reform (votes for illiterates and enlisted men), and university reform (abolition of lifetime professorships). Finally, the President urged that the Congress consider holding a national plebiscite on the question of basic reforms. As if to underline the ultimatum behind this suggestion, Goulart noted that the "institutional shackles" had divided the country into two groups: "the small nucleus of the privileged," as opposed to the "disinherited, from whom everything is demanded without even offering them the reassuring certainty of a better future." The moment was one of urgency, he warned, similar to the eras of "Independence, Abolition of Slavery, the proclamation of the Republic, and the promulgation of the Workers' Legislation," when "our ancestors" proved to have the "wisdom and the greatness to renovate the basic institutions of the Nation that had become obsolete, thus guaranteeing the peaceful progress of the Brazilian people." [68]

In the central area of "structural reforms" the Goulart government in its new phase relied primarily on slogans, buttressed by ill-coordinated administrative fiats. For agrarian reform, the President had produced the decree of March 13, characterizing it as "merely a first step." [69] But there was no sign of a systematic program to study the agrarian problem as a whole. This hastily drafted decree was vehemently attacked by the conservatives and considered woefully inadequate by the radical left. Meanwhile, scattered groups of landless peasants were invading lands, some already occupied by small farmers. Armed conflict broke out in the countryside, and there were reports of runs on guns and ammunition by the *fazendeiros* in response to the growing militancy of the rural unions. Goulart wanted to capitalize on this tension, but his government had failed to come up with a comprehensive agrarian program. Having neither organized nor taken over the newly formed rural unions (despite some belated efforts in the northeast), Goulart had also failed to offer a blueprint which would give direction to their ill-organized attacks on the established agrarian order.

Here, as elsewhere, Goulart was unable to articulate a coherent program for the left, the more radical (Brizola) wing of which he

appeared to have endorsed after March 13. He was therefore to have
the worst of all worlds. He had never organized a base of mass political support for a reform government. Nor had he mobilized a base of
support for revolutionary attack against the constitutional structure
which lay behind the political impasse. And he had not formulated a
coherent position that could be described as unequivocally leftist,
much less revolutionary. Yet he allowed himself after March 13 to be
drawn into a radical stance. Having lacked a base of democratic support during the Dantas-Furtado phase of 1963, he now stood before a
carefully primed crowd on March 13, 1964, apparently believing that
a revolutionary phalanx, created without any clear direction from
him, would carry him to victory against a nearly united opposition of
the military and the politicians of the center and right, who still controlled the ramparts of political power.

The massive rally of March 13 had served to strengthen the overconfidence of the "Jacobin" left, inducing euphoria over the "irreversible" popular mobilization now in process. Within many quarters on
the left there occurred a collapse of any ability to assess objectively
the true power situation: the wish became father to the conclusion.
The "popular forces" had now awakened—the *tomada de consciência*
was the central fact of politics, or so it was thought the left. In fact,
the left was as divided as ever after March 13.

Brizola continued his own bid for power. He repeated his demand
for a Constituent Assembly, thereby running directly counter to
Goulart's strategy (outlined in the "Introduction to the Presidential
Message to Congress") of bringing pressure to bear on the *existing*
Congress.[70] Brizola added to the tension by confessing that *he*
doubted that there would be any elections in 1965.[71] On March 20
he told a PTB convention in Brasília that it should not be afraid of
"washing its dirty linen" in public because criticism would help
strengthen the party. He urged cautious support for the government
because "we think the Jango of the [March 13] rally returned to
being the Jango of the Ministry of Labor."[72] Brizola's paper,
Panfleto, threw cold water on the popular front efforts, preferring
an independent stance.[73] Brizola seemed certain that the "popular
forces" enjoyed a natural advantage over the "reactionaries." "The
golpista spirit" had already "twice been loudly defeated by the people
—in the crisis of 1961 and the plebiscite."[74] Close observers of the

mood on the left reported in late March that the lower ranks of the lefts chafed at their leaders' (CGT, UNE, PCB) willingness to follow Goulart's legalistic approach to Congress. They preferred Brizola's radicalism. In fact, they were deeply suspicious of Goulart's "continuist" motives.[75]

Dantas, on the other hand, doggedly continued his attempt to unite the left after the March 13 rally, but he knew time was running out. On March 23 the front published its program, which presupposed a continued attempt to work through the Congress to achieve "basic reforms." [76] The atmosphere had changed rapidly, however. The air was full of charges of coup and continuism. Dantas grew alarmed over the overconfidence of the Jacobins within the presidential palace and among the lefts. He warned that "those who try to demoralize the Congress and ridicule it in the eyes of the people are, above all, the enemies of the people and are probably only interested in working for what Brazil most needs to avoid, which is the risk of a revival of personalistic power." [77] Arraes, one of the leftist leaders who retained some objectivity as the political polarization accelerated, pointedly denied that there was any plot afoot to close the Congress.[78] The fact that he felt it necessary to issue a denial only confirmed the rumors and fears.

The Prestes-led Communist Party (PCB) met feverishly to set its own policy in the midst of the rapidly growing political confrontation. On March 17, Prestes analyzed the situation at length, reiterating the party's support of the popular front and the policy of exercising "growing pressure on Congress." The objective remained "the conquest of a government which, although still under the present system and prior to the victory of the revolution, would be capable of initiating, and moving forward with, the structural reforms that are being demanded." The legalistic, cautious approach was underlined by Prestes, who argued that the "peaceful pathway" was the "possibility in the best interests of the workers." To achieve a "nationalistic and democratic government" would require that the "patriotic and democratic forces in our country be unified. And that is a slow and difficult process. It is no easy task to unify the very wide-ranging patriotic and democratic forces in our country." These forces, Prestes added, "reach even into the urban middle classes and into the national bourgeoisie." [79]

From Conspiracy to "Revolution": The Fall of Goulart

The very centrist forces to which both Prestes and Dantas worriedly looked were already moving rapidly toward the radicals on the right.[80] The radical turn on March 13 solidified the opposition to Goulart by strengthening the belief that he had rejected the rules of the democratic game. The shift in opinion was most significant within the group that had held the balance of power during every civilian political impasse in the history of the Republic: the officer corps. The sight of elite Army military police, backed by tanks, serving as the shock troops to maintain order at the March 13 rally, brought officers of centrist opinion (pro-"legality") to the painful realization that the military was being drawn into tacit support of measures that these officers thought ill-advised and perhaps even subversive. If the people want the President's reforms, they began to ask, then why does he need so much protection for his public appearances?

The active conspirators among the military had gone much farther; they now decided to shift from a defensive to an offensive status. Events were moving fast. Goulart, they reasoned, had irrevocably committed himself and would have to be removed. Their attention now turned to questions of detail: the timetable for the coup, the exact pattern of loyalties in the Army commands, the problem of supplies in case of civil war, the reliability of the anti-Goulart civilian politicians.

But the moderates among the military were still reluctant to depose the constitutional head of state, in whose legitimization the Army had played a crucial role by tacitly underwriting the plebiscite of January 1963. Would such a move not be a violation of the Constitution? This dilemma was a real one for many officers, and provoked long debates in the barracks and clubs. It was the uneasy conscience of these moderates—among the civilian plotters as well as the military—which tempted them to overemphasize the ideological coherence of Goulart's final option on March 13. They felt they had perfectly justifiable reasons for regarding the government as dangerously incompetent: the haphazard economic policy that held no promise of success against either accelerating inflation at home (now exceeding an annual rate of 100 percent) or the threat of payments default abroad, the recourse to exclusively statist solutions to social and economic problems (e.g., land reform), and the growing complicity with organized violence. In short, the moderate opposition—the buffeted and confused center of yesteryear—had begun to believe the Goulart-baiters whose warnings of catastrophe were first heard when their arch-enemy, Vargas, appointed Jango as Labor Minister in June 1953. Favoring reform but fearing too rapid a change in the status quo, they now shared the fear, becoming widespread since late 1963, that all of Goulart's moves had no further purpose than to create a revolutionary situation in which the President would emerge as the Brazilian Perón.

As in 1954, the cranking up of the military machine to move against its Commander in Chief was a slow process. Although long-time conspirators such as Odílio Denys and Cordeiro de Farias needed no convincing, it was still an arduous task to mobilize the individual Army commanders. In fact, the conspirators were certain of the support of only one of the four generals commanding the four principal Army regions—General Justino Bastos (Fourth Army—the Northeast). The other three—General Amaury Kruel (Second Army —São Paulo), General Âncora (First Army—Rio de Janeiro), General Galhardo (Third Army—Rio Grande do Sul)—were known to be stubbornly pro-legality and loyal to Goulart in varying degrees. But many of their officers had proved receptive to the conspirators' arguments. In the Third Army, for example, where pro-Goulart pressure had made possible his succession to the presidency in 1961 and the advancing of the date for the plebiscite in 1962, anti-Goulart sentiment was running high among the officers, especially in the interior of Rio Grande do Sul.[81]

The military conspiracy against Goulart gained impetus on March 20, when Castello Branco, chief of the Army General Staff, circulated a memorandum to his staff. This brief statement quickly became known to the wavering moderate officers and offered a clear-cut justification for opposing the President's apparent plan to use the government-controlled labor unions as a political base for overturning the constitutional structure. The memorandum, which became a central document of the anti-Goulart conspiracy, began by mentioning the March 13 rally as the cause of "worry and inquiries among my subordinates."

Castello Branco went on to attack the idea of a Constituent Assembly as the prelude to a dictatorship. "Are the Brazilian people request-

ing a military or civilian dictatorship and a Constituent Assembly?"
he asked. "Not yet, it would appear." There must be no compromise,
with the "historic role" of the armed forces as the defender of the
constitutional order and the enforcer of the laws, "including those
which guarantee the electoral process." [82]

A respected leader of the moderates had given Goulart an unmistakable warning: pull back from your embrace with the radical left or
lose your military support as President. How the military conspirators would move against Goulart if he ignored this warning (the memorandum quickly reached presidential hands) was not yet clear. The
opposition was still in the awkward position of waiting for some further maneuver by Goulart that would finally discredit his formidable
asset of "legality." Incredibly enough, Goulart soon obliged with just
such a move.

What finally galvanized the moderates into action was Goulart's
outright challenge to the principle of military discipline during the
Easter weekend of March 27–29. On March 25 the Navy Minister,
Admiral Mota, had ordered the arrest of a sailor who was active in
organizing a Sailors' Association. This group was a labor union of the
enlisted men, demanding an improvement in working conditions from
their commanders. They had gained the sailors' support by champion-
ing their demands for better pay and the right to marry and to wear
civilian clothes while off duty.

However spontaneous the support for the movement, its leadership
was directly linked to the radical leftists who had talked the President
into the new strategy of March 13. José Anselmo, the arrested sailor,
was a university student who earlier had been active in the radical
leftist student organization (UNE) and had entered the Navy to do
his compulsory military service, which most university students managed to avoid. Anselmo, however, had joined the Navy, anxious to
extend the mobilization of the "popular forces" to the Navy proletariat. When the Navy Minister moved against Anselmo and the Sailors'
Association, as well as Admiral Aragão, the leftist commander of the
Marines (whose appointment in late 1963 had caused protests from
conservative naval officers),[83] over one thousand sailors and marines
revolted on March 26, and barricaded themselves in the headquarters
of the metallurgical workers' union.

The following day, Good Friday, Goulart hurriedly returned from what he had hoped would be a long holiday weekend in Rio Grande do Sul. He was immediately buffeted by conflicting advice on how to handle the crisis. Darcy Ribeiro and Raul Riff finally caught the President's ear and convinced him to dismiss Mota. He named as the new minister, Paulo Rodrigues, a fragile and aged retired admiral, who had been chosen from a short list of candidates submitted by the leaders of the CGT. The military opposition could hardly have asked for the issue to be posed more clearly: the Communist-infiltrated labor leadership exercising a veto over the chief of one of the three services. The worst fears of the opposition were confirmed almost immediately. The new Minister was told by Goulart that he had a free hand to solve the problem of the rebels. Rodrigues immediately ordered a full amnesty for the besieged sailors. This move hit the officer corps like a bombshell. The Military Club and an ad hoc group of admirals issued manifestos denouncing the attack on the principle of military discipline.

During the sergeants' revolt in September 1963 Goulart had drawn back at the crucial moment, allowing the commanders to discipline the rebels. But events in March had moved too quickly for the President's usual stop-and-go tactics. He was now associated irrevocably with the declared enemies of the higher military. As happened in the crisis leading to Getúlio's suicide in 1954, the military was being drawn toward direct intervention by an incident challenging the "honor" and autonomy of the officer corps itself. In 1954 it was the politically motivated assassination of an Air Force major; now, ten years later, it was the mobilization of the sailors against their officers —a move of far greater significance. Both involved, interestingly enough, the lesser services—the Air Force and the Navy. The Army was inexorably brought in, however, through feelings of class solidarity among the officers and a common fear that their role as the "moderating power" in the political system was at stake.

As the military conspiracy now reached its climax, center civilian political opinion was also being mobilized. The rally of March 13 convinced many pro-legalists that Goulart had ceased to believe in the democratic process. To understand their reaction one must recall that the Brazilian political system rested upon a delicate equilibrium.[84] The balance of forces carried with it the assumption that no sector would attempt to displace totally any other sector. By late 1963 Goulart had already convinced many of the most traditional elements—large landowners, conservative military, and merchants—that the "established order" was threatened by radical change, not mere reform. They therefore concentrated their attacks upon the *nouveaux* whom they feared would be the exclusive beneficiaries of the new order: radical labor leaders (CGT) and peasant organizers (progressive priests, Arraes, student radicals).

Added to the concern of the traditional sectors was the growing panic among the middle class and the nervous industrialists and bankers. The middle class of the center-south region, for example, feared for its position vis-à-vis the new proletariat, for whom Goulart's radical advisers claimed to speak. Could Brazil become another Cuba, where the middle class had been relegated to exile or impotence? Nor was the middle class prepared to accept without a struggle the imposition of a syndicalist regime, reducing them to an inferior role. This fear was the civilian counterpart to the military's concern that a trade union phalanx might displace *them* as the ultimate arbiters of the political process.[85]

Both the traditional and the "middle" sectors therefore contemplated with alarm the apparent breakdown of the republican institutions created in 1945–46. The elitist political system had proved unable to adjust to the widening popular participation that had increased so rapidly since 1945. The President had decided to carry his struggle for "reforms" beyond the Congress and into the streets. Now the middle class was about to answer with its own mobilization.[86]

On March 19, a hastily organized public march, led largely by women's religious groups, was called to demonstrate the militancy of the middle-class opposition to Goulart. A crowd estimated at more than 500,000 jammed the streets of São Paulo, under the banner of embattled religion, to protest Goulart's Rio rally of the 13th, and all that the marchers thought the rally signified. Higher military of the Second Army, headquartered in São Paulo, were said to observe carefully the size of the crowd.[87]

The civilian elements now leading the opposition to Goulart included diverse groups. They ranged from a small but articulate extreme right-wing position that deeply feared the mass-based democracy being created by an industralized Brazil, to centrists who feared that Goulart was endangering orderly economic growth on the pattern of a mixed economy. The former were represented by newspapers such as *Tribuna da Imprensa* (no longer owned by Lacerda but still under his influence) and Cardinal Dom Jaime Câmara, while the latter were represented by groups such as IPES, the São Paulo businessmen's movement, and *Síntese,* the organ of the reform-minded but moderate Catholic position.

Also prominent among the opposition by late March were the governors of every major state—São Paulo (Adhemar de Barros), Minas Gerais (Magalhães Pinto), Guanabara (Carlos Lacerda), and Rio Grande do Sul (Ildo Meneghetti). Unlike 1937, when Vargas had carefully laid the growndwork for his coup among the principal governors, Goulart had almost totally isolated himself from the most powerful regional political leaders.

Well before the Easter revolt, General Castello Branco had told the civilian conspirators that the dismissal of the Navy Minister would be the signal to depose Goulart. When he heard of the dismissal, Adaúto Cardoso, a leader of the UDN and of the civilian conspirators, called Castello Branco and learned that the signal for the revolt had indeed been confirmed. By Sunday, March 29, the date for the overthrow of Goulart had been set for the following Thursday, April 2, when another massive opposition rally, patterned after the anti-Goulart rally in São Paulo on March 19, was to be held in Rio. This demonstration of civilian opposition would, it was hoped, give the military further political "cover" to intervene.

It was now merely a matter of ensuring the adherence of the principal military commands. The key command about which the conspirators were uncertain was the Second Army in São Paulo. General Kruel, the commander, continued to waver. Although he had denounced left-wing labor leaders in São Paulo, his close personal friendship with Goulart and his stubborn devotion to "legality" delayed his adherence to the conspiracy.

By Monday, March 30, the timetable for Goulart's overthrow had become known even to the CGT, whose directorate issued a denunciation of the "coup" set for April 2. But Goulart's *dispositivo militar* had ceased to function. Even fate seemed to have joined the conspiracy against the President. His War Minister, General Dantas Ribeiro, was immobilized in the hospital for intestinal surgery throughout the crisis. The Army was now a "body without a head," all the more significant since the War Minister was a figure still held in considerable respect by many centrist officers.

As if to give his enemies their final justification, the President agreed to address a gathering of sergeants at the Automobile Club on Monday night, March 30. It was a decision little short of political suicide. Discarding his prepared text, he refused to dissociate himself from attacks on military discipline. The tone of his talk was that of a belligerent farewell speech. Even General Assis Brasil, until now a voice urging the President on, realized that Goulart had gone too far.[88]

Goulart's speech was televised nation-wide. One viewer, a military conspirator of long standing, decided the time had come to act. General Mourão Filho, purveyor of the infamous "Cohen Plan" in October 1937, mobilized his troops in Juíz da Fora (part of the First Army stationed in Minas Gerais). At dawn he told his men they were marching on Rio. The Governor of Minas Gerais, Magalhães Pinto, had already issued a manifesto on March 30 pledging Minas Gerais to "the restoration of the constitutional order, which is now compromised." The conspirators had previously agreed that the revolt should begin in Minas, not São Paulo. "We began it in 1932," argued the Paulistas, remembering Minas' failure to aid the Constitutionalist Revolution, "now it's your turn to start." [89]

As Mourão Filho's troops moved toward Rio, where resistance from General Âncora's First Army was expected, the conspirators anxiously awaited public confirmation from São Paulo that Kruel was also joining the revolt. The conspirators thought that he had finally decided to join them on Sunday, March 29, but either he changed his mind again, or they were misinformed, because during Tuesday Kruel was still making repeated pleas by telephone to Goulart, urging him to renounce the Communist CGT. If he did, Kruel implied, he might yet "save his mandate." But Goulart could not turn back. He finally answered, "I cannot cast aside the popular forces that support me." This outright refusal finally set Kruel's conscience at ease: "Then, Mr. President, there is nothing we can do." [90] On the evening of March 31, Kruel finally ordered his tanks to move on Rio. This maneuver was essential to the revolt because of the strategic importance of the Paraíba valley in case of battle.

Meanwhile in Rio, Governor Lacerda, strangely silent over the tense Easter weekend, had barricaded himself into the gubernatorial palace. He had ordered the state's orange-and-gray garbage trucks to form road blocks across the palm-lined avenues offering access to the palace. Inside, Lacerda was dressed in a leather jacket and armed with two submachine guns and a pistol. He was busily engaged in telephoning police posts around the city, awaiting confirmation of the rumor that Admiral Aragão's marines were about to attack the palace.

Goulart now began to learn how disastrously the radical lefts, and his military advisers, had overestimated their real strength. The CGT had called for a general strike on March 30, but the workers did not respond. Trains and buses operated normally on the 31st, service slowing down on April 1 only when the news of the military movements became generally known. The *dispositivo sindical* was in fact paralyzed because the handful of radical leftist labor leaders had either been arrested on March 30 (by Lacerda's political police, DOPS) or gone into hiding. The gap, both in lines of command and in political sentiment, between the overconfident leaders and their passive rank and file had become painfully obvious. On the morning of April 1, Justice Minister Jurema took command in the studios of the government-owned radio station and began broadcasting frantic appeals for the "people" to take to the streets against the "golpistas." Many cariocas were indeed in the streets, but out of curiosity; they listened impassively on their transistor sets to Jurema's entreaties.[91]

The only question remaining was the position of the First Army command, headquartered in Rio. The troops which Goulart had sent on March 31 from Rio to "crush" the "insignificant rebellion" in Minas Gerais were proving curiously unable to find their enemies. In the late morning of April 1, Goulart saw that his position was hopeless; at noon he flew to Brasília, where he hoped to make a stand. General Âncora, the First Army commander, telephoned the presidential palace for instructions, and found the President gone. He did, however, reach Assis Brasil, who disclaimed any authority to speak for the President, but then informed Âncora that Goulart had left word that he wanted no military clash. That settled the question. The First Army and the Second Army quickly reached an agreement precluding any fighting. The loyalist units sent to block Mourão Filho's march on Rio had already joined the rebel column. The heartland of center-south Brazil was securely in rebel hands.

Goulart found the situation in Brasília equally hopeless. On the night of April 1, only hours after fleeing Rio, he continued his flight to Pôrto Alegre. That same night in Brasília the President of the Senate, Auro de Moura Andrade, declared the presidency vacant. There was no constitutional basis for this unilateral act, although it offered a logical and expedient way out of the crisis now dictated by the pressure of military rebellion. Goulart's congressional opponents had long known that they lacked the votes to impeach the President (under Articles 88 and 89), and the congressional leaders were in no mood to wait until he fled the country (thereby violating Article 66, which required congressional approval for presidential travel abroad).

Once Moura Andrade had declared the office vacant, he was following constitutional procedure by swearing in as Acting President Ranieri Mazzili, who as president of the Chamber of Deputies was next in line for succession under Article 79.

Arriving in Pôrto Alegre, Goulart found his brother-in-law, Brizola, demanding a last-ditch fight. General Ladário, commander of the Third Army, was maintaining an ambiguous stand.[92] Governor Meneghetti, a hesitant conspirator who feared civil war in his capital city, had fled to the interior. Brizola argued bitterly with his brother-in-law, even weeping in the attempt to convince him that Rio Grande do Sul could hold out, but Goulart refused to sanction further resistance.[93]

The next day Brizola appeared on the balcony of the Town Hall calling for his fellow gaúchos to take up arms. Only minor disturbances ensued, and before the end of April 2 the Third Army in its entirety had joined the revolt. Goulart fled to the interior of Rio Grande do Sul with Assis Brasil, where they shuttled among Goulart's border ranches. On April 4, Assis Brasil finally convinced the former President to take asylum in Uruguay. As if to underline his courage and independence, Brizola eluded his pursuers by moving mysteriously through the border fazenda country until the end of April, when he reluctantly followed the route to Uruguay.[94]

EPILOGUE

The Search for a New Political Order

The overthrow of João Goulart was proof that normal constitutional processes had failed in Brazil. It was not the first time the Army had intervened to suspend combat among the politicians. The obvious precedent was 1954; but 1964 was profoundly different for several reasons.

The Army was for the first time united in an ideological stance against populism. This position was first clearly spelled out in February 1954 when "the colonels' memorandum" made an implicit case for Goulart's dismissal as labor minister. Their anti-populism was, however, muted in the subsequent generals' ultimatum, which brought about Vargas' suicide in August 1954. Now, even the pro-legality moderates had been forced to the conclusion that populist politicians could not be trusted to preserve the delicate social equilibrium on which Brazilian democracy rested.

It was the apparent breakdown of this equilibrium which had converted the moderate military to an offensive conspiracy. They believed that the Goulart regime had decided to incorporate a new guard into the political elite while threatening to exclude the old guard altogether. The "old guard" comprised the leadership of the hybrid political system created by Vargas. It included old-style politicians (typified by the PSD), middle-class spokesmen (most prominent in the UDN), and the journeymen functionaries of the PTB—a labor party created by Vargas and not the outgrowth of an independent working-class movement. The "new guard" were the leaders of the radical left, such as the left-wing labor leadership (CGT, PUA), radical nationalist student cadres (UNE, AP), and the professional politicians of the radical left (Leonel Brizola, Max da Costa Santos, and other members of the *Frente Parlamentar Nacionalista*). The violent language of the new guard indicated that they sought a monopoly of political power which would forever end the politics of compromise. Whether true or not, this is what the old guard and the moderate military had come to believe in March 1964. The Army, therefore, prepared to fight a civil war against whatever cadres the radical left could mobilize.

The Victors and the Vanquished

The Goulart government collapsed so quickly that even the "revolutionaries" were surprised. Instead of taking a stand in Rio de Janeiro, or in Brasília, or in Rio Grande do Sul, Goulart fled Brazil, leaving his bewildered supporters isolated in the face of the rapidly mobilizing revolutionaries. But the political forces that brought down the Goulart government were far from united. That soon became evident as the revolutionaries contemplated the sudden vacuum of power created by their boldness.

Who were the victors of March 31? Most important among their number were the aggressive young military. Adamant in their anti-political attitude, they had no desire to finish their intervention by simply delivering power to a different group of civilian politicians, as had happened in 1954, 1955, and 1961. The "hard-line" military had been the earliest conspirators and had waged a long campaign to convert their moderate elders. The latter thought in terms of the Army's traditional role as the guardian of the political equilibrium, and could not contemplate the vision of a Brazil governed indefinitely by men in uniform. It was the aggressive younger officers who pushed their senior colleagues to a more militant position.

Although it was the military who had intervened to rescue Brazil from "corruption" and "communism," there were some civilians who believed they were the victors. These were the anti-getulista civilians of neo-liberal views. They were led by conservative politicians, such as Bilac Pinto, who had been long-time conspirators, and public figures such as Júlio Mesquita Filho, owner of *O Estado de São Paulo*.

The civilian conspirators believed they had at last triumphed over the legacy of Getúlio Vargas. Their claim of victory was another expression of the syndrome of 1937—compounded with frustration over the incomplete victory of 1954, the setback of 1955 and the bitter frustration of 1961. When Getúlio Vargas committed suicide, the lines of conflict were drawn: on one side the populist politicians mobilizing the new mass vote; on the other side, the military, the middle class, and the old elite who feared that the populists might push Brazil toward a realm of conflict in which the traditional techniques of political compromise would be scrapped in favor of more radical methods of government.

The apparent influence of the populists was magnified by the failure of the democratic left to find any significant institutional expression in the two decades after 1945. This failure was briefly disguised by Kubitschek's *tour de force* of improvisation, but the lack of responsible leadership in the early 1960's brought the crisis to the surface. When the "positive left" attempted its brief experiment in early 1963, San Tiago Dantas found that there was no organized political base to sustain his program. The PTB remained in the hands of unresponsive manipulators, and the "progressive" wings of the PSD and UDN were but ineffectual minority movements within their own parties. There was neither time nor leadership to organize a new party of the left. Furthermore, the center, representing middle-class opinion which wanted both honesty and reform, was also debilitated by disorganization. Seen in these terms, the failure of Quadros in 1961, combined with the lack of a "respectable" democratic left, led directly to the clash of March 1964.

When the clash came, however, even the radical left collapsed. Its leaders had overestimated the militancy and organization of the masses and underestimated the panic they had provoked in the center. Put to the test, radical nationalism proved to lack both inner coherence and a firm social basis.

Coup or Revolution?

Was the political trauma of 1964 an authentic revolution? If defined in terms of a radical shift in the distribution of power among social classes or sectors, only time could answer that question. Could one at least conclude that the victory of the "Movement of March 31" portended a radical transformation of political institutions? That question received a partial answer less than two weeks after the coup.

Goulart had been deposed by a military revolt. His flight was not the result of action by the civilian political elite. On the contrary, the Goulart opponents in the Congress had not even attempted impeachment proceedings because they knew they lacked the necessary votes to win such a test, just as the anti-getulista opponents had lacked the votes in 1954. Although a majority of congressmen had grown deeply suspicious of Goulart's intentions, they were still not ready to try him on the grounds outlined in the Constitution. Their reluctance was hardly surprising. As professional politicians they were fearful of what an impeachment might bring in its wake. As a result, there was no centrist congressional leader prepared to champion a campaign to impeach the President. And the UDN militants who favored such a move, such as Bilac Pinto, were suspect figures to the majority leadership, made up of PSD stalwarts, who feared that an ouster of Goulart might turn into a general purge of the "ins."

In the days immediately following Goulart's flight from Brasília, there was a period of apprehensive maneuver among the old-style political elite. Many politicians, especially among the PSD and moderate wing of the UDN, attempted to act as if 1964 would be little different from the earlier crises of 1954, 1955, and 1961. The first sign of a real difference came, however, when the Congress conspicuously declined to formalize Goulart's ouster by failing to vote (no resolution was even introduced) that he had been *impedido* (the constitutional term meaning "obstructed" or "prevented") from continuing to exercise presidential powers. Marshal Lott had been able to extract such a vote against both Carlos Luz and Café Filho in November 1955. It had not been necessary in 1954 or 1961, when Vargas and Quadros had removed themselves from office. Why did the Congress in 1964 not attempt to repeat the vote of 1955? In part it was because the majority—still PSD-PTB as it had been in 1954—was highly apprehensive about its own future, and far more interested in thinking about the next President than in ratifying the inglorious exit of the last President. (In 1955 the President had already been elected and represented the PSD-PTB alliance.) The fact was that in 1964 the initiative lay with the soldiers, and the politicians knew it.

The Constitution provided for an election within thirty days if both the presidency and vice presidency should fall vacant. Political crises had come with such rapidity in the early 1960's that Brazil now lacked a Vice President who could succeed to the presidency. Unlike the crisis of 1954 when the Army endorsed Vice President Café Filho's inauguration, or 1961 when the advocates of legality got Vice President Goulart into the presidential palace, some new figure would have to be found. The politicians began to make soundings. Would it be an experienced PSD leader of center-left, such as Tancredo Neves, or an old-style politician, such as Gustavo Capanema? Perhaps a centrist general such as Amaury Kruel? Or a military-civilian patriarch such as Dutra?

What the speculation ignored was the more significant struggle in progress behind the scenes. The extremist military, soon known as the "hard-line" (*linha dura*), were now anxious to seize control of Brazilian politics. In their view the recurrent interventions of the military since 1945 had solved nothing. They were determined not to repeat the mistake of delivering power to another subgroup of the political elite who might lead Brazil back to the cul-de-sac of "corruption" and "subversion." There would be no presidential election before the military "revolutionaries" could make certain that the political rule had been changed to their satisfaction.

From the moment he took office in the early morning hours of April 2, Acting President Mazzilli and the old-line congressional leadership were under intense pressure to expel from their legislative ranks those whom the military branded as unacceptable, and get from Congress emergency anti-subversive legislation. On April 7 the demand of the three military ministers, appointed by Mazzilli (except Costa e Silva, the War Minister, who had literally appointed himself on April 2[1] and was merely "retained" in his post by Mazzilli), became public knowledge. The legislation demanded by the military would give the Executive sweeping powers to purge the civil service, and revoke the mandates of members of the federal and state legislatures.

The leaders of Congress were not, however, ready to surrender their powers. The conservative leaders of the UDN and PSD drafted their own version of an emergency act which made it clear that they did not share the hard-liners' diagnosis of Brazil's political problem.

In short, the civilian politicians were unwilling to carry out the "surgery" to the extent and in the manner that the military demanded.[2]

The uniformed revolutionaries therefore took matters into their own hands. On April 9, 1964, the three military ministers, simply ignoring the politicians' draft of an emergency act, issued, on the authority which they arbitrarily assumed as the Supreme Revolutionary Command, an Institutional Act. The Act, which had been drawn up by Francisco Campos (author of the Constitution of 1937), gave the Brazilian Executive extraordinary powers to break the political deadlock. It began by stating that the Constitution of 1946 and the state constitutions were to remain in force subject to the modifications included in the articles of the Institutional Act. The new powers granted to the Executive included the following: (1) The power to submit constitutional amendments to the Congress, which would have only thirty days in which to consider the proposals, and need only approve them by a majority vote rather than the two-thirds vote required in the 1946 Constitution. The President was also given exclusive power to propose expenditure bills to Congress, and the Congress was denied the right to increase expenditures on any bills proposed by the President. The President was also given the power to declare a state of siege or to prolong such a state of siege for a maximum period of thirty days without congressional approval. (2) The Executive was given sweeping powers to suppress the political rights of political undesirables for ten years. This included the right to cancel the mandates of members of state, municipal, or federal legislatures. There was also an article suspending for six months the constitutional guarantees of job security in the civil service.

This act by the Supreme Revolutionary Command was a new response to the crisis of political authority that had been evident in Brazil since the mid-1950's. Quadros had complained that he lacked powers to deal with the Congress. Goulart repeated this complaint, had even proposed a state of siege in October of 1963 and had in early 1964 put forward a number of specific proposals for strengthening the hand of the Executive. The Institutional Act was therefore a new and decisive response to the apparent inability of the Brazilian Executive to command the necessary authority.

The action of the military in 1964 thus went beyond any other intervention since 1945 because the Army now came close to repudiating the political elite as a whole. The Institutional Act temporarily changed the rules of democratic politics. The implication was obvious: the politics of compromise had been discredited by Goulart's "overplaying" the democratic game. The Army intervention was a throwback to the anti-political message preached by Jânio Quadros: it was the "politicians" whose irresponsibility had brought Brazil to the edge of chaos.

The Awkward Electorate

The Institutional Act stipulated that an election of a new President and a Vice President should be held within two days of the Act's publication. It also specifically canceled the ineligibility clause in the Constitution, thereby making eligible for election military officers on active duty. This change was intended to make possible the prompt election of General Castello Branco, the coordinator of the military conspiracy, who was the overwhelming choice of the revolutionaries, both military and civilian. Castello Branco was duly elected as the new President on April 11. As if to assert its independence, the Congress elected as Vice President José Maria Alkmin, a PSD leader from Minas Gerais who had become a civilian ally of the military conspirators only as Goulart neared the end of his presidency.

Castello Branco soon proved to be a mediator between the hardline military and the pro-constitutionalists among the revolutionaries. The two months from Castello Branco's election until the expiration on June 15 of Article X of the Institutional Act (giving the President time to revoke legislative mandates and suspend political rights), was the period of purge designated by the new government. Castello Branco was under pressure from the hard-line military to suspend the political rights of some 5,000 "enemies" of the new regime. By June 15, when the deadline ran out under the Institutional Act, the political rights of 378 persons had been suspended.[3] They included three former Presidents—Kubitschek, Quadros, and Goulart—as well as six state governors, 55 members of the federal Congress, and assorted diplomats, labor leaders, military officers, intellectuals, and public officials. The accused were given no right of self-defense. Their punishment was frankly acknowledged by the government as an arbitrary act necessitated by the emergency conditions in Brazil. The fact that only a few hundred were involved represented a considerable victory for the moderates among the revolutionaries, who wished to keep the list of the purged to a minimum. Actually, there had been pressure to extend the time limit of Article X to November 9, which was the cutoff date for Article VII, the article that provided for purges within the Civil Service. Marshal Taurino de Rezende, the head of the general investigating commission, had publicly requested Castello Branco to extend the life of Article X, but the moderates won out and the article lapsed, as stipulated, on June 15.

The new government included a combination of political conservatives and technocrats. There were several ministers identified with the UDN, and the head of the Civil Household, Luis Vianna Filho, was an UDN stalwart. Economic policy was in the hands of Finance Minister Octávio Bulhões and Planning Minister Roberto Campos. Both were identified as outspoken advocates of vigorous anti-inflation measures.

The fundamental question was, of course, what political position the new government would take. During his initial months as President, Castello Branco attempted to dissociate his regime from the reactionary position of the extreme right-wing revolutionaries. He explained that the revolution had been made in order to ensure continued economic development and social justice for all. But the government's heavy emphasis on anti-Communism, coupled with the suspension of the rights of a national figure such as Kubitschek, suggested that the influence of the "hard-line" was great. It appeared that the extremists were poised to demand the resumption of emergency powers for use against any opposition that threatened the new government's monopoly of power.

From the outset, the Castello Branco government faced the problem of finding a political base. The regime soon realized that the program of economic stabilization, on which the President placed utmost priority, would take longer than the year and a half remaining of the Presidential mandate, then due to expire on January 20, 1966. The "gradualist" deflationary policy of Campos and Bulhões would not have achieved its objectives by the time of the presidential election scheduled for October of 1965. In July 1964, President Castello

Branco reluctantly agreed to a congressional amendment which extended his term until March 15, 1967, at the same time setting the election for November 1966. This was explained as an extension of the temporary "cure" during which preparations could be made for a return to normal political life.

The first electoral test came in March of 1965, with the election for the mayor of São Paulo. The victor was Brigadier Faria, who had been publicly supported by Jânio Quadros. Although the prestige of the federal government was not directly at stake in the election, there were rumblings of discontent among the hard-line military, who argued that the government should not permit itself to undergo a direct electoral test in October, when the governorships of eleven states would fall vacant.

In July 1965 the political crisis deepened. Of the eleven states in which there were to be gubernatorial elections, two were of major importance—Guanabara and Minas Gerais. The incumbent governor (unable by law to succeed himself) was in each case a prominent UDN leader—Carlos Lacerda in Guanabara and Magalhães Pinto in Minas Gerais. Both had been prominent supporters of the anti-Goulart conspiracy, but both had grown outspokenly critical (Lacerda violently critical) of the economic stabilization program, which had become an enormous electoral liability because all sectors were being squeezed simultaneously. It was thus inevitable that in both states the election should be considered a test of the popularity of the federal government.

During July the Castello Branco government moved to increase its control over the electoral system by two measures. The first was an "ineligibility law" that barred from candidacy in the upcoming elections any former ministers who served in the Goulart presidency after the plebiscite of January 1963. This was a measure clearly designed to limit the effectiveness of the opposition and to make it less likely that the government would suffer important reverses in its first major electoral test. The second measure was a new Statute of Political Parties that was intended as the framework for a major reorganization of political activity in Brazil. This was a long-term measure that, it was hoped, would overcome the splinter party phenomenon and help give Brazil the quality which its new government said it had most notably lacked since the war—stability.

In August, as preparations for the elections became intense, the opposition in Guanabara and Minas Gerais attempted to nominate figures who soon proved anathema to the hard-line revolutionaries. In Guanabara the choice had first fallen to Hélio de Almeida, who was promptly ruled ineligible under the act passed by Congress in July. The second choice of the opposition was clearly intended to inflame the anger of the military hard-liners. It was the nomination of Marshal Lott, the "nationalist" general of 1955 and the ill-fated presidential candidate of 1960. Marshal Lott's nomination was narrowly victorious in a tumultuous PTB convention, but his candidacy was soon quashed by the electoral tribunal on the grounds that he lacked the necessary residence in the state of Guanabara. The tribunal, however, deliberated under intense pressure from the government, including a warning by President Castello Branco that declared enemies of the revolution would not be permitted to reach high office.

In Minas Gerais, the opposition attempted to nominate Sebastião Pais de Almeida, a leading PSD politician in Minas Gerais and Kubitchek's last Finance Minister. He was also a *bête noire* to the hard-line military because of his widespread reputation for buying votes. After Pais de Almeida was ruled ineligible, the PSD nominated another long-term Kubitschek protégé in Minas, Israel Pinhero. In Guanabara the PTB joined with the PSD and nominated Negrão de Lima, a PSD scion and a former official in the Kubitschek government. In both states the incumbent UDN governors endorsed their party's candidates—Roberto Resende in Minas Gerais and Flexa Ribeiro in Guanabara. The contest was, therefore, between Kubitschek-inspired PSD politicians and UDN politicians whom the electorate tended to identify with the Castello Branco government, despite the incumbent governors' attempts to establish an independent position for their nominees.

When the votes had been counted, Negrão de Lima and Israel Pinhero had won handily, although in the other nine states the prestige of the federal government was not compromised by the results. The reaction of the hard-line military was immediate and vehement to what they regarded as the electoral success of the opposition. They pressed President Castello Branco strongly during October to annul the results of the elections. There was even pressure to subject the winners to investigation by military tribunal. As a result, the President was forced to issue a new (Second) Institutional Act on October 27, restoring many of the special powers that had expired under the first Institutional Act. In return, the President was allowed to ensure the peaceful inauguration of the two newly elected PSD governors, but at the same time his wide-ranging second Institutional Act again revised the rules for politics in Brazil.

All political parties were to be dissolved. The presidential election of 1966, as well as the gubernatorial elections, would be indirect (by the Congress for the President and by the state legislatures for governors), and the President regained the right, on his own discretion, to remove the political rights of Brazilians considered to be a threat to the security of the government. There were many other provisions to the new Institutional Act, including an increase in the membership of the Supreme Court from eleven to sixteen, the additional judges to be appointed by the President. This packing of the Court was a response to the Court's repeated rulings in favor of the liberation of political prisoners.

At the same time that the government had capitulated to the hard-line military, it attempted to institutionalize these changes and to establish clear limits. The new Institutional Act was to remain in force until March 15, 1967, the date on which President Castello Branco's successor would be inaugurated. The Act was therefore a compromise between the hard-line and the constitutionalists. It was also clear recognition by the government that in its search for a political base it would need to manipulate the political scene more fully than the "constitutionalist" revolutionaries had hoped would be necessary. For them the implication was deeply disturbing: for how long must the electorate be deprived of the right to choose directly their governors and President? And for whose benefit would the manipulation be used? Might this coup prove "revolutionary" by devouring its own children?

Development and Stabilization vs. Democracy: Brazil's Dilemma?

After Goulart's fall all of Brazil's essential problems remained to be tackled: the immediate problem of economic stabilization; social reform in agriculture and education; and most important of all, rationalization of the economy to promote further growth.

But what rationale would emerge to sustain an attack on these

problems? How would a new social consensus be created and maintained? Since the late 1950's Brazil's ideology, insofar as it had one,
was nationalism in the ambiguous form which enlisted support from
both growth-minded neo-liberals and the moderate left. Kubitschek
had proved able to govern in part because he took care *not* to give his
government any clear ideological identification. Quadros had embraced
a frenetic moralism, but combined it with a conspicuously independent foreign policy—including an outright refusal to follow American
policy in Cuba. Goulart, as we have seen, played with the ideologies
of both the moderate and radical left, finally appearing to opt for the
latter. *No* elected President since 1950 had ignored the ideology of
nationalism and the left which put it forward. Which way would Brazil go now?

In the twenty years since the end of the second world war, Brazil
had experienced an alternation between expansion and attempted
stabilization. Since the exhaustion of foreign exchange reserves in
1947, the country had incurred growing foreign indebtedness. This foreign financing was a predictable and necessary result of the industrialization drive. Still, it deferred part of the cost of development and represented an increasing burden which amounted to a growing political
liability for successive governments. From 1951 until 1964 one could
characterize Brazil as caught in a deepening "credit crisis." The economic growth rate remained high, one of the highest in the world until
1962, but the extensive use of foreign financing meant that a growing
percentage of scarce foreign exchange had to be used to service the
debt. This credit crisis, which first became severe in 1959, recurred in
1961 when the Quadros government attempted orthodox stabilization
measures. It was the single most important policy problem for the
Goulart regime. The serious shortage of foreign exchange, a direct
result of the declining price for Brazil's exports, as well as Brazil's
failure to diversify her exports, became evident in the early 1950's. It
was to be a principal restraint on continued development after the
early 1960's. In short, Brazil was unable to find a new method of
financing her development once she had incurred a level of indebtedness that reached the maximum of tolerance for her foreign creditors.

Along with the incurring of heavy foreign indebtedness, went a
growing sentiment of political nationalism. This attitude, which had

historic roots in Brazil and was now being nurtured by the organized left, blamed foreign incomprehension and ill will for Brazil's difficulties in maintaining economic development. In practice, the nationalist explanation was often little more than the search for a convenient scapegoat. What it concealed was the inherent difficulty of mobilizing domestic resources for economic growth, particularly for an ambitious rate of growth.

As with so many developing economies, a full-scale mobilization of resources is what Brazil conspicuously lacked during its "developmentalist" drive of the 1950's. In order to mobilize resources, three steps are necessary: (1) a sound technical assessment of the situation; (2) the selection of a strategy for action; (3) the construction of a reliable political base for the strategy adopted.

The first step requires a determination of the stage of development reached and of the potentials and bottlenecks for the next stage. There was considerable agreement in the early 1950's about the proper diagnosis of the Brazilian economic situation. The studies of ECLA, the BNDE, and the Joint Brazil-United States Economic Development Commission laid the groundwork for the industrialization drive that produced successful results in the Kubitschek presidency. The specific barriers were identified: the lack of sophisticated technology, the lack of equipment, and the lack of incentives for domestic and foreign producers. These barriers were overcome by an intelligent combination of government policies that encouraged the rapid development of a sophisticated industrial base in Brazil. One can say with confidence that the technical assessment of the economic situation in Brazil in the early 1950's—despite minor disagreements—was virtually unanimous among the technocratic elite. Indeed, it is difficult to find another country in Latin America where the diagnosis was so widely shared or the government policy so fully supported.

The second step involves the selection of a strategy for development. In the Brazil of the early 1950's, governments alternated between a nationalist and a moderately "cosmopolitan" policy, an alternation most dramatic during the presidency of Vargas between 1951 and 1954. The Kubitschek government proved willing to embrace a mixed strategy based on maximum use of public and private resources both domestic and foreign. The nationalist emphasis was less pronounced than in the Vargas period, although the credit crisis of

1958–59 found Kubitschek taking a nationalist way out. It was his political gamble for the preservation of his own image and the fulfillment of his "target program." The 1950's, then, may be seen as a period in which Brazil pursued a mixed strategy, relying on private and public investment, both foreign and domestic, to develop the industrial base and the social capital necessary for an industrializing economy.

The third step requires the devising of a political strategy to ensure the public support for the development strategy adopted. This necessitates in the first instance an assessment of the lines of party support and secondly an evaluation of the class and sectional basis underlying the party structure It is at this point that the Brazilian case becomes interesting and complex. The political base chosen for the developmentalist drive of the 1950's was first articulated by Vargas in 1950. By forming an unlikely alliance of the PSD and the PSP, along with his own PTB, Vargas was able to achieve a near majority in the presidential election of 1950. But he failed thereafter to strengthen the political base for a continuation of the developmentalist drive he had begun by 1953. Kubitschek merely extended the Vargas strategy to its ultimate potential without developing any new line of political strategy. What this strategy lacked most conspicuously was any clear-cut party commitment, either to the diagnosis of the economic situation or to the policy chosen for development. Kubitschek's principal support was the PSD, a notably non-ideological party whose support he maintained by a generous use of political rewards for the "ins." In the short run, this pragmatic attitude toward basic questions in economic analysis and developmental strategy was advantageous. It helped to submerge latent disagreements and to avoid policy conflicts over relative class roles in the developmentalist drive. In the long run, however, the avoidance of basic questions in politics was to prove disastrous when the character of political leadership deteriorated under Quadros and Goulart.

An illuminating way to look at the "revolutionary" regime, and to compare it with past governments, is to examine the way the Castello Branco regime has been tackling these three steps in the basic task of mobilizing resources for development. As for the first step, it has merely endorsed a technical assessment of the economic situation which had been in the air since the early 1960's. This diagnosis laid priority on the need to achieve a slowdown in the rate of price increase as an essential prerequisite for further economic development. It had been inherent in the Quadros stabilization policy in 1961 and had been the basis of Furtado's Three-Year Plan, outlined in December 1962. But no government had spelled out the assessment in such detail as did Roberto Campos and Octávio Bulhões in mid-1964. They went farther than the previous diagnoses in fixing the federal government's responsibility for controlling inflation and in emphasizing the need to diversify Brazil's export trade as the key to breaking the foreign exchange bottleneck. There was also a clearer emphasis upon bottlenecks in Brazilian institutional structure: the obsolete capital market, the privileged groups within the organized labor movement, the ill-organized monetary system, and the faulty distribution structure for agricultural products. All these weaknesses had been stressed previously, especially in the Furtado Three-Year Report, but there was a new single-mindedness on the part of the government to carry out the changes to which the diagnosis pointed.

In the strategy for development, the Castello Branco government diverged sharply from the policies of previous regimes. There was first of all a strong emphasis on the need to satisfy the international financial authorities and principal foreign creditors as a prerequisite for further development in Brazil. This meant the commitment to a rigorous anti-inflation program. At the same time, the new government sought to rehabilitate the role of the private sector, which it thought had been denigrated by the Goulart regime. The Goulart regime had emphasized the public role in a mixed strategy. The Castello Branco regime sought to emphasize the private role.

There was at the same time a new commitment to strengthening and improving the machinery of public administration. Tax collection —long notorious for its laxness—was tightened by introducing techniques of automated record-keeping. Delinquents were subjected to more prompt prosecution; they found themselves not only subject to fines but also forced to pay a percentage premium (computed according to a government-established rate under a policy called "monetarization") to compensate for the decline in the real value of the tax bill caused by inflation in the interval since the bill had been originally incurred.

A potentially powerful new government instrument for inducing change in the agrarian sector was the Agrarian Reform Bill passed by the Brazilian Congress in November 1964. The law placed primary reliance on a progressive land tax as a stimulus to more efficient utilization of land. Although the law gave many safeguards to rural landowners (strict limits on the government's power to expropriate, guarantees against currency depreciation for holders of government bonds paid in compensation), the amount of real reform would obviously depend on the attitude and determination of the administering authorities. As a first step, the Agrarian Reform Institute (IBRA) in 1965 began an ambitious computer-aided cadastral survey of all rural land holdings. When completed, this would be the first such nation-wide survey ever conducted in Brazil. It was a further example of the "technocratic" approach that characterized the Castello Branco government's approach to social problems.[4]

It was in the third area—of political support for the new strategy— that the Castello Branco government found most difficulty. In essence, it encountered the same problem which every postwar Brazilian government had faced: the overwhelming political unpopularity of any effort at anti-inflation policies. This became obvious to Vargas in 1953, the Café Filho government in 1955, the Kubitschek government in 1958–59, the Quadros government in 1961, and Goulart, especially after early 1963. The Castello Branco government chose as its way out a policy which the Goulart government appeared to have been considering in 1964: a frankly anti-democratic solution. Since the economic diagnosis suggested that there was no alternative to a rigorous anti-inflation program and a constant attention to the need to renegotiate and settle foreign accounts, the Castello Branco government relegated the return to constitutional government to a secondary level. It carried through what seemed to be the logic inherent in the desperate measures of both Quadros and Goulart: a suspension of the normal democratic process during a period of economic emergency. The suspension of the political system existing between 1945 and 1964 therefore had a direct connection with the rhythm of economic development and economic crisis which has been evident since the Second World War. Faced with the problem of electoral reversals while pursuing an anti-inflation program, the Castello Branco government chose to change the rules of the electoral game so that it could not suffer defeat.

The recurrent historical question that arises out of an examination of the period from 1945 to 1964 is: when did an authoritarian solution to Brazil's political cul-de-sac seem the only possibility? At what point did the suspension of the democratic system become unavoidable? Even if one acknowledges that Brazil was extraordinarily ill-served by its two Presidents after 1960, the fact remains that the need for unpopular and painful choices in economic policy-making imposed grave limits on the potential for either charismatic or populist political leadership. What all political leaders discovered in this political system was the inadequacy of the party structure, the inability to control the political elite in the midst of a highly controversial policy-making crisis. In short, the lines of political authority were not sufficient to sustain the tasks of political leadership demanded by the crisis of the early 1960's.

Instead, there was a steady poisoning of the political atmosphere as the possibility of negotiation and compromise faded. The arguments of the extreme left and the extreme right bore a great similarity. Both accused their enemies of delivering Brazil to a foreign power. The left charged *entreguismo,* meaning a "sellout" to capitalist powers, particularly the United States. The right charged subversion and communism—a sellout to the Communist bloc. In between, there were varying charges of bad faith and anti-democratic sentiments that ranged from the suspicion of Peronism on the left to suspicion of reactionary militarism on the right. Essentially, there was a collapse of the belief that differing interests could be harmonized. The "creative tension" of the Kubitschek period dissolved into an increasingly acrimonious conflict between differing visions of Brazil's problems and potential.

Most important, during the last year of the Goulart presidency there was a growing suspicion that the equilibrium upon which Brazilian politics rested was about to be destroyed. Could it have become possible that Brazilian politics was a zero-sum game in which there were only winners and losers in the absolute sense but no negotiated solutions? The trauma of Goulart's overthrow in 1964 led to a suppression of open political bargaining and an attempt to impose short-term emergency solutions that included not only economic stabilization but also institutional reform.

What of the deeper causes of the breakdown in the political system so carefully constructed in 1945–46? At that time Brazil reaffirmed her democratic ideals by rejecting the authoritarian system under which so much economic change and institutional innovation had taken place. In the following two decades the implicit goal was wider political participation—bringing a larger number of the public into the active political process. In 1964 the trend toward increasing public participation was cut short. In its place was substituted a semi-authoritarian system. The revolutionaries increasingly feared that they could not justify to a majority of the electorate their programs or their basic ideas. Elections were thus made indirect—not only the election for governor of twelve states in September 1966, but also the election of a new President in October 1966. When the Castello Branco government encountered serious resistance in attempting to impose its own candidates (under the label of the new government party, called ARENA) in the 1966 gubernatorial elections, it did not hesitate to purge the state legislature, as in Rio Grande do Sul in July 1966, or even to remove the governor, as in São Paulo, where the deposing of Adhemar de Barros in August removed the last of the leading civilian revolutionaries who still held high office.

By the fall of 1966 it was clear that the Castello Branco government had chosen (or felt itself forced) to close the political system farther and farther. The immediate justification was the need to continue an anti-inflation and economic development program that was acknowledged to be unpopular but nonetheless essential. It was the one issue on which Castello Branco demanded a commitment from General Costa e Silva, the consensus candidate of the military and therefore the certain successor. Only after Costa e Silva had effectively promised to continue the stabilization program did he receive Castello Branco's unqualified support in the presidential campaign. The election of Costa e Silva by the Congress in October 1966 was a foregone conclusion since the government party held a majority of Congressional seats. The opposition party, MDB, registered its protest by refusing to appear in the Congress for the *pro-forma* vote.

The government's turn away from the electorate, whatever its short-term justification, seemed to develop its own momentum. A regime that so pointedly refused to practice the arts of electoral politics found itself developing a rationale for longer-term authoritarianism. Above all, the closing of the political system—the purges of elected politicians, the constant changing of the rules to prevent significant victories for the opposition—made clear that any eventual return to open political competition would find the political elite and the public ill-prepared. The organization of new political groups appeared virtually impossible in the manipulated atmosphere created by the revolutionaries.

One question remains. What of the opposition? How could the forces of the left and center have fallen silent so quickly? The two important centers of consistent political opposition after 1964 were the radical university students and the progressive Roman Catholic clergy. It is significant that these were the only groups which remained secure in their respective ideological positions. The fact is that the left was deeply divided in the early 1960's, never more so than in the last year of Goulart's presidency. Among politicians and intellectuals identified with the left there lurked deep uncertainties about the soundness of their ideas and the reliability of their political strategy. Their apparent confidence had become recklessness in early 1964. The center? It was outflanked, outshouted, and disorganized. The voice of the center which represented the majority of the politically aware public (especially in the urban sector), failed to carry any significant weight either in the final crisis of 1963–64 or in the aftermath of the coup of March 31.

Three factors contributed to the increasing authoritarianism of the revolutionary government. Most important was the attitude of the military, which had been the direct cause of Goulart's fall and immediately emerged as the active censor of Brazilian political life. Despite frequent conflicts between the moderates and the "hard-liners" within the officer corps, the majority of the military agreed on the absolute need to prevent a return to populist politics. They constantly pressed Castello Branco to restrict the opposition whenever it threatened the monopoly of power that the revolutionaries claimed for themselves. A second factor was the disorganization and opportunism of the political elite that logically should have comprised the opposition. A third was the profoundly skeptical attitude of the general public. Arbitrary suspension of the political rules, for example, brought a minimal response. The public, disillusioned by the blunders and opportunism of the "politicians," appeared to be resigned, for the time being at least, to rule by technocrats under military tutelage.

APPENDIX

THE UNITED STATES ROLE
IN JOÃO GOULART'S FALL

What was the role of the United States government in the political upheaval of March 31, 1964? The Jacobin left and the Communists were quick to attribute the outcome of the political trauma to American intervention in Brazil, as one such account explained in its title, *The Coup Began in Washington*.[1] This interpretation began by arguing that the United States had changed its Latin American policy since the inception of the Alliance for Progress in 1961. The radical left argued that Assistant Secretary of State Thomas Mann, in contrast to his predecessors since 1961, had adopted a policy which was more sympathetic to military governments in Latin America. The United States, it was alleged, had forgotten the ideals of social reform outlined in the Alliance for Progress and had returned to its traditional postwar policy of obsessive anti-communism. At its most extreme, this explanation claimed that the Brazilian conspirators who overthrew Goulart were acting under direct instructions from the United States government.

The apparent disorganization of the Goulart government, and its complete unwillingness to stage a last-ditch stand, makes the "conspiracy" theory implausible as an explanation of how the open political system designed in 1945 could have broken down. The political upheaval of 1964 is explicable in terms of the political forces that have struggled for the control of Brazil since 1945. Nonetheless, it is worth examining the attitude of the United States government toward the Goulart regime in an attempt to see what influence it may have exerted in the course of events during 1963 and 1964.

The United States government had been deeply disappointed over the debacle of Quadros' mere seven months as President. At the outset of his term in 1961, Quadros appeared to have the rare talents of leadership that would enable him to carry out a vigorous stabilization program while at the same time maintaining a viable political base in Brazil. When Quadros resigned, the United States had to face the awkward fact that Brazilians were deeply divided over Goulart's accepitibility as a President. Once the succession question was settled in 1961, the U.S. government decided to adopt a cautiously cooperative attitude toward the Goulart government, a policy which continued until the middle of 1963. Until then, the Kennedy administration encouraged Goulart to follow up his interest in social reform, but also constantly pressed him to undertake the politically unpopular attack on inflation, which was becoming more and more unavoidable.

The turning point in the attitude of the United States government came during the course of 1963. The Dantas-Bell agreements of March 1963 gave Brazil clear warning that it must carry out a stabilization program and begin social reform in order to qualify for further financial assistance. The failure of the Dantas-Furtado experiment and the apparent unwillingness of Goulart to support similar measures as proposed by Finance Minister Carvalho Pinto aroused doubts in the American government that Goulart would be willing under any circumstances to carry out a painful anti-inflation program, a step considered indispensable by the international financial authorities, as well as by virtually all economists, however they may have differed on details. After the middle of 1963, the American government became increasingly wary of Goulart. No new aid agreements were signed with the federal government, except for the surplus wheat agreements (under Public Law 480) and the assistance to the SUDENE program in the Northeast. Instead, the U.S. government followed a policy of negotiating directly with those state governors who were willing to meet the terms of United States agencies. In states such as Guanabara and Rio Grande do Norte, UDN governors were happy to accept American money while carrying out programs of economic development.

The deterioration in relations between the Goulart government and the United States became obvious when the new coordinating committee of the Alliance for Progress met in São Paulo in November

1963. President Goulart gave a speech in which he virtually ignored the Alliance for Progress and concentrated instead upon the upcoming World Trade Conference in Geneva. During the rest of the São Paulo meetings, the Brazilian government was conspicuously uncooperative in the efforts to develop a new multilateral mechanism for the administration of the Alliance for Progress.

By early 1964, the U. S. government had become preoccupied with the possibility of a sharp leftist turn in Brazil. The American ambassador, Lincoln Gordon, later made no secret of his own belief in early 1964 that Goulart was on the verge of attempting a Peronist solution to the Brazilian political cul-de-sac. This view was also held by Secretary of State Rusk, who explained soon after the coup of 1964 that the American government had been concerned over leftist infiltration in the Goulart regime.

It is clear, therefore, that the United States government had from mid-1963 decided to withhold any further direct financial assistance to the federal government, although it was willing to continue cooperation with the state governors who would conform to the procedures of the Alliance for Progress. As for Brazil's large foreign indebtedness, the American government in late 1963 explained that it was prepared to enter into negotiations for a rescheduling of Brazil's debt but that the initiative would have to come from the Brazilian government; and the first stage of approval would need to come from the European creditors, who held a larger share of Brazil's indebtedness than the United States. In other words, the United States would wait until the Goulart regime was able to satisfy its European creditors before it would enter into negotiations for debt refinancing. The Goulart government had begun negotiations in Paris in March 1964, just before the President was overthrown. In the course of March, however, the American government became deeply concerned over the *political* trend of the Goulart regime. There was, therefore, great tension in the American Embassy and in high administration circles in Washington over the possibility of political violence in Brazil.

What of the American role at the time of the military revolt itself? Was the U. S. government a direct sponsor of the military rebels, as it had been in Guatemala in 1954, or the Bay of Pigs in 1961? The answer is undoubtedly no. There is no evidence to support the claim that the military conspirators were sponsored or directed by the United States government. The intervention of the Brazilian military in 1964 was in principle no different from their previous interventions of 1955 or 1954 or 1945.

As one would expect, the American ambassador and the Secretary of State denied that the United States had played any role in the coup. Their language was unequivocal, and strikingly similar. Ambassador Gordon, during his testimony before the Senate Foreign Relations Committee in 1966, explained: "Certainly in Brazil in these last four years I have been very aware of the limitations on our influence. Brazil is a very large country with a very active political life of its own, and the American voice, although a significant one, is in no sense whatsoever a controlling one. And the Brazilian revolution of 1964 was a purely 100 per cent Brazilian product, not a hidden U. S. product in any way, shape, or manner." [2] In his press conference on April 3, 1964, Secretary of State Rusk was equally adamant in his denials. He was asked about the Cuban charge that the Brazilian revolution was prepared, ordered, and paid for in the United States. Said Rusk: "Well, there is just not one iota of truth in this. It's just not so in any way, shape, or form." [3] Former Ambassador Gordon was questioned in detail about the possible role of American personnel in Brazil and he replied: "The movement which overthrew President Goulart was a purely 100 per cent—not 99.44—but 100 per cent purely Brazilian movement. Neither the American Embassy nor I personally played any part in the process whatsoever." Gordon was asked whether the CIA was included in his disavowal of any U. S. role. He replied: "Yes. In the Brazilian situation, whatever may have been the case in other countries at other times, there was no lack of coordination, and there is none, among the CIA personnel, the military attachés, the political officers of the Embassy, the AID mission, the USIS mission, and the Ambassador. This was and is all one team." [4]

It seems clear, however, that the American Embassy was *well informed* about the efforts of the conspirators. The U. S. Army attaché in the U. S. Embassy, Colonel (later promoted to General) Vernon Walters, was an exceedingly knowledgeable liaison with the Brazilian officer corps. A gifted linguist and one of the most effective attachés in the United States military, Walters had served as an interpreter for the U. S. Fifth Army in its contacts with the Brazilian expe-

ditionary force in Italy during the Second World War. In Italy he had
become a personal friend of Lieutenant Colonel Castello Branco, who
was now a General and the coordinator of the anti-Goulart military
conspiracy. Although the victorious revolutionaries were circumspect
about the contacts that they had maintained with the Embassy before
March 31, 1964, some later accounts included details of conversations with Embassy representatives. The series of documentary articles
published in the *O Estado de São Paulo,* for example, included a description of three contacts between military conspirators and the Embassy before March 31, 1964. The last contact is described as follows: "A high [Brazilian] official was asked about the possibility of
meeting with one of the members of the military section of the Embassy of the United States. He agreed to hold a conversation at the
office of the latter. The meeting took place, and on that occasion he
received, couched in diplomatic language, an offer of war materiels in
case of necessity. His response was one of sincere thanks and it was
accompanied by the following explanation: 'Brazil, sir, is a country
different from all others. In the decisive moment, I am certain that we
here, with our own forces, will know how to resolve the situation.
Arms we do not need. We have enough for an action, even if it is a
long one. But I admit that we may face the need for fuel, and in that
case perhaps I will contact you.' " [5] A sympathetic American journalistic account of the conspiracy (published in *Fortune* magazine)
states that in early 1964 the conspirators were making plans for an
armed rebellion: "They sent an emissary to ask U. S. Ambassador
Lincoln Gordon what the U. S. position would be if civil war broke
out, who reported back that Gordon was cautious and diplomatic, but
he left the impression that if the Paulistas could hold out for 48 hours
they would get U. S. recognition and help." [6] Evidently these conspirators were at that time thinking in terms of a possible secession of São
Paulo, as in 1932. The fact is that this assistance (never, according to
this account, actually promised—its availability was deduced from an
"impression") was never needed, and therefore the American authorities *could* afterward state unequivocally that they had not assisted the
rebels. That their sympathy lay with the conspiracy seems undeniable.

After the overthrow of Goulart, the American government made
clear that it was delighted with the turn in Brazilian politics. Within
hours after President Ranieri Mazzilli had been sworn in as the Acting

President of Brazil in the early morning hours of April 2, President Lyndon Johnson sent a message expressing "warmest good wishes" and stating that "the American people have watched with anxiety the political and economic difficulties through which your great nation has been passing, and have admired the resolute will of the Brazilian community to resolve these difficulties within a framework of constitutional democracy and without civil strife." [7] The surprising rapidity of the American recognition of Goulart's overthrow helped to reinforce the suspicion that the United States had played some role in the Brazilian coup.

It is known that there were disagreements within the State Department over the propriety of recognizing immediately a government that had come to power through a military coup. Despite objections in Washington, the views of the American Embassy in Rio prevailed. This position rested on the assumption that the transfer of power had been constitutional, reasoning that since Goulart had "vacated" the presidency, it was entirely in line with constitutional procedure for the president of the Senate, Auro de Moura Andrade, to swear in Mazzilli, the next in line, as President. This was the explanation given by Secretary of State Rusk in his press conference on April 3, 1964. The enthusiasm and speed of the American recognition, however, caused second thoughts in Washington. On April 3 Arthur Krock, the well-known *New York Times* columnist of conservative views, had commended the American government on its apparent policy of "letting the dust settle" before passing judgment on events in Brazil. By the time his column had appeared, however, the message of President Johnson had already been sent. Krock was dismayed that the American government had acted so quickly. On April 7 he reported that the career officers in the State Department had attempted to convince their superiors that "the Latin American people are quick to find and resent an implication in any Washington statement praising their revolutionary changes, that these have primarily served the United States interest. And another lesson of experience is that it is best to await the development of the policies of new Latin American governments before praising them; and, as in the instance of Brazil, initiating renewed offers of cooperation." Krock then put his troubling question: "In view of these familiar sequels to a revolution in Latin America and considering the fact that—though constitutional government was maintained by the replacement of a fugitive President with the Head of the Chamber of Deputies—Goulart was overthrown by military force, why did President Johnson and Secretary Rusk not only reject the counsels of experienced subordinates, but reject them with such haste and highlighted publicity?"

On the basis of his own information, Krock answered: "An authoritative explanation given to this department today is that the President and Rusk acted on recommendations from Ambassador Lincoln Gordon in Rio de Janeiro and his 'country team'—the United States officials who labored intelligently and effectively to keep the United States out of any involvement in the events which led up to the revolution. Since they made this good record in a delicate situation, and are on the scene, it is comprehensible why their counsels prevailed over colleagues in Washington of longer and continental experience in the ways of Latin America. Nevertheless, the indications are mounting that the locals [i.e., the State Department officers in Washington] were better advisors." [8]

Undoubtedly one factor motivating the Embassy in Rio de Janeiro was a desire to strengthen the hand of the moderates against the "hardliners" in the struggle among the revolutionaries. Ambassador Gordon may have argued that immediate. recognition of a new civilian head of government would undercut the more extreme military who had little patience with constitutional formalities. If this was the reasoning, then the gamble of immediate recognition yielded disappointing results. The pressure of the hard-line officers, combined with the fact that the revolutionaries found the professional politicians so uncooperative, led directly to the first Institutional Act on April 9, 1964, (an arbitrary edict that contradicted the "constitutional" rationale which the United States so pointedly praised in justification of early recognition) and the increasingly frequent "supplementary" Acts over the following two and a half years. Born out of what was essentially a military coup, the Revolution of 1964 could not be contained within normal constitutional limits, whatever the United States government may have hoped and labored for.

There is no doubt that Ambassador Lincoln Gordon was an enthusiastic champion of the new government in Brazil. On April 23, he spoke in Pôrto Alegre, announcing that the overthrow of Goulart had presented Brazil with the opportunity for a fresh start toward the realization of the ideals of the Alliance for Progress. On May 5 he gave a major speech to the Higher War College in Rio de Janeiro, extolling the Brazilian Revolution. He explained that "this event can indeed be included along with the Marshall Plan proposal, the Berlin Blockade, the defeat of Communist aggression in Korea, and the resolution of the missile crisis in Cuba as one of the major turning points in world history in the middle of the twentieth century." [9] Ambassador Gordon continued, during his ambassadorship in Brazil until early 1966 (when he was appointed Assistant Secretary of State for Inter-American Affairs), to defend the Brazilian regime against its critics abroad. He expressed faith in the Castello Branco government's commitment to restore democratic procedures, and he continued to regard the government as compatible with the principles of U. S.-Latin American policy as outlined by President Kennedy. Ambassador Gordon's attitude was fully endorsed in the policy statements and actions of official Washington.

The Brazilian government began, after April 1, 1964, to enjoy much fuller cooperation from the United States in receiving economic and financial assistance. At the same time, the Castello Branco government adopted an unequivocally pro-American foreign policy. Brazil became an enthusiastic supporter of the intervention in the Dominican Republic in April 1965, and contributed a military force to the OAS peace-keeping operation there. Indeed, the Brazilian foreign office attempted to press the American government into exercising a veto in the United Nations in order to prevent the sending of a representative to investigate the Dominican situation. It was not, however, successful in the effort, and the secretary general of ECLA, José Mayobre, went to the Dominican Republic to prepare a report for the United Nations in the summer of 1965. The total effect of the Brazilian change in foreign policy was to repudiate the "independent" foreign policy of the Quadros-Goulart period and to implement instead the "pro-Western" philosophy that had been spelled out in the courses and lectures of the Higher War College.

There is a more fundamental sense in which one can ask about the U. S. role in the political upheaval of March 31, 1964. Granted that the American government in no way "sponsored" the anti-Goulart rebels, whose actions were explicable in terms of the dynamics of Brazilian politics since 1930, to what extent was the mentality of the "revolutionaries" influenced indirectly by the United States? This is a difficult as well as an interesting question, which goes beyond the scope of an appendix and would require a detailed study of U. S.-Brazilian relations over the last several decades.

One special area in which evidence of this more subtle U. S "influence" must be sought is the Higher War College, founded in 1949 under the inspiration and leadership of General Cordeiro de Farias, a leading anti-getulista in the postwar era. Under the U. S.-Brazilian military agreements of the early 1950's, the U. S. Army received exclusive rights to render assistance in the organization and operation of the college, which had been modeled on the National War College in Washington. In view of the fact that the Brazilian War College became a rallying point for leading military opponents of civilian populist politicians, it would be worth examining the extent to which the strongly anti-Communist ideology—bordering on an anti-political attitude—of officers such as Generals Cordeiro de Farias and Jurandir Mamede was reinforced (or moderated?) by their frequent contacts with United States officers. There was also the fact that the Brazilian military had been supplied since the early 1950's with a considerable amount of U. S. military assistance in the form of equipment and training. To what extent did this relationship transform previous attitudes of Brazilian officers toward their role in the Brazilian political process? If, as appears likely, the Brazilian military has committed itself to a much deeper involvement in politics, students of contemporary Brazil will have to examine more carefully the forces which have shaped officer opinion.

Chapter I

1. The historiography on the "Old Republic" (1889–1930) is relatively meager. The standard account is José Maria Bello, *História da República: 1889–1954* (São Paulo, 1959), now available in an American edition (Stanford, Calif., 1966). A stimulating but generally underestimated essay is Charles Morazé, *Les trois ages du Brésil* (Paris, 1954). One of the most profound critiques of the Old Republic was published by a monarchist on the eve of the Revolution of 1930: José Maria dos Santos, *A Política geral do Brasil* (São Paulo, 1930). Two general accounts with much valuable information are: Sertório de Castro, *A República que a revolução destruio* (Rio de Janeiro, 1932); and Dormund Martins, *Da república á dictadura* (Rio de Janeiro, 1931). For invaluable bibliographical suggestions see Américo Jacobina Lacombe, *Brasil: Período nacional* (Mexico City, 1956).
2. The classic study of the "colonels" in back-country politics is Victor Nunes Leal, *Coronelismo, enxada e voto: O município e o regime representativo no Brasil* (Rio de Janeiro, 1948). For a study showing how *coronelismo* has persisted in a backward northeastern state, see Edilson Portela Santos, "Evolução da Vida Política no Município de Picos, Piauí," *Revista Brasileira de Estudos Políticos,* No. 10 (Jan. 1961), 160–83. A collection of case studies of "colonels" with much colorful detail is Marços Vinicios Vilaça and Roberto Cavalcanti de Albuquerque, *Coronel, Coronéis* (Rio de Janeiro, 1965). Undoubtedly one of the best ways to understand the atmosphere of *coronelismo* is through novels by writers who grew up in these back-country areas. One of the best-known fictionalized accounts of a "colonel" is Mário Palmério, *Vila dos Confins* (Rio de Janeiro, 1956).
3. The Liberal Alliance was a pact formed for the presidential election

of 1930 by the leaders of the states of Minas Gerais, Rio Grande do Sul, and Paraíba. The pact was supported also by the recently founded *Partido Democrático* of São Paulo, which opposed the *Partido Republicano Paulista*, the dominant force in that state. The platform of the Liberal Alliance, issued on January 2, 1930, is in Getúlio Vargas, *A Nova Política do Brasil* (Rio de Janeiro, 1938), I, 19–54.

4. Reprinted in Paulo Nogueira Filho, *Ideais e lutas de um burguês progressista: O Partido Democrático e a Revolução de 1930* (São Paulo, 1958), II, 718–20.

5. The literature on the Revolution of 1930 is very extensive, and there is as yet no critical bibliography available. I have drawn heavily on the excellent survey by Edgard Carone, *Revoluções do Brasil Contemporâneo, 1922–1938* (São Paulo, 1965). For useful secondary accounts, see Glauco Carneiro, *História das Revoluções Brasileiras* (Rio de Janeiro, 1965), II, 363–94; and Hélio Silva, *1930: A Revolução Traída* [O Ciclo de Vargas, v. III] (Rio de Janeiro, 1966). The most penetrating contemporary accounts are Barbosa Lima Sobrinho, *A verdade sobre a revolução de outubro* (São Paulo, 1933); and Virgílio de Mello Franco, *Outubro, 1930* (Rio de Janeiro, 1931). For an important memoir with much detail on the origins of the Aliança Liberal (whose candidate was Vargas), see João Neves da Fontoura, *Memórias, Volume II: A aliança liberal e a revolução de 1930* (Rio de Janeiro, 1963). For details on the role of Minas Gerais in the Revolution, see Afonso Arinos de Melo Franco, *Um Estadista da República* (Rio de Janeiro, 1955), III, 1300–1363. On two special aspects of the revolution, see John D. Wirth, "Tenentismo in the Brazilian Revolution of 1930," *Hispanic American Historical Review*, XLIV, No. 2 (May 1964), 161–79; and Jordan Young, "Military Aspects of the 1930 Brazilian Revolution," in the same issue of the *Hispanic American Historical Review*, 180–96. In stating (p. 181) that there were practically no purges among the higher military after the revolution, Young appears to contradict Wirth's analysis (p. 169), where it is argued that many resentful victims of the purges later joined the São Paulo revolt of 1932. On the assassination of João Pessoa, see Ann Quiggins Tiller, "The Igniting Spark—Brazil, 1930," *Hispanic American Historical Review*, XLV, No. 3 (August 1965), 384–92.

6. Vargas, *A Nova Política*, I, 59–63.

7. Tristão de Alencar Araripe, *Tasso Fragoso: Um Pouco de História do Nosso Exército* (Rio de Janeiro, 1960), 543, 545, 547. For details on the Army's increasingly "political" role in the 1920's, see Estêvão

Leitão de Carvalho, *Dever Militar e Política Partidária* (São Paulo, 1959).

8. *Ibid.*, 557.

9. There is a detailed account of the Cardinal's dramatic intervention in Irmã Maria Regina do Santo Rosário (Laurita Pessôa Raja Gabaglia), *O Cardeal Leme* (Rio de Janeiro, 1962), 216–26.

10. Araripe, *Tasso Fragoso*, 611.

11. For the history of Riograndense politics during the Old Republic, see A. Fay de Azevedo and F. Contreiras Rodrigues, "Os Partidos Políticos no Rio Grande do Sul: Dois Pontos de Vista," *Revista Brasileira de Estudos Políticos,* No. 2 (July 1957), 76–98. Useful also is Neves da Fontoura, *Memórias*, I: *Borges de Medeiros e Seu Tempo* (Rio de Janeiro, 1958); and João Pio de Almeida, *Borges de Medeiros* (Pôrto Alegre, 1928). Mr. Joseph Love of the University of Illinois is engaged in a study of Riograndense politics under the Old Republic.

12. For an analysis of these two currents, see Afonso Arinos de Melo Franco, *Um estadista da República*, III, 1421; and his more recent *Evolução da crise brasileira* (São Paulo, 1965), 76–82. There is an interesting analysis of the diverse ideological currents in the Revolution of 1930 by a later apologist for the Estado Nôvo in Azevedo Amaral, *O estado autoritário e a realidade nacional* (Rio de Janeiro, 1938), 80–105.

13. The history of liberal constitutionalism in Brazil is primarily, although certainly not entirely, one aspect of the history of politics and political thought in São Paulo. Among the sources on the *Partido Democrático* is the memorial volume dedicated to the party's first president, Antonio Prado: Nazareth Prado, ed., *Antonio Prado no Império e na República* (Rio de Janeiro, 1929); and the memoirs of the party's secretary-general: Paulo Nogueira Filho, *Ideais e lutas de um burguês progressista: O Partido Democrático e a Revolução de 1930* (São Paulo, 1958), 2 vols. For an example of the classic liberal position, see A. de Sampaio Doria, *O espírito das democracias* (São Paulo, 1925). The Achilles' heel of liberal constitutionalism in Brazil has been the "social question," a problem which was apparent well before the Revolution of 1930. See F. Contreiras Rodrigues, *A questão social e o Partido Democrático Nacional* (Rio de Janeiro, 1928). Oliveira Vianna criticized the Partido Democrático soon after its founding for "reflecting only the Paulista environment." Francisco José de Oliveira Vianna, *O idealismo da constituição* (Rio de Janeiro, 1927), 114. The most famous representative of liberal constitutionalism outside of São Paulo was the Riograndense politician, J. F. de Assis Brasil, whose

political vehicle in Rio Grande do Sul was the *Partido Libertador*. Among his influential works was *Democracia representativa: Do voto e do modo de votar*, 4th ed. (Rio de Janeiro, 1931).

14. The best secondary accounts of the tenentes' revolts are Carneiro, *História das Revoluções Brasileiras*, i, 223–309; and Carone, *Revoluções do Brasil Contemporâneo*, 21–67. There is invaluable detail in Hélio Silva's first two volumes of his series "O Ciclo de Vargas": *1922: Sangue na Areia de Copacabana* (Rio de Janeiro, 1964) and *1926: A Grande Marcha* (Rio de Janeiro, 1965).

15. The best brief analysis of tenentismo is to be found in Wirth, "Tenentismo in the Brazilian Revolution of 1930." The earlier classic study is Virginio Santa Rosa, *O sentido do tenentismo* (Rio de Janeiro, 1933), which was republished under the title *Que foi o tenentismo?* (Rio de Janeiro, 1963). See also Robert J. Alexander, "Brazilian Tenentismo," *Hispanic American Historical Review*, XXXVI, No. 2 (May 1956), 229–42. For an interesting Marxist analysis, see Leoncio Basbaum, *História sincera da República*, III (São Paulo, 1962), 21 ff. The elitist character of tenentista thinking is very clear in Juarez Távora's reply to Luís Carlos Prestes' Communist Manifesto of May 1930, reprinted in Nogueira Filho, *Ideais e Lutas*, ii, 714–18.

16. Lídia Besouchet, *História da Criação do Ministério do Trabalho* (Rio de Janeiro, n.d.), 57. Luís Carlos Prestes, who was in exile in Buenos Aires, issued a Manifesto on May 30, 1930, denouncing the "placebo program [*programa anódino*]" of the Liberal Alliance and warning that the election had been merely a contest "between the conflicting interests of two oligarchic camps." Two leading tenentes, João Alberto and Siqueira Campos, had gone to Buenos Aires to try to win the support of the "cavalier of hope" for the impending revolt. They were unable to convince Prestes, whose Manifesto of May 30 calling for an "agrarian and anti-imperialist revolution" was a declaration of his conversion to communism. The manifesto is printed in Paulo Nogueira Filho, *Ideais e Lutas*, ii, 710–13. Details of the tenentista mission to Buenos Aires, during which Prestes tried unsuccessfully to convert his visitors to communism, are in João Alberto Lins de Barros, *Memórias de um Revolucionário* (Rio de Janeiro, 1953), 222–26. On the early history of the Communist Party in Brazil, see Astrojildo Pereira, *Formação do PCB: 1922–1928 Notas e documentos* (Rio de Janeiro, 1962). Pereira is one of Brazil's most widely respected Communist intellectuals. For the history of the Communist Party, see also Abguar Bastos, *Prestes e a revolução social* (Rio de Janeiro, 1946); Rollie E. Poppino, *International Communism in Latin America* (Glencoe, Ill.,

1964), 70–77; and Robert J. Alexander, *Communism in Latin America* (New Brunswick, N. J., 1957), chapter VII.

17. Araripe, *Tasso Fragoso*, 582.

18. General Tasso Fragoso, one of the junta that deposed Washington Luiz, had been irritated by the President's rejection of his suggestion for more funds. *Ibid.*, 525–26. Increased appropriations for the military was a specific provision in the platform of the Liberal Alliance.

19. There is a summary of the case of the forged Bernardes letters in José Honório Rodrigues, *Teoria de História do Brasil*, 2nd ed. (São Paulo, 1957), II, 509–19.

20. The platform of the Liberal Alliance also favored a general amnesty for all political and military rebels, some of whom had spent years in exile in Uruguay and Argentina. Washington Luiz had stubbornly refused to grant an amnesty to the rebels of the Bernades era (1922–1926).

21. Júlio Prestes had been leader of the majority in the Senate in 1926, when he presented to the Congress the Monetary Reform Law that was the basis of Washington Luiz' financial policy. Prestes was, therefore, irrevocably identified with the incumbent government. There is a detailed explanation of Brazil's financial plight as of 1930 in Agnes Waddell, "The Revolution in Brazil," *Foreign Policy Association Information Service*, VI, No. 26 (March 4, 1931), 489–506. A spirited defense of Washington Luiz' financial policies is offered in Francisca Isabel Schurig Vieira, "O Pensamento político-administrativo e a política financeira de Washington Luís," *Revista de História*, XI, No. 41 (Jan.-March 1960), 105–46. The fundamental study of Brazilian coffee-marketing policy is Antônio Delfim Netto, *O Problema do Café no Brasil* [Faculdade de Ciências Econômicas e Administrativas: Universidade de São Paulo, Boletim No. 5] (São Paulo, 1959). Celso Furtado argues that the revolution "was a reaction against the excessive predominance of the coffee groups—and their allies in international finance involved in the valorization policy—in the federal government." *The Economic Growth of Brazil* (Berkeley, 1963), 221. This is certainly not true of the year immediately before the revolution, when the coffee growers bitterly attacked the federal government's maintenance of a high value for the Brazilian currency and its failure to do more to cushion the effects of the collapse of world coffee prices. By describing the Revolution of 1930 as a revolt against São Paulo and all it symbolized in the political system of the Old Republic, Furtado fails to note how the coffee growers had turned against the Washington Luiz government (and its presidential candi-

date, Júlio Prestes) in 1929. The irony lay in the fact that both men were from the principal coffee-growing state. The role of the coffee question in 1930 is well described in Barbosa Lima Sobrinho, *A Verdade,* chapter IX, entitled "O Marechal Café."

22. It is possible to view the Revolution of 1930 as part of the struggle between reformers, especially the tenentes, and the state "oligarchies." This is the theme of Carone, *Revoluções do Brasil contemporâneo.* Seen from this standpoint, Vargas finally achieved domination by using the oligarchies against the reformers. Amaral, *O estado autoritário,* 107 ff.

23. There is no general history of politics in either the city or the state of São Paulo. Much information can be found in Richard M. Morse, *From Community to Metropolis* (Gainesville, 1958). The memoir of the important Paulista politician, Altino Arantes, *Passos do meu caminho* (Rio de Janeiro, 1958), is an important source, as is the memorial volume *Centenário de Júlio Mesquita* (São Paulo, 1964). Interesting examples of works extolling São Paulo's unique virtues are A. Carneiro Leão, *São Paulo em 1920* (Rio de Janeiro, 1920); and Ruy Ribeiro Couto, *Espírito de São Paulo* (Rio de Janeiro, 1932). The history of Paulista separatism goes back to the Empire and is closely associated with the growth of Republicanism. On this little-studied phenomenon, see Luís Washington Vita, *Alberto Sales: Ideólogo da República* (São Paulo, 1965), 35 ff. On the existence and role of the middle class in modern Brazilian history, see John J. Johnson, *Political Change in Latin America: The Emergence of the Middle Sectors* (Stanford, 1958), Chapter 8. Some rough data on social mobility under the Old Republic are presented in João Camillo de Oliveira Tôrres, *Estratificação Social no Brasil* (São Paulo, 1965), 151–77.

24. For an example of an early (Nov. 1930) demand for an immediate Constituent Assembly by a spokesman for liberal constitutionalism, see A. de Sampaio Doria, *Democracia; A Revolução de 1930* (São Paulo, 1930).

25. The decree is reprinted in Nogueira Filho, *Ideais e Lutas,* ii, 741–43.

26. Carone, *Revoluções do Brasil Contemporâneo,* 99–100; a brief account of the origins of the Ministry of Labor is given in Besouchet, *História da Criação do Ministério do Trabalho.*

27. The influence of the tenentes between 1930 and 1932 is clearly explored in Wirth, "Tenentismo."

28. Vargas, *A Nova Política,* ii, 17–19.

29. For examples of the angry response by Paulista revolutionaries to what they considered the deliberate abuse of São Paulo and the failure

to carry through their program, see Paulo Duarte, *Que é que ha?* . . .
Pequena historia de uma grande pirataria (São Paulo, 1931); and
Vivaldo Coaracy, *O Caso de São Paulo* (São Paulo, ,1931). The
Partído Republicano Paulista was a favorite target for both authors.

30. Theodorico Lopes and Gentil Torres, *Ministros da Guerra do Brasil:*
1808-1946 (Rio de Janeiro, 1947), 193-96.

31. Lacking sufficient arms, the Paulistas fought back with words. The
resulting memoir literature is vast and very *engagé*. For a bibliography
of the Constitutionalist Revolution of 1932, see Aureliano Leite,
"Causas e objectivos da Revolução de 1932," *Revista de História,*
XXV, No. 51 (July-Sept. 1962), 139-66. Typical of the exuberant
literature is Alfredo Ellis Júnior, *A nossa guerra* (São Paulo, 1933);
and Menotti Del Picchia, *A Revolução Paulista* (São Paulo, 1932).
For an interesting review of Paulo Duarte, *Palmares pelo Avesso* (São
Paulo, 1947), a memoir by a Paulista rebel, see Florestan Fernandes,
Mudanças sociais no Brasil (São Paulo, 1960), Chapter IX. The
memoirs of João Alberto Lins de Barros, *Memórias de um revolu-*
cionário were the subject of a long review by Júlio de Mesquita Filho,
Memórias de um revolucionário: Notas para um ensaio de sociologia
política (São Paulo, 1954). João Alberto was the disastrously unpopular interventor in São Paulo in 1930-31. Júlio de Mesquita Filho
is the scion of the famous family which owns the influential daily,
O Estado de São Paulo, a pillar of liberal constitutionalism. For the
Paulista mobilization effort in which Roberto Simonsen played a central role, see Clovis de Oliveira, *A Indústria e o Movimento Consti-*
tucionalista de 1932 (São Paulo, 1956). The best secondary account
of the Revolt of 1932 is Carneiro, *História das Revoluções Brasileiras,*
II, 396-413.

32. For an example of the attempt by a Riograndense to rally Rio Grande
do Sul and Rio de Janeiro to the support of São Paulo, see João
Neves da Fontoura, *Por São Paulo e pelo Brasil* (n.p., 1932). A
representative of the liberal constitutionalist position, Neves da Fontoura vigorously attacked the tenentes, 46. In his memoirs he later
charged that Vargas welcomed their activity in 1930-31, *Memórias,*
II, 481 ff. Soon after the collapse of the Paulista revolt, Neves da
Fontoura published his own analysis of where the Revolution of 1930
had gone wrong in *Acuso!* 2nd ed. (Lisboa, 1933). Flores da Cunha's
ambiguous position before the outbreak of the revolt in São Paulo
made him vulnerable politically after the Paulistas' military defeat.
In an effort to prove that he had been loyal to Vargas, he appointed
a "Tribunal of Honor" whose findings were published in *O General*

Flores da Cunha e a Revolução Paulista: Decisão do tribunal de honra e outros documentos (Pôrto Alegre, 1933).

33. On the reforms in the electoral system, see Barbosa Lima Sobrinho, "Evolução dos sistemas eleitorais," *Revista de Direito Público e Ciencia Política,* IV, No. 3 (Sept.-Dec. 1961), 29–40; Nunes Leal, *Coronelismo, enxada e voto,* chapter 6; and Edgard Costa, *A Legislação Eleitoral Brasileira* (Rio de Janeiro, 1964).

34. For an analysis of the Constitution of 1934 by a noted student of European and North American constitutional history, see Karl Loewenstein, *Brazil Under Vargas* (New York, 1942), 21–26. See also Fábio Lucas, *Conteúdo social nas constituições brasileiras* (Belo Horizonte, 1959), 65–71; and Hamilton Leal, *História das instituições políticas do Brasil* (Rio de Janeiro, 1962), 469–505. A liberal Catholic evaluation of political events between 1930 and the Constitution of 1934 may be found in Alceu Amoroso Lima, *Indicações políticas da revolução à constituição* (Rio de Janeiro, 1936). For an account of the activities of the *Liga Eleitoral Católica,* which urged progressive measures on social and economic affairs in the new Constitution, see Irmã Maria Regina, *O Cardeal Leme,* 309–22.

35. The October 3rd Club, which had been the most continuous organized voice of tenentismo, began to suffer a sharp decline in its influence in April 1933, after issuing a manifesto opposing the elections set for the following month. Carone, *As Revoluções do Brasil Contemporâneo,* 133–34. Elsewhere Carone has pointed out that although the tenentes were disorganized and lacked a "definite ideology," they nonetheless exercised an important influence. He attributes the following items to the efforts of the tenentes: the Code of Mines, the assessment of real estate, the "struggle" against Light [the foreign-owned public utility in Rio de Janeiro], the Water Code, the election and government of Pedro Ernesto as prefect of the Federal District, and the work of Lindolfo Collor in the Ministry of Labor. The latter seems a questionable case of tenentista influence. Review of Nelson Werneck Sodré, *Introdução à Revolução Brasileira* (Rio de Janeiro, 1958) by Carone in *Revista Brasileira de Estudos Políticos,* No. 7 (Nov. 1959), 150.

36. Afonso Arinos de Melo Franco, *História e Teoria do Partido Político no Direito Constitucional Brasileiro* (Rio de Janeiro, 1948), 86–87.

37. Prestes' account of the founding and direction of the ANL was later given in a speech delivered in 1945: Luís Carlos Prestes, *Problemas Atuais da Democracia* (Rio de Janeiro, n.d.), 167–82.

38. Details of the ANL may be found in Affonso Henriques, *Vargas: O*

maquiavélico (São Paulo, 1961), which covers the period up to the Estado Nôvo. The author, who was the treasurer of the ANL, in 1966 published two more volumes on the Vargas era, including the 1951–1954 presidency.

39. The sources on *Integralismo* are limited. Olbiano de Melo, a former Integralista, has given us his account in *A marcha da revolução social no Brasil* (Rio de Janeiro, 1957). Plínio Salgado, the Integralista leader, has been a prolific author. See his *O Integralismo perante a Nação*, 3rd. ed. (Rio de Janeiro, 1955), which includes his principal manifestos. Also useful is *Enciclopédia do Integralismo*, 11 vols. (Rio de Janeiro, 1957–61). An excellent contemporary account of the growth and doctrine of the Integralistas is Karl Heinrich Hunsche, *Der brasilianische integralismus; geschichte und wesen der faschistischen bewegung Brasiliens* (Stuttgart, 1938). The Hunsche dissertation was completed just before the coup of November 1937.

40. One of the most interesting secondary accounts of the 1930's is Basbaum, *História sincera*, III. An indispensable primary source is the frank memoir of Góes Monteiro, the general whose support was essential for the coup of 1937: Lourival Coutinho, *O General Góes depõe* . . . (Rio de Janeiro, 1955). A contemporary analysis which has proved to be of enduring value is Horace B. Davis, "Brazil's Political and Economic Problems," *Foreign Policy Reports*, XI, No. 1 (March 13, 1935), 2–12. There is an interpretation of the entire period from the Revolution of 1930 to the end of the Estado Nôvo in Rollie E. Poppino, "O processo político no Brasil: 1929–1945," *Revista Brasileira de Estudos Políticos*, No. 17 (July 1964), 83–94.

41. Quoted in Carone, *As Revoluções do Brasil Contemporâneo*, 143.

42. The process of radicalization is described in detail in Henriques, *Vargas, o maquiavélico*. Henriques attributes the discrediting of the Aliança Nacional Libertadora to Vargas' ubiquitous "agents." A similar conspiracy theory is presented in Basbaum, *História sincera*, III. Mr. Robert Levine (formerly a doctoral student at Princeton University) is engaged in a study of political radicalization during the 1930's. I have drawn heavily upon Carone, *As Revoluções do Brasil Contemporâneo* for my own analysis. Historians who have done research on the 1930's report that the disorganization of contemporary police records suggests that the police were hardly capable of the Machiavellian manipulations with which they are often charged. The intelligence services of the Army may have been more efficient. Vargas' own sources of information were probably supplemented by the generosity of the British secret service, as well as the Gestapo. Both

were keeping track of Communist activities in Brazil and both had their own reasons for wanting to help prevent a sharp turn to the left in Brazil.

43. There is no detailed historical study of the Communist revolt of 1935, which has been described as "the one serious attempt to seize power by force in the history of Latin American communism": Ernst Halperin, "Latin America," *Survey* (Jan. 1965), 165. An account of the revolt may be found in Carneiro, *História das Revoluções Brasileiras,* II, 415–35; and Poppino, *International Communism in Latin America,* 143–44. For the account of a participant, see Agildo Barata, *Vida de um revolucionário* (Rio de Janeiro, n.d.). Robert J. Alexander, *Communism in Latin America,* chapter VII, has a useful account of the Aliança Nacional Libertadora, but fails to distinguish clearly between the "legalist" and "revolutionary" wings of the Communist Party. The distinction is made clear in Basbaum, *História sincera,* III, 77–103. Basbaum was an active Communist of the period. In later years Luís Carlos Prestes was at pains to explain how the Communists could have so gravely overestimated Brazil's revolutionary potential in 1935. "Our error," he explained in a speech in 1945, "was not in taking up arms" but in "not having succeeded in widening the front, the National Union, and in not having succeeded in completely unmasking the fascist propaganda." Prestes, *Problemas Atuais da Democracia,* 169. See also Bastos, *Prestes e a Revolução Social,* 297–336.

44. Armando de Salles Oliveira, *Jornada democrática: Discursos políticos* (Rio de Janeiro, 1937), XIX; 7–9, 10, 17–18.

45. For his campaign speeches, see José Américo de Almeida, *A palavra e o tempo: 1937–1945–1950* (Rio de Janeiro, 1965).

46. Lourival Coutinho, *O General Góes Depõe,* 231–327. The continuous and effective pressure on Vargas from the military is stressed in John D. Wirth, *Brazilian Economic Nationalism: Trade and Steel Under Vargas* (Ph.D. dissertation, Stanford University, 1966).

47. For a brief analysis of the incident of the "Cohen Plan" and its origins, see José Honório Rodrigues, *Teoria da História do Brasil, II,* 519–24.

48. Vargas' daughter, Alzira, described sarcastically the desire of Dutra and Góes Monteiro to stage "their" coup on the anniversary of the fall of the Empire, thereby emulating Deodoro da Fonseca and Floriano Peixoto, the architects of the coup of 1889. Alzira Vargas do Amaral Peixoto, *Getúlio Vargas, meu Pai* (Rio de Janeiro, 1960), 162–230. Dutra's efforts to re-establish "discipline" in the Army after 1936 are described in José Caó, *Dutra: O Presidente e a Restauração Democrática* (São Paulo, 1949), 63.

49. Armando de Salles Oliveira, *Diagrama de uma situação política: Manifestos políticos do exílio* (São Paulo, 1945), 5–19.
50. Salles Oliveira, *Jornada Democrática*, 10, 21.
51. Salles Oliveira, *Diagrama*, 13.
52. Vargas, *Nova Política*, V, 17–32.
53. On coffee policy in the 1930's, see Benedicto Mergulhão, *O General Café na revolução branca de 37* (Rio de Janeiro, 1944); and Sergio Milliet, *Roteiro do café* (São Paulo, 1941), as well as the authoritative economic analysis of Delfim Netto, *O Problema do Café*.
54. An earlier example of the anti-democratic critique of "romantic liberalism" may be found in Virgínio Santa Rosa, *A desordem* (Rio de Janeiro, 1932), 99 ff. A similar indictment of the "fossilized" liberalism inherent in the Revolution of 1930 was offered in Martins de Almeida's influential *Brasil Errado: Ensaio Político sôbre os Erros do Brasil como País* (Rio de Janeiro, 1932). By 1935 such critics felt that their diagnoses had been amply confirmed by the actions of the Constituent Assembly and the resulting Constitution of 1934. See, for example, Azevedo Amaral, *A Aventura Política do Brasil* (Rio de Janeiro, 1935). Amaral announced that "economic individualism and liberal democracy have been reduced to two cadavers over which the paid mourners murmur their impotent lamentations. . . ." *A Aventura*, 6. Salles Oliveira's campaign speeches in 1937 revealed a well-justified preoccupation with the question of the viability of democracy in Brazil.
55. The character of Vargas' authoritarian regime was analyzed in Loewenstein, *Brazil Under Vargas*. Although Loewenstein's study is the best available analysis of the Estado Nôvo, it suffers from an overly legal approach and from having been published in 1942, before some of the most lasting features of the corporatist structure, such as the labor union system, had undergone the further development that was begun in 1942. For an angry view of the Estado Nôvo by a foreign friend of Brazil, see Samuel Putnam, "The Vargas Dictatorship in Brazil," *Science and Society*, V (1941), 97–116. Historical accounts of the Estado Nôvo have tended to minimize the police terrorism of the era, perhaps in part because Vargas later succeeded in replacing his image as a dictator by his democratic phase after 1945, especially his presidency from 1951 to 1954. The dictator's persecution of intellectuals produced at least one famous work of literature: Graciliano Ramos, *Memórias do Cárcere* (Rio de Janeiro, 1953), 4 vols.
56. The best secondary account of the Integralista attack is Glauco Carneiro, *História das Revoluções Brasileiras*, II, 437–57. Alzira Vargas gave her own witty account of the suspicious inability of the higher

military to defend the President—Góes Monteiro "surrounded" in his apartment (as he reported to Alzira by telephone), Chief of the Military Cabinet Canrobert Pereira da Costa abducted in his pajamas, Cordeiro de Farias, commanding the relief column) bogged down in logistical problems, War Minister Dutra reaching the palace and then asking helplessly for instructions. Alzira Vargas do Amaral Peixoto, *Getúlio Vargas*, 117-33. A prominent young non-Integralista officer involved in the attack was Lieutenant Severo Fournier, whose diary was published in David Nasser, *A Revolução dos Covardes* (Rio de Janeiro, 1947).

57. The author of the Constitution of 1937 and the chief theoretician of the Estado Nôvo was Francisco Campos. See his *O Estado Nacional: Sua estructura, seu conteúdo ideológico*, 3rd ed. (Rio de Janeiro, 1941). Azevedo Amaral, *O estado autoritário*, is a lucid defense of the Estado Nôvo as the first Brazilian regime which was not simply a copy of an inappropriate foreign model, such as the ineffectual "liberal-democratic" regimes of the past. Amaral later described Vargas as the "Chief of the Nation" whose "supreme and irrevocable authority" has a "beneficial educational effect" on the "popular mind." Azevedo Amaral, *Getúlio Vargas: Estadista* (Rio de Janeiro, 1941), 92. Amaral's role as an apologist for the Estado Nôvo is all the more interesting in view of the fact that he endorsed Júlio Prestes during the campaign of 1930. See, for example, Amaral's *Ensaios Brasileiros* (Rio de Janeiro, 1930), 229-45. One of the first essayists to support a fascist solution for Brazil after the Revolution of 1930 was Octávio de Faria in his *Maquiavel e o Brasil* (Rio de Janeiro, 1931). Oliveira Vianna, who also proved sympathetic to the authoritarian turn in 1937, had long criticized Brazil's penchant for uncritically copying foreign political forms. See, for example, his *O Idealismo da Constituição*, 12-15, where he argues that the lack of organized public opinion in Brazil made democracy, as known in the United States and Europe, impossible. The government-inspired works by Isaias Alves, *Educação e Brasilidade: Idéias-Forças do Estado Nôvo* (Rio de Janeiro, 1939) and Severino Sombra, *Forças Armadas e Direção Política* (Rio de Janeiro, 1941) are merely collections of excerpts from Vargas' public speeches.

58. The phrases "clientelistic politics" and "notary state" (*Estado Cartorial*) were coined by Hélio Jaguaribe in his influential analyses of the Brazilian political system under the Republic. The first published version was "Política de Clientela e Política Ideológica," *Digesto Econômico*, VI, No. 68 (July 1950), 41-62. Among his later works

see: *O problema do desenvolvimento econômico e a burguesia nacional* (São Paulo, 1956), esp. 51 ff; *Condições institucionais do desenvolvimento* (Rio de Janeiro, 1958), esp. 18 ff; *O nacionalismo na atualidade Brasileira* (Rio de Janeiro, 1958), esp. 37 ff.

59. For a collection of articles by prominent critics of the political, economic, social, and intellectual world of the Old Republic, see A. Carneiro Leão, et al., *Á Margem da Historia da República* (Rio de Janeiro, 1924). The intellectual ferment of the 1920's is described in João Cruz Costa, *A History of Ideas in Brazil* (Berkeley, 1964), 239–71.

60. Wirth, "Tenentismo," 172–75; Delfim Netto, *O Problema do Café*, 123–40; Henry William Spiegel, *The Brazilian Economy: Chronic Inflation and Sporadic Industrialization* (Philadelphia, 1949), 220–24.

61. G. Wythe, R. A. Wight, and H. M. Midkiff, *Brazil: An Expanding Economy* (New York, 1949), 34, 263–66. One foreign economist who studied Brazil in the early 1930's concluded from his survey of modern Brazilian economic history that "the main problem remains unchanged: to extend the territory of the 'economic Brazil,' and to inject an economic substance into the political area." J. F. Normano, *Brazil: A Study of Economic Types* (Chapel Hill, N.C., 1935), 222.

62. Mário Wagner Vieira da Cunha, *O sistema administrativo brasileiro, 1930–1950* (Rio de Janeiro, 1963); Gilbert B. Siegel, "The Strategy of Public Administration Reform: The Case of Brazil," *Public Administration Review*, XXVI, No. 1 (March 1966), 45–55.

63. The highly personal character of Vargas' dictatorship is emphasized In Jacques Lambert, *Os Dois Brasís* (Rio de Janeiro, 1959), 270–75. This assessment was challenged by Florestan Fernandes in *Revista Brasileira de Estudos Políticos*, No. 7 (Nov. 1959), 143–45.

64. Among the interventors of the early 1930's, Juracy Magalhães was particularly effective in Bahia, while João Alberto turned out to be an extremely unfortunate choice in São Paulo. Both had been tenentes. Speeches during Juracy Magalhães' years as interventor may be found in his *Minha vida pública na Bahia* (Rio de Janeiro, 1957), 81–171. Among other interventors who became prominent figures in postwar Brazilian politics were Adhemar de Barros, Amaral Peixoto (Vargas' son-in-law and later leader of the PSD), and Benedito Valladares. The recently published memoirs of Valladares, whom Vargas named interventor in Minas Gerais in 1933 and who became a key figure in Minas politics for the next thirty years, should prove to be an interesting source. Benedito Valladares, *Tempos Idos e Vividos: Memórias* (Rio de Janeiro, 1966).

65. For an example of an eulogistic pamphlet by a leading writer, see Gilberto Amado, *Perfil do Presidente Getúlio Vargas* (Rio de Janeiro, 1936). This noted intelléctual's admiration for Vargas was not dimmed by the coup of 1937, as he demonstrated in his preface to an official publication in 1938 written by Epitacio Pessoa Cavalcanti de Albuquerque, *Getúlio Vargas: Esboço de biografia* (Rio de Janeiro, 1938). For an example of pro-Vargas propaganda before the coup of 1937, see José Pereira da Silva, *Getúlio Vargas* (Rio de Janeiro, 1934), and the same author's collection of Vargas' early speeches: *Os melhores discursos de Getúlio Vargas* (Rio de Janeiro, 1934). For a speech by a young politician in praise of Getúlio on the occasion of the second anniversary of the Estado Nôvo, see Alexandre Marcondes Filho, *O Presidente Getúlio Vargas: Um Estadista Como Ainda não Surgira no Brasil* (D. I. P., n.d.). Marcondes Filho was later to become Vargas' Labor Minister and an important collaborator in the development of the doctrine of *trabalhismo*. On Vargas' birthday (April 19) in 1941 there was public celebration with speeches lauding Getúlio by Góes Monteiro, João Neves da Fontoura and others. *Um Grande Data* (D.I.P., Rio de Janeiro, 1941).

66. The explanation was in a speech given by Vargas in January 1947 at a PTB rally in Rio de Janeiro. Getúlio Vargas, *A Politica Trabalhista no Brasil* (Rio de Janeiro, 1950), 130.

67. John Gunther, *Inside Latin America* (New York, 1941), 362–66; Loewenstein, *Brazil Under Vargas*, 363–67. The enigmatic political personality of Vargas will undoubtedly intrigue his biographers for years to come. A one-dimensional portrait of Getúlio is presented in Henriques, *Vargas: O maquiavélico*. The thesis that Vargas was able to use others because they wished to be used is argued in Claudio de Araujo Lima, *Mito e realidade de Vargas* (Rio de Janeiro, 1955). For the personal aspect, see Luiz Vegara, *Fui secretário de Getúlio Vargas: Memórias dos anos de 1926–1954* (Rio de Janeiro, 1960); and the memoir (the first of what is promised as a series of volumes) of Vargas' daughter, Alzira Vargas do Amaral Peixoto, *Getúlio Vargas, meu pai*. An earlier work written during the Estado Nôvo and favorable to Vargas is Paul Frischauer, *Presidente Vargas* (São Paulo, 1943). The treatment of Vargas in Tad Szulc, *Twilight of the Tyrants* (New York, 1959), 41–98, covers primarily Vargas' career up to 1945. Professor J. W. F. Dulles has completed a biography of Vargas to be published by the University of Texas Press in 1967.

68. Alexandre Marcondes Filho, *Trabalhadores do Brasil! Palestras do Ministro Marcondes Filho na Hora do Brasil em 1942* (Rio de

Janeiro, 1943). Marcondes Filho was bitterly attacked by a former labor official who resigned in 1943 because of a disagreement over the new labor policies. The critic was Cupertino de Gusmão, whose attack, *Do Bôjo do Estado Nôvo: Memórias de um Socialista na República de Trinta e Sete* (Rio de Janeiro, 1945), contains much valuable information on the origins of the labor union structure and the compulsory membership dues (*impôsto sindical*). Marcondes Filho was responsible for reorganizing the entire Labor Code in 1942–43, thereby consolidating the work of his predecessors, especially Waldemar Falcão, who was Labor Minister from 1937 to 1941. The standard secondary account, although very brief, is Robert J. Alexander, *Labor Relations in Argentina, Brazil, and Chile* (New York, 1962), 59–62. The paternalistic character of the government-sponsored union organization is brought out clearly in Azis Simão, "Industrialisation et syndicalisme au Brésil," and Alain Touraine, "Industrialisation et Conscience Ouvrière a São Paulo," *Sociologie du Travail*, 3, No. 4 (Oct.-Dec. 1961), 66–76, 77–95. Useful also, although now dated and based on English-language sources, is Sarah Elizabeth Roberts, *A History of Trade Unionism in Latin America* (Ph.D. dissertation, George Washington University, 1948), 174–228. The most recent study is Leôncio Martins Rodrigues, *Conflito Industrial e Sindicalismo* (São Paulo, 1966).

69. Vargas, *A Nova Política*, v. X, 178, 290.

70. My use of the term "liberalism" in discussions of Brazilian economic history and economic policy-making refers to Manchester-school or laissez-faire liberalism.

71. The principal secondary work on Brazilian economic history is Celso Furtado, *The Economic Growth of Brazil*. For a contemporary attack on the policy of coffee protection, begun by the Convention of Taubaté in 1906, see J. Pandiá Calógeras, *A Política Monetária do Brasil* (São Paulo, 1960), 410–31. Calógeras' book was first published in French in 1910. For the views of a Manchester-school liberal who was several times finance minister during the Old Republic, see Augusto de Bulhões, *Leopoldo de Bulhões: Um Financista de Princípios, 1856–1928* (Rio de Janeiro, n.d.).

72. For a study of the struggle between advocates of industrialization and the defenders of Brazil's traditional position under the law of comparative advantage, see Nícia Vilela Luz, *A luta pela industrialização do Brasil: 1808–1930* (São Paulo, 1961); and the same author's "O Industrialismo e o Desenvolvimento Econômico do Brasil: 1808–1920," *Revista de História*, XXVII, No. 56 (Oct.-Dec. 1963), 271–

285. Cotton manufacturers were remarkably successful in gaining protection by means of tariffs and later even by restrictions on machinery imports. Stanley J. Stein, *The Brazilian Cotton Manufacture: Textile Enterprise in an Underdeveloped Area, 1850–1950* (Cambridge, Mass., 1957).

73. Wythe, *Brazil: An Expanding Economy*, 296. See also Valentim F. Bouças, *História da dívida externa*, 2nd ed. (Rio de Janeiro, 1950), 337 ff.

74. The standard account of this inadvertent maintenance of domestic demand is Furtado, *Economic Growth of Brazil*, 203–24. Details on the mechanism of coffee support may be found in Delfim Netto, *O Problema do Café*, 136–46. There are relatively few detailed studies of Brazilian industrial development before 1945. See Francisco Iglésias, *Periodização do Processo Industrial no Brasil* [Faculdade de Ciências Econômicas da Universidade de Minas Gerais: Textos de História: No. 1] (Belo Horizonte, 1963, mimeo). An early survey, written by an influential advocate of Brazilian industrialization, is Roberto Simonsen, *Brazil's Industrial Evolution* (São Paulo, 1939). See also George Wythe, "Brazil: Trends in Industrial Development," in Simon Kuznets, Wilbert E. Moore, and Joseph J. Spengler, eds., *Economic Growth: Brazil, India, Japan* (Durham, N. C., 1955), 29–77; Henri van Deursen, "L'émancipation industrielle du Brésil," *Révue Economique Internationale*, XXVI, No. 2 (August 1934), 275–335; Preston E. James, "Industrial Development in São Paulo State, Brazil," *Economic Geography*, XI (July 1935), 258–66. The startling view that Paulista entrepreneurs actually "hindered industrial growth" is advanced in Warren Kempton Dean, *São Paulo's Industrial Elite, 1890–1960* (Ph.D. dissertation, University of Florida, 1964, Univ. Microfilms, Ann Arbor, Mich.). There is a wealth of data in Octávio A. Dias Carneiro, *Past Trends of Structural Relationships in the Economic Evolution of Brazil, 1920–1965* (Center for International Affairs, Harvard University, Cambridge, Mass., 1966).

75. Seabra Fagundes, "O poder econômico da União e as suas repercussões sôbre a autonomia política dos Estados," *Revista Brasileira de Estudos Políticos*, No. 5 (Jan. 1959), 30–55. Wythe, *Brazil: An Expanding Economy*, 135.

76. Humberto Bastos, *A Conquista Siderúrgica no Brasil* (São Paulo, 1959).

77. Frederic William Ganzert, "Industry, Commerce, and Finance" and "Wartime Economic Conditions" in Lawrence F. Hill, ed., *Brazil* (Berkeley, 1947), 254–322.

78. An account of the diplomatic history is J. Lloyd Mecham, *A Survey of United States-Latin American Relations* (Boston, 1965), 139–40, 450–53. The chief of the American Technical Mission, Morris Llewellyn Cooke, published his account in *Brazil on the March: A Study in International Cooperation* (New York, 1944). For an account that views skeptically the extent to which the Roosevelt administration's economic aid to Brazil represented a significant break with traditional U.S. policies, see Lloyd C. Gardner, *Economic Aspects of New Deal Diplomacy* (Madison, Wis., 1964), 129–32; 212–213.

79. Vargas, *Nova Política*, v. X, 1968; 300. The lateness of Vargas' commitment to industrialization is stressed in Dean, *São Paulo's Industrial Elite*, 130–32.

80. Arguments in support of economic nationalism came from both the right and the left. For an Integralista (and outspokenly anti-Semitic) attack on foreign bankers, see Gustavo Barroso, *Brasil: Colonia de Banqueiros: História dos Emprestimos de 1824 a 1934*, 6th ed. (Rio de Janeiro, 1937). For an interesting analysis of this period by a leading Marxist historian in Brazil, see Nelson Werneck Sodré, *História da Burguesia Brasileira* (Rio de Janeiro, 1964), 290–324. Scholarly studies of the history of economic nationalism in Brazil are, not surprisingly, almost nonexistent. For a stimulating treatment of this subject for the 1930's, see John D. Wirth, *Brazilian Economic Nationalism: Trade and Steel Under Vargas*. Barbosa Lima Sobrinho, *Desde Quando Somos Nacionalistas?* (Rio de Janeiro, 1963), is a polemical pamphlet written to prove that Brazilians have been struggling against economic "imperialism" since the colonial era.

81. The nationalization of foreign-owned enterprises in certain key sectors such as mineral resources and railways was first introduced after the Revolution of 1930. The legal basis during the Estado Nôvo was article 144 of the Constitution of 1937, which provided for "the progressive nationalization of mines, mineral deposits and waterfalls and other sources of power, as well as the industries considered as basic or essential to the economic and military defense of the Nation." Loewenstein, *Brazil Under Vargas*, 208; Wythe, *Brazil: An Expanding Economy*, 189, 306–7. The Constitution of 1934 had contained a similar, although milder provision, whose inclusion could be traced to the influence of Juarez Távora. Even before the Revolution of 1930, the Constitution of the Old Republic had been amended in 1926 to include a provision (Article 72, Paragraph 17) prohibiting foreigners from acquiring mines "necessary for national security and

defense." This amendment resulted in part from the long political controversy over the Itabira Iron concession in Minas Gerais, acquired in 1920 by the colorful but tactless American investor Percival Farquhar. President Arthur Bernardes (1922–26) became an irreconcilable opponent of the Itabira concession and pressed for its cancellation. The origins of later domestic political conflict over issues of economic nationalism can be seen in the arguments put forward during the Itabira controversy. Bernardes' "Jacobinism" was attacked by Assis Chateaubriand, a Brazilian lawyer whose legal fees from foreign investors such as Farquhar helped make possible the founding of what soon became a huge publising empire. Assis Chateaubriand, *Terra Deshumana: A Vocação Revolucionária do Presidente Arthur Bernardes* (Rio de Janeiro, n.d.). The case for Bernardes is presented in Paulo Amora, *Bernardes: O Estadista de Minas na República* (São Paulo, 1964), 201–16. For a useful but eccentric study of Farquhar, see Charles A. Gauld, *The Last Titan: Percival Farquhar, American Entrepreneur in Latin America* (Stanford, 1964). After the last concession of Farquhar was canceled in 1942, a state enterprise, the Companhia do Vale do Rio Doce, was founded to exploit the mining areas of the Itabira concession.

82. Beginning in 1943, a series of national conferences was organized and promoted by government-endorsed advocates of industrialization and economic planning. The *Primeiro Congresso Brasileiro de Economia* was held in 1943, and was succeeded in 1944 by the *Primeiro Congresso Brasileiro de Indústria* and then in 1945 by the *Primeira Conferência das Classes Produtoras*. The latter two conferences both issued statements calling for a vigorous state role in promoting economic growth. Humberto Bastos, *O Pensamento Industrial no Brasil* (São Paulo, 1952). Roberto Simonsen was the leader of the advocates of industrialization and was instrumental in organizing the first two conferences and drafting proposals for them. His career as a successful industrialist, economic historian, and publicist was central to all industrialization efforts in Brazil after the early 1920's. A starting point for the study of his career is the chapter by Heitor Ferreira Lima on Simonsen in *Homens de São Paulo* (São Paulo, 1955). An indispensable bibliographical guide is Annibal Freire da Fonseca, *Filinto de Almeida e Roberto Simonsen: Notas biliográficas* (Rio de Janeiro, 1952). The obvious parallel between Simonsen and the 19th century pioneer of industrialization, Mauá, has been developed in Heitor Ferreira Lima, *Mauá e Roberto Simonsen: Dois pioneiros do desenvolvimento* (São Paulo, 1963). Simonsen,

in *A indústria em face da economia nacional* (São Paulo, 1937), made a plea for industrialization as the only way for Brazil to avoid poverty.

83. In 1945, however, there was a bitter exchange between the arch-industrializationist, Roberto Simonsen, and Eugênio Gudin, a leading spokesman for economic liberalism. Gudin had tried to discredit the idea of planning and cast serious doubt on Brazil's potential for industrialization in a report to a recently created National Planning Commission: Eugênio Gudin, *Rumos de Política Econômica* (Rio de Janeiro, 1945). Simonsen replied two months later, charging angrily that Gudin had distorted the views (and even the basic concepts, such as "National Income") of his opponents: Roberto Simonsen, *O Planejamento da Economia Brasileira* (São Paulo, 1945). There is much analysis of the controversies over industrialization in Octavio Ianni, *Estado e Capitalismo: Estrutura Social e Industrialização no Brasil* (Rio de Janeiro, 1965).

Chapter II

1. Generals Dutra and Góes Monteiro first began to discuss the inevitability of "reconstitutionalization" with Vargas and the civilian politicians in late 1944. Coutinho, *O General Góes Depõe*, 395–409. Caó, *Dutra*, 215–16.
2. Vargas, *Nova Política*, v. X, 178.
3. *New York Times,* April 16, 1944.
4. Virgílio A. de Mello Franco, *A campanha da U.D.N.: (1944–1945)* (Rio de Janeiro, 1946), 103–11. This volume includes a valuable collection of documents on the last year of the Estado Nôvo.
5. *Ibid.,* 133.
6. José Américo de Almeida, *1945* (Rio de Janeiro, 1945), 13–35.
7. Caó, *Dutra*, 225–26.
8. Mello Franco, *A campanha da U.D.N.,* 243–49.
9. Prestes, *Problemas Atuais,* 77–94.
10. Alexander, *Communism in Latin America,* 116–19.
11. Later Vargas blandly explained (to Góes Monteiro) that Berle had read the speech to him beforehand in such "badly masticated Portuguese" that he couldn't remember if it was the same version as the speech Berle subsequently delivered. Coutinho, *O General Góes Depõe,* 430–32.
12. The decree was drafted by Justice Minister Agamemnon Magalhães,

whose Asian physiognomy led Chateaubriand to label the decree the "Malayan Law" (*Lei Malaia*). The text of the decree and the UDN's response is in Mello Franco, *A campanha da U.D.N.*, 288–307. For an "anti-imperialist" account of the struggle over the decree, see Osny Duarte Pereira, *Que é a Constituição?: Crítica à Carta de 1946 com Vistas a Reformas de Base* (Rio de Janeiro, 1964), 21–24. There is a very useful analysis of the Brazilian political scene as of August 1945 in Olive Holmes, "Brazil: Rising Power in the Americas," *Foreign Policy Reports*, XXI, No. 15 (Oct. 15, 1945), 209–19.

13. Mello Franco, *A campanha da U.D.N.*, 345–48.

14. On October 15 Getúlio urged all workers to join the PTB. Since the PTB was a hotbed of *queremismo*, Vargas was in effect endorsing the movement to keep him in the presidential palace. Caó, *Dutra*, 233.

15. Benjamin Vargas was bragging to his friends that he would soon be police chief. Rumor also had it that he had already ordered three hundred extra mattresses to accommodate the "conspiring" generals whom he would soon arrest. Vargas' private secretary, Luiz Vergara, who knew Benjamin well, found the rumor credible. Vergara, *Fui Secretário de Getúlio Vargas*, 175–76.

16. Góes Monteiro gave a detailed account of the events of October 29 in Coutinho, *O General Góes Depõe*, 440–67. Vargas' secretary gave his version in Vergara, *Fui Secretário de Getúlio Vargas*, 173–89. For a popularized anti-getulista account, see Hernane Tavares de Sá, *The Brazilians: People of Tomorrow* (New York, 1947), 209–17.

17. Mello Franco, *A campanha da U.D.N.*, 375–76; 383.

18. The reminder came right after Vargas' election to the presidency in October 1950. In an ironical speech on October 27, 1950, in which he derided the opportunism of Vargas' former opponents, Góes Monteiro said he knew in October 1945 that Vargas could have won an election even then because "the people were on his side" despite "all his errors and faults." *Diário do Congresso Nacional*, October 1950, 7229–36.

19. The political consequences of this contrast led one observer to see two distinct systems in Brazil: the "politics of backwardness" and the "politics of development." Gláucio Ary Dillon Soares, "The Political Sociology of Uneven Development in Brazil," in Irving Louis Horowitz, ed., *Revolution in Brazil: Politics and Society in a Developing Nation* (New York, 1964), 164–95. The best-known analysis of the "lags" within modern Brazilian society is Lambert, *Os dois Brasís*. This book was subjected to a blistering review by Caio Prado Júnior in *Revista Brasiliense*, 26 (Nov.-Dec. 1959), 213–16. Lambert's analy-

sis is probably the best-known and most widely discussed version of the "dualistic" interpretation of modern Brazil. For a Brazilian sociologist's critique of this kind of interpretation, see Ianni, *Estado e Capitalismo*, 73–82.

20. There is as yet no study which surveys the history of Brazilian political parties since the Second World War. A useful starting point as background is Afonso Arinos de Melo Franco, *História e Teoria do Partido Político*. Octavio Ianni, Paulo Singer, Gabriel Cohn, and Francisco C. Weffort, *Política e revolução social no Brasil* (Rio de Janeiro, 1965) is a collection of interpretive essays. There is a brief survey of the party system, with emphasis on its functioning in the early 1960's in Bela C. Maday, et al., *U. S. Army Area Handbook for Brazil* (Washington, D. C., 1964), 312–28. The most detailed analysis is to be found in an unpublished doctoral dissertation: Phyllis Peterson, *Brazilian Political Parties: Formation, Organization, Leadership, 1945–1959* (Ph.D. dissertation, University of Michigan, 1962). See also the same author's chapter on Brazil in Martin C. Needler, ed., *Political Systems of Latin America* (Princeton, N. J., 1964), 463–510. An indispensable source, which includes analysis of the presidential elections, is *Brazil: Election Factbook*, No. 2 (Washington, D. C., 1965), edited by Charles Daugherty, James Rowe, and Ronald Schneider, and published by the Institute for the Comparative Study of Political Systems. It covers the elections from 1945 through 1962. For an interesting analysis of post-war Brazilian politics—seen from the perspective of the post-Goulart era—see James W. Rowe, "The 'Revolution' and the 'System': Notes on Brazilian Politics," *American Universities Field Staff Reports Service,* East Coast South America Series, XII, Nos. 3 & 4 (Brazil).

21. Orlando M. Carvalho, "Os Partidos Políticos em Minas Gerais," *Revista Brasileira de Estudos Políticos*, No. 2 (July 1957), 104. Afonso Arinos de Melo Franco, *História e Teoria do Partido Político*, 101. Vargas, *Política Trabalhista*, 112.

22. Góes Monteiro was an alternate member of the first national PSD Directorate. He was subsequently elected a PSD senator from Alagóas. His career illustrates the problems for any historian who accepts uncritically the widely held view of the Brazilian higher military as "non-political." Coutinho, *O General Góes Depõe*, 423.

23. Vargas, *A Política Trabalhista*, 112.

24. The principal source on the origins of the UDN is Mello Franco, *A campanha da U.D.N.* One of the "melancholy generation" that lived through the Estado Nôvo while rejecting its authoritarianism was

Aliomar Baleeiro, who was to become a leader of the UDN. In 1943 he gave a speech in Bahia attacking the heirs of Oliveira Vianna (which included many members of his generation, explained Baleeiro) for their lack of faith in Brazil's democratic potential. Aliomar Baleeiro, *A Política e a Mocidade: Ensaios,* 2nd ed. (Bahia, 1957), 151–73. For the angry anti-getulismo of a long-time liberal constitutionalist, see Paulo Duarte, *Prisão, Exílio, Luta* (Rio de Janeiro, 1946). Duarte had been a journalist with *O Estado de São Paulo* since 1916. He was forced into exile in 1938, returning to Brazil after the end of the Estado Nôvo in 1945. For a campaign biography of Gomes, see Gastão Pereira da Silva, *Brigadeiro Eduardo Gomes* (Rio de Janeiro, 1945). His campaign speeches may be found in Major Brigadeiro Eduardo Gomes, *Campanha de libertação* (São Paulo, 1946).

25. Armando de Salles Oliveira, *Diagrama de uma Situação Política: Manifestos Políticos do Exílio* (São Paulo, 1945), 108–11.

26. *Ibid.,* 147.

27. The middle-class character of the Army as of 1945 is stressed in M. Seabra Fagundes, "As Forças Armadas na Constituição," *Revista Militar Brasileira,* XLVIII, Nos. 3–4 (July-Dec. 1948), 333–77. Considering its importance in modern Brazilian history, the Army has been relatively unstudied. The most valuable starting point is the two chapters on Brazil in John J. Johnson, *The Military and Society in Latin America* (Stanford, 1964), which includes a very useful bibliography. For a stimulating survey by an extreme nationalist officer, see Nelson Werneck Sodré, *Historia Militar do Brasil* (Rio de Janeiro, 1965).

28. Mello Franco, *A campanha da U.D.N.,* 405–10.

29. *Ibid.,* 349.

30. Holmes, "Brazil: Rising Power."

31. Gomes, *Campanha da Libertação,* 42–46; Mello Franco, *A Campanha da U.D.N.,* 322; Herbert V. Levy, *O Brasil e os novos tempos: Considerações sôbre o problema de reestruturação política, econômica e social do Brasil* (São Paulo, 1946), 23.

32. Prestes, *Problemas Atuais,* 84, 92.

33. Poppino, *International Communism in Latin America,* 77; and Poppino, "Communism in Postwar Brazil" (unpublished paper presented to the American Historical Association, December 1962, mimeo); Alexander, *Communism in Latin America,* 114–21. Fiúza soon became the hapless target for the first of many sensational journalistic campaigns by the vitriolic ex-Communist, Carlos Lacerda. In late November Lacerda ripped into Fiúza, accusing him of scandals during his administration of DNER (the federal road construction authority). Carlos Lacerda, *O Rato Fiúza* (Rio de Janeiro, 1946).

34. The UDN in mid-1945 encompassed three principal positions. The right wing was represented by such figures as Herbert Levy, a Paulista. In the center were such figures as Octávio Mangabeira, while the left (which called itself the *Esquerda Democrática* and soon broke away), led by Hermes Lima and Domingos Vellasco, backed Gomes for President but ran independently in the congressional elections. For the views of Domingos Vellasco, who had been a leading Integralista in the 1930's, see his *Rumos Políticos* (Rio de Janeiro, 1946).

35. Coutinho, *O General Góes Depõe*, 425-26.

36. Vargas, *Política Trabalhista*, 15-16; Caó, *Dutra*.

37. *Brazil: Election Factbook;* Peterson, *Brazilian Political Parties.* For an analysis of the elections of 1945 by a former member of the PCB, see Basbaum, *História sincera*, III, 199-210.

38. For a useful biographical guide to the members of the Constituent Assembly of 1946, see Gastão Pereira da Silva, *Constituintes de 46: Dados biográficos* (Rio de Janeiro, 1947). The composition of the Assembly was notable for its relative youth and the predominance of the professions, especially law and medicine. One of the leading members of the commission that drafted the new Constitution was Raul Fernandes. Antônio Gontijo de Carvalho, *Raul Fernandes: um Servidor do Brasil* (Rio de Janeiro, 1956), 309-13. For a leftist critique of the "reconstitutionalization" of 1945-46, which includes interesting detail from the debates of the Constituent Assembly, see Osny Duarte Pereira, *Que é a Constituição?*

39. For an analysis of the constitutional structure and electoral system as it was reorganized in 1945-46, see: Themistocles Cavalcanti, Carlos Medeiros Silva, and Victor Nunes Leal, *Cinco estudos* (Rio de Janeiro, 1955); Barbosa Lima Sobrinho, ed., *Sistemas eleitorais e partidos políticos* (Rio de Janeiro, 1956); Raul Machado Horta, ed., *Perspectivas do federalismo brasileiro* (Belo Horizonte, 1958); Leal, *História das instituições políticas*, 575-99; Lucas, *Conteúdo social nas constituições*, 77-82. The economic provisions of the Constitution of 1946, like the Constitution of 1934, combined so many "contradictory ideological tendencies" that they were soon known as the "goulash" amendments. Themistocles Brandão Cavalcanti, *Manual da Constituição* (Rio de Janeiro, 1960), 13. Cavalcanti was the member of the drafting commission in charge of the section on the "Economic and Social Order."

40. Examples of the appeals may be found in the presidential *Mensagem Apresentada ao Congresso Nacional* (Rio de Janeiro, 1948), 5; and the *Mensagem* for 1949, 373. In the latter, Dutra asked for "serenity" and "reconciliation" because "the Nation is tired of sterile quarrels

and demagoguery as an end in itself." Excerpts from Dutra's speeches as President have been collected in José Teixeira de Oliveira, ed., *O Governo Dutra* (Rio de Janeiro, 1956).

41. UDN leader Juracy Magalhães argued unsuccessfully that in order to save Brazilian democracy, "democrats of all parties" ought to unite "for the conscientious and careful continuation of sound finance and the preservation of the widest public freedom." Magalhães, *Minha Vida Pública*, 187.

42. Vargas, *Política Trabalhista*, 58, 68.

43. Osny Duarte Pereira, *Que é a Constituição?*, 45-51.

44. Poppino, *Communism in Latin America*, 77.

45. The prosecutor's briefs and a collection of contemporary press opinion (only pro-suppression views are represented) on the suppression of the Communist Party may be found in Alceu Barbedo, *O fechamento do Partido Comunista do Brasil* (Rio de Janeiro, 1947).

46. Wythe, *Brazil: An Expanding Economy*, 239-40; Jover Telles, *O Movimento Sindical no Brasil* (Rio de Janeiro, 1962), 40-41. The latter is a collection of articles published in the Communist newspaper, *Novos Rumos*. The Dutra government at first announced that it would hold elections to replace the deposed union leaders, but later explained that this had proved "inconvenient" in the "abnormal situation" because the Congress was about to reorganize the entire union structure. General Eurico Gaspar Dutra, *Mensagem Apresentada ao Congresso Nacional* (Rio de Janeiro, 1949), 165. The legislation never materialized.

47. Vargas, *Política Trabalhista*, 183.

48. Azis Simão, "O Voto Operário em São Paulo," *Revista Brasileira de Estudos Políticos*, No. 1 (Dec. 1956), 130-41.

49. The concept of "populism" has come to be used frequently in analyses of post-World War II politics in Latin America. It appears often, for example, in the collection of articles edited by Claudio Veliz, *Obstacles to Change in Latin America* (London, 1965). In the chapter on "Populism and Reform in Latin America," Torcuato di Tella has trouble, however, fitting the Brazilian case into his schema for Latin America. There are no Brazilian examples in either of his tables (57; 73), and the discussion of Brazil (59-60) is distorted by a preoccupation with parties rather than leaders. The leading student of populism in Brazil is Francisco Weffort. See his "Estado y masa en el Brasil," in *Revista Latinoamericana de Sociología*, I (No. 1, March 1965), 53-71; "Política de masas," in Octavio Ianni, *Política e revolução social*, 161-98; and "Raízes Sociais do Populismo em São Paulo,"

Revista Civilização Brasileira, I, No. 2 (May 1965), 39–60. The latter is a comparative analysis of the electoral followers of Adhemar de Barros and Jânio Quadros in the São Paulo gubernatorial election of 1962. For other analyses of postwar Brazilian politics that stress populism, see Luciano Martins, "Aspectos Políticos da Revolução Brasileira," in the same issue of *Revista Civilização Brasileira* with Weffort's article; and Juarez R. B. Lopes, "Some Basic Developments in Brazilian Politics and Society," in Eric N. Baklanoff, ed., *New Perspectives of Brazil* (Nashville, Tenn., 1966), 59–77. Charles Morazé, in *Les trois ages du Brésil,* draws an interesting parallel between *coronelismo* and populism. What he ignores is the fact that coronelismo rests on a manipulable political system whose results are predictable. Populism, on the other hand, presupposes an open political system with less predictable results.

50. Clovis Leite Ribeiro, "A Classe Média e as Eleições de 19 de janeiro," *Digesto Econômico,* III, No. 29 (April 1947), 71–77. One of the first analyses of the political style of Adhemar and its significance for the Brazilian political system was Hélio Jaguaribe's "Que é o Adhemarismo?" *Cadernos do Nosso Tempo,* 2 (Jan.-June 1954), 139–49.

51. Adhemar's free-spending campaign tactics and corrupt administration made him a bête noire of the moralists among the traditional Paulista political elite. For an example of their ire, see F. Rodrigues Alves Filho, *Um homem ameaça o Brasil: A história secreta e espantosa da "caixinha" de Adhemar de Barros* (São Paulo, 1954). Adhemar was defended in a long-winded (and no doubt subsidized) book by Lopes Rodrigues, *Adhemar de Barros perante a nação* (São Paulo, 1954), who adopted the straightforward tactic of arguing that "in Brazil there are only two alternatives for a politician: either he does nothing and is thought honest or he does something and is thought a thief," 305.

52. For a collection of violently anti-getulista newspaper articles written in 1945–47, see David Nasser, *Para Dutra Ler na Cama* (Rio de Janeiro, 1947). Nasser chafed at the continued influence of the Vargas "system." For a study that found only political opportunism and financial scandal during the Dutra era, see Milcíades M. Mourão, *Dutra: História de um governo* (Rio de Janeiro, 1955).

53. In this and subsequent discussions of postwar Brazilian economic history, I have drawn heavily upon "Fifteen Years of Economic Policy in Brazil," *Economic Bulletin for Latin America,* IX, No. 2 (Dec. 1964), 153–214; "The Growth and Decline of Import Substitution in Brazil," *Economic Bulletin for Latin America,* IX, No. 1 (March 1964), 1–59; Werner Baer, *Industrialization and Economic Develop-*

ment in Brazil (Homewood, Ill., 1965); Dorival Teixeira Vieira, *O Desenvolvimento Econômico do Brasil e a Inflação* (São Paulo, 1962); and Pedro C. M. Teichert, *Revolución Económica e Industrialización en América Latina*, 2nd ed. (Mexico, D. F., 1963), 201–30. For the Dutra period valuable accounts are Romulo de Almeida, "Experiência Brasileira de Planejamento, Orientação e Contrôle da Economia," *Estudos Econômicos*, I, No. 2 (June 1950), 6–115; and Wythe, *Brazil: An Expanding Economy*, 333–49.

54. Ministério da Fazenda, *Relatório: 1946* (Rio de Janeiro, 1948), 9, 156, 172.

55. Baer, *Industrialization and Economic Development*, 45–48; Furtado, *Economic Growth*, 239–40.

56. The Dutra regime as a whole was not overtly anti-industrialization; on the contrary, the President reported proudly on his government's efforts at regional development, which were intended to make certain that "Brazil possesses, on a continuously functioning basis, indispensable basic industries." *Mensagem* (1948), 117. The point here is that the government gave no evidence that it understood the connection between measures such as exchange controls and the process of industrialization.

57. Almeida, "Experiência Brasileira," 33–34; Furtado, *Economic Growth*, 240–41; "Fifteen Years of Economic Policy," 155–57; *The Development of Brazil: Report of the Joint Brazil-United States Economic Development Commission* (Washington, D. C., 1954), 5. Dutra's presidential message for 1949 noted that it had been a "constant preoccupation of the government, while fighting inflation, not to contribute to any economic decline that might cause unemployment. For this reason it avoided deflation and did not reduce the money supply." *Mensagem* (1949), 187. A similar attitude, conditioned by the political impossibility of pursuing a genuinely deflationary policy, has characterized virtually every Brazilian government since the war.

58. The plan's name derived from the first letters of the Portuguese words designating the principal areas of expenditure: *Saúde* (Health), *Alimentação* (Food), *Transportação* (Transportation), *Energia* (Energy).

59. Baer, *Industrialization and Economic Development*, 61–63.

60. Almeida, "Experiência Brasileira," 41–42. Details on the origins of regional planning in Brazil may be found in Albert Hirschman, *Journeys Toward Progress* (New York, 1963), 13–58. The development authority for the Northeast (*Superintendência do Desenvolvimento do Nordeste* or SUDENE) was not organized until 1959. See a brief account of central planning in Brazil since the Second World War in

Robert T. Daland, "La planificación central como un instrumento de desarrollo: Problemas de aplicación en el Brasil," *Anales de Facultad Latinoamericana de Ciencias Sociales,* I, No. 1 (Jan.-Dec. 1964), 169–186.

61. *Report of the Joint Brazil-United States Technical Commission* (Washington, D. C., 1949), iii, 12, 35–36.

62. "Relatório Abbink," *Estudos Econômicos,* I, No. 1 (March 1950), 175–91. Two of the economists responsible for this critique were Ewaldo Correia Lima and Rômulo de Almeida, who were later to become important government planners. They had been on one of the sub-commissions that prepared technical studies in connection with the Abbink Report. See also Almeida, "Experiência Brasileira," 77. Octávio Gouveia de Bulhões, *Á Margem de um Relatório* (Rio de Janeiro, 1950). Bulhões stressed the central role to be played by private enterprise ("no less strong in Brazil than it is in the United States") rather than government: "Why, then, should the establishment of financial relations between the two countries be entrusted to government channels, if, at this time, private individuals on both sides are better qualified for this purpose than government leaders?" Bulhões, "Inflation and Industrialization: A Brazilian Viewpoint," in *Four Papers Presented in the Institute for Brazilian Studies, Vanderbilt University* (Nashville, 1951), 55. Bulhões lagged behind opinion in both Brazil and the United States, as the events of the Vargas era (1951–54) were soon to make clear. It was the viewpoint of the younger planners that on balance prevailed.

63. Vargas, *Política Trabalhista,* 61, 69–115.

64. *Ibid.,* 58, 165.

65. *Ibid.,* 68.

66. Vargas' closest collaborators in building the PTB in Rio Grande do Sul were José Loureiro da Silva and Alberto Pasqualini. A. Fay de Azevedo, "Balanco das eleições de 58 no Rio Grande do Sul," *Revista Brasileira de Estudos Políticos,* No. 8 (April 1960), 274–75. A few years later Pasqualini explained his political philosophy to a reporter: "I am not a man of the left or the right. I am certainly not a socialist. I just think the bourgeoisie should give a little. There is a lot of selfishness among the rich. It seems to me the bourgeois are growing steadily blinder and deafer." Nertan Macedo, *Aspectos do Congresso Brasileiro* (Rio de Janeiro, 1957), 159.

67. Coutinho, *O General Góes Depõe,* 494–500.

68. When Gustavo Capanema, a PSD chieftain in Minas Gerais, was campaigning for Machado he would often confess to his audience: "Well,

you're right, Getúlio really is the best of the three [presidential candidates]." Macedo, *Aspectos do Congresso*, 135–36.
69. Gomes, *Campanha de Libertação*, 351. Gomes' remarks on the minimum wage were made in the concluding speech of the 1950 campaign. *O Estado de São Paulo*, October 1, 1950.
70. Coutinho, *O General Góes Depõe*, 500.
71. Getúlio Vargas, *A Campanha Presidencial* (Rio de Janeiro, 1951), 379, 634, 217–18.
72. *Ibid.*, 362. In 1947 Vargas attacked Silveira Filho when the latter was president of the Bank of Brazil: "The public was convinced that it had elected General Dutra President of the Republic. But the man directing the country is the President of the Bank of Brazil, imposing a program whose only objective is to increase the value of money." Vargas, *Política Trabalhista*, 268.
73. Vargas, *Política Trabalhista*, 58; *Campanha Presidencial*, 511.
74. *Ibid.*, 101.
75. There is an interesting study of the campaign tactics of the three major candidates in Morazé, *Les Trois Ages*, 153–77. One of the best contemporary analyses is Clarence H. Haring, "Vargas Returns in Brazil," *Foreign Affairs*, XXIX, No. 2 (January 1951), 308–14.

Chapter III

1. Vargas complained at the time that Adhemar was asking for much bigger payment for his support in the election campaign. Coutinho, *O General Góes Depõe*, 512.
2. The urban-rural trend in Brazil was illustrated by the fact that between 1940 and 1950 the rural population increased by only 17.4 percent while the population of urban areas grew 41.5 percent and that of suburban areas 58.3 percent. Thomas Pompeu Accioly Borges, "Relationships between Economic Development, Industrialization and the Growth of Urban Population in Brazil," in Philip M. Hauser, ed., *Urbanization in Latin America* (New York, 1961), 155. For an interesting (if perhaps overschematized) analysis of Brazilian social structure and its implications for politics in the early 1950's, see the article by Hélio Jaguaribe, "A Crise Brasileira," in *Cadernos do Nosso Tempo*, No. 1 (Oct.-Dec. 1953), 120–60. For a general analysis of post-1945 Brazilian class structure, see L. A. Costa Pinto, "As Classes Sociais no Brasil," *Revista Brasileira de Ciências Sociais*, III, No. 1 (March 1963), 217–47; and Charles Wagley, "The Brazilian Revolu-

tion: Social Changes Since 1930," in Lyman Bryson, ed., *Social Change in Latin America Today* (New York, 1960).

3. Many industrial workers in Brazil retain mental attitudes conditioned by the patriarchal atmosphere of the rural sector from which they have migrated. This "lag" tends to make them less militant and less inclined to collective action than workers who have grown up in urbanized industrial communities. This point is emphasized in Juarez Rubens Brandão Lopes, "O Ajustamento do trabalhador à indústria: mobilidade social e motivação," [a study of workers in a São Paulo factory] in Bertram Hutchinson, ed., *Mobilidade e Trabalho* (Rio de Janeiro, 1960); and Lopes' more recent *Sociedade Industrial no Brasil* (São Paulo, 1964). See also the articles by Lopes, Alain Touraine, Azis Simão, and Fernando Henrique Cardoso in *Sociologie du Travail*, III, No. 4 (Oct.-Dec. 1961).

4. John J. Johnson prefers the term "middle sectors" to "middle class" in his *Political Change in Latin America* (Stanford, 1958), which includes a chapter on Brazil. See also L. C. Bresser Pereira, "The Rise of the Middle Class and Middle Management in Brazil," *Journal of Inter-American Studies*, IV, No. 3 (July 1962), 313–26; Thales de Azevedo, *Social Change in Brazil* [University of Florida Latin American Monograph Series: No. 25] (Gainesville, 1963), 46–56.

5. For a brief analysis of the political attitude of the Brazilian middle class in the early 1960's, see Charles Wagley, "The Dilemma of the Latin American Middle Classes," *Proceedings of the Academy of Political Science*, XXVII, No. 4 (May 1964), 2–10. Claudio de Araujo Lima, *Imperialismo e Angústia: Ensaio sôbre as Bases de uma Sócio-psiquiatria da classe média brasileira na era imperialista* (Rio de Janeiro, 1960) does not deliver what its provocative subtitle promises.

6. Details on postwar government coffee policy may be found in Delfim Netto, *O Problema do Café;* Marek Skowrónski, *La Politique Brésilienne du Café Après la Deuxième Guerre Mondiale* (Rio de Janeiro, 1961); and Salvio Pacheco de Almeida Prado, *Dez Anos na Política do Café, 1945–1955* (São Paulo, 1956).

7. The initial economic policies of the Vargas government were sketched out in the presidential message presented to Congress in March 1951, reprinted in Getúlio Vargas, *O Govêrno Trabalhista do Brasil* (Rio de Janeiro, 1952), I, 161 ff. The study of the Economic Commission for Latin America was published under the title *Recent Developments and Trends in the Brazilian Economy* (Mexico City, 1951, mimeo) [E/CN 12/217/Add 2], 24.

8. The history of industrial growth in São Paulo, and especially the his-

tory of individual enterprises and entrepreneurs, is largely unwritten. A pioneering effort is Warren Dean, "The Planter as Entrepreneur: The Case of São Paulo," *Hispanic American Historical Review*, XLVI, No. 2 (May 1966), 138–152, which draws on research done for the same author's doctoral dissertation, *São Paulo's Industrial Elite*. Dean stresses the extent to which the native-born Paulista entrepreneurs failed to foim a new class as compared to the planter class from which so many of them had come and with which they remained identified. For other sources on economic development in São Paulo, see Chapter I, footnote 74.

9. There is a discussion of these formulae, labeled somewhat differently, in Ianni, *Estado e Capitalismo*, 215–56; and in Hélio Jaguaribe, *Desenvolvimento Econômico e Desenvolvimento Político* (Rio de Janeiro, 1962), 184–213.

10. Eugênio Gudin has written widely, contributing to *O Globo* and the publications of commercial associations. For a sample of his views, see Eugênio Gudin, *Análise de Problemas Brasileiros: Coletânea de Artigos, 1958–1964* (Rio de Janeiro, 1965). Gudin was bolstered in his neo-liberal doctrines by the periodic visits to Brazil of like-minded economists from the United States such as Gottfried Habeler and Jacob Viner. Another Brazilian economist with less doctrinaire neo-liberal views was Octavio Gouvêa de Bulhões. The ablest younger economist associated with this position was Roberto Campos, who had hardly begun his professional career in Brazil in 1951 and was later to prove far too eclectic and pragmatic to be pigeonholed.

11. The developmentalist-nationalist position is often referred to as the "structuralist" school, although that phrase immediately calls to mind the technical debate over the causes of inflation. Certainly the advocates of what came to be called "developmentalist nationalism" were more interested in growth than price stability and were willing to tolerate a higher level of inflation (which they considered inevitable in a developing economy) than the neo-liberals. Among the most influential spokesmen for this viewpoint were the young economist-administrators who were in 1951 to make up Vargas' Economic Advisory Staff (*Assessoria Econômica da Presidência da República*), such as Rômulo de Almeida. Perhaps the leading writer of this position was Celso Furtado in such works as *A Economia Brasileira* (Rio de Janeiro, 1954) and *Uma Economia Dependente* (Rio de Janeiro, 1956).

12. One study group of young intellectuals was known as the "Itatiaia group," for the national park near Rio de Janeiro where they held

their meetings. It was first organized in 1952, and by 1953 was publishing a journal, *Cadernos do Nosso Tempo* (five issues appeared between 1953 and 1956), with systematic analyses of the political, economic, social, and cultural problems of Brazil. This group, led by writer-social scientists such as Hélio Jaguaribe, Guerreiro Ramos, and Ewaldo Correia e Lima, was the nucleus from which grew the later Higher Institute of Brazilian Studies (*Instituto Superior de Estudos Brasileiros*, more commonly known by its initials of ISEB). For an analysis of this group, see Frank Bonilla, "A National Ideology for Development: Brazil," in K. H. Silvert, ed., *Expectant Peoples: Nationalism and Development* (New York, 1963), 232–64.

13. The spokesmen for radical nationalism were much less well organized in 1950 than they were to become by the later 1950's. In 1955 the *Revista Brasiliense* began publication and became a principal forum for radical nationalism. Its publisher, Caio Prado Júnior, was a Marxist, and a number of the contributors were present or former members of the Communist Party, although the journal was independent of any party line. For an editorial explaining the views of the founders, see the first issue (Sept.-Oct. 1955), 1–3. Another influential writer of the radical nationalist position was Nelson Werneck Sodré. For an example of this position at the outset of the new Vargas era, see Moacyr Paixão, "Capitais estrangeiros dominam a economia nacional," *Digesto Econômico*, VI, No. 70 (Sept. 1950), 29–35.

14. Hélio Jaguaribe has distinguished two principal formulae: "cosmopolitanism" and "nationalism," the former attributing to foreign capital "the largest possible participation" and assigning to it "the major share of responsibility and initiative in the growth and increased productivity of the national economy." The "nationalist" camp, on the other hand, believes that "Brazilian development must be sustained by national capital, however scarce," as part of "the operation of the Brazilian economy by Brazilians, at the service of the Brazilian national interest." The "cosmopolitan" group is further divided into "liberal" and "developmentalist" wings, and the "nationalist" group into "socializing" and "developmentalist" wings. These positions and their chief representatives are described in Jaguaribe, *Desenvolvimento Econômico*, 201–10. A rich source for articles expressing the viewpoints of all positions is the journal *Digesto Econômico*, especially for the late 1940's and early 1950's, before the appearance of the more specialized publications representing each position. In the pages of this monthly journal, edited by Antonio Gontijo de Carvalho and sponsored by the Commercial Association of São Paulo and the Fed-

eration of Commerce of the State of São Paulo, could be found contributions from such diverse figures as Eugênio Gudin, Hélio Jaguaribe, and Nelson Werneck Sodré.

15. For the views of an UDN leader who looked askance on state intervention in the economy (quoting with approval Hayek's *Road to Serfdom*), see Herbert Victor Levy, *Problemas Básicos da Nação: Economia, Finanças, Política Nacional e Internacional* (São Paulo, 1950). An UDN politician who expressed more doubts over the adequacy of neo-liberal doctrines was Aliomar Baleeiro, *A Política*, esp. 53-54, 62-63, and 223. For the views of a well-known journalist of liberal constitutionalist views who had decided by 1950 that democratic socialism was the answer for Brazil, see Paulo Duarte, "Justiça Social, por que Preço?" *Anhembi*, I, No. 1 (Dec. 1950), 3-27. One UDN leader who lamented his party's failure to overcome its excessively legalistic bias was Afonso Arinos de Melo Franco, *A Escalada: Memórias* (Rio de Janeiro, 1965), 49-50.

16. The best introduction to the problems of Brazil's economic development as of 1953 is probably *The Development of Brazil: Report of the Joint Brazil-United States Economic Development Commission*, published in 1954. For the following analysis I have drawn also on the *Economic Survey of Latin America* for 1951-52 (New York, 1954) and 1953 (New York, 1954), published by the Economic Commission for Latin America. The statistics are from the tables in Baer, *Industrialization and Economic Development*.

17. In early 1951 Vargas pointed to the creation of this commission as proof of the good relations that Brazil enjoyed with the United States. Vargas, *Govêrno Trabalhista*, I, 55.

18. *The Development of Brazil*, vi.

19. Banco Nacional do Desenvolvimento Econômico, *Exposição Sôbre o Programa de Reaparelhamento Econômico: Exercício de 1955* (Rio de Janeiro, n.d.), 1. For details on the history and operation of the BNDE, see Cleantho de Paiva Leite, "Brazilian Development: One Problem and Two Banks," *Inter-American Economic Affairs*, XIV, No. 1, (Summer 1960), 3-24.

20. *The Development of Brazil*, vi.

21. Vargas, *Govêrno Trabalhista*, I, 252.

22. Baer, *Industrialization and Economic Development*, 51-55. The exchange system is explained in Alexandre Kafka, "The Brazilian Exchange Auction System," *Review of Economics and Statistics*, XXXVIII, No. 3 (Aug. 1956), 308-22.

23. A collection of Vargas' speeches on the oil question has been pub-

lished in Getúlio Vargas, *A política nacionalista do petróleo no Brasil* (Rio de Janeiro, 1964). There is, to my knowledge, no study of the long political controversy that led up to the creation of Petrobrás. For radical nationalist accounts, see Werneck Sodré, *História Militar,* and Almir Matos, *Em Agôsto Getúlio Ficou Só* (Rio de Janeiro, 1963).

24. The speech is reprinted in Vargas, *Govêrno Trabalhista,* II, 65–79.

25. The figures on profit remittances are from *A Remessa de Lucros: Um Problema Nacional* [Pareceres do Deputado Daniel Faraco e do Senador Mem de Sá] (Rio de Janeiro, 1963), 17, which are based on the figures of SUMOC. Vargas later claimed that the balance of foreign capital movements for the years 1939–53 was a net outflow of $800 million: *Mensagem ao Congresso Nacional* (Rio de Janeiro, 1954), 92.

26. An excerpt from this speech is printed in Afonso César, *Política, Cifrão e Sangue,* 3rd ed. (Rio de Janeiro, 1956), 113–14.

27. *O Estado de São Paulo,* November 30, 1950.

28. For an interesting estimate of the significance of the elections of 1950 in the perspective of modern Brazilian history, see Roland Corbisier, "Reflexões sôbre o momento político," *Digesto Econômico,* VI, No. 72 (Nov. 1950), 5–24. See also the analysis in "Jornal de 30 Dias," *Anhembi,* I, No. 1 (Dec. 1950), 125–39.

29. The UDN efforts were the subject of many news stories in *O Estado de São Paulo* in late October and throughout November. See, for example, the issues for November 4, 7, and 9, 1950.

30. *Ibid.,* November 18, 1950.

31. *Ibid.,* November 19 and 22, 1950.

32. I have drawn heavily here upon the analysis in *Cadernos do Nosso Tempo,* No. 1 (Oct.-Dec. 1953), 90–98.

33. Werneck Sodré, *História Militar,* 304–55, gives much information on the political battles within the officer corps during the first three years of the Vargas presidency. The author was a leading member of the radical nationalist camp.

34. Coutinho, *O General Góes Depõe,* 496.

35. Robert J. Alexander, "Brazil's CP: A Case Study in Latin American Communism," *Problems of Communism,* IV, No. 5 (Sept.-Oct. 1955), 17–26.

36. *O Estado de São Paulo,* November 24, December 8, 13, 16, 1950.

37. One leading opponent of the nationalists, General Canrobert Pereira da Costa, had a straightforward explanation: "The hand of the Communists is in every corner and we must cut it off. I am in favor of the government's taking drastic measures against the Communist in-

filtration so that we can get back to working in peace." *O Estado de São Paulo*, March 26, 1952.

38. The conflict within the military was widely reported in the Brazilian press. *O Estado de São Paulo*, for example, gave details on the charges and counter-charges, while taking an editorial position in support of the "anti-communist" group. The text of the speeches given by Estillac Leal and Santo Cardoso on the occasion of the latter's assuming the war ministry are printed in *O Estado de São Paulo*, March 28, 1952.

39. The incumbent president was General Horta Barbosa, a "nationalist" who had been elected to the Directorate of the Club in 1950 at the same time that Estillac Leal was elected president. The latter resigned the presidency in 1951, being succeeded by Horta Barbosa. For a list of the officers of the Military Club up to 1962, see Gerardo Mojella Bijos, *O Clube Militar e Seus Presidentes* (Rio de Janeiro, n.d.).

40. Werneck Sodré, *História Militar*, 327–28. The "Democratic Crusade" had accused the nationalists of "trying to push the [Military] Club into serving interests of groups or ideas [*correntes*] alien to the social order." *O Estado de São Paulo*, March 12, 1952. When accepting the honorary presidency of the "Democratic Crusade" in April, Eduardo Gomes explained that "as nationalists we shall not compromise with any foreign influences incompatible with the self-respect and honor of our citizens who are anxious to direct their own destinies, nor shall we compromise with those who wish to destroy the established legal order and our Christian way of life. . . ." *Ibid.*, April 20, 1952.

41. Estillac Leal had called for a "sound nationalism, not sterile Jacobinism." His objective was "active vigilance in defense of national sovereignty." *O Estado de São Paulo*, March 8, 1952. During the election campaign he challenged his opponents to define their views on economic policy, charging that ambiguities in this area would "only play into the hands of the international trusts and their agents, who are interested in dividing the Nation in order to facilitate their appropriation of its riches." *Ibid.*, April 15, 1952.

42. In March and April, 1952, *O Estado de São Paulo* reported many arrests and raids on "Communist" and "subversive" cells. On March 29, for example, it reported the arrest (by DOPS, the political police) of several printing shop operators in Rio de Janeiro, as well as arrests in Salvador, Pôrto Alegre, and Pelotas.

43. I am indebted here to the analysis in *Cadernos do Nosso Tempo* No. 2 (Jan.-June 1954), 103–20.

44. Amora, *Bernardes*, 201–19.

45. This point is emphasized in the article analyzing moralism and middle-class alienation in *Cadernos do Nosso Tempo*, No. 2 (Jan.-June 1954), 150–59; and in Plínio de Abreu Ramos, *Brasil, 11 de Novembro* (São Paulo, 1960), 108.

46. Vargas explained the basis for the December 1951 wage increase, and at the same time attacked the Dutra government for having frozen the minimum at the same level that "I assured the workers more than eight years ago," while their life had become "constantly more difficult and expensive." Vargas, *Govêrno Trabalhista*, II, 57–62. Details on wage levels—in both money and real terms—may be found in Baer, *Industrialization and Economic Development*, 119–25; and Oliver Onody, *A Inflação Brasileira, 1820–1958* (Rio de Janeiro, 1960), 255–74.

47. Early in his presidency Vargas had repeatedly called upon the workers (whom he always addressed in the intimate second-person form) to show patience. In his Christmas Eve speech in 1951, for example, he urged: "You don't need strikes or appeals to extreme methods; don't let yourselves be moved by agitators and those who disrupt order and entice you with ideologies that conceal ambitions of a very different kind." He repeated his appeal on May 1, 1952 for cooperation with the government's "systematic and coherent plan of economic reconstruction, which is designed to increase our wealth for the benefit of all social classes." Vargas, *Govêrno Trabalhista*, II, 60, 460–62.

48. Secondary sources on union activities in the early 1950's are difficult to come by. For a Communist account, see Telles, *O Movimento Sindical*, 44–77.

49. For a laudatory biography by a fellow Riograndense, see Limeira Tejo, *Jango: Debate sôbre a crise dos nossos tempos* (Rio de Janeiro, 1957).

50. In his annual message to Congress for 1953, Vargas outlined the rationale for his change in political strategy that was to come several months later: "Brazil today has an economy on the way to furnishing its population with a level of consumption comparable to the developed countries. In order to reach this objective in the near future, however, it will be necessary to overcome insufficiencies and remove obstacles, in order to achieve an accelerated and directed transformation by means of deliberate government action, based on a consensus [*assentimento*] of national opinion. The building of this consensus, on democratic foundations, is precisely the political problem of our day and its solution requires a commitment by the representative forces of the country to the objective of overcoming national underdevelop-

ment." Vargas, *Mensagem ao Congresso Nacional* (Rio de Janeiro, 1953), 11. An interesting analysis of the political forces as they appeared at the outset of the last year of the Vargas presidency may be found in Michèle Langrod, "Les forces politiques au Brésil," *Révue Française de Science Politique*, III, No. 3 (Sept. 1953), 511–532.

51. There is a very useful analysis of this trend and the Brazilian government's response in *The Brazilian Balance of Payments* (London, 1956), a pamphlet published by The Bank of London & South America Ltd.

52. *Economic Survey of Latin America: 1953* (New York, 1954), 15–16, 79–82, 183–86, 211–12. Lafer's speech is reprinted in *O Estado de São Paulo*, June 19, 1953.

53. Augusto de Bulhões, *Ministros da Fazenda do Brasil, 1808–1954* (Rio de Janeiro, 1955), 223. Aranha, Vargas' faithful lieutenant of many battles in the past (although Aranha had quarreled bitterly with Vargas during the war), had not lost his enthusiastic faith in Brazil. After describing the "temporary" financial troubles, he predicted that "Brazil will be one of the great leaders by the end of this century and will make contributions to the new human order that will not be surpassed by any other peoples, even those who today appear more advanced and powerful." *O Estado de São Paulo*, June 19, 1953.

54. Not to be confused with the unsuccessful "Aranha Plan" to refinance the foreign debt in the early 1930's.

55. Some of the ideas behind the plan were explained in Aranha's replies to questionnaires on the stabilization effort sent to him by Deputies Raimundo Padilha and Bilac Pinto: *Exposição Geral do Ministro Oswaldo Aranha Perante a Câmara dos Deputados* (Oct. 1, 1953, mimeo.).

56. One close presidential adviser who channeled the ideas of the radical nationalists to Vargas was Lourival Fontes. Brazilian reaction to the termination of the Joint Commission is reported in *The New York Times*, July 19, 23, 29, 1953; and a retrospective story on May 9, 1955. American irritation with Vargas' nationalist moves is reflected in the account by a former American member of the Joint Commission: Thomas W. Palmer, Jr., *Search for a Latin American Policy* (Gainesville, 1957), 197–98.

57. Hélio Damante, "O Movimento de 22 de Março de 1953 em São Paulo," *Revista Brasileira de Estudos Políticos*, 18 (Jan. 1965), 105–112. The election is also analyzed in Oliveiros S. Ferreira, "Comportamento Eleitoral em São Paulo," *Revista Brasileira de Estudos*

Políticos, 8 (April 1960), 162–228. Jânio's working-class following is examined in Simão, "O Voto Operário em São Paulo." Information on Jânio's earlier political career may be found in Castilho Cabral, *Tempos de Jânio e outros tempos* (Rio de Janeiro, 1962), 47–141.

58. Carvalho, "Os Partidos Políticos em Minas Gerais."

59. In a book written in 1947, Afonso Arinos de Melo Franco, a leading figure in the UDN, was already lamenting Brazil's failure to develop a more responsible and representative party system. Significantly, however, he seemed most worried about the lack of a "more consistent socialist movement" which might have prevented "the tradition of the working-class movement from being, as it is, Communist in character." *História e Teoria do Partido Político,* 112, 144–45. A visiting American economist observed that "On the whole it is probably correct to say that those political groups in Brazil which are most firmly attached to the *political* tenets of the Western liberal tradition, that is, those groups which cherish civil liberties and the political prerogatives of the individual, tend to be skeptical of a more active role of the government in the economic sphere. Those groups, on the other hand, whose arsenal of economic policies contains more than the traditional devices of old-time liberal action or inaction, tend to be 'interventionists' also in the political sphere. In other words, there does not seem to exist a 'progressive' party which would combine an active program in the realm of economics with the restraint observed by old-time liberals in the political sphere." Henry William Spiegel, "Brazil: The State and Economic Growth," in Simon Kuznets, Wilbert E. Moore, and Joseph J. Spengler, eds., *Economic Growth: Brazil, India, Japan* (Durham, N. C., 1955), 413.

60. *Cadernos do Nosso Tempo,* No. 2 (Jan.-June 1954), 104–5.

61. Any attempt to describe coherent positions within the officer corps is bound to ascribe greater consistency and homogeneity to the supposed groups than in fact existed. Nonetheless, such rough categories are indispensable until further research clarifies the spectrum of officer opinion.

62. César, *Política, Cifrão e Sangue,* 117–20.

63. The Joint U.S.-Brazilian Commission had noted in 1953 that the ability to control inflation "was weakened by the lack of an effective, independent and nonpolitical body entrusted with the supervision of the banking system and the coordination of monetary and credit policies." *The Development of Brazil,* 42.

64. In October 1953 Aranha, known to be an opponent of Goulart's generous inclinations on minimum wage levels, had explained that

"these readjustments, whether for civil servants, clerks, or workers, are results and not causes of inflation, unless they are set above the level and share attributed to these sectors in the redistribution of national income." Aranha, *Exposição Geral*, 22–23. *O Estado de São Paulo,* certainly no friend of Goulart, expressed the editorial view that the minimum wage adjustment should "correspond to the increase in the cost of living between the end of 1951 [the date of the last adjustment] and the present." *O Estado de São Paulo,* February 24, 1954.

65. *O Estado de São Paulo,* June 19, 1953.

66. In 1952 there had appeared a "Brazilian Anti-Communist Crusade" that claimed some 600,000 members. *Ibid.,* March 29, 1952. By 1954 there was a "Popular Alliance Against Theft and a Coup" led by Carlos Lacerda and Adaúto Cardoso. *Ibid.,* July 9, 1954.

67. For examples of the attacks on Goulart as the "alter ego" of Vargas and the "chief of Brazilian Peronism," see *ibid.,* January 14, 21, February 16, 1954.

68. Information on the origins of the congressional investigation may be found in Nelson de Souza Sampaio, *Do Inquérito Parlamentar* (Rio de Janeiro, 1964), 109–44.

69. The Higher War College (*Escola Superior de Guerra*), founded in 1949 under the leadership of General Cordeiro de Farias, was a principal meeting ground for members of the military and civilian elites. The college ran a one-year course attended by senior military officers, higher bureaucrats, and leading figures from the civilian political sector. In his address to the graduating class in 1953, Juarez Távora called for greater "planning, and, above all, effective coordination of public programs and, insofar as democratically possible, private activities in the economic sphere." At the same time, however, he warned against the "surreptitious and disloyal propaganda, systematic and persistent, that tries to agitate and divide the democratic nations of the western bloc, and to alienate the mass from the elite." Equally pernicious, he charged, was the Communist attempt to "belittle the cooperation which can be given us by foreign initiative, technology and capital in order to accelerate our economic and social development." Juarez Távora, "Escola Superior de Guerra," *A Defesa Nacional,* XLI, No. 475 (Feb. 1954), 111–20. In his address to the first graduating class in December 1950, General Cordeiro de Farias made anti-communism a keynote, denouncing the "communist infiltration" that disguises itself as "ultra-nationalist" and the "defender of the weak." There could be no avoiding the choice between "a Com-

munist hemisphere and a Christian hemisphere" because the world was moving toward "a painful and, as it appears, unfortunately inevitable . . . clash of two worlds which cannot coexist because they are conflicting and incompatible." *O Estado de São Paulo*, December 23, 1950.

70. *O Estado de São Paulo*, January 27, 1954. The memorandum is reprinted, along with the complete list of signatories, in Oliveiros S. Ferreira, *As Fôrças Armadas e o Desafio da Revolução* (Rio de Janeiro, 1964), 122–29. Ferreira's book is an important source on the political currents within the officer corps, especially in the early 1960's.

71. For an analysis of the salary grievances, see General Miguel de Castro Ayres, "O Memorial dos Coronéis," *A Defesa Nacional*, XLI, No. 478 (May 1954), 113–15. Undoubtedly anti-getulista opinion was even stronger within the Air Force and the Navy, whose officers were known to be more conservative in their political views than the Army.

72. An interview with Vargas in *O Globo* reprinted in *O Estado de São Paulo*, February 23, 1954.

73. *Ibid.*

74. *Ibid.*, January 12, February 2, 1954.

75. *Ibid.*, February 23, 1954.

76. Getúlio Vargas, *Mensagem ao Congresso Nacional* (Rio de Janeiro, 1954), 79 ff.

77. *O Estado de São Paulo*, February 27, 1954.

78. The interview is reprinted in João Neves da Fontoura, *Depoimentos de um Ex-Ministro* (Rio de Janeiro, 1957). For an analysis of the political implications of the interview, see *Cadernos do Nosso Tempo*, No. 2 (Jan.-June 1954), 83–100. It is worth remembering that João Neves had been a leading opponent of Getúlio in the early 1930's, when he joined the "Constitutionalist Revolution" in São Paulo.

79. Macedo, *Aspectos do Congresso*, 149.

80. *Correio da Manhã*, May 4, 1954.

81. *Ibid.*

82. Vergara, *Fui Secretário*, 246–48.

83. Morton Baratz, "The Crisis in Brazil," *Social Research*, XII, No. 3 (Autumn 1955), 347–61.

84. Matos, *Em Agôsto Getúlio Ficou Só*, 47–48. Monthly figures (by quantity and value) for coffee exports to the U.S.A. in 1953 and 1954 are given in *Conjuntura Econômica* (International edition), II, No. 1 (Jan. 1955), 2.

85. The following account of Vargas' fall is based upon John V. D.

Saunders, "A Revolution of Agreement Among Friends: The End of the Vargas Era," *Hispanic American Historical Review*, XLIV, No. 2 (May 1964), 197–213, which draws upon the extensive personal testimonials published in the contemporary press. One of the most dramatic personal testimonials is José Américo de Almeida, *Ocasos de Sangue* (Rio de Janeiro, 1954). Also useful for information and documentation are F. Zenha Machado, *Os últimos dias do governo de Vargas* (Rio de Janeiro, 1955), and César, *Política, Cifrão e Sangue*. For the later version of the radical nationalist student movement see Matos, *Em agôsto Getúlio Ficou Só*. One of the most penetrating analyses of Vargas' fall is "O golpe de Agosto," *Cadernos do Nosso Tempo*, No. 3, (Jan.-Mar., 1955), 1–22. For the accounts of two American scholars, see Baratz, "The Crisis in Brazil," and Alan K. Manchester, "Brazil in Transition," *South Atlantic Quarterly*, LIV, No. 2 (April 1955), 167–76. There is a dramatic reconstruction of Vargas' last day in Araken Távora, *O Dia em que Vargas Morreu* (Rio de Janeiro, 1966).

86. An idiosyncratically edited collection of documents on the assassination attempt is Hugo Baldessarini, *Cronica de uma época: Getúlio Vargas e o crime de Toneleros* (São Paulo, 1957).

87. Cited in Saunders, "A Revolution of Agreement," 204; and Baldessarini, *Getúlio Vargas e o Crime*, 221.

88. César, *Política, Cifrão e Sangue*, 163–64.

89. The speech is reprinted in Machado, *Os Ultimos Dias*, 157–61. The forthcoming memoirs of João Café Filho will be an important source on the August crisis. See the interview in *Visão*, July 15, 1966, 22–25.

90. Machado, *Os Ultimos Dias*, 81–82.

91. The manifesto is reprinted in Bento Munhoz da Rocha Netto, *Radiografia de Novembro*, 2nd ed. (Rio de Janeiro, 1961), 118–19.

92. Saunders, "A Revolution of Agreement," 209.

93. The text of the suicide letter, as released to the press, is reprinted in César, *Política, Cifrão e Sangue*, 219–20. The slightly garbled English translation, published in the *New York Times* of August 25, 1954, is reprinted in E. Bradford Burns, ed., *A Documentary History of Brazil* (New York, 1966), 368–70. The authenticity of the testament-letter is upheld in John W. F. Dulles, "Farewell Messages of Getúlio Vargas," *Hispanic American Historical Review*, XLIV, No. 4 (Nov. 1964), 551–53; and by Lourival Fontes in Glauco Carneiro, "A Face Final de Vargas," *O Cruzeiro*, May 15, 1965.

Chapter IV

1. *Keesing's Contemporary Archives*, p. 13774.
2. General Lott, the War Minister, assigned officers and troops to more than 200 locations in 19 states to assure the freedom of "electoral publicity" and to "guarantee the free exercise of the vote and the honest counting of the ballots." The War Minister later congratulated his men for the "impeccable manner" in which they fulfilled their assignment. Lott's statement was published in the *Diário Official* of December 13, 1954, and reprinted in *A Defesa Nacional*, XLII, No. 487 (Feb. 1955), 113.
3. The election results are analyzed in *Cadernos do Nosso Tempo*, No. 3 (Jan.-March, 1955), 31–48. For the effect of Vargas' suicide on the election, including Goulart's defeat in Rio Grande do Sul, see Baratz, "The Crisis in Brazil," 360; Tejo, *Jango*, 142. Vargas' suicide and the conspicuously indecisive congressional elections only two months later led to a number of calls for constitutional and electoral reform. See, for example, Hermes Lima, *Lições da Crise*, 2nd ed. (Rio de Janeiro, 1955); and Ruy Bloem, *A Crise da Democracia e a Reforma Eleitoral* (São Paulo, 1955). Bloem argued for a tightening of the requirements for the voting franchise, along with an increase in party discipline. Orlando Carvalho called for a profound reform of the "centrist parties," such as the UDN, PSD, and PR. "Os Partidos Políticos em Minas Gerais." There are interesting portraits of a number of congressmen and senators who retired or were defeated in 1954, such as Marcondes Filho, in Macedo, *Aspectos do Congresso*.
4. For a stimulating analysis of the preelection maneuvering in 1955, see the article in *Cadernos do Nosso Tempo*, No. 4 (April-Aug. 1955), 1–23.
5. *Tribuna da Imprensa*, February 18, March 31, 1955. F. Rodrigues Alves Filho, *Democracia Corrompida ou Golpe de Estado?* (São Paulo, 1955), 50, 56.
6. *O Estado de São Paulo*, August 2, 1955.
7. *Ibid.*, August 6, 1955.
8. *Ibid.*, September 3, 1955.
9. Kubitschek's ideas on economic policy were summarized in a volume privately circulated during the campaign and published immediately after his election: Juscelino Kubitschek de Oliveira, *Diretrizes Gerais do Plano Nacional de Desenvolvimento* (Belo Horizonte, 1955).
10. Admiral Pena Boto was the president of a "Brazilian Anti-Communist Crusade" that regularly published newspaper advertisements, such

as one that warned: "It cannot be possible that the very men who humiliated and dragged down this country should return to power by means of dishonest elections." *O Estado de São Paulo,* September 6, 1955.

11. Munhoz da Rocha, *Radiografia de Novembro,* 160–61; *O Estado de São Paulo,* September 6, 1955.

12. Tribunal Superior Eleitoral, *Dados Estatísticos:* Eleições Federais Estaduais e Municipais, v. III, pt. 2 (Rio de Janeiro, n.d.).

13. *Tribuna da Imprensa,* October 5, 1955. In August 1955 the Brazilian Communist Party had endorsed Kubitschek and Goulart.

14. *O Estado de São Paulo,* October 26, 1955.

15. Lott's views were expressed in a statement to the Congress by Deputy Armando Falcão on October 7. *Jornal do Comercio,* October 8, 1955.

16. The interview was published by *O Globo* on October 29, 1955 (the tenth anniversary of Vargas' fall in 1945), and reprinted in *O Estado de São Paulo* on October 30.

17. General Canrobert Pereira da Costa had been War Minister during the Dutra presidency and a former chief of the general staff of the armed forces. He was an aggressive anti-Communist and had been a leading member of the "Democratic Crusade" that supported General Etchegoyen's successful campaign for president of the Military Club in 1952 against the "Nationalist Crusade" of Generals Estillac Leal and Horta Barbosa. At the time of his death General Canrobert was president of the Military Club, a position to which he was elected in 1954 as successor to General Etchegoyen. Canrobert had been a leading conspirator against Vargas in August 1954 and in August 1955 he denounced the political elite for what he saw as their failure to provide "stability."

18. The speech is reprinted in Ferreira, *As Forças Armadas e o Desafio da Revolução,* 130–33.

19. Details on the Mamede case are in Munhoz da Rocha, *Radiografia de Novembro,* 71–80.

20. The text of the military ministers' memorandum is in *ibid.,* 132–33.

21. Lott had grown embarrassed over the delay on the Mamede case, which was rapidly becoming a *cause célèbre* in the press, and on November 5 the war ministry issued a statement denying the claim in Lacerda's *Tribuna da Imprensa* that Café Filho had already refused Lott's request for Mamede's transfer. The statement is reprinted in José Loureiro Júnior, *O Golpe de Novembro* (Rio de Janeiro, 1957), 238–39.

22. This account is drawn principally from Munhoz da Rocha, who par-

ticipated in the cabinet meeting. *Radiografia de Novembro,* 75–80.
Carlos Luz later gave his account, which stressed the unwillingness
of the command of the *Escola Superior de Guerra* to release Mamede:
Carlos Luz, *Em Defesa da Constituição* (Rio de Janeiro, 1956).

23. This position, for which the well-known sociologist Gilberto Freyre
was also an apologist, is described in Munhoz da Rocha, *Radiografia,*
29–30, 58–70.

24. UDN Congressman Aliomar Baleeiro once again, as in 1950, presented
detailed legal arguments purporting to prove that the Constitution
required an absolute majority of votes in presidential elections. The
UDN maneuvers after the election in October were extensively reported in the columns of *O Estado de São Paulo.*

25. Afonso Arinos and some other UDN congressmen thought that the
introduction of a parliamentary system might be a compromise solution allowing Kubitschek to assume the presidency. *Ibid.,* October 28,
1955. Of course this would have greatly reduced the new President's
power, which is precisely what the UDN sought to accomplish. Back
in March 1955 Otávio Mangabeira, expressing his despair over the
inability to find a "non-partisan" unity candidate for the presidential
campaign, confessed in a congressional speech: "Imagine, Mr. President [of the Chamber of Deputies], the distress and sadness with
which a soldier of democracy—and that is the title I prize most in
my public life—begins to assume a position that can in any way
appear anti-democratic. But if I am doing so, or if I should do so, it
will be precisely out of a love for our liberties." Otávio Mangabeira,
A Situação Nacional: Três Discursos (Rio de Janeiro, 1956), 31.

26. *Tribuna da Imprensa,* November 4, 9, 1955.

27. *Ibid.,* October 24, 1955.

28. An example of the pro-legality viewpoint among the military was a
lecture, with the indicative title "Let Us Be Optimistic in Analyzing
the National Situation," delivered in the Naval College in August
1955. The speaker, a naval captain, argued that by her history Brazil
had already demonstrated "an authentic, noble, and instinctive talent
for democracy." Election campaigns always produce "confusion and
unrest" but this is "natural and part of the democratic system," he
explained. Those "idealists" who "call for emergency governments
as the only way out of the drama perplexing us . . . forget that
History has shown us the terrible sequence of calamities unleashed
by the destruction of the constitutional order." Corruption? "In any
single nation the corrupt and the morally afflicted are evenly distributed through all social classes." Against corruption "the popular

vote" is the "only morally acceptable weapon." This optimistic captain left no doubt about the firmness of his views: "What would be the solution for the problem created by the 'allegation' that there existed a corruption so unlimited that it had shaken the very structure of the state? We would answer that the worst government is better than the best revolution." Francisco de Souza Maia Júnior, "Sejamos Otimistas na Análise da Conjuntura Nacional," *A Defesa Nacional,* LXIII, No. 497 (Dec. 1955), 61–65.

29. The "legalist" group was led by General Zenóbio da Costa, who had previously spoken out repeatedly in favor of Vargas' inauguration during the UDN's campaign to nullify the presidential election result in 1950. He had also served as Getúlio's last War Minister, when he proved unable to stem the tide of anti-Vargas opinion among the higher military during the crisis of August 1954. Lott had dismissed Zenóbio from his post as inspector general of the Army on October 18, 1955, because Zenóbio had once again begun speaking out in favor of the inauguration of the elected candidates, Kubitschek and Goulart, thereby violating Lott's repeated injunctions against officers taking *any* public political positions. Another officer pushing Lott toward the preventive coup on the night of November 10 was General Odílio Denys, commander of the Army garrison in Rio de Janeiro.

30. The Air Minister, Eduardo Gomes, had fled to São Paulo, where he hoped to make preparations so that Carlos Luz and his loyalist ministers could continue as the "legitimate" government. São Paulo Governor Jânio Quadros proved uncooperative, however. The officer in command of the "Tamandaré" during her abortive flight was Vice Admiral Pena Botto, Commander in Chief of the Fleet and also president of the Brazilian Anti-Communist Crusade. Other passengers on board included Colonel Mamede and Navy Captain Sílvio Heck. A list of the important passengers is in Munhoz da Rocha, *Radiografia,* 115–16.

31. *Keesing's Contemporary Archives,* p. 14530.

32. In Munhoz da Rocha's *Radiografia* a vigorous defense is made of Café Filho's devotion to legality but a similar defense of Carlos Luz does not emerge. Munhoz da Rocha joined the flight on the "Tamandaré."

33. The debate in the Chamber of Deputies on November 11 is reprinted in Loureiro Júnior, *O Golpe de Novembro,* 241–317.

34. See, for example, the speeches on November 11 and 14 by Afonso Arinos de Melo Franco reprinted in the pamphlet, *Episódios de História Contemporânea: Dois Discursos do Sr. Afonso Arinos* (Rio de Janeiro, 1956).

35. On November 14 the three military ministers—Antônio Alves Câmara (Navy), Vasco Alves Seco (Air), and Henrique Lott (War)—sent the President (Nereu Ramos) a memorandum requesting a state of siege. The coup of November 11 ("the movement to return to existing constitutional methods") had been necessary, they explained, "principally in order to prevent the imminent carrying out of the subversion of the constitutional order, insultingly preached by bad Brazilians in Congress, in the press, over radio and television, and made possible by the connivance of certain military chiefs and high officials in the Executive branch." They accused Acting President Carlos Luz of having "within his few hours in office shown himself to be under the influence of those plotting against the government and to be an efficient instrument in the service of their subversion. The President was by his deliberate acts, which undermined discipline, aggravating the existing crisis [Mamede case]; at the same time he was trying to staff the higher posts in military administration with those who would open the doors to the movement destructive of legality and thus he provoked the lightning manifesto [*pronunciamento fulminante*] by which the Armed Forces were able, once again, thanks to God, to preserve public order and the representative system from a coup d'etat that was being unleashed from the top down and lacked support among the people or the troops, serving only the purposes of personal ambition and political revenge." The ministers of Navy and Air who signed this memorandum were appointed by Nereu Ramos after the coup of November 11, thereby replacing Amorim do Valle and Eduardo Gomes, who had remained loyal to Carlos Luz. The memorandum is reprinted in Loureiro Júnior, *O Golpe de Novembro*, 319–22.

36. Luz's speech, with details on the cruise of the "Tamandaré," was published in Carlos Luz, *Em Defesa da Constituição*.

37. The following analysis has drawn heavily upon ECLA's *Economic Survey of Latin America* for 1954 and 1955; *The Brazilian Balance of Payments* published by the Bank of London and South America; and José Maria Whitaker, *Seis Mêses, de Nôvo, no Ministério da Fazenda* (Rio de Janeiro, 1956). Statistics are from Baer, *Industrialization and Economic Development*.

38. Augusto de Bulhões, *Ministros da Fazenda*, 230–33.

39. As head of the Brazilian Commission that participated in the preparation of the "Abbink Report" in 1948, Bulhões had been a target for the criticism of the younger Brazilian economists who were later known as "structuralists."

40. Gudin defended his policies in a speech given in mid-April, when

his successor assumed office. The speech is reprinted in Whitaker, *Seis Meses*. Gudin defended his anti-inflationary credit policies in "Nota Sôbre as Apreciações da CEPAL," *Carta Mensal do Conselho Técnico da Confederação Nacional do Comércio,* II, No. 9 (September 1956), 287–95.

41. Whitaker gave a detailed defense of his policies, especially the proposed abolition of the "exchange confiscation" for coffee, in his *Seis Mêses*.

42. Lincoln Gordon and Engelbert L. Grommers, *United States Manufacturing Investment in Brazil: The Impact of Brazilian Government Politics 1946–1960* (Boston, 1962), 19 ff. SUMOC Instruction #113 subsequently became the focus of a bitter debate between "nationalists" and those who favored incentives for foreign investment in Brazil. There is a study of Brazilian businessmen's attitude toward foreign private investment, and especially the effects of SUMOC Instruction #113 in Raimar Richers, *et al., Impacto da Ação do Govêrno Sôbre as Empresas Brasileiras* (Rio de Janeiro, 1963), 105–121. Eugênio Gudin often defended Instruction #113, as in "A Reforma Cambial," *Carta Mensal do Conselho Técnico da Confederação Nacional do Comércio,* II, No. 7 (July 1956), 219–28. As a visiting American writer noted in 1955, "there is no consensus in Brazil on the desirability of private foreign investment. In this situation the only certainty for importers of long-term capital is the uncertainty of governmental policy." Baratz, "The Crisis in Brazil," 361.

Chapter V

1. A very useful source on the official activities of the presidency during the Kubitschek era is the *Síntese Cronológica* published by the Presidência da República for the years 1956, 1957, 1958, and 1959 (Rio de Janeiro, 1959–60). It includes a day-by-day summary of speeches and official acts issuing from the presidential palace.

2. Francisco Medaglia, *Juscelino Kubitschek, President of Brazil: The Life of a Self-Made Man* (n.p., 1959). As the subtitle would indicate, this short biography was published as part of a public relations effort in the United States.

3. Celso Furtado, *Diagnosis of the Brazilian Crisis* (Berkeley, 1965), 88–90. Detailed analyses of the economic policies of the Kubitschek period may be found in Baer, *Industrialization and Economic De-*

velopment, and the two ECLA-sponsored studies cited earlier: "Fifteen Years of Economic Policy in Brazil" and "The Growth and Decline of Import Substitution in Brazil." There is also a cogent study of economic policy-making in Brazil between 1954 and 1963 in the Economic Commission for Latin America's *Economic Survey of Latin America: 1964* (New York, 1966), 288–309.

4. Kubitschek, *Diretrizes Gerais do Plano Nacional de Desenvolvimento.*

5. One Brazilian observer has compared the use of the "executive groups" during the Kubitschek presidency to the corporatist structure that Vargas created in the later years of the Estado Nôvo. In both cases, the Executive sought new means of entering into direct contact with the entrepreneurial sector in order to "dynamize" it. Ianni, *Estado e Capitalismo,* 233–34.

6. An American consulting firm published a study in 1958 that was very optimistic about "the dynamic new spirit in Brazil." It found that "the fever of industrialization has caught hold in Brazil; it is in industrial production that the greatest gains have been made, and where the great hopes and aspirations for the future reside." William B. Dale, *Brazil: Factors Affecting Foreign Investment* (Stanford Research Institute, Menlo Park, Calif., 1958), 4.

7. *The Economic Development of Brazil: A Study Prepared by the Joint Working Group of the Banco Nacional do Desenvolvimento Econômico and the Economic Commission for Latin America* (New York, 1956). A version of this report was published by the BNDE in 1955 under the title *Esboço de um Programa Preliminar de Desenvolvimento da Economia Brasileira.* Celso Furtado, then working for ECLA, was instrumental in drawing up this report. Brazil's chief source of public financing from abroad was the Export-Import Bank of the United States.

8. Upon assuming the presidency, one of Kubitschek's first acts was to create a Development Council (*Conselho do Desenvolvimento*), directly subordinate to the President. The council was empowered, among other things, to "study methods necessary for the coordination of the country's economic policy, especially as regards its economic development, to draw up plans and programs aimed at increasing the efficiency of government activities, and to stimulate private initiative." *Síntese Cronológica: 1956,* 18. One of the council's most important activities was the sponsorship of the drafting of the Target Program (*Programa de Metas*), which established goals in the fields of energy, transportation, agriculture, basic industries, and education. The pro-

gram is spelled out in Conselho do Desenvolvimento, *Programa de Metas,* 3 vols. (Rio de Janeiro, 1958).

9. On the eve of the Kubitschek presidency an anonymous article in the journal edited by Hélio Jaguaribe, who was a political adviser to the new President, outlined the political problems that any "developmentalist" policy would have to confront: *Cadernos do Nosso Tempo,* No. 5 (Jan.-March 1956), 1–17.

10. Kubitschek's first message to Congress in March 1956 was typical of this approach. He attempted to conciliate the opposition by noting that it included "eminent public figures and enlightened patriots." He even reassured the military officers who had attempted an abortive revolt against the new government in February 1956 that he harbored no "grievances or vendettas of any kind." In the last election campaign he had seen "the irrepressible desire of our people for democratic government." He concluded on a characteristic note: "Let us make this hour a constructive hour. Let us remember, by putting aside our transitory personal interests for the benefit of a common labor of national greatness, the ancient Biblical truth: 'one generation passeth away, and another generation cometh; but the earth abideth forever.' " Juscelino Kubitschek de Oliveira, *Mensagem ao Congresso Nacional* (Rio de Janeiro, 1956), 552–57.

11. For speeches of a nationalist intellectual, explaining the importance of Brasília for Brazil's past and future, see Roland Corbisier, *Brasília e o desenvolvimento nacional* (Rio de Janeiro, 1960). A very different view of the new city, as seen by a *nordestino* migrant, is offered in José Marques da Silva, *Diário de um Candango* (Rio de Janeiro, 1963). *Candango* was the name given the migrants who streamed into the new Federal District to furnish the labor for the overnight construction of the capital. Many of the more traditional circles bitterly criticized the building of Brasília. Opinion in Rio de Janeiro, which stood to lose the economic and cultural benefits it had enjoyed as the capital city, was understandably unenthusiastic. Some critics, such as Eugênio Gudin, argued that the funds consumed in the construction of Brasília could better be used for other forms of public expenditure. What these critics denied was the possibility or value of a change in national mentality that might both be symbolized and further stimulated by moving the capital to an inland pilot city. For an example of the national debate on Brasília, see the letters to the editor in the issues of *Visão* for April, 1959. The Kubitschek regime was gratified by the favorable impression that the construction of Brasília created abroad. The government published four volumes of laudatory com-

ment in *Brasília e a Opinião Mundial* (Rio de Janeiro, 1958–59), as well as a book by André Malraux, *Brasília—La Capitale de l'Espoir* (Rio de Janeiro, 1959).

12. The magazine, sponsored by the *Confederação Nacional da Indústria*, was *Desenvolvimento & Conjuntura*, the first issue of which was dated July 1957. The lead editorial in the first issue ("Bases de uma Política para o Desenvolvimento") spelled out a position favorable to a mixed economy in terms very similar to those being put forward by the Kubitschek government. The same issue included an article analyzing the availability of foreign exchange for industrialization and warning against the "denationalization" of Brazilian industry that might result from the operation of SUMOC Instruction #113. As for the latter question, see the survey of Brazilian businessmen's views, on the whole favorable to foreign participation, in Richers, *et al., Impacto da Ação do Govêrno*, 105–21. On April 6, 1958, the *New York Herald Tribune* published the results of an opinion poll (interviews conducted only in Rio de Janeiro and São Paulo) that showed Brazil to have, of all countries polled, the lowest level of opinion (14 percent) that regarded foreign private investment as "bad" for the country and the highest ratio of favorable to unfavorable attitudes on the role of private foreign investment. Twelve countries were included in the poll, including two in Asia, two in Latin America, seven in Europe, and Canada. Cited in Dale, *Brazil: Factors Affecting Foreign Investment*, 32.

13. For an analysis which cast grave doubt on the Brazilian entrepreneurial elite's potential for independent action in support of industrialization, see Fernando Henrique Cardoso, *Empresário Industrial e Desenvolvimento Econômico* (São Paulo, 1964). On the eve of the Kubitschek presidency Hélio Jaguaribe appealed to Brazilian industrialists to assume a dynamic roll in the impending new phase of industrialization. The lecture was delivered in the "Forum Roberto Simonsen" and published in Hélio Jaguaribe, *O Problema do Desenvolvimento Econômico e a Burguesia Nacional* (São Paulo, 1956).

14. Nonetheless there were bitter criticisms of government coffee policy from the coffee growers, including a protest march (in automobiles!) by coffee growers in October 1958. But the *principle* of extensive purchase of surplus coffee stocks was maintained by the Kubitschek government. The disagreements came over exchange rate policies (coffee growers favoring depreciation so as to increase their cruzeiro earnings) and the continuation of the policy of "exchange confiscation."

15. In his first message to Congress, Kubitschek included a strongly

worded section on agriculture that seemed to presage far-reaching proposals. He noted that industrialization would need "a solid agrarian base" and an "expanding internal market." The rural market was weak, he explained, because of an "inadequate agrarian structure as regards the ownership of land: a disequilibrium between the small number of rural landowners and the large number of those working on land they do not own." Kubitschek, *Mensagem ao Congresso Nacional* (1956), 152. This question was never raised again, however, in any of the subsequent messages to Congress. I am indebted to Márcio Rego Monteiro for this reference.

16. The cost of Brasília became a favorite subject for debate among Kubitschek's opponents. Brasília was never included in the Target Program. There was no accounting rendered for the project, thereby giving rise to the wildest rumors. One of the few sources is "Gastos Públicos em Brasília," *Conjuntura Econômica*, XVI, No. 12 (Dec. 1962). I am indebted for this information to an unpublished manuscript of Mr. Nathaniel Leff on "Economic Policy and Economic Development in Brazil, 1947–1962," which presents a very interesting interpretation of the influence of nationalism and pro-industrialization doctrines among Brazilian policy makers.

17. The best single source on the intellectual rationale for "developmentalism" is Bonilla, "A National Ideology for Development." For an analysis of the Brazilian "developmentalists" and the rethinking of their position that began after the end of the Kubitschek presidency, see Michel Debrun, "Nationalisme et politiques du développement au Brésil," *Sociologie du Travail*, VI, No. 3 (July-Sept. 1964), 235–57, and No. 4 (Oct.-Dec. 1964), 351–80. There is a brief discussion of the ISEB group in Arthur P. Whitaker and David C. Jordan, *Nationalism in Contemporary Latin America* (New York, 1966), 79–88. It is impossible to understand the influence of the "developmentalist" intellectuals unless one realizes that many of their number were also influential in actually shaping government policies after 1951, especially in the sphere of economic policy. Social scientist-administrators such as Celso Furtado, Rômula de Almeida, Ewaldo Corrêa Lima, Roberto Campos, and Hélio Jaguaribe were engaged not only in spelling out a rationale for rapid industrialization, but also in planning and administering important parts of the governmental role in this process. They were a younger generation (primarily in their 30's) combining the roles of an administrative and an intellectual elite. An excellent survey of the views of the group that shaped ISEB thinking at the outset is the collection of lectures delivered at the institute's course

in 1955: *Introdução aos Problemas do Brasil* (Rio de Janeiro, 1956).

18. There is an account of the Air Force revolt in Carneiro, *História das Revoluções Brasileiras*, II, 504–17.

19. The elections for the presidency of the Military Club in May 1956 resulted in the victory of General João de Segadas Viana, identified by one expert on the politics of the military as a "nationalist." Werneck Sodré, *História Militar*, 367. This undoubtedly strengthened the hand of Lott within the higher ranks of the Army officer corps.

20. In a speech in 1953, for example, Juarez Távora endorsed the idea of building a new capital in the interior, which would bring the federal government into contact with the "reality of the Brazilian interior" and thereby "liberate the national activities of the government from the constant and powerful pressure of problems that are much more local than general." Távora, "Escola Superior de Guerra," 113–14. Távora's view is all the more interesting since he was an intransigent anti-getulista and was to be Kubitschek's principal opponent in the presidential election in 1955. General Edmundo de Macedo Soares e Silva, a pioneer in the development of the Volta Redonda steel complex, was a leading example of pro-industrialization opinion among the higher military. In a speech delivered not long before Kubitschek's inauguration, he called upon Brazilians to insure the "conditions" that make possible the "creation of modern industry," such as "a clear understanding by the elites" and "a devotion to the common cause" by "leaders in economic and political life" who "will not oppose their petty interests to those of a national program." "A Indústria Pesada e o Progresso do Brasil," *A Defesa Nacional*, LXIII, No. 498 (Jan. 1956), 85.

21. Goulart's leadership of the PTB was repeatedly challenged during the Kubitschek presidency by party "reformers" such as Congressman Fernando Ferrari. They accused Goulart of failing to give the PTB a new ideological orientation and of merely living off the Vargas legend for short-term electoral gain. See, for example, the report by Tad Szulc in the *New York Times*, March 3, 1957. As for Goulart's connection with the Communists and the basis of Kubitschek's working-class politics, one scholar who has studied carefully the history of the Brazilian labor movement in this period concludes: "In 1956 they [the Communists] dropped their opposition to the 'union tax' since, as an important part of the labor leadership, they were benefiting from it. The PTB allowed the Communists to run some candidates under PTB labels. In return the Communist Party provided disciplined cadres which the PTB sorely needed. Goulart and the PTB controlled

the distribution of government jobs in labor courts and social security institutes. These jobs made it possible for labor leaders to live in the middle class, from which a great many had come. The support of the Communist and PTB labor leaders helped Kubitschek maintain the Vargas alliance between labor, middle class, and industrialists, as well as landowners, to the end of his presidency in 1960." Timothy F. Harding, "Revolution Tomorrow: The Failure of the Left in Brazil," *Studies on the Left,* IV, No. 4 (Fall 1964), 36.

22. There was undoubtedly occasional friction between the President and his Labor Minister over labor policies. In September 1959, for example, the President issued a statement denouncing "a movement organized and directed by known agitators intending to create conditions that would threaten the peace and order of the Brazilian people by calling illegal strikes and similar demonstrations." The next day the President had to issue another statement explaining that his previous remarks had not been meant to pertain to "any parties or political personalities, above all not personally to my loyal friend and sincere ally, Dr. João Goulart." *Síntese Cronológica: 1959,* v. II, 88, 94.

23. Details on the origins of "Operation Pan-America" are provided in Licurgo Costa, *Uma Nova Política para as Américas: Doutrina Kubitschek e OPA* (São Paulo, 1960). The Brazilian government published a series of documents in *Operação Pan-Americana,* 5 vols. (Rio de Janeiro, 1958–59).

24. In his speech proposing the "Alliance for Progress," President Kennedy announced that "our approach itself must be bold—an approach consistent with the majestic conception of Operation Pan America." *New York Times,* March 14, 1961. One American economist later observed: "If any one person can be regarded as the father of the program, it was President Kubitschek, who proposed it in its original form as Operation Pan American." William Withers, *The Economic Crisis in Latin America* (Glencoe, Ill., 1964), 35. It should be noted that the Eisenhower administration had begun to alter its rigid Latin American policy in 1959, laying the groundwork for the more dramatic policy changes of Kennedy.

25. The ECLA-BNDE study of 1956, *The Economic Development of Brazil* (p. 29), warned that the growth rate of "recent past" could "probably not be achieved during the period 1955–1962." In fact, predicted the study, "on the assumption that Brazil will lose, during the next five years, all the improvement in the terms of trade that characterized the previous five years (1949–54), the economy's rate of growth would be even slower." The deterioration did not turn out to

be quite so disastrous. Taking 1953 as a base year (coffee exports worth 100), the dollar price of coffee, Brazil's most important foreign exchange earner, had declined to 61 by 1960, whereas it had been 47 in 1949. This loss in the capacity to earn badly needed foreign exchange came just at the time that Brazil was undertaking the greatest industrialization drive in her history. The Bank of London and South America gauged the future more correctly by suggesting in 1956: "The eventual solution of Brazil's more pressing problems would seem to depend not so much on an increase in export earnings—though this would naturally be welcome—as on priority being given to the development of basic production which, to the extent that it supplied the country's needs, would relieve the import bill of burdensome essentials." *The Brazilian Balance of Payments,* 29. Nonetheless, the critical shortage of foreign exchange eventually caught up with the Kubitschek government. The data are from Baer, *Industrialization and Economic Development.*

26. The entire issue of the *Revista Brasileira de Estudos Políticos,* No. 8 (April 1960) was devoted to an analysis of the 1958 elections. Brizola's election as governor of Rio Grande do Sul marked the emergence of a populist politician to the front rank of leading national political figures. His election technique is analyzed in A. Fay de Azevedo, "Eleições de 58 no Rio Grande do Sul," in *ibid.* Another significant trend in the gubernatorial contests was Cid Sampaio's election as governor of Pernambuco, which represented an unprecedented victory of the urban and coastal voters over the traditionally dominant oligarchy of the interior. The campaign and election is analyzed in Gláucio Veiga, *et al.,* "Geografia eleitoral de Pernambuco," in *ibid.,* 50–85. For a brush-stroke analysis of the 1958 elections, see *Síntese Política Econômica Social,* I, No. 1 (Jan.-March 1959), 53–59.

27. Ministério da Fazenda, *Programa de Estabilização Monetária para o Período de Setembro de 1958 a Dezembro de 1959* (Rio de Janeiro, 1958), 11.

28. *Ibid.,* 1, 7.

29. The figures are from the basic outline of a later stabilization effort: Ministério do Planejamento e Coordenação Econômica, *Programa de Ação Econômica do Govêrno: 1964–1966: Síntese* (Rio de Janeiro, 1964), 29.

30. *Programa de Estabilização Monetária,* 12–13.

31. The following account of the attempt at economic stabilization in 1958–59 is based upon the ECLA *Economic Survey of Latin Amer-*

ica: 1958 (Mexico, 1959); Economist Intelligence Unit, *Three-Monthly Economic Review: Brazil,* No. 28 (December 1958), No. 36 (Nov. 1960); and the monthly news summaries in the *Hispanic American Report.*

32. In early 1959 the Brazilian Communist Party decided to launch a more aggressive attack on the "politics of conciliation" in Brazil. As party leader Luis Carlos Prestes explained in January 1959, "Our entire analysis leads us to the conclusion that during 1958 the world scene witnessed an acceleration in the decline of imperialism, while the socialist camp became stronger as the struggle continued for the national emancipation of the colonial and dependent peoples. These fundamental trends are reflected in Brazil and influence the development of its internal situation, creating more favorable conditions for the struggle against North American imperialism." Luís Carlos Prestes, *A Situação Política e a Luta por um Govêrno Nacionalista e Democrático* (Rio de Janeiro, 1959), 15. On February 28, 1959, there appeared the first issue of a new Communist Party weekly newspaper, *Novos Rumos.* On the front page was a cartoon lampooning Roberto Campos as a stooge of Wall Street.

33. The conflict in Brazil over the costs and purposes of an anti-inflation program came in the midst of a general controversy in Latin America between "monetarists" and "structuralists." These conflicting positions, which had their advocates among academic economists and government policy-makers, are described in Roberto de Oliveira Campos, "Two Views on Inflation in Latin America" and David Felix, "An Alternative View of the 'Monetarist'-'Structuralist' Controversy," in Albert O. Hirschman, ed., *Latin American Issues* (New York, 1961). The Kubitschek government and Brazilian public opinion were very aware of the Chilean government's having undertaken a strict monetarist program in early 1959 in agreement with the IMF. Argentina had also agreed to an austerity program in late 1958. This undoubtedly strengthened the Brazilian resolve not to "give in" to the orthodox school. The Chilean case is the subject of one chapter in Hirschman, *Journeys Toward Progress.* The limitation of orthodox methods in combating inflation in Brazil, as well as elsewhere in Latin America, was emphasized at the time by a number of outside observers. The Economist Intelligence Unit, for example, warned that "while a good deal can be said in favour of stabilization, its cost in terms of economic stagnation and political unrest may well be too high." *Three-Monthly Economic Review: Brazil,* No. 31 (Aug. 1959), 4. In August 1959, Sir George Bolton, chairman of the Bank of London and South America, criticized the use of strict credit controls as an anti-

inflationary instrument in Latin America: "It may even be argued that anything that checks the volume of production, in however good a cause, is bound in such precarious economies to be inflationary." *Times* (London), August 10, 1959, cited in *ibid.*, 4.

34. The Communist press became especially shrill. Roberto Campos, whom they knew to be one of the key figures urging continuation of the stabilization effort, was charged with following "the teachings of Fouché, Goebbels and Himmler" in his supposed attempts to suppress criticism from within the government. *Novos Rumos,* May 8–14, 1959. A more effective attack on Campos was mounted by the radical nationalist university students' association (UNE), which sponsored protest marches that ended by burning Campos in effigy. "Go Home, Bobby Fields [Roberto Campos in American]!" was their cry. For an account of this campaign as given by an UNE source, see Zuleika Alambert, *Estudantes Fazem História* (Rio de Janeiro, n.d. [1963?]), 64–68.

35. The conflict within ISEB centered ostensibly on Hélio Jaguaribe's *O Nacionalismo na Atualidade Brasileira* (Rio de Janeiro, 1958), published by the institute. The radical nationalists found it too pragmatic in its consideration of the role of foreign capital and, especially, on the question of possible foreign participation in the Brazilian oil industry. The controversy between radical nationalists and moderate nationalists led to the resignations in late 1958 and early 1959 of Jaguaribe (who had been the director of the Department of Political Science), Candido Antônio Mendes de Almeida (who had been director of the Department of History), and Guerreiro Ramos (who had been the director of the Department of Sociology). ISEB thereafter reflected the views of radical nationalists such as Nelson Werneck Sodré, Roland Corbisier (who continued as the executive director) and Álvaro Vieira Pinto. A further point of conflict had been the extent to which the institute should become involved in the coming presidential election campaign. The moderates who resigned had unsuccessfully argued that the institute should not involve itself directly in the political maneuverings.

36. A brief description of their position is given in Roberto de Oliveira Campos, *A Moeda, o Gôverno, e o Tempo* (Rio de Janeiro, 1964), 106–7. Roberto Campos had earlier spelled out his views on the proper strategy for economic development in speeches and essays, the more important of which are reprinted in *Ensaios de História Econômica e Sociologia* (Rio de Janeiro, 1963) and *Economia, Planejamento e Nacionalismo* (Rio de Janeiro, 1963).

37. The politically moderate Brazilian magazine *Visão* explained that

Kubitschek's confrontation with "the financial orthodoxy of the
Fund's technicians" was of "decisive political importance," and noted
that "it was impossible to compromise [*conciliar*] the developmentalist 'style' of JK's government with the inflexible rules of this orthodoxy. Sooner or later, JK had to choose his course: compromise or
opposition. It was certain that he would not accept the rigid advice of
the Fund's technicians." *Visão,* June 19, 1959, 12.

38. *New York Times,* June 28, 1959.

39. As *Visão* noted in its article analyzing the domestic political implications of Kubitschek's break with the IMF, "the desire to capitalize on
the emotional prestige of nationalism could lead JK, as the maneuver
develops, farther than he wants to go." Issue of June 19, 1959. Details
on the messages of support sent the government may be found in *Síntese Cronológica: 1959* for the month of June. On June 30, for example, Kubitschek received a personal expression of support from
Oscar Augusto de Camargo, president of the Federation of Industries
of the State of São Paulo. *Síntese Cronológica: 1959,* v. I, 368.

40. The Kubitschek government managed to ride out the remainder of its
term by resorting to a large number of short-term financing arrangements, such as the "swap" transactions, which were a kind of barter
An improvement in the price of coffee in late 1959 also helped. Brazil's
bravado in defying the IMF was not without admirers abroad. The
London Financial Times gave Brazil its Oscar of 1959 for "the most
defiant move of the year." Economist Intelligence Unit, *Three-
Monthly Economic Review: Brazil,* No. 33 (February 1960), 2. During the long negotiations with the IMF and the American authorities,
there was a strong feeling in Brazil that the country was not being
accorded its proper measure of attention and respect. This sentiment
was obvious in Kubitschek's later explanation of his government's failure to achieve economic stabilization in 1959: "We have not yet obtained from international financial authorities the cooperation which
we might expect, given our importance in the contemporary world,
and which would have greatly facilitated the internal task of monetary
stabilization, as well as contributing to an acceleration in our economic development." Juscelino Kubitschek de Oliveira, *Mensagem ao
Congresso Nacional* (Rio de Janeiro, 1960), 51. At the end of his
term Kubitschek gave a detailed defense of his economic policies in
a speech reprinted in *Revista do Conselho Nacional de Economia,* X,
Nos. 1–2 (Jan.–June 1961), 94–109.

41. The War Minister, General Lott, who was a possible contender for the
PSD-PTB nomination (which he eventually received), had taken an

aggressively anti-IMF position, as had João Goulart, who was later to become his running mate in the presidential election.

42. In 1955 Roberto Campos spelled out, with remarkable frankness, what was to be the rationale of the Kubitschek era: "Opting for development implies the acceptance of the idea that it is more important to maximize the rate of economic development than to correct social inequalities. If the rate of development is rapid, inequality can be tolerated and corrected with time. If the rate of development falls because of inadequate incentives, the practice of distributive justice [*justiça distributiva*] becomes a sharing of poverty. Obviously this does not mean that one can leave uncontrolled the predatory instincts occasionally present in certain capitalist sectors. It merely implies that, at our stage of cultural evolution, preserving incentives for the growth of output ought to have priority over measures aimed at its redistribution." This lecture, part of the ISEB course in 1955, was included in *Introdução aos Problemas do Brasil*, published by ISEB. The passage quoted is on p. 233.

43. Soon after taking office as Governor of Rio Grande do Sul in early 1959, Brizola had expropriated the local electric power utility that was a subsidiary of American and Foreign Power. This led to a campaign for expropriation of other AMFORP subsidiaries in Minas Gerais and Pernambuco. *Visão*, May 22, 1959.

44. Kubitschek visited Belo Horizonte and found he got little support for his opposition to the movement in favor of expropriating the local foreign-owned electric power company. Such incidents helped convince him that there was wide public support for a "nationalist" break with the IMF. *Visão*, June 19, 1959.

45. The activities of the Peasant Leagues in the Northeast gained increased national publicity with the articles published by Antônio Callado in the *Correio da Manhã* (Rio de Janeiro) in late 1959. The articles have been republished, along with other documents of the controversy which they provoked, in Antônio Callado, *Os industriais da Sêca e os "Galileus" de Pernambuco* (Rio de Paneiro, 1960). Two articles by Tad Szulc in the *New York Times* on October 31 and November 1, 1960, did much to arouse interest in the United States. The drought of 1958, one of the worst on record, also dramatized the endemic misery in the Northeast.

46. The creation of SUDENE furnishes one of the three case studies in Albert Hirschman's *Journeys Toward Progress*.

47. This point is stressed in the "Introduction to the American Edition" of Celso Furtado, *Diagnosis of the Brazilian Crisis*, xix-xx.

48. The background of an unsuccessful attempt to reform the educational system is given in Roberto J. Moreira, "Sociologia política da Lei de Diretrizes e Bases da Educação Nacional," *Revista Brasileira de Estudos Políticos,* No. 9 (July 1960), 176–212.

49. For an analysis of the "lags" in Brazilian development as they had become apparent by the end of the decade of the 1950's, see Werner Baer, "Socio-Economic Imbalances in Brazil," in Eric N. Baklanoff, ed., *New Perspectives of Brazil* (Nashville, Tenn., 1966), 137–54.

Chapter VI

1. Details of Jânio's earlier career may be found in the sources cited in footnote 57 in Chapter III.

2. The social composition and political implications of Quadros' following are analyzed in the articles of Francisco Weffort and Oliveiros Ferreira, cited in footnote 49 in Chapter II, and footnote 57 in Chapter III.

3. For news reports on Quadros' attempts to win PTB support in his campaign for the governorship of São Paulo in 1954, see *O Estado de São Paulo,* January 28 and February 4, 1954.

4. Whitaker was quite frank in acknowledging that he had become Finance Minister because of Quadros' influence. Whitaker, *Seis Meses, passim;* Cabral, *Tempos de Jânio,* 69–73.

5. Details of the convention may be found in Vidal dos Santos and Luiz Monteiro, *Diário de uma campanha* (São Paulo, n.d.), 61–84.

6. *Ibid.,* 85–123. Quadros' brief renunciation of his nomination touched off an abortive revolt by a group of right-wing Air Force officers at the remote interior base of Aragarças. The revolt was launched by the same elements that had attempted the revolt of Jacareacanga against newly inaugurated President Kubitschek in January-February 1956. The rebellion was motivated by despair at the certain prospect of the getulista "ins" winning another election. The rebels later claimed that they were also acting to block an imminent leftist coup planned by Governor Brizola of Rio Grande do Sul. Carneiro, *História das Revoluções Brasileiras,* II, 519–31.

7. Accounts of the campaign are included in Cabral, *Tempos de Jânio,* 142–210; and Vidal dos Santos and Monteiro, *Diário,* 85–281. After Quadros' election, one politically conservative Paulista economics professor gave a series of lectures confidently predicting what the new President's economic policy would be. He explained that Jânio, "like

all neo-liberals, seeks by a combination of doctrines to conserve the liberal system of free enterprise, purging it of the errors and distortions that disfigure it." He noted that the victorious candidate believed "it is only possible to achieve economic development by promoting the balanced growth of all the existing sectors of the national economy." The logical result would be to "abandon the idea of the 'great drive' and replace it with a balanced national development." Dorival Teixeira Vieira, *A Futura Política Econômica e Financeira do Brasil* [Faculdade de Ciências Econômicas e Administrativas: Universidade de São Paulo: Boletim No. 17] (São Paulo, 1961), 135, 141.

8. Quadros' campaign style and the contraditions of his campaign message are well analyzed in Frank Bonilla, "Jânio vem aí: Brazil Elects a President," *American Universities Field Staff Reports Service*, East Coast South America Series, VII, No. 2 (Brazil), reprinted in Robert D. Tomasek, ed., *Latin American Politics: Studies of the Contemporary Scene* (Garden City, N. Y., 1966), 468–82.

9. Gláucio Ary Dillon Soares, "Classes sociais, strata sociais e as eleições presidenciais de 1960," *Sociologia*, XXIII, No. 3 (Sept. 1961), 217–38; and the same author's "Interêsse político, conflito de pressões e indecisão eleitoral," *Síntese Política, Econômica e Social* (Jan.-March 1961), 5–34.

10. *Brazilian Election Factbook: 1965*, 56–57.

11. The speech is reprinted in *O Estado de São Paulo*, February 1, 1961.

12. Economist Intelligence Unit, *Three-Monthly Economic Review: Brazil*, No. 38 (May 1961); *O Estado de São Paulo*, March 14, 1961; *New York Times*, March 15, 1961. The most important policy decision was the issuing of SUMOC Instruction #204 on March 13, 1961, which spelled out the de facto devaluation of 100 percent. The Brazilian government published an informative pamphlet in December, 1961, explaining the changes in financial policies instituted since the beginning of the year: *A Nova Política Financeira do Brasil* (n.p., 1961).

13. *New York Times*, May 18, 1961.

14. A leading "developmentalist" who became a principal presidential adviser and palace staff member in March 1961 was Cândido Antônio Mendes de Almeida. He had been active in ISEB (he was a moderate nationalist who had resigned during the ideological and political quarrels within the institute in 1958–59) and had supported Lott in the campaign of 1960. His appointment, made despite the fact that Mendes de Almeida had supported Lott, was a sign that Quadros was becoming interested in the "developmentalist" approach.

15. In his message to Congress in March, for example, Quadros had im-

plicitly downgraded the role of public investment when discussing the problems of financing industrial development: "There is no doubt that [the government's] major contribution will lie in the achieving of monetary stability, which is the only climate conducive to the growth of the capital market, the permanent and final solution for this problem." Jânio Quadros, *Mensagem ao Congresso Nacional* (Brasília, 1961), 46–47. The message was notable for its neglect of any long-term considerations on economic development. The document itself was considerably shorter (104 pages) than any presidential message since the Dutra era. On the thorny question of agrarian reform, the message recommended a "system of penalties" to force the exploitation of under-utilized land, but there was no mention of a possible change in Article 141 of the constitution that required prior compensation in cash for expropriation, 85–86. The most far-reaching idea in the message was the proposal to eliminate the compulsory union dues (the *impôsto sindical,* which was the basis of the government-manipulated labor structure) and to replace the entire labor legislation with "authentic freedom for the unions" so that the worker could reach "his political maturity," 68. The political implications of such a move, which never got beyond the planning stage, were enormous.

16. Interview with Octávio Dias Carneiro, Cambridge, Mass., December 1965.

17. One of the most interesting analyses of the changes in the institutional context of Brazilian politics that became evident with the election of Quadros is Guerreiro Ramos, *A Crise do Poder no Brasil* (Rio de Janeiro, 1961), especially 21–104.

18. *New York Times,* May 23, 1961.

19. Quadros explained his foreign policy in an article which appeared one month after his resignation: Jânio Quadros, "Brazil's New Foreign Policy," *Foreign Affairs* (October 1961), 19–27. The roots of the policy are examined in Frank Bonilla, "Operational Neutralism," *American Universities Field Staff Reports Service,* East Coast South America Series, IX, No. 1 (Brazil). Quadros' Foreign Minister was Afonso Arinos de Melo Franco, a moderate UDN leader and a member of a distinguished *mineiro* family. His retrospective analysis of the Quadros foreign policy may be found in his *Evolução da Crise Brasileira,* 244–58. For an explanation (first published in 1962) of the new "independent" policy by a leading Brazilian historian who was one of its principal defenders, see José Honório Rodrigues, "Uma Política externa própria e independente," *Política Externa Independente,* I, No. 1 (May 1965), 15–39. The same author also published a very interesting

study of Brazilian-African relations which was intended in part as a historical justification for the Quadros government's attempt to reverse Brazil's traditional support for Portuguese policy in Africa and to replace it with a more dynamic policy toward the new Afro-Asian nations with whom Brazil, in Quadros' words, had much in common "because of the characteristics of its economy and its racial origins." José Honório Rodrigues, *Brasil e África: outro horizonte* (Rio de Janeiro, 1961), also published in an American translation: *Brazil and Africa* (Berkeley, 1965).

20. News report and a separate analysis (in the section: "News of the Week in Review") by Tad Szulc, *New York Times,* March 5, 1961.

21. At an UDN national convention in Recife in May 1961 Carlos Lacerda warned President Quadros that he "must not forget to listen to the UDN and confide in it." He pointedly concluded that "there exists a constant effort, using every possible means, to separate me from President Jânio Quadros; and despite his acuteness and lucidity, I do not know whether he believes that this effort is really being made or whether he thinks it is simply the product of imagination or sham." The speech is in Carlos Lacerda, *O Poder das Idéias* (Rio de Janeiro, 1963), 121–37.

22. The speech is reprinted in *ibid.,* 329–43.

23. *New York Times,* September 12, 1961.

24. The most searching analysis of the Quadros resignation crisis is Hélio Jaguaribe, "A Renúncia de Jânio Quadros e a Crise Política Brasileira," *Revista Brasileira de Ciências Sociais,* I, No. 1 (Nov. 1961), 272–311, although the author overemphasizes the cohesion which Quadros' opposition had gained by August 25, 1961. This article has been published in English, but the incompetence of the translation (attributed to Ruth Horowitz) unfortunately makes it unusable: Irving L. Horowitz, *Revolution in Brazil,* 138–64. The importance of Quadros' difficulties in domestic politics is stressed in Charles Morazé, "La démission de Jânio Quadros," *Revue Française de Science Politique,* XII, No. 1 (Mar. 1962), 39–53. A very useful collection of documents has been published in Gileno dé Carli, *Anatomia da Renúncia* (Rio de Janeiro, 1962). The author concludes that the evidence does not support the view that Quadros was overthrown by any of the groups (foreign economic interests, the Congress, the military) which have been singled out as "golpistas." The study by Ivo A. Canduro Piccoli, *As Pressões na Renúncia de Jânio* (Rio de Janeiro, 1962), is a negligible contribution to the study of the crisis.

25. In June Quadros had used federal troops to quell a strike by students

at the Law Faculty in Recife when the Dean banned a meeting where Che Guevara's mother was to speak. *New York Times,* June 9, 11, 18, 1961. This move strengthened the hand of those radical nationalists who argued that Quadros' "independent" foreign policy was only a cover for his "reactionary" domestic policies.

26. Quadros sent Castilho Cabral, the former president of the MPJQ, an oblique message on the day of the resignation, suggesting that Cabral "act in accordance with his conscience." Their subsequent efforts at protest were ill-coordinated and ineffectual, cut short by the lack of any clear leadership from Jânio and by the fact that martial law had been imposed immediately by the military ministers. Cabral, *Tempos de Jânio,* 230.

Chapter VII

1. There is a useful, although by no means inclusive, chronology of the crisis in Mário Victor, *Cinco anos que abalaram o Brasil: de Jânio Quadros ao Marechal Castelo Branco* (Rio de Janeiro, 1965), 287–416. Jaguaribe, "A Renúncia de Jânio Quadros," includes an analysis of the forces at work in insuring Goulart's succession to the presidency.

2. Victor, *Cinco Anos,* 307–10.

3. *Ibid.,* 311–12.

4. *Ibid.,* 315.

5. *O Estado de São Paulo,* August 26, 1961.

6. Mazzilli's message is in Victor, *Cinco Anos,* 337. There was heated debate in the Congress over the difference between the situation in 1955 and 1961. Naturally it was the left which stressed the difference most. But even a figure such as Adauto Cardoso, a strongly legalist UDN leader, denounced what he saw as a plot between the military ministers and Acting President Mazzilli. *Ibid.,* 335.

7. The manifesto is printed in *ibid.,* 347–48. The ministers predicted that Goulart's succession to the presidency would "unleash a period of unrest, agitations upon agitations, tumults and even bloody conflict in city and country, and armed subversion which would finally destroy democratic institutions themselves and with them, justice, liberty, social peace, and all the high values of our Christian culture."

8. Lott's manifesto is reprinted in Werneck Sodré, *História Militar,* 374, along with details on the role of the pro-Goulart military.

9. There is a detailed account of this crucial period in Gileno dé Carli, *JQ, Brasília e a Grande Crise* (Rio de Janeiro, 1961).

10. This view was clearly expressed by Munhoz da Rocha, former governor of Paraná and Minister of Agriculture (in the Café Filho government), when he said in the congressional debate, "I did not vote for João Goulart and I do not admire his political style. I voted for Milton Campos for Vice President and I worked for his victory. I am, however, prepared to defend a man for whom I did not vote, but who has certain inalienable political rights. I am saying, therefore, that without giving up or abdicating my political convictions, I shall accept the parliamentary amendment as an emergency solution so that Brazil will not catch fire and be shaken by a civil war." Victor, *Cinco Anos*, 402.

11. The introduction of the parliamentary system had been repeatedly proposed and discussed since the "reconstitutionalization" of 1945. Raul Pilla was a federal deputy from Rio Grande do Sul and leader of the *Partido Libertador*, which, like the *Partido Republicano*, was a historical relic from the Old Republic.

12. One analyst has termed this the "neo-Bismarckian" alternative. Jaguaribe, "A Renúncia de Jânio Quadros."

13. There is no satisfactory study of Goulart's earlier career. The political biography by Tejo is a panegyric by a fellow Riograndense. The author did note prophetically, however, that Goulart needed to transform the "getulista methods," which were already being "superseded" when Vargas committed suicide, due to the "political demands" of a "new economic and social cycle," Tejo, *Jango*, 140–41.

14. Ferrari was one of the most active proponents of a more "authentic" *trabalhismo* within the PTB. Expelled from the party, he tried to build his *Movimento Trabalhista Renovador* as an independent political movement. Ferrari was nominated by the PDC as its vice presidential candidate in 1960, but came in third behind João Goulart and Milton Campos (UDN). He ran for governor of Rio Grande do Sul in 1962, and succeeded in drawing enough votes away from the PTB candidate (Egydio Michaelsen) to help elect Ildo Meneghetti, the coalition candidate of the PSD, UDN, and PL. Ferrari's career, which illustrated the difficulties facing any leader attempting to reorganize the democratic left, was cut tragically short by an air crash in 1963. Details on the 1960 campaign may be found in Fernando Ferrari, *Minha Campanha* (Pôrto Alegre, 1961); information on his efforts to organize rural labor is in his posthumous volume: *Escravos da Terra* (Pôrto Alegre, 1963).

15. Despite his moralistic rhetoric, Quadros proved to be a "flexible" politician during the campaign of 1960 by tacitly endorsing the local "Jan-Jan" (Jânio-Jango) committees that were urging voters to split their ballots, voting for the UDN-PDC candidate for President, and the

PTB-PSD candidate for Vice President. These committees were in most cases an attempt by the PTB "ins" to salvage some political capital out of what loomed as the inevitable defeat of their nominal presidential candidate, Lott.

16. Goulart's brother-in-law (married to Goulart's sister), Governor Leonel Brizola of Rio Grande do Sul, was the most outspoken and rapidly rising radical on the left. He was already making extravagant claims for his role in blocking the military ministers' veto in the August-September crisis.

17. As the vehemently anti-Goulart *O Estado de São Paulo* expressed it the day after Quadros' resignation: "The future of our nationality is in their [the military's] hands." August 26, 1961.

18. Despite the politico-military trauma surrounding the creation of the new parliamentary regime, the staff that Quadros had begun to assemble in the last months of his presidency continued to draw up the outline of an "Economic Policy for Development with Stability," spelled out in detail in a document that surpassed Quadros' message to Congress the previous March in its attention to long-range economic planning and social reform. Conselho de Ministros, *Programa de Govêrno: Bases: Análise da Situação Econômica e Social do Brasil* (Brasília, Sept. 1961). The document even suggested that parliamentarism would be "a more appropriate instrument . . . for realizing the basic reforms that the country needs, and the postponement of which has been unjustly blamed on the National Congress," vi-vii.

19. dé Carli, *JQ, Brasília, e a Grande Crise,* 148.

20. Goulart also stressed the need for "structural reforms." In his short (47 pages) message to Congress in March 1962, he called for reforms in banking, public administration, taxes, and "the great Brazilian aspiration—agrarian reform," which he described as "an irresistible intellectual force." João Goulart, *Mensagem ao Congresso Nacional* (Rio de Janeiro, 1962), xi, xiii.

21. The Brazilian ambassador in Washington, Roberto Campos, and the American ambassador to Brazil, Lincoln Gordon, gave their accounts of Goulart's visit in Alberto Dines, et al., *O mundo depois de Kennedy* (Rio de Janeiro, 1965), 110–11; 192–200. According to Campos, President Kennedy "for a fleeting moment" thought he had found in Goulart "a reforming leader of the center, able to communicate with the masses and capable of assuming the missing leadership of the Alliance for Progress in Latin America, which rightfully belonged to Brazil, not only as the largest country, but also because it had initiated Operation Panamerica," 110. Goulart's speeches during the trip are

reprinted in João Goulart, *Desenvolvimento e Independência: Discursos: 1962* (Brasília, 1963).

22. The speech is reprinted in *ibid.,* 75–81.
23. The divisions within the left will be discussed in greater detail below. The phrases "negative left" and "positive left" were coined by San Tiago Dantas.
24. Resignations were necessary because of the constitutional requirement that cabinet ministers resign their posts at least three months before running for election.
25. A collection of speeches and congressional debates, in which Dantas defended and explained his foreign policy, may be found in San Tiago Dantas, *Política externa independente* (Rio de Janeiro, 1962).
26. The radical leftist labor leadership had issued a series of manifestos in late June and early July culminating in the order for a general strike on July 4. The documents are reprinted in Telles, *O movimento Sindical no Brasil,* 158–82. It had become obvious by mid-1962 that Goulart no longer had the control over the labor movement that he had enjoyed as Vice President. This was in part because of the increasing radicalization within the labor movement, acute since 1960, in part because it was impossible to combine the roles of President and patron of the labor leadership, especially as long as Goulart continued to pursue the "politics of conciliation." Harding, "Revolution Tomorrow," 40; and the same author's "An Analysis of Brazil's Third Labor Congress," *Hispanic American Report,* XIII, No. 8 (October 1960), 567–72; Abelardo Jurema, *Sexta-Feira, 13* (Rio de Janeiro, 1964), 59.
27. The *Instituto Superior de Estudos Brasileiros* (ISEB), now under the control of radical leftist intellectuals, in October 1962 published a pamphlet giving a detailed answer to the question *Por que votar contra o parlamentarismo no plebiscito?* (Rio de Janeiro, 1962).
28. Victor, *Cinco Anos,* 441–45.
29. The speech is in Cabral, *Tempos de Jânio,* 297–309.
30. On the election of 1962 in São Paulo, see Oliveiros S. Ferreira's two studies: "A Crise do Poder do 'Sistema' e as Eleições Paulistas de 1962," *Revista Brasileira de Estudos Políticos,* No. 16 (Jan. 1964), 179–226; and "São Paulo" in Themistocles Cavalcanti & Reisky Dubnic, eds., *Comportamento Eleitoral no Brasil* (Rio de Janeiro 1964), 229–62. There is an analysis of the social basis of the differing "populist" styles of Jânio and Adhemar in Weffort, "Raízes Sociais do Populismo em São Paulo."
31. The elections were subjected to a state-by-state analysis (ten states

covered, with the most notable omission being Guanabara) in a special number of the *Revista Brasileira de Estudos Políticos,* No. 16 (Jan. 1964). For an important examination of the regional variations in the ideological character of the major parties, see Hélio Jaguaribe, "As Eleições de 62," *Tempo Brasileiro,* No. 2 (Dec. 1962), 7–38. Another collection of detailed studies on the elections of 1962 (including Guanabara) may be found in Cavalcanti and Dubnic, eds., *Comportamento Eleitoral no Brasil.* One foreign observer, commenting on the political scene after the congressional elections, concluded: "Brazilians today, in their impatience and disillusionment, are in a dangerous mood. Their feeling is that it is the politicians who have been digging democracy's grave. If, after next January's referendum, the political rough house continues, the army may be forced to intervene." Andrew Marshall, "Brazil: Democracy's Last Chance?" *The World Today* (London) (Nov. 1962), 467.

32. The chief sources on which I have drawn for the factual outline of the remainder of the Goulart presidency are *O Jornal do Brasil, Correio da Manhã, O Estado de São Paulo,* and *O Cruzeiro,* as well as reports in the *New York Times* and *Le Monde.* Monthly summaries consulted were the *Hispanic American Report* (Stanford University), and the very useful "Analysis of Government Background in Brazil" prepared from 1962 to 1964 by Professor George W. Bemis of the School of Public Administration of the University of Southern California. Professor Bemis' news summaries were part of a project of the United States Agency for International Development (USAID) in Brazil.

33. "Radicalization" is used here in the sense in which Brazilians use the word "radicalização." It refers to the growth of extremism and intransigence among political sectors. In short, it signifies the loss of faith in the democratic process of negotiation and compromise.

34. Details on the anti-Goulart conspiracy may be found in the series of documentary articles first published in *O Estado de São Paulo* and later issued in book form: José Stacchini, *Março 64: Mobilização da Audácia* (São Paulo, 1965).

35. Details on the *Frente Patriótica* may be found in the book by a journalist (on the staff of *O Estado de São Paulo*) who sympathized with the movement: Ferreira, *As Forças Armadas e o Desafio da Revolução.* Admiral Sílvio Heck, the Navy Minister at the time of Quadros' resignation, was the leader of this movement, whose manifesto was published in the *Correio da Manhã* for December 19, 1963.

36. Philip Siekman, "When Executives Turned Revolutionaries," *Fortune,*

LXX, No. 3 (Sept. 1964), 147–49, 210–21. For an account of IPES by one of its founders, see Paulo Ayres Filho, "The Brazilian Revolution," in Norman A. Bailey, ed., *Latin America: Politics, Economics, and Hemispheric Security* (New York, 1965), 239–60.

37. The CGT was in fact extralegal under the Vargas labor legislation (still valid) of the 1940's. Vargas had sought to prevent any horizontal organization of labor, although vertical integration was greatly promoted. Vargas' objective had been to ensure government control of labor while preventing the formation of an independent labor front. For an analysis of the labor movement as of early 1963, see Neuma Aguiar Walker, "The Organization and Ideology of Brazilian Labor," in Horowitz, *Revolution in Brazil*, 242–56. The Communists within the labor movement were extremely active in attempting to organize a horizontal command. For details on their efforts, see Telles, *O movimento sindical no Brasil*.

38. The FPN issued its manifesto of principles on February 3, 1963, which is reprinted in Sérgio Magalhães, *Prática da Emancipação Nacional* (Rio de Janeiro, 1964), 155–58. The president of the Organizing Committee was Sérgio Magalhães and one of the vice presidents was Leonel Brizola.

39. For a history of its efforts, published by UNE, see Zuleika Alambert, *Estudantes Fazem História*. There is a lurid "exposé" of UNE in Sonia Seganfreddo, *UNE: Instrumento de Subversão* (Rio de Janeiro, 1963). A bitter battle over student politics in Belo Horizonte, an important center of radical student activities, is described by the former director of the economics faculty in Yvon Leite de Magalhães Pinto, *O Movimento "estudantil" de 1960 na Faculdade de Ciências Econômicas da Universidade de Minas Gerais* (Belo Horizonte, 1963). The Communist Party (the Moscow wing led by Luís Carlos Prestes) had an on-again-off-again relationship with the student movement. In 1962 a Party spokesman explained that "in recent years the reactionaries have sought to weaken the student movement and to divert it from the path of revolutionary struggle. At the same time the Communist Party underestimated this movement and frowned upon it on the unsound pretext that it challenged the leading role of the working class." P. Motta Lima in *World Marxist Review*, V, No. 2 (Feb. 1962), 75. The most detailed analysis of the political position of university student organizations (focusing on the situation in early 1964) is Leonard Therry, "Dominant Power Components in the Brazilian University Student Movement Prior to April, 1964," *Journal of Inter-American Studies*, VII, No. 1 (Jan. 1965), 27–48.

40. The phrase "Jacobin left" has been used by Robert Alexander to describe those "political parties and groups which have many of the attributes of the Jacobins of the French Revolution. They favor social revolution at whatever cost, and they are excessively nationalistic to the point of xenophobia." They are to be distinguished from the orthodox Communist parties by their rejection of the democratic process and their reluctance to accept outside discipline. Robert J. Alexander, *Today's Latin America* (Anchor paperback, Garden City, N. Y. 1962), 9–10; 157–59. For an important discussion of the distinctions among the left in Brazil, as well as the rest of Latin America, see Ernst Halperin's article in *Survey* (Jan. 1965), 154–67. There is an interesting analysis of the relationship between nationalists and Communist parties in Latin America in the same author's *Nationalism and Communism in Chile* (Cambridge, Mass. 1965), Chap. 1. A position akin to the "Jacobin" left was evident in many of the volumes in the pamphlet series "Cadernos do Povo Brasileiro," directed by Álvaro Vieira Pinto (who remained as a leading force in ISEB after the resignation of the moderate nationalists in 1958–59) and Ênio Silveira, and published by Silveira's publishing house (Editôra Civilização Brasileira) starting in 1962. The first title was Francisco Julião, *Que São as Ligas Camponesas?* (Rio de Janeiro, 1962).

41. Shortly before the elections of October 1962, *Novos Rumos*, the weekly organ of the PCB, published a detailed analysis of the political situation in Brazil, offering the Communist Party's strategy for attaining a "nationalist and democratic government." According to a précis in an official English-language Communist publication, the document warned against two dangerous tendencies: "First, the 'Left' tendency not to lay the emphasis on struggle against imperialism and its domestic agents, not to differentiate between the pro-imperialist and the national wing of the bourgeoisie, and to ignore the contradictions between the two groups instead of utilizing these contradictions for intensifying the struggle against imperialism and latifundism, furthering the mass movement and thus paving the way to a national and democratic government. Second, the 'right' tendency to identify the interests of the working class and the people generally with the interests of the bourgeoisie as represented by João Goulart, to ignore the dual, conciliatory character of the national bourgeoisie and to abstain from consistent struggle against its policy of compromise with imperialism and the diehard reactionaries." "Communists Review the Situation in Brazil," *World Marxist Review,* V, No. 11 (Nov. 1962), 42.

42. Impressionistic judgments on public opinion are an unsatisfactory substitute for scientific investigations. My assessment is based on,

among other sources, Lloyd A. Free, *Some International Implications of the Political Psychology of Brazilians* [Institute for International Social Research] (Princeton, N. J., 1961). Free's data were the result of a careful opinion survey done in both urban and rural areas in late 1960 and early 1961. It therefore reflects the national self-confidence that was soon to be shaken by the prolonged political crisis that began with Quadros' resignation. Another American social scientist (a research psychiatrist) conducted surveys among Brazilian university students in early 1964 and found that there were three principal political positions—"the conservative, reformist, and revolutionary positions," using these terms as "purely descriptive." He noted that "they are not the terms used by the students themselves who are more apt to speak in terms of rightist or leftist position; interestingly, there is no common term for the moderate reformist position although this certainly represents the operational stance of the majority of students." The author divided the students into those who were "active" and "passive" in their attitude toward politics. Based on his interviews with university officials, student leaders, and Brazilian social scientists, he estimated that at the nine universities (in five cities) he studied, the distribution of student opinion was as follows: of the 15 per cent classified as "active," 3 percent were "conservative," 7 percent "moderate reformist," and 5 per cent "revolutionary." The other 85 percent were classified as "passive," made up of 15 percent "conservative," 60 percent "moderate reformist," and 10 percent "revolutionary." Bryant Wedge, *Problems in Dialogue: Brazilian University Students and the United States* [Institute for the Study of National Behavior] (Princeton, N. J., 1965), 154–55. The success of the "revolutionaries" in gaining control of the student organizations such as UNE was undoubtedly due to their superior organizing efforts and dedication. In the course of 1963, a carefully administered poll was conducted in middle and upper class neighborhoods of Rio de Janeiro to determine opinion on a key reform issue—granting the franchise to illiterates. The investigators found (contrary to what they had expected!) that a majority (56.5 percent) opposed this reform, with a sizable minority (38.7 percent) in favor and the remainder (4.7 percent) of no opinion. Allowing illiterates to vote would, of course, have radically increased the electorate and was therefore perhaps the most far-reaching of all the reforms currently proposed. Hermínio Augusto Faria, ed., *Três Pesquisas* [Escola Brasileira de Administração Pública] (Rio de Janeiro, 1964), 5–67.

43. Economist Intelligence Unit, *Three-Monthly Economic Review: Brazil,* No. 43 (Sept. 1962), 3–4.

44. The struggle over the profit remittances law would make an excellent

case study in the politics of economic nationalism in Brazil. The reports of a deputy and a senator, both opposed to the bill as passed, were published in *A Remessa de Lucros: um problema nacional. Pareceres do Deputado Daniel Faraco e do Senador Mem de Sá* (Pôrto Alegre, 1963). On November 6, 1963, *O Jornal do Brasil*, a Rio de Janeiro daily of the center-right, ran a feature article on "Concepções errôneas sôbre o investimento privado estrangeiro e remessas de lucros." The views of the radical nationalists, who led the fight for the bill, are clearly stated in Sérgio Magalhães, et al., *A Questão da Remessa de Lucros* (Rio de Janeiro, 1962); and Magalhães, *Prática da Emancipação Nacional*, 51–66, 76–81. A collection of interviews with opponents of the bill, before its final passage, was published in *O Cruzeiro*, XXXIV, No. 11 (Dec. 23, 1961), 155–61. In 1961 Jânio Quadros had begun the action in Congress by calling for "an immediate disciplining of all profit remittances, which are at an immoderate level. . . ." *Mensagem ao Congresso Nacional*, 85. For an important study of the economics of U.S. private investment in Brazil, see Hélio Jaguaribe's chapter in Raymond Vernon, ed., *How Latin America Views the U.S. Investor* (New York, 1966), 67–93. The level of profit remittances is doubly significant because of the burden they place on the balance of payments—always a crucial consideration in Brazil.

45. In his first months as governor in early 1959, Brizola had consolidated his position of leadership among the radical nationalists by expropriating a subsidiary of American and Foreign Power in Rio Grande do Sul.

46. Land invasions in the state of Rio de Janeiro are reported in the *New York Times*, June 23 and 26, 1963, and the *Correio da Manhã*, December 3, 1963.

47. For the political situation in the countryside, see Frank Bonilla, "Rural Reform in Brazil," *Dissent*, IX, No. 4 (Autumn 1962), 373–82. As the Goulart presidency continued, Bonilla grew concerned over the possible disappearance of the oft-praised Brazilian ability to compromise. He noted: "Danger signs that this kind of social entente may be crumbling, particularly in the rural areas, can be seen in all regions of the country though they are concentrated in the famine-ridden northeast." Frank Bonilla, "Brazil" in James S. Coleman, ed., *Education and Political Development* (Princeton, N.J., 1965), 213. Non-Brazilian observers were inclined to overestimate (perhaps because of a lag in information) the leadership and influence of Julião, who was by early 1963 being overshadowed by other rural organizers. One of the grossest overestimates of Julião was in Horowitz, *Revolution in Brazil*,

13–34. For an analysis of Francisco Julião as a member of the "new guard," see Anthony Leeds, "Brazil and the Myth of Francisco Julião," in Joseph Maier and Richard W. Weatherhead, eds., *Politics of Change in Latin America* (New York, 1964), 190–204. A sociologist who found the rural protest movements to be heavily influenced by the patrimonial atmosphere of traditional Brazilian rural society is Benno Galjart, "Class and Following in Rural Brazil," *America Latina*, VII, No. 3 (July-Sept. 1964), 3–24. Galjart was accused of downplaying class conflict too much by Gerrit Huizer, "Some Notes on Community Development and Rural Social Research," *America Latina*, VIII, No. 3 (July-Sept. 1965), 128–44. Galjart replied in the same issue, 145–52. The controversy is important because it concerns the extent to which the new rural movements could survive the loss of a few key leaders. A general account of rural discontent in the Northeast in the early 1960's may be found in Josué de Castro, *Sete Palmas de Terra e Um Caixão* (São Paulo, 1965).

48. This phenomenon has been described as the "progressive inauthenticity" of party representation. Pompeu de Souza, "Eleições de 62: Decomposição Partidária e Caminhos da Reforma," *Revista Brasileira de Estudos Políticos*, No. 16 (Jan. 1964), 7–19.

49. Ramos, *A Crise do Poder no Brasil*, 94–98; Pedreira, *Março 31*, 84–89. The best recent discussion of party lines is Octávio Ianni, et al., *Política e Revolução Social no Brasil*. Any discussion of the social basis or exact ideological position of the parties is greatly handicapped by the lack of reliable monographic studies.

50. The basic sources on the elections of 1962 are the January 1964 issue (No. 16) of *Revista Brasileira de Estudos Políticos;* and Cavalcanti and Dubnic, eds., *Comportamento Eleitoral no Brasil;* and *Brazil: Election Factbook*, 61–68.

51. IBAD became the subject of a congressional investigation in early 1963 and was abolished by federal decree in the same year. *Correio da Manhã*, December 21, 1963. For an attack on IBAD from the left, see Eloy Dutra, *IBAD: Sigla da Corrupção* (Rio de Janeiro, 1963).

52. In July 1962 a National Conference of Brazilian Bishops had issued a strongly worded statement in support of reforms. Their suggestions, including possible expropriation of rural lands for redistribution, were spelled out in greater detail in a document published on April 30, 1963. A leader in these activities was the Auxiliary Archbishop of Rio de Janeiro, Dom Helder Camara, an outspoken advocate of rapid social change. *New York Times*, August 15, 1963; Houtart and Pin, *The Church and the Latin American Revolution*, 216–18. A center of

moderate reformist sentiments was the Instituto de Estudos Políticos e Sociais of the Catholic University of Rio de Janeiro, which began publishing in 1959 a quarterly journal: *Síntese: Política Econômica Social.* For an attack on radical reformers within the Church, see Manoel Cardozo, "The Brazilian Church and the New Left," *Journal of Inter-American Studies,* VI, No. 3 (July 1964), 313–21. Cardozo charged that the weekly newspaper *Brasil Urgente,* edited by the Dominican Carlos Josaphat, "aped the vocabulary and followed, in so far as it could, the ideology of Communism," 313.

53. A large number of the congressional delegation of the PTB were unimaginative electoral bureaucrats, anxious to benefit from the party's empire of patronage in the Ministry of Labor and the social security and insurance institutes. Alexander's description of the PTB as one of "the parties of the Jacobin Left" is certainly inaccurate: Alexander, *Today's Latin America,* 9, 102. There was a small group of PTB congressmen (*Grupo Compacto*) attempting to give the party a more aggressive and ideologically cohesive leftist stance after 1961. But even these leftists within the PTB were divided. One of their number, Guerreiro Ramos, gave an interesting critique of Vargas' *trabalhismo* and the need for its updating in *A Crise do Poder no Brasil* (Rio de Janeiro, 1961), 89–94. Ramos subsequently proved to be a moderate among the PTB reformers, and carried on a bitter battle with his "Jacobin" colleagues, which contributed to his failure to win a seat from Guanabara in the congressional election of 1962. For details, see Guerreiro Ramos, *Mito e Verdade da Revolução Brasileira* (Rio de Janeiro, 1963), 9–15. In the midst of the campaign, he demanded that the Guanabara PTB specifically renounce Marxism-Leninism. His proposed manifesto is included on pp. 217–18. Elsewhere Alexander has given a more accurate picture of the divisions within the PTB: Robert J. Alexander, "The Emergence of Modern Political Parties in Latin America," in Maier and Weatherhead, eds., *Politics of Change in Latin America,* 119–20.

54. Details on the creation and first years of SUDENE, including much information on Furtado's role, may be found in Hirschman, *Journeys Toward Progress,* chapter one. For details on Furtado's earlier career, see the cover story in *Visão,* June 26, 1959.

55. The first use of the terms "positive" and "negative" left by Finance Minister San Tiago Dantas evidently occurred in his reply to attacks by Leonel Brizola in April 1963. *Hispanic American Report,* XVI, No, 4 (June 1963), 404. Dantas developed the distinction in "A Evolução da Política Brasileira," *O Digesto Econômico,* 174 (Nov.-Dec.

1963), 77–85. Dantas later explained the distinction thus: "The forces of the left are not inherently negative or positive, but the left sometimes assumes attitudes that are positive and negative. The negative attitudes are provocations that serve to strengthen the right." Press conference reported in *O Jornal do Brasil,* February 15, 1964.

56. Dantas had written a brilliant study of Ruy Barbosa's policies as Finance Minister (1889–91), showing him to be "a social reformer . . . who ought to be considered the statesman of progress in our society, where previously the greatest public figures incarnated prudence, moderation, and a conservative attitude." San Tiago Dantas, *Dois Momentos de Ruy Barbosa* (Rio de Janeiro, 1949), 44–45. It seems fair to say that Dantas had conceived a similar role for himself in 1964. Ramos, *Mito e Verdade da Revolução Brasileira,* 60. Dantas' speech upon assuming the finance ministry was printed in *O Jornal do Brasil,* January 25, 1963.

57. *Plano Trienal do Desenvolvimento Econômico e Social, 1963–1965: Síntese* (Rio de Janeiro, n.d.). The *Plano Trienal* was subjected to detailed analysis by a number of economists in a special issue of the *Revista Brasileira de Economia,* XVI, No. 4 (Dec. 1962). The Plan was drawn up hurriedly by Furtado in the last three months of 1962. Many of its technical deficiencies (which both its sympathizers and its enemies were quick to point out) were the result of haste in preparation. Goulart was anxious to be able to present the United States and the multilateral authorities of the Alliance for Progress (the "Nine Wise Men" who were empowered to screen plans submitted by the Latin American nations) with evidence of Brazilian long-term planning.

58. *Plano Trienal,* 18.

59. The "bottleneck" rationale for reforms was closely connected with a stagnation theory that attributed the slowdown in economic growth, since 1962, to the fact that industrialization had reached a stage of vertical integration, resulting in a declining capacity to absorb labor in the face of a constantly growing labor supply. This, in turn, put a ceiling on the size of the market. To enlarge the market would require "structural" changes, especially in the agrarian sector. The most carefully documented and researched presentation of the stagnation model of the Brazilian economy was Maria Conceição Tavares, et al., "The Growth and Decline of Import Substitution in Brazil," *Economic Bulletin for Latin America,* IX, No. 1 (March 1964), 1–59. The stagnation model was often advanced by the writers and social scientists earlier categorized as the "developmentalists." The rationale of "social

justice" was advanced, as one might expect, by the radical nationalists, who knew that promises of immediate income redistribution had more political appeal than complicated theories purporting to explain the slowdown in economic growth. Their analysis of the latter amounted to a neo-Leninist explanation.

60. The concluding section of the Three-Year Plan outlined the "basic reforms required for economic development," explaining that "genuine qualitative modifications in the economic system presuppose reforms that can be formulated through planning, but which are beyond its direct control." The reforms suggested were of two kinds: "i) rationalization of government activity, which in Brazil requires administrative and banking reforms; ii) elimination of institutional restraints on the optimal utilization of the factors of production, especially fiscal and agrarian reforms." *Plano Trienal,* 189.

61. *Ibid.,* 39–42.

62. *Ibid.,* 19–22, 34–38.

63. The *Plano Trienal* expressed the point epigrammatically: "It is a question of planning stabilization in conditions of development, so that we may, in a later phase, plan a speed-up in development without compromising stability," 18. The stabilization plan of 1958–59, drawn up by Lucas Lopes and Roberto Campos, had a similar purpose but gave less attention to the problems of institutional reform and social justice.

64. For the following analysis of economic policy-making in the first six months of 1963 I have drawn heavily upon the Economist Intelligence Unit, *Three-Monthly Economic Review: Brazil,* No. 44 (Dec. 1962); No. 45 (Feb. 1963); No. 46 (June 1963); No. 47 (August 1963).

65. Economist Intelligence Unit, *Three-Monthly Economic Review: Brazil,* No. 45 (Feb. 1963), 4–5.

66. Goulart's annual presidential message to Congress did call for increased trade with the eastern bloc. Its publication on March 15 (the traditional date of the message) came just after Dantas had arrived in Washington.

67. The negotiations were reported in detail in the *New York Times,* March 11, 12, 14, 18, and 25, 1963.

68. The Washington negotiations were clouded by a leak in the testimony of the U.S. ambassador to Brazil, Lincoln Gordon, before the House Foreign Affairs Committee. Because of an unexplained lack of coordination between the State Department and the Foreign Affairs Committee, a part of the testimony in which the ambassador stated that the Brazilian labor movement and student organizations were extensively

"Communist-infiltrated" was released to the press. There were immediate protests in Brazil, led by Brizola. The matter was finally settled when the American government managed to convince Goulart that the incident had no connection with the negotiations and did not signify any sudden shift in the U.S. attitude toward Brazil. *New York Times,* March 18, 19, 21, 1963.

69. Campos has given his version of these conversations in Alberto Dines, et al., *O mundo depois de Kennedy,* 115–17.

70. The diplomatic significance of the Dantas mission to Washington was the subject of an interesting analysis by Geraldo Banas in *O Cruziero,* April 13, 1963.

71. Economist Intelligence Unit, *Three-Monthly Economic Review: Brazil,* No. 46 (June 1963), 2–3.

72. *Desenvolvimento & Conjuntura,* VII, No. 4 (April 1963), 3–5; *Conjuntura Econômica,* XVIII, No. 2 (Feb. 1964) contains a complete review of the official statistics for 1963.

73. The increase took effect on January 1, 1963, by which time it was estimated to represent a 60% increase in money terms. *Conjuntura Econômica,* XVIII, No. 2 (Feb. 1964), 71.

74. The military protests are reported in *O Cruzeiro,* May 11, and June 8, 1963.

75. Goulart's relations with the senior Army officers are analyzed in *ibid.,* April 27 and May 4, 1963.

76. Dantas spelled out his views in his first speech as Finance Minister. *Jornal do Brasil,* January 25, 1963.

77. *Wall Street Journal,* April 23, 1963.

78. Furtado's Three-Year Plan was also a target for attack by the radical left. An UNE-sponsored publication concluded: "The Three Year Plan is an attempt to conciliate imperialism and large landowners as a part of an overall policy which the national bourgeoisie is carrying out through the government of João Goulart. Its failure is inevitable, because it is arousing, and must arouse with increasing force, the opposition of the Brazilian people." Mario Alves and Paul Singer, *Análise do Plano Trienal* (Rio de Janeiro, 1963), 90. A similar critique may be found in José de Souza Martins, "O Plano Trienal e a Marcha da Revolução Burguesa," *Revista Brasiliense,* No. 49 (Sept.-Oct. 1963), 41–52. In radical leftist circles Furtado was accused of having succumbed to the "Gudinizing" of Brazil's economic planning. Eugênio Gudin was the conservative economist who advocated orthodox stabilization measures and had been Finance Minister for the first six months of the Café Filho regime.

79. The political deadlock over "reforms" is analyzed by Benedito Coutinho in *O Cruzeiro*, June 1, 1963. The leader of the majority in Congress (Deputy Oliveira Britto—PSD, Bahia) favored an amendment to Constitutional Article 141, which required prior compensation in cash for expropriation. Britto expressed his views in an interview published in *O Cruzeiro*, May 25, 1963.

80. François Houtart and Emile Pin, *The Church and the Latin American Revolution* (New York, 1965), 216.

81. The political battles of April-May were reported in detail in the *New York Times*, which I have used as a source, along with the monthly news summaries in the *Hispanic American Report* and the monthly "Analysis of Government Background in Brazil" prepared by Professor George W. Bemis.

82. *O Cruzeiro*, April 13, 1963. From the left came this description of the Dantas mission: "The courageous Minister of Finance appeared, jumped out of the trench and bounded across the no-man's land for a 'commando' operation in the very fortress of our traditional and generous friends, the Shylocks of Wall Street." Paulo Motta Lima, "A Viagem do Ministro da Fazenda," *Revista Brasiliense*, No. 46 (March-April 1963), 122.

83. *New York Times*, May 23, 1963.

84. The principal opposition to the compulsory loan provision had come from the UDN congressional delegation, which claimed that stricter collection procedures would eliminate the need for new taxes.

Chapter VIII

1. There were at least four separate literacy campaigns underway in 1963. One was an experimental campaign, directed by Professor Paulo Freire of the University of Pernambuco in Recife. Freire had pioneered a method for teaching illiterates to read quickly by using graphic illustrations from their own surroundings. His intention was to arouse a "critical consciousness" in the newly literate. Naturally, these surroundings were miserable, and therefore Freire was soon accused of using the literacy campaign to spread "subversive" ideas. The rightist newspaper *O Globo* led the attack. The second group sponsoring literacy campaigns was the National Conference of Bishops, which commissioned the preparation of a special instruction booklet (published in early 1964) along the lines of the Paulo Freire method. The third group was operating directly out of the federal Ministry of Education, and the fourth was the *Movimento de Educação de Base* (MEB), a

program partially sponsored by the Ministry of Education and staffed by volunteers, who only began working in late 1963. Interview with Paulo Freire, Cuernavaca, Mexico, January 4, 1966.

2. The process of awakening in the rural sector was greatly stimulated by the extension of the right of unionization to the countryside. The Constitution of 1946 had specifically provided for agricultural workers' unions, but they had remained a legal fiction. Francisco Julião's organizing efforts at the end of Kubitschek's presidency stimulated competition among rival organizers, such as leftist politicians and progressive priests, who sought to enforce their own direction on the channeling of peasant protest. In March 1963 the Congress passed a law legitimizing the formation of rural unions. As in the case of all other unions recognized under Brazilian law, the Ministry of Labor was given the power to grant certification of the lawful syndicate in each region. Thus the 1963 law was an extension of the Vargas-inspired corporatist structure to the rural sector. There was immediate competition to see which groups would gain control of this powerful new economic and political instrument in the countryside. For background on the legal and social context see Richard Adams, "Rural Labor" in John J. Johnson, ed., *Continuity and Change in Latin America* (Stanford, 1964), 66; J. V. Freitas Marcondes, *First Brazilian Legislation Relating to Rural Labor Unions: A Sociological Study* (Gainesville, Florida, 1962); and Caio Prado Júnior, "O Estatuto do Trabalhador Rural," *Revista Brasiliense*, No. 47 (May-June 1963), 1–13. The best general study of the syndicates, as of December 1963, is Robert E. Price, *Rural Unionization in Brazil* [Research Paper: Land Tenure Center, University of Wisconsin] (Madison, Wisconsin, August 1964, mimeo). Useful also is the excellent brief study on Pernambuco done in October 1963 by Mary E. Wilkie, *A Report on Rural Syndicates in Pernambuco* (Centro Latinoamericano de Investigaciones en Ciencias Sociales, Rio de Janeiro, April 1964, mimeo). A general view of rural organization in the Northeast may be found in Furtado's chapter on "The Revolutionary Process in the Northeast" in *Diagnosis of the Brazilian Crisis*, 125–62. For further sources, see Chapter VII, footnote 47.

3. Stacchini, *Março 64: Mobilização da Audácia*, documents the conspiratorial efforts of the anti-Goulart forces.

4. This reorganization was another attempt to create a viable institution of economic planning. The last major organizational change had come with Quadros' decree of August 5, 1961 (which created the group known as COPLAN). Quadros' effort, in turn, was an attempt to create a successor institution to Kubitschek's planning apparatus.

5. My analysis of economic policy-making from mid-1963 to the end of

the Goulart presidency has drawn on the Economist Intelligence Unit, *Quarterly Economic Review*, No. 48 (Dec. 1963), No. 49 (Feb. 1964), No. 50 (June 1964).

6. Carvalho Pinto's report to the President and Cabinet was reprinted in *Correio da Manhã*, July 5, 1963.

7. Valentim F. Bouças, *História da Dívida Externa* (2nd ed.; Rio de Janeiro, 1950) gives basic historical data on Brazil's foreign debt.

8. *New York Times*, August 31 and September 3, 1963.

9. Furtado's Three-Year Plan had stressed the need to expand exports. *Plano Trienal*, 34–38. Figures for wheat and oil imports in 1962 are given in *Conjuntura Econômica*, XVIII, No. 2 (Feb. 1964), 53.

10. Details on the Sergeants' Revolt may be found in Carneiro, *História das Revoluções Brasileiras*, II, 533–50; and *O Cruzeiro*, October 5, 1963.

11. The interview, the published version of which Lacerda afterward repudiated as unauthentic, was with Julian Hartt, Rio correspondent of the *Los Angeles Times*.

12. *Correio da Manhã*, October 6, 1963.

13. *Ibid.*, October 8, 1963.

14. A knowledge of the movement of officers and opinions within the Army is essential for an understanding of Goulart's final ten months in office. One of the most authoritative sources is Carlos Castelo Branco, who was political columnist for *O Jornal do Brasil* in Brasília. See his chapter, "Da Conspiração à Revolução," in Alberto Dines, et al., *Os Idos de Março e a Queda em Abril* (Rio de Janeiro, 1964). The book is a collection of eight articles by journalists on the staff of *O Jornal do Brasil* and published only a few months after the events. Another important source on military opinion is Fernando Pedreira, *Março 31: Civis e Militares no Processo da Crise Brasileira* (Rio de Janeiro, 1964), especially the first two chapters. After the successful coup of March 31, 1964, many of the conspirators were anxious to reveal the details of their movement. See, for example, the accounts in Stacchini, *Março 64: Mobilização da Audácia;* the interviews of Armando Falcão in *O Cruzeiro*, May 2, 1964; Marshal Odílio Denys in *Fatos & Fotos*, May 2, 1964; and General Carlos Luiz Guedes in *O Cruzeiro*, April 16, 1966.

15. General Bevilacqua explained his position in an interview in *Fatos & Fotos*, January 4, 1964. He favored amending Constitutional Article 141, which required prior compensation in cash for any expropriation of land.

16. The interview was in the issue of *Manchete* for November 30, 1963,

which was published on November 20. The reaction expressed in the editorial of the *Correio da Manhã* on November 21 was typical of center opinion: "In truth everyone has the responsibility to cooperate with the federal government in applying emergency measures. But it is the responsibility of the federal government to propose them. And this is what the President failed to do in his interview." Immediately after Goulart's abortive state-of-siege request in early October, the *Correio da Manhã* had taken a similar position, urging the federal government to "draw up a plan, a program, or at least a scheme for resolving the problems of inflation, foreign indebtedness, and economic development. To draw it up and put it into practice." *Correio da Manhã,* October 8, 1963.

17. The Brazilian foreign ministry had taken the lead among Latin American countries in the preparations for the United Nations Conference on Trade and Development that was scheduled for March 1964 in Geneva. The Latin American viewpoint, as spelled out in a special report written by Raúl Prebisch, *Nueva Politica Comercial para el Desarrollo* (Mexico, 1964), stressed the urgent need for a revision in the rules of world trade so as to ease the limited capacity to import of the developing countries. Goulart's speech in São Paulo was therefore part of the diplomatic buildup for the Geneva Conference. Details on the Brazilian role may be found in *Revista Brasileira de Política Internacional,* VII, No. 28 (Dec. 1964).

18. For reports on rumors of Brizola's possible appointment, see *Correio da Manhã,* December 17, 1963. In late December the walls in Rio de Janeiro suddenly blossomed forth with the slogan: "Contra a inflação, Brizola é a solução!!!"

19. For an analysis of the PSD's desire to continue cooperation with Goulart in order to pave the way for the return of their leader, Kubitschek, in the presidential election of 1965, see the article in *O Cruzeiro,* September 14, 1963. In late November, Goulart met with PSD leaders Tancredo Neves and Amaral Peixoto to discuss the continuation of the PSD-PTB alliance in the next session of Congress, scheduled to begin in March 1964. *Jornal do Brasil,* December 1, 1963.

20. *Jornal do Brasil,* October 23, 1963.

21. The workability of the compulsory Treasury certificate scheme was questioned in the Economist Intelligence Unit, *Three-Monthly Economic Review: Brazil,* No. 49 (February 1963), 2, which suggested that the issuing of the certificates had so disrupted the capital market that Carvalho Pinto himself would have had to scrap the plan if he had remained Finance Minister. Nonetheless, it had been one possible tech-

nique for restricting the money supply and at the same time channeling private savings into essential investment areas. The scheme's failure only highlighted the government's lack of any method to achieve this stated purpose.

22. See, for example, Carvalho Pinto's plea for "more time," not "more dollars," as reported in the *New York Times,* October 25, 1963.

23. Jurema describes his efforts in his memoir, *Sexta-Feira, 13,* 49–56.

24. The effects of the exchange reforms, the most important of which was SUMOC Instruction #263, were analyzed by Gilberto Paim in *Correio da Manhã,* March 1, 1964.

25. In 1963, the deficit had declined to $220 million from $345 million in 1962. The sharp increase in coffee prices beginning in September 1963, as a result of the international coffee agreement and the frost damage in Brazil, improved the balance and seemed likely to continue to do so in 1964. For 1964 Brazil was actually anticipating the first surplus (on current account) in its balance of payments since 1961. This optimistic outlook may have led Goulart to believe that Brazil's bargaining position with her foreign creditors had significantly improved. *Conjuntura Econômica,* XVIII, No. 2 (Feb. 1964), 61–68. The efforts at the end of the Goulart government to renegotiate the foreign debt are described in "Brazil Tries Again: Independence Without Inflation?" *The Banker,* CXIV, No. 458 (April 1964), 228–33. The article noted that the "deepening deficit in public finances reflects the widely held view, both inside the government and outside it, that the establishment of economic independence is more important than victory over inflation." But as the anonymous correspondent pointed out, "unfortunately these sentiments are not shared so enthusiastically by Brazil's foreign creditors, whose attitudes towards inflation, moreover, are a good deal less fatalistic than those of the average Brazilian." 229. On March 9 Goulart gave a radio speech in which he described very optimistically Brazil's prospects in the impending debt renegotiations in Paris. *Correio da Manhã,* March 10, 1964.

26. See, for example, the report of Nahum Sirotski, North American correspondent of *Jornal do Brasil,* published on January 22, 1964. See also the column of Arthur Krock in the *New York Times,* February 11, 1964, which reports on the concern in U.S. government circles over the political radicalization in Brazil. The U.S. ambassador in Brazil, Lincoln Gordon, later explained during a Senate Foreign Relations Committee hearing his own assessment of Goulart's intentions in early 1964: "It had become clear for many months before his deposition that his purpose was to put an end to constitutional government in

Brazil in the interest of establishing some sort of a personal dictatorship. I myself believe it would be one copied from the models of Peron in Argentina, and of Vargas between 1937 and 1945 in Brazil." Under pointed questioning by Senator Gore, Gordon continued: "I had hoped, Senator, like many Brazilians, including, I believe the present President [Castelo Branco], that some means could be found of preventing the President, constraining the President, from his intention of subverting the regime from the top, some means which would make it possible for the rest of his term to be lived through or struggled through in peace without a disturbance in the normal constitutional chain of circumstances. As late as January 1964 I still hoped that that might be possible although I was becoming increasingly dubious of the possibility. I would say that sometime between January and the actual overthrow I became convinced that it simply wasn't possible because he would not permit it under any circumstances. He was bound and determined to overthrow the regime himself unless he were prevented by others from so doing." *Hearing Before the Committee on Foreign Relations, United States Senate, on the Nomination of Lincoln Gordon to be Assistant Secretary of State for Inter-American Affairs: February 7, 1966, 7, 11–12.*

27. Goulart's speech at the time he issued the decree is in *Correio da Manhã*, January 18, 1964. The *New York Times* attacked the decree in an editorial entitled "Brazilian Boomerang" on January 27, 1964.

28. Details on the Hanna holdings in Brazil may be found in "Brazil: Hanna's Immovable Mountains," *Fortune*, LXXI, No. 4 (April 1965), 55–64.

29. After Goulart's pessimistic interview in *Manchete* in November, the UDN leadership announced that the President was engaged in a plot to prolong his term beyond January 1966, when it was legally scheduled to end. *Jornal do Brasil*, November 22, 1963. The principal officers of the Congress, President Auro de Moura Andrade of the Senate and President Ranieri Mazzili of the Chamber of Deputies, both of whom were PSD politicians suspicious of Goulart's motives, arranged for the Congress to remain in permanent session through the normal Brazilian summer recess, from December until March. They feared some move to close the Congress (à la 1937) as part of a "continuist" plot. The militantly anti-Goulart congressmen (such as UDN leader Bilac Pinto) began to consider impeachment proceedings against the President, but knew they lacked the votes for such a move. Their plight closely resembled the situation in June 1954 when the UDN unsuccessfully attempted to impeach Vargas. The general fear of a "sudden

interruption of the constitutional process" was described in the *Jornal do Brasil* of February 15, 1964: "This is really a new situation: the officially sanctioned spread of the fear, or better, the conviction, that the country is in a state of abnormality and is heading, as if fatally, toward an abnormal solution of its institutional problems."

30. The PSD was worried enough about Goulart's intentions so that it moved ahead its presidential nominating convention a full year to March 1964, and the UDN had done the same, scheduling their convention for April. Even the PTB congressional leadership felt it necessary to get reassurances about his intentions from Goulart in January 1964, and to make clear their opposition to any coup, as well as their reservations about the "ideological, political, and administrative efficiency of the government." Column of Carlos Castelo Branco, *O Jornal do Brasil,* January 28, 1964. See also the coverage in the *Correio da Manhã* for January 25 and 26.

31. Kubitschek's dilemma over whether or not to break with Goulart was analyzed in the column of Carlos Castelo Branco in *Jornal do Brasil,* March 1, 1964.

32. For the analysis of an opinion survey on attitudes toward Lacerda (taken in early 1964, before Goulart's fall) among students in Guanabara, see Gláucio Ary Dillon Soares, "As Bases Ideológicas do Lacerdismo," *Revista Civilização Brasileira,* No. 4 (September 1965), 49–70. From his data Soares concluded: "Lacerdismo is predominantly liberal, non-interventionist, and favorable to foreign capital, therefore rejecting the nationalist position on this point." 69.

33. Bilac Pinto enunciated this theory in a speech in the Chamber of Deputies on January 23, 1964. It is reprinted in his *Guerra Revolucionária* (Rio de Janeiro, 1964). A similar theory is presented in a pamphlet published sometime in early 1964 by *O Globo* under the pseudonym of Pedro Brasil: *Livro Branco sôbre a Guerra Revolucionária no Brasil* (Pôrto Alegre, 1964). It is written in the style of a general staff paper.

34. On Magalhães Pinto's political position in early 1964, see the articles by Hermano Alves in *Correio da Manhã,* January 29 and 30, 1964. On March 13, the *Correio da Manhã* reported that Magalhães Pinto had decided to remain a presidential candidate regardless of the result of the UDN national convention that was scheduled for April. On March 1 he made a detailed analysis of the political deadlock, warning against the "leftist extremism" that "aims at the destruction of democracy," but added that he was equally disturbed over the "process of hypnosis that is engulfing sectors of the population in an irrational and fanatical

anti-communism." The target for this campaign, he noted, was "the Brazilian middle class." *Correio da Manhã,* March 1, 1964. One of Magalhães Pinto's principal rivals for the leadership of the center was Carvalho Pinto, former Finance Minister and former Governor of São Paulo. Carvalho Pinto was also a presidential hopeful, but his unhappy and ineffectual term as Finance Minister (June-December 1963) had gravely weakened his political position. Furthermore, he lacked any political base. His most reliable party support came from the Christian Democratic Party, a relatively small force in national politics.

35. One of Arraes' admirers thought the Governor was setting a new pattern in the Northeast for a responsible left-wing movement embracing elements ranging from progressive priests to Communist Party members: Antônio Callado, *Tempo de Arraes: Padres e Communistas na Revolução sem Violência* (Rio de Janeiro, 1964). This is the book edition of a series of articles published in *O Jornal do Brasil* in December 1963 and January 1964. The book includes an interesting preface and epilogue written after Goulart's fall and Arraes' imprisonment. See also the strong support for Arraes in Caio Prado Júnior, "Um Discurso Marca Época," *Revista Brasiliense,* No. 46 (March-April, 1963), 1–9. For other sources on Arraes, see Adirson de Barros, *Ascensão e Queda de Miguel Arraes* (Rio de Janeiro, 1965) and the collection of Arraes' speeches in *Palavra de Arraes* (Rio de Janeiro, 1965).

36. Arraes' presidential candidacy was launched in January 1964 by Almino Afonso, former Labor Minister during the January-June 1963 government. *Correio da Manhã,* January 17, 1964. Arraes' worries over Goulart's possible plans for a coup are described in Carlos Castelo Branco's column, *Jornal do Brasil,* January 26, 1964.

37. The speech is reprinted in *O Jornal do Brasil,* January 1, 1964.

38. The constant editorial warnings in *O Jornal do Brasil* and *Correio da Manhã* were typical of this center position.

39. For a post-mortem on Goulart's fall that stresses the divisions within the left, see Maia Neto, *Brasil: Guerra-Quente na América Latina* (Rio de Janeiro, 1965), 3–7. The author was the director of radio station Mayrink Vega, controlled by Brizola.

40. See, for example, Murilo Melo Filho, "Os Três Caminhos das Esquerdas," *Manchete,* March 21, 1964. The three roads were: (1) Jango—reelection; (2) Arraes—the vote; (3) Brizola—arms.

41. In early February Goulart announced the proposed program for the *Frente Única,* as drawn up by Dantas. It included constitutional amendments giving the vote to illiterates and revising Articles 141 (which required prior compensation in cash for land expropriation),

as well as legalization of the Communist Party and the negotiation (or, if necessary, unilateral declaration) of a moratorium on the foreign debt. *Correio da Manhã,* February 6, 1964. Dantas explained that the United Front had the following goals: "(1) Preservation of the democratic system and the constitutional order, and, therefore, repudiation of a coup; (2) support for basic reforms as an indispensable part of any policy of economic development or inflation control; (3) the resulting guarantee of the process of presidential succession until the election of 1965." *Jornal do Brasil,* February 15, 1964. The prospects for the popular front were analyzed in an article in *Manchete* for February 1, 1964. Later, Dantas explained that the purpose of the popular front was to unite the "left" and the "progressive forces of the center." *Correio da Manhã,* March 1, 1964.

42. See, for example, the editorial in *Novos Rumos,* the PCB weekly, for February 28-March 5, 1964.

43. The cautious approach of Prestes was evident in his statement in early 1963, published in *World Marxist Review,* VI, No. 5 (May 1963), 50–51. His caution was repeated in an interview in late 1963. Prestes explained that "We Communists want a solution without civil war, and we think it is possible." As for a "revolution," Prestes warned, "the conditions do not exist for calling the masses to an insurrectionary uprising. . . . The Brazilian bourgeoisie makes great profits and knows how to make concessions. In the last strike in São Paulo [November 1963] they agreed to an 80 percent increase in wages. So that the crisis is not an economic one but a financial one." The interview was first published in the Mexican magazine *Siempre!,* January 1, 1964, and later reprinted in an English translation in Victor Rico Galan, "The Brazilian Crisis," *Monthly Review,* XV, No. 12 (April 1964), 657–74. The PCB line in late 1963 could be found also in Giocondo Dias, "Some Problems of the Class Struggle in Brazil," *World Marxist Review,* VII, No. 1 (Jan. 1964), 21–25. Dias explained: "We believe that the basic task of the vanguard forces in the struggle for structural reforms now is to build up the national and democratic movements. It is along these lines that we envisage the possibility of a peaceful revolution," 24.

44. For examples of leftist critiques of the PCB, see Ramos, *A Crise do Poder no Brasil,* 106–18; and Edmar Morel, *O Golpe Começou em Washington* (Rio de Janeiro, 1965), 63–65. One independent radical leftist criticized the PCB for having failed to appreciate the far-reaching significance of the newly legal rural syndicates. Instead, he charged, the party was still preaching the obsolete and irrelevant (in

Brazil) doctrine of land redistribution. Caio Prado Júnior, "Marcha da Questão Agrária no Brasil," *Revista Brasiliense,* No. 51 (Jan.-Feb. 1964), 1–9.

45. The chief organ of the PC do B was the bi-weekly newspaper *A Classe Operária.* In the issue of February 16–29, 1964, for example, João Amazonas attacked the PCB as a "mere appendage of the bourgeoisie" and accused it of "shamefully flattering the government that represents the latifundists and great capitalists." The front-page editorial contemptuously rejected Dantas' proposed popular front as a "sack of crabs." The negotiations had revealed the "revisionists of the party of Prestes" to be "docilely following the beckonings of Professor Dantas in the hope of gaining their much-prized legality and perhaps a post in the government."

46. In December 1963 Sérgio Magalhães, president of the *Frente Parlamentar Nacionalista,* explained his "leftism": "We understand a move toward the left [*esquerdização*] as an attempt at development with economic emancipation, and we consider the phenomenon much more as a readiness to fight for the lower classes and the country than the implementation of an ideological position. Communists, laborites, socialists, and even Catholics are active as leftists. For this reason we are unhappy with the designation of "left," which can confuse the people. Many are led to think that to be a leftist is to be a Marxist. As can be seen, however, the so-called Brazilian lefts do not demand the socialization of the means of production. They are not, therefore, Marxists in their actions. In truth, what we want is a reinvigoration of democracy and the placing of first priority on social [welfare] laws, basic reforms, and the necessary reforms in the Constitution." Magalhães, *Prática da Emancipação Nacional,* 146. Magalhães was one of the regular contributors to the weekly newspaper *O Semanário,* which represented this independent leftist position. It was receptive to the popular front proposals of Dantas. See, for example, the editorial in the issue of March 5–11, 1964, which urged support for the *Frente Única* as the only way the "center, moderate-left and left" can "survive in face of the enormous danger represented by despair and by the power of the right."

47. On student politics in 1963–64, see Therry, "Dominant Power Components in the Brazilian University Student Movement Prior to April, 1964"; and Harding, "Revolution Tomorrow," 51–52.

48. The weekly newspaper *Política Operária* (not to be confused with the magazine of the same name, which also appeared to follow the PC do B line) often represented the views of some militant UNE leaders and

other radical leftists who favored a revolutionary position akin to the PC do B, thereby rejecting the "conciliatory" politics of the PCB. See, for example, the editorial in *Política Operária*, February 27-March 4, 1964, attacking Dantas and the popular front and demanding instead a "working-class program."

49. These leaders were a favorite target for journalistic exposés after Goulart's fall. See, for example, "CGT: Império da Corrupção," *O Cruzeiro*, May 16, 1964; and "Os 'Generais' da Derrota," *O Cruzeiro*, May 2, 1964. The growing influence of the CGT leaders within the presidential palace greatly alarmed center opinion. The editorial "Assalto ao Regime" in *Jornal do Brasil*, March 18, 1964, is typical of this growing alarm.

50. In an interview in late 1963, Brizola explained his relations with Goulart: "He and I met through politics, and we had the same ideas. He is a reformist, one of those people who wants to paint the walls of peasant huts and leave them looking beautiful, but who remain in possession of the big house themselves. He is not aware that the big house must become the headquarters of the local cooperative. I began to abandon my old ideas, to understand things clearly; meanwhile he turned to a policy of conciliation; so that now our dialogue is increasingly difficult. There is no formal rupture of relations, but a dialogue that leads nowhere is futile." Galan, "The Brazilian Crisis," 674.

51. On February 25 Brizola was the target of a riot in Belo Horizonte where he tried to address a political rally. One day earlier Admiral Heck had addressed a rally of the rightist *Movimento de Mobilização Democrática*, where another speaker, General Bragança, urged his listeners to break up the Brizolistas' meeting scheduled for the next day. The Brizola rally was in fact invaded by crucifix-swinging women (led by Father Caio de Castro) before Brizola arrived, and the local police prevented him from entering the hall. *Correio da Manhã*, February 26, 1964. *O Cruzeiro* for March 21 carried photographs of the melee. The incident immediately became a *cause célèbre*, seized upon by the right (*O Globo*, for example) as evidence that the "democratic, Christian" forces were finally to take a real stand against the "communizers," while the radical left (see, for example, *Panfleto* for March 2, 1964) charged that the golpistas were so frightened that they had resorted to violence, thus proving that the left must be prepared for "revolutionary" action. Centrist opinion, on the other hand, was appalled by the evident breakdown in the democratic process. See, for example, the editorial "O direito de reunião" in *Jornal do Brasil*, February 27, 1964.

52. The first issue of *Panfleto* was dated February 17, 1964. Seven issues

were published, the final one dated March 30. The editorial board included Brizola, Sérgio Magalhães, Neiva Moreira, Almino Afonso, Demistócles Baptista, Adão Pereira Nunes, Paulo Alberto, and Alvaro Vieira Pinto. As can be seen from this list, there was considerable overlap among the principal contributors to the many publications on the radical left. Brizola's strong hand in *Panfleto* was evidenced, however, by the fact that his article was the lead editorial in each issue. Furthermore, the president-director of *Panfleto* was Maio Neto, who was also the director of Radio Mayrink Vega, which Brizola controlled.

53. *Panfleto,* March 23, 1964, 4.
54. In early January, for example, Brizola attacked Goulart for failing to govern and warned that the people were waiting for Jango to return to being "the Jango of the time for Getúlio Vargas." *Correio da Manhã,* January 10, 1964. Since Brizola became such an important figure in the 1963–64 crisis, it is worth examining his views in greater detail. In the interview in late 1963, Brizola explained that the economic crisis produced by "imperialist plundering" was causing the "ruling classes, supported by imperialism" to unify themselves "for a rightist coup, in order to establish a government of force, a dictatorship either open or concealed. It would of course be difficult to impose a dictatorship, because it is no longer easy to deceive the people. We are willing to fight, we are prepared, and this will be the beginning of the revolutionary struggle for national liberation. The example of 1961 shows that the people will fight, together with their brothers in the army—the sergeants, the corporals, the privates, and the nationalist officers." Such a struggle, Brizola continued, would require "organization and unity. We have had problems, due to the errors committed by the Communist Party and by Francisco Julião. However, we must acknowledge that Julião possesses the great merit of having awakened the most oppressed sector of the population, the peasantry. And we believe that all the errors will be overcome. We are not anti-Communist, we welcome any Brazilian who comes as a patriot to struggle for the liberation of his country. The Latin American problem must be stated in terms of national liberation. Without national liberation there can be no basic reforms, because poverty cannot be reformed." Galan, "The Brazilian Crisis," 673. In his lead editorial in *Panfleto* for March 2, 1964, Brizola pronounced on the "authenticity of leadership," attacking the "tens of leaders, born in the PTB, who preach accommodation and patience and who divert the people from the path of their social conquests." Goulart was the obvious target. Brizola concluded

ominously: "The best advice that I give the people in trying to help them judge their leaders is that the people concentrate not on the words but on the actions of those they follow. Because a courageous action is worth a thousand times more than a million words, however courageous."

55. *Panfleto,* February 17, 1964. The editorial ridiculed Dantas' effort to include in the popular front the "old foxes of the PSD."

56. Arraes had also assumed an outspokenly "anti-imperialist" position, attacking "exploitation" by foreign capital, as well as what he thought was the ill-conceived basis of United States assistance to the Northeast. In his inauguration speech as governor in January 1963, he noted: "The cancer of the Northeast is preoccupying the Northamericans, who think that our sickness might be politically contagious and could contaminate our neighbors, and so they give powdered milk, whether ingenuously or not I don't know, as if our hunger were different from theirs, as if it were not, as everywhere else in the world, a living hunger." *Palavra de Arraes,* 13–14. In early 1963, he appointed a commission to study the state's contracts with USAID. The commission's report of May 1963, which recommended that the state terminate the contracts, included a critical analysis, on radical nationalist lines, of the assumptions and practice of American aid. The report was published by Editôra Brasiliense: *"Aliança Para o Progresso": Resultado de Inquérito* (São Paulo, 1963).

57. Jurema reported that the labor leaders became much more important in the palace as the preparations for the rally of March 13 got under way. *Sexta-Feira 13,* 143. Goulart was undoubtedly in a much less strong position vis-à-vis the labor leaders than he had been as Vice President. This point is stressed in Harding, "Revolution Tomorrow," 40.

58. Assis Brasil's four-hour testimony before the subsequent military investigating tribunal on May 26, 1964, is an important source on Goulart's final weeks in power. Assis Brasil's assessment of the President's personality and the details of the conflict among his advisers are especially valuable. This testimony will need to be balanced against that of other participants, such as Justice Minister Jurema, and many who have yet to publish their accounts. Assis Brasil's testimony was published in *O Estado de São Paulo* for July 2 and 3, 1964.

59. In mid-February Pedro Aleixo, an UDN congressman from Minas Gerais and the leader of the opposition in the Chamber of Deputies, admitted freely to a journalist that Castelo Branco was his source of

information on anti-Goulart sentiment among Army officers. *Correio da Manhã*, February 19, 1964. This paralleled the recurrent rumors that Castelo Branco was about to be transferred from his key position as Chief of the Army General Staff, as reported in *Correio da Manhã*, February 22 and March 27, 1964.

60. For an example of a news report on Assis Brasil's reassurances to the President that the "nationalists" were in a majority in the officer corps, see *Correio da Manhã*, March 17, 1964.

61. For a journalistic feature story published on the eve of the March 13 rally, see "Riff: O Braço Esquerdo," *Fatos & Fotos*, March 14, 1965. On February 13, 1964, Darcy Ribeiro gave a long television address to the nation, explaining the President's plans and intentions. The text was published in *O Jornal do Brasil* on February 14, 1964. The speech provoked an immediate reply from Bilac Pinto, the UDN leader who was waging a campaign to prove that the Goulart government was fomenting a "revolutionary war" to prepare for a "continuist" coup.

62. It is difficult to establish exactly who was most instrumental in planning the rally. Jurema said that Goulart chose the planners, and that they were José Gomes Talarico and Gilberto Crockatt de Sá,"old and loyal friends who had nothing to do with ideology, but who were specialists in labor affairs working exclusively for the President." *Sexta-Feira 13*, 143. Talarico, who was vice president of the state legislature of Guanabara, was named as the chief organizer, along with representatives of UNE, CGT, CNTI, and the FPN in *Correio da Manhã*, February 15, 1964.

63. Assis Brasil claimed that Goulart "was so surprised at the fact that former Governor Brizola was going to speak at the rally that he delayed to see if he could arrive after Brizola had spoken. But they held up the rally and he finally arrived and had to listen to Brizola's speech." Assis Brasil testimony in *O Estado de São Paulo*, July 2, 1964. At one point in his speech Brizola resorted to the dramatic device of asking all those who wished to scrap the "politics of conciliation" in favor of a "nationalist and popular government" to raise their hands. A forest of arms arose across the Praça da República. He went on to call for a plebiscite to decide on the need for a Constituent Assembly. There was no threat of "continuism," Brizola explained, because "I have already received the President's personal word of assurance that if there were elections for a Constituent Assembly, excluding the economic interests [*grupos econômicos*] and the alienated press, but including the vote for illiterates, soldiers and sailors and with the press democratized, the President would end his term." Bri-

zola concluded defiantly: "Our path is peaceful but we shall know how to answer violence with violence." The speech is reprinted in *Panfleto,* March 16, 1964; differing versions, in more colorful language, were published in the daily press of March 14. Brizola's reference to "democratizing" the press evidently referred to the kind of rationale that was behind the proposal (circulating within presidential circles) that the federal government should establish a monopoly over the importation and distribution of newsprint. This would have given the federal regime a powerful instrument for influencing the formation of public opinion. For examples of press protests against the proposal, see the editorials in *Correio da Manhã,* March 19 and 20, and in *Jornal do Brasil,* March 25, 1964.

64. Senhora Goulart's appearance on the platform a few moments before Brizola finished his rousing speech helped to divert some attention from her husband's chief rival. Several uninspired orators spoke between Brizola and Goulart, so the President was spared an undiluted contrast between himself and his brother-in-law.

65. The speech was reprinted in the *Jornal do Brasil,* March 14, 1964.

66. For an editorial questioning the logic of expropriating the privately owned refineries, which was in the air in late 1963, see *Correio da Manhã,* November 10, 1963.

67. Goulart had devoted far more time in his March 13th speech to agrarian reform than any other question. The mood of the landowners was hardly one of conciliation, as illustrated by the comment of Último de Carvalho, leader of the PSD delegation from Minas Gerais in the Chamber of Deputies, who is reported to have said, "If the President confiscates our properties or permits anyone else to confiscate them, someone will also confiscate his mandate as President." Column of Carlos Castelo Branco in *Jornal do Brasil,* February 7, 1964.

68. João Goulart, *Os Novos Tempos e as Novas Tarefas do Povo Brasileiro: Introducção à Mensagem Presidencial de Abertura da Sessão Legislativa de 1964* (Brasília, 1964), V–VII, XLIX, LIX–LX. The complete *Mensagem* for 1964 was never published.

69. João Pinheiro Neto, *SUPRA Começa a Reforma* (Rio de Janeiro, 1964), 66. Pinheiro Neto was the director of SUPRA, the federal agrarian reform agency empowered to carry out the decree. This book, published by UNE in late March 1964, includes the decree of March 13, and Pinheiro Neto's analysis of the agrarian problem.

70. *Correio da Manhã,* March 17, 1964.

71. *Ibid.,* March 21, 1964.

72. Brizola rubbed salt into the wounds left from the Dantas-Furtado ex-

periment of early 1963: "If there had been a strong PTB there would never have been a Three-Year Plan nor the scandal of the purchase of the public utilities. The government would never have embarked in that leaky canoe." *Jornal do Brasil*, March 21, 1964.

73. See, for example, the column by Maia Neto in *Panfleto*, March 23, 1964.

74. Brizola's editorial, which bore the revealing title "A Violência não Partiu de Nós" in *Panfleto*, March 30, 1964.

75. See, for example, the column of Wilson Figueiredo in *Jornal do Brazil*, March 26, 1964. The battles within the left during March are well described in Figueiredo's chapter "A Margem Esquerda," in Dines, *Os Idos de Março*, 193–245.

76. The program was published in *Correio da Manhã*, March 24, 1964.

77. *Ibid.*, March 20, 1964.

78. *Jornal do Brasil*, March 17, 1964. Arraes had gone to Minas Gerais after the March 13 rally to confer with Governor Magalhães Pinto. They had a three-hour session. This was one of the UDN governor's last attempts to explore the ill-fated "opening to the left."

79. Prestes' speech was reprinted in *Novos Rumos*, March 20–26, 1964.

80. The principal secondary source on the immediate background and the history of overthrow of Goulart is Alberto Dines, et. al., *Os Idos de Março*, written by eight journalists on the staff of the *Jornal do Brasil* and published only a few months after the events. The most objective, as well as the most perceptive analysis by a foreigner is found in the two reports of James W. Rowe, "Revolution or Counterrevolution in Brazil," *American Universities Field Staff: Reports Service*, East Coast South America Series, XI, Nos. 4 and 5 (Brazil). For an interesting analysis that sharply revises the assessment of Brazilian political forces given in his earlier book [*Revolution in Brazil*, written shortly before Goulart's overthrow], see Irving Louis Horowitz, "Revolution in Brazil: The Counter-revolutionary Phase," *New Politics*, III, No. 2 (Spring 1964), 71–80. Another useful article by an American scholar is Harding, "Revolution Tomorrow." An analysis extremely antipathetic to the "revolutionaries," may be found in Ruy Mauro Marini, "Contradicciones y conflictos en el Brasil contemporáneo," *Foro Internacional*, V, No. 4 (April-June 1965), 511–46. There is an enormous and constantly growing body of Brazilian publications on the political crisis that led to Goulart's overthrow. One bibliography is already available: "Bibliografia sôbre a Revolução de 31 de Março," *Boletim da Biblioteca da Câmara dos Deputados*, 13 (2), Jul./Dec. 1964, 499–514.

81. The chief sources on the military conspiracy to depose Goulart are Dines, *Os Idos de Março;* Stacchini, *Março 64: Mobilização da Audácia;* and the special editions of *O Cruzeiro, Manchete,* and *Fatos & Fotos,* published immediately after Goulart's overthrow.

82. The memorandum is printed in Dines, *Os Idos de Março e a Queda em Abril,* 392–93. In view of the extreme importance assumed by the military, it is essential to investigate their views *before* the overthrow of Goulart. Although Castelo Branco had the reputation of being a "non-political" general, he had by no means been unwilling to speak on the question of "ideologies" in Brazil. On December 15, 1961, for example, he gave a speech explaining the difference between democracy and totalitarianism, concluding: "These two ideologies are engaged in a world conflict. Not to realize this is to divorce oneself from the world and to overlook Brazil. . . . This ideological struggle has crossed the Atlantic and one can say that it is already under way in our country." The speech is reprinted in the *Boletim do Diretório Central da Liga da Defesa Nacional,* No. 4 (November 1962). Upon assuming command of the Army General Staff in late 1963, Castelo Branco warned that the General Staff must not become so "absorbed in day-to-day business" that it grows "detached from the evolution of national politics." He attacked the "opportunistic reformers" who were trying to change the structure of the Army "by a continuous and treacherous undermining." They wished to introduce, he charged, "a Popular Army, a pseudo-militia with an ambiguous ideology designed to stir up the country with threadbare rhetorical pronouncements and to disrupt the public with bloodless subversion [*subversões brancas*] and mutinies. In their work of destruction, they attempt to discredit professional standards by pushing aside those who honor the profession and by belittling the emphasis on standards, as well as by discreetly fomenting discord among the military." Humberto de Alencar Castelo Branco, "Papel do Estado-Maior do Exército," *Revista do Instituto de Geografia e História Militar do Brasil,* XXXI, No. 44 (2° semester 1963), 29. Castelo Branco's memorandum of March 20 became such public knowledge that it was even mentioned in the national press, such as in the column of Carlos Castelo Branco (no relation to the General), *Jornal do Brasil,* March 26, 1964.

83. The protest of the conservative naval officers against Aragão's appointment is reported in the *New York Times,* December 5, 1963.

84. My analysis at this point owes much to Charles W. Anderson, *Toward a Theory of Latin American Politics.* [*Occasional Paper No. 2: The Graduate Center for Latin American Studies, Vanderbilt University*] (Nashville, Tenn., February 1964).

85. The growing alarm expressed in the editorials of the *Correio da Manhã* and *Jornal do Brasil,* Rio dailies of centrist opinion, was an index of this political polarization. On March 20, for example, the *Jornal do Brasil* announced that "this is the hour for democratic resistance. It is also the hour for democratic reform. Let us return the nation to its lost peace and tranquillity, thereby regaining the initiative from the radicals who are burning all the bridges to a democratic solution."

86. In mid-February the *Jornal do Brasil* had commented sympathetically on Dantas' efforts to form a popular front, noting, "It would be better, while there is still time, to shift the center of the pro-reform bloc into the Congress, channeling the reform movement, which until now has been a subject for agitation in the streets and fields, onto the appropriate ground. . . ." *Jornal do Brasil,* February 15, 1964.

87. Among the speakers at the rally were Deputies Herbert Levy, a leading UDN congressman, Plínio Salgado, the ex-Integralista leader of the 1930's, and Senate President Auro de Moura Andrade. *Correio da Manhã,* March 20, 1964.

88. Extensive excerpts from the speech were printed in *Jornal do Brasil,* March 31, 1964 and *Manchete,* April 11, 1964.

89. Magalhães Pinto's manifesto is printed in Dines, *Os Idos de Março,* 393–94. The Paulista conspirators had not forgotten their bitter experience of 1932.

90. *Ibid.,* 144.

91. On April 1 the PCB newspaper *Novos Rumos* published a special edition, calling for massive support of the CGT-ordered general strike. But the cautious pro-government attitude that had characterized the PCB attitude throughout the battles within the left was still evident: "This is the moment to demand from the President of the Republic effective and immediate measures against the civilian and military golpistas, many of whom still occupy command posts, and to support firmly all acts of the federal government designed to eliminate the conspiracy from the extreme right." As the PCB leaders knew, the situation was already well beyond the control of Goulart, and the prospects for the success of any general strike were virtually nil. Wilson Figueiredo, "A Margem Esquerda," in Dines, *Os Idos de Março,* 241–42. On March 27 *Novos Rumos* had published a special supplement, "Teses para Discussão." An article in *O Jornal do Brasil,* "Rumos Comunistas Ditavam Rumos ao Brasil Janguista" (April 12, 1964), after the revolution, analyzed this supplement, attempting to show that the Goulart government and the entire left was following a coherent line that matched the views of the PCB. In fact, the PCB was

feverishly attempting to keep up with events, which had become hope-
lessly confused by the disorganization and miscalculation within the
deeply divided left, as well as within the government.

92. General Ladário arrived in Pôrto Alegre to take over the command of
the Third Army from General Benjamin Galhardo only on the morning of April 1. It was a desperate last-minute move by Goulart, but the
loyalty of the rest of the command could not be assured, since the
conspirators had already converted so many of the officers.

93. Assis Brasil, in his testimony, gave his account of the encounter. For
a journalist's version, see "Brizola Queria Sangue," *O Cruzeiro,* May
16, 1964. There is a detailed chronology of the last days of the
Goulart era in Pôrto Alegre in "A Revolução Vista do Rio Grande,"
Revista do Globo, 872 (May 9–22, 1964), 34–48.

94. The Army was embarrassed not to be able to capture Brizola as he
moved among the border fazendas in the interior of Rio Grande do
Sul. On May 3, 1964, the *Correio da Manhã* printed a letter, allegedly
from Brizola, announcing his decision to go into exile in Uruguay.

Epilogue

1. Sometime on the night between April 1 and 2, General Costa e Silva
simply announced to a group of assembled officers that he was assuming "the functions of Commander in Chief of the National Army."
This was reported in *Correio da Manhã,* in its issue for April 2, 1964.
Later, Costa e Silva claimed that he had already assumed command of
the conspiracy on March 16, 1964. His claim was immediately disputed by General Mourão Filho, who considered himself the father of
the revolt. *O Estado de São Paulo,* April 4, 1965.

2. General Costa e Silva was later remarkably frank in describing this
struggle with the congressional leadership, which he said had "consumed more of our energy than the actual military operation." Costa e
Silva's comments were in a speech given in early May 1964 to the
Chamber of Deputies, excerpts of which were reprinted in the *Boletim
Informativo,* No. 86 (May 7, 1964), published by the Brazilian Embassy in Washington, D.C.

3. Evidently no official summary has been published of the number of
persons whose political rights were suspended by the Castelo Branco
government. Many different totals have appeared in press reports. The
figure of 378, for the suspension of political rights in the period from
April 1 to June 15, 1964, was given in a feature story in *Correio da*

Manhã, April 1, 1965. The story also noted that approximately 10,000 government officials had been dismissed or forcibly retired, and that about 5,000 investigations (involving 40,000 persons) had been initiated. The suspension of political rights resumed after the government gave itself back its arbitrary powers by the second Institutional Act (October, 1965). It was under the latter that Adhemar de Barros was deposed as Governor of São Paulo in 1966.

4. The new law is analyzed in Robert E. Price, *The Brazilian Land Reform Statute* [Research Paper: Land Tenure Center, University of Wisconsin] (Madison, Wisc., April 1965, mimeo). See also James W. Rowe, "The 'Week of the Land' in the Brazilian Sertão," *American Universities Field Staff Reports Service,* East Coast South America Series, XII, No. 1 (Brazil).

Appendix

1. Edmar Morel, *O Golpe Começou em Washington* (Rio de Janeiro, 1965).
2. *Hearing Before the Committee on Foreign Relations, United States Senate,* February 7, 1966, 9.
3. *Department of State Bulletin,* L, No. 1295 (April 20, 1964), 614.
4. *Hearing Before the Committee on Foreign Relations, United States Senate,* February 7, 1966, 44–45.
5. Stacchini, *Mobilização da Audácia,* 87–89.
6. Siekman, "When Executives Turned Revolutionaries," 214.
7. *New York Times,* April 3, 1964.
8. *New York Times,* April 7, 1964.
9. I have translated this passage from the Portuguese text published in *O Estado de São Paulo,* May 4, 1964.

Selected Bibliographical Index

This is an index of works cited more than once. References are to first citation (for example, III, 12 is Chapter III, footnote 12), where full publishing information may be found. Because of possible confusion due to multiple names in Portuguese, the reader may need to look in more than one place. Excluded from this index are newspapers and magazines.

Cabral, *Tempos de Jânio*, III, 57.

Caó, *Dutra*, I, 48.

Carneiro, *História das Revoluções Brasileiras*, I, 5.

Carone, *Revoluções do Brasil Contemporâneo*, I, 5.

Carvalho, "Os Partidos Políticos em Minas Gerais," II, 21.

Cavalcanti and Dubnic, eds., *Comportamento Eleitoral no Brasil*, VII, 30.

César, *Política, Cifrão e Sangue*, III, 26.

Coutinho, *O General Góes depõe*, I, 40.

Dale, *Brazil: Factors Affecting Foreign Investment*, V, 6.

Dean, *São Paulo's Industrial Elite*, I, 74.

dé Carli, *JQ, Brasília, e a Grande Crise*, VII, 9.

Delfim Netto, *O Problema do Café*, I, 21.

Development of Brazil, The, III, 16.

Dines, et al., *O mundo depois de Kennedy*, VII, 21.

————, *Os Idos de Março*, VIII, 14.

Economic Development of Brazil, The, V, 7.

Ferreira, *As Fôrças Armadas e o Desafio da Revolução*, III, 70.

————, "A Crise do Poder do 'Sistema,' " VII, 30.

"Fifteen Years of Economic Policy," II, 53.

Fontoura, *Memórias*, Volume I: *Borges de Medeiros e Seu Tempo*, I, 11.

————, *Memórias*, Volume II: *A aliança liberal e a revolução de 1930*, I, 5.

Franco, Afonso Arinos de Melo, *Evolução da crise brasileira*, I, 12.

————, *História e Teoria do Partido Político*, I, 36.

————, *Um Estadista da República*, I, 5.

Franco, Virgílio A. de Mello, *A campanha da U. D. N.*, II, 4.

Furtado, *Diagnosis of the Brazilian Crisis*, V, 3.

————, *The Economic Growth of Brazil*, I, 21.

Galan, "The Brazilian Crisis," VIII, 43.

Gomes, *Campanha de libertação*, II, 24.

"Growth and Decline of Import Substitution in Brazil, The," II, 53.

Harding, "Revolution Tomorrow," V, 21.

Hearing Before the Committee on Foreign Relations, United States Senate, VIII, 26.

Henriques, *Vargas: O maquiavélico*, I, 38.

Hirschman, *Journeys Toward Progress*, II, 60.

Holmes, "Brazil: Rising Power," II, 12.

Horowitz, *Revolution in Brazil*, II, 19.

Houtart and Pin, *The Church and the Latin American Revolution*, VII, 80.

Ianni, *Estado e Capitalismo*, I, 83.

————, *Política e revolução social,* II, 20.
Introdução aos Problemas do Brasil, V, 17.
Jaguaribe, *Desenvolvimento Econômico,* III, 9.
————, "A Renúncia de Jânio Quadros," VI, 24.
Jurema, *Sexta-Feira, 13,* VII, 26.
Kubitschek, *Diretrizes gerais do Plano Nacional de Desenvolvimento,* IV, 9.
Lambert, *Os dois Brasís,* I, 63.
Leal, Hamilton, *História das instituições políticas,* I, 34.
Leal, Nunes, *Coronelismo, enxada e voto,* I, 2.
Lima Sobrinho, *A verdade,* I, 5.
Loewenstein, *Brazil Under Vargas,* I, 34.
Loureiro Júnior, *O Golpe de Novembro,* IV, 21.
Lucas, *Conteúdo social nas constituições,* I, 34.
Luz, *Em defesa da Constituição,* IV, 22.
Macedo, *Aspectos do Congresso,* II, 66.
Machado, *Os últimos dias,* III, 85.
Magalhães, Juracy, *Minha vida pública,* I, 64.
Magalhães, Sérgio, *Prática da Emancipação Nacional,* VII, 38.
Maier and Weatherhead, eds., *Politics of Change in Latin America,* VII, 47.
Matos, *Em Agôsto Getúlio Ficou Só,* III, 23.
Mensagem apresentada ao Congresso. This is the most common title for the President's annual message to Congress, further identifiable by the name of the President and the year it was sent.
Morazé, *Les trois ages du Brésil,* I, 1.
Nogueira Filho, *Ideais e lutas,* I, 4.
Oliveira, *Diagrama,* I, 49.
————, *Jornada democrática,* I, 44.
Palavra de Arraes, VIII, 35.
Pedreira, *Março 31,* VIII, 14.
Peixoto, *Getúlio Vargas,* I, 48.
Pereira, *Que é a Constituição?* II, 12.
Peterson, *Brazilian Political Parties,* II, 20.
Plano Trienal, VII, 57.
Poppino, *International Communism in Latin America,* I, 16.
Prestes, *Problemas Atuais da Democracia,* I, 37.
Ramos, *A Crise do Poder no Brasil,* VI, 17.
————, *Mito e Verdade da Revolução Brasileira,* VII, 53.
Regina, *O Cardeal Leme,* I, 9.
Richers, et al., *Impacto da Ação do Govêrno,* IV, 42.

Rocha, *Radiografia de Novembro,* III, 91.

Rodrigues, *Teoria de História do Brasil,* I, 19.

Santos and Monteiro, *Diário,* VI, 5.

Saunders, "A Revolution of Agreement," III, 85.

Siekman, "When Executives Turned Revolutionaries," VII, 36.

Simão, "O Voto Operário em São Paulo," II, 48.

Síntese Cronológica: 1956, 1957, 1958, 1959, V, 1.

Sodré, *História Militar,* II, 27.

Stacchini, *Março 64: Mobilização da Audácia,* VII, 34.

Távora, "Escola Superior de Guerra," III, 69.

Tejo, *Jango,* III, 49.

Telles, *O Movimento Sindical,* II, 46.

Therry, "Dominant Power Components in the Brazilian University Student Movement Prior to April, 1964," VII, 39.

Vargas, *A Campanha Presidencial,* II, 71.

————, *O Govêrno Trabalhista,* III, 7.

————, *A Nova Política,* I, 3.

Vegara, *Fui secretário de Getúlio Vargas,* I, 67.

Vianna, *O idealismo da constituição,* I, 13.

Victor, *Cinco anos,* VII, 1.

Weffort, "Raízes Sociais do Populismo em São Paulo," II, 49.

Whitaker, *Seis Mêses,* IV, 37.

Wirth, *Brazilian Economic Nationalism: Trade and Steel Under Vargas,* I, 46.

————, "Tenentismo in the Brazilian Revolution of 1930," I, 5.

Wythe, *Brazil: An Expanding Economy,* I, 61.